From the library of
Danny Doyle
Raised on songs and stories

THE ENGLISH TRAVELLER
IN
IRELAND

THE
ENGLISH TRAVELLER
IN
IRELAND

Accounts of Ireland and the Irish
through five centuries

Compiled and edited by
John P. Harrington

WOLFHOUND PRESS

U.S. DISTRIBUTOR
DUFOUR EDITIONS
CHESTER SPRINGS.
PA 19425-0449
(215) 458-5005

First published 1991 by
WOLFHOUND PRESS,
68 Mountjoy Square,
Dublin 1.

British Library Cataloguing in Publication Data

The English traveller in Ireland : English
descriptions of Ireland and the Irish from
the Elizabethan to the Victorian eras.
1. Ireland. Description and travel, history
I. Harrington, John P.
914.15'04

ISBN 0-86327-189-8 hb

Cover illustration: Erskine Nicol (1825-1904), Seafront at Bray, Co. Wicklow. Courtesy National Gallery of Ireland.

Cover design: Jan de Fouw
Typesetting: Redsetter Ltd., Dublin.
Printed and bound by Billings & Sons Ltd., Worcester.

CONTENTS

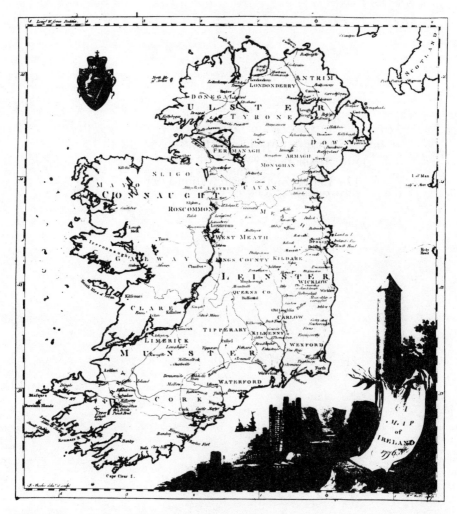

Frontispiece to *A Tour in Ireland 1775* by Richard Twiss.

O thievish Night,
Why shouldst thou, but for some felonious end,
In thy dark lantern thus close up the stars,
That nature hung in heaven, and filled their lamps
With everlasting oil, to give due light
To the misled and lonely traveller?

— Milton, *Comus*

ACKNOWLEDGEMENTS
The editor and publisher would like to thank the following for permission to reproduce illustrations: National Library of Ireland; National Gallery, Dublin; Ulster Museum, Belfast; National Portrait Gallery, London.

INTRODUCTION

Four years after he published the 'elucidated' edition of Cromwell's speeches, and just after the worst of the Irish potato famine, Thomas Carlyle recorded a confused impulse in his journal. 'Am thinking of a tour in Ireland', he wrote on May 17, 1849, 'unhappily have no call I *desire* that way, or any way, but am driven out somewhither (just now) as by the point of bayonets at my back. Ireland really *is* my problem'. Carlyle did indeed tour Ireland that summer, travelling around the country from late June until late July. Only after his 'long confused wayfarings of the summer', as he described them in his journal on October 4, 1849, did he decide to 'endeavor to write down with all dispatch what I can remember of them'. This he did with great dispatch indeed, finishing in less than two weeks the work later published as *Reminiscences of My Irish Journey 1849*. That work done, he returned to his journal on November 11, 1849, and wrote: 'have forcibly recalled all my remembrances, and thrown them down on paper since my return. Ugly spectacle: sad health, sad humor; a thing unjoyful to look back upon. The whole country figures in my mind like a ragged coat; one huge beggar's gabardine, not patched or patchable any longer: far from a joyful or beautiful spectacle'.

These incidental notes of an interesting writer present in especially vivid form the mechanics of the literary occasion that is the subject of this anthology. These are all *Accounts of Ireland* by English visitors to the country over the course of three centuries. The writers represented here journeyed through Ireland in many different political, military, commercial, and private capacities, and they left behind written records that vary widely in form and style. But all these writers and their works have in common preoccupations concisely represented in Carlyle's journal. Preeminent among them is the sense that Ireland is a problem, and for Carlyle even 'my problem'. Two and a half centuries earlier, the poet Edmund Spenser made his attempt to explain the Irish problem, and almost a half century after Carlyle the final, anonymous author represented here actually disguised himself as an Irishman in order to find 'the problem'. As that sad history might suggest, another feature common to all these works is persistent confusion: these writers perceive Ireland as a 'spectacle' essentially different from England, and they hazard explanations for it, usually based like Carlyle's on 'confused wayfarings' and in the form of generalizations about the national character. These writers also all confront Ireland with their own vested interests, whether they are political appointees seeking preferment, adventurers seeking fortune, or travel writers seeking

9

picturesque material. In Carlyle's case, he came for confirmation of ideas already posited in *Chartism*. These interests help control what they report about Ireland, and they also help explain some of the most egregious failures of self-knowledge on the parts of these writers. Finally, as writers these visitors, like Carlyle, record their reactions in some literary fashion. At times they are explicit in their reactions — 'ugly spectacle'. At other times they are less than explicit, and their reactions are often most provocative when embedded in ostensible scientific objectivity or cast in figures like Carlyle's image of the 'beggar's gabardine'.

As one might expect, the history of Irish complaints about these sorts of English accounts is a long one, which in itself points to the political dynamics of these texts. As early as 1632 Geoffrey Keating, author of the first general history of Ireland written in Irish Gaelic, attacked 'foreign beetles', among them English writers on Ireland included here such as Richard Stanihurst, Edmund Spenser, and Fynes Moryson. Keating chose the metaphor with relish: 'it is in the nature of the beetle, raising its head in summer, to move to and fro without alighting on flower of field or garden, roses or lilies, but rolling itself in the dung of horses and cows'. Just so, he wrote, 'the chronicles of the foreigners . . . dwell entirely on the habits and customs of the baser sort, ignoring the more worthy'. It is certainly true that the image of the Irish presented in these accounts is less than flattering. Most of these writers dwell with evident satisfaction on their disgust at what the visitors saw, though *pace* Keating that disgust is likely to be shared by modern readers of these frequently graphic descriptions of very primitive Irish dietary and hygenic habits. It is also certainly true that these writers are sometimes far from credible — John Dunton describes domesticated otters that fetched their masters salmon, and J. C. Curwen matter-of-factly reports that in her last years the 140-year-old Countess of Desmond grew new teeth. But there is a persuasive corroborative power to the descriptions of daily life in this selection of accounts. It is also true that 'the chronicles of the foreigners' were probable enough to upset. When Richard Twiss criticised the Irish for indelicacy they responded by painting his portrait inside chamberpots.

These are all informative records of life in Ireland in different historical periods. There is an attractive anecdotal quality, for example, in Edmund Campion's report in 1571 that Irish rebels left the right arms of their sons unchristened to deliver a more 'deadly blow'. There is a wealth of factual information here on matters such as the diet, clothing, and cabins of the people of Ireland at different times. But useful compilations already exist of documentary descriptions of Ireland by Irish and English writers. Several are listed in the bibliography to this volume. This anthology stresses instead that these are also self-conscious accounts and records of forms of English encounters with Ireland, forms of concern, forms of confusion, and forms of expression. It is on this level that they provide special insight into past and present relations between the English and the Irish in particular, and between colonizers and the colonized in general.

Keating's attack on 'foreign beetles' underscores a fundamental dynamic of the works collected here: these are descriptions of visits to Ireland written by outsiders. Swift, for example, is excluded because of his Dublin birth and residence, as is the remarkably popular Mrs. Hall. Furthermore, the writers represented here all travelled in Ireland and recorded their impressions as eyewitness reports. Thus many notable English documents on 'The Irish Question' such as government papers or expository essays of writers like John Stuart Mill and Matthew Arnold are excluded because they are not informed by immediate personal encounters with Ireland. There are slight complications in the cases of Richard Stanihurst, born in Dublin though educated in England and one of Keating's foreign beetles, and in the case of Carlyle, a Scot. But all of these visitors did write from a distinctly English perspective on Ireland. They were visitors to Ireland for periods ranging from a few years in the case of the early political appointees to a few weeks or even less in the case of the later tourists. Each was, as John Carr identified himself in his account, *The Stranger in Ireland* (1805). In fact, one of the salient qualities of these works is the persistent sense of being an outsider, even an intruder, despite the proximity of the two islands and the facts of political governance. In 1617 Fynes Moryson, one of the many English visitors to suffer from an Irish version of 'Montezuma's revenge', wrote that in Ireland 'strangers are troubled with looseness of the body, the country disease'. The first true English road book of Ireland, though not a prose account, had as its title *A Guide for Strangers in the Kingdome of Ireland* (1647). John Stevens, a Williamite soldier, observed of the Irish in 1689, 'few strangers love them better or pity them more than I do'. In 1800 the Act of Union presumably brought Ireland and England into a closer harmony, but John Carr chose his title after that, and Henry Inglis began his tour in 1834 with a description of being 'a stranger arriving in Dublin in Spring'. There is far more than coincidental recurrence of that term and ones congruent with it in these works, in which personal experience frequently belies public policy, enlightened historiography and journalism, and aloof ethics.

Like Carlyle, what these strangers did when confronted with this difference, this 'spectacle' of Ireland, was write an account of it. These are 'accounts' of Ireland in several senses of the word. First, they are subjective *versions*, or personal accounts, of the condition of Ireland at specific times. This is evident in the disagreements between accounts written at the same time, such as the divergent descriptions of the religious life of the people recorded by the Catholic Edmund Campion and the Protestant Edmund Spenser. Second, they are *explanations* that hope to account for the habits of the Irish, largely through citation of religious and social customs. Different explanations suit different purposes, and so these accounts are frequently quite contentious, as in the running feud between Stanihurst and Barnaby Rich. Third, these are *apologies* that hope to account for English treatment of Ireland, which they generally begin to do by dismissing what John Carr called 'the ridiculous misrepresentations' of predecessors. Finally, these are also *reckonings* of a colonial property, proprietary accounts of its character, worth, and proper management. That may be explicit, as in the case of the plantation manager Robert Payne, but it is also implicit in the later tourists' comments on how, for example, glimpses of poverty can spoil a visit to the lakes of Killarney. Moreover, these writers are generally quite aware of these problematic dimensions of ostensibly objective works of physical description, though they also generally think themselves privileged. In 1764, in *Hibernia Curiosa*, John Bush boasted that he 'copied immediately from nature, without the least implicit reliance on any accounts whatsoever'. The anonymous author of the hale and hearty *Sportsman in Ireland* (1840) arrived for a tramp in Ireland determined 'at once to be convinced of the truth or falsehood of the accounts put forth' of the people as well as of the fishing.

The agriculturalist Edward Wakefield called his 1812 description of the country *An Account of Ireland, Statistical and Political*, a title appropriate to all these works. These are all both statistical and political, both factual and ideological. They are not sufficient as studies in Irish history, and after Elizabethan times these writers attempt little history in their accounts. Nor are they sufficient as descriptions of Ireland, and statistical anatomies, too, become rare in these works long before Wakefield's day. Instead, these accounts of Ireland are partial: they are incomplete, insufficiently researched and considered, and also biased, limited in perspective. But as records of encounters of English writers with Ireland these works are valuable for, not despite, their partiality. They mix fact and ideology and confuse social and natural law in instructive ways.

In his account Wakefield confessed that 'there is, perhaps, a secret delight in protecting the prescriptive prejudices of our forefathers, in cherishing with the same acrimony those national reflections that feed our own consequence'. Of course, he thought himself quite immune to that delight. But the evidence of these works suggest that some ideological constructs are perpetuated in just that inherited fashion, that predecessors narrow the field of vision. The first selection in this anthology, Edmund Campion's account of 1571, addresses itself to earlier chroniclers of Ireland. Stanihurst relies on Campion, and Arthur Young relies on both in his *A Tour in Ireland 1776-1779*. Twiss, in 1775, borrows from Young and also Fynes Moryson's *Itinerary* of 1613. Carr, writing in 1805, refers to Spenser, who wrote in 1596. John Dunton goes to Ireland in 1698 with a copy of Laurence Echard's *Exact Description of Ireland*, published seven years before, and quotes it as an authority though he is in and looking at Ireland itself. These cross-references are not always in agreement, but they do indicate one kind of fairly systematic perpetuation of the 'prescriptive prejudices' mentioned by Wakefield.

However, over 300 years one would scarcely expect the particular prejudices of English visitors to remain absolutely monolithic. In addition to continuities there are historical phases to the images of Ireland presented here. In fact, there is a continuing evolution of images of the Irish that appears to proceed almost independently of the actual, quite stable condition of most of the population. These accounts are controlled by the conventions of different centuries, by successive episodes in Irish history, and by the changing circumstances of the English presence in Ireland, and so some historical survey here may be useful as a context for the chronologically-arranged selections themselves.

These accounts were composed with some regularity from the late 1500s to the late 1800s, a period marked by very regular military, political, and natural catastrophies for the people of Ireland. The end of the Elizabethan period is marked by the collapse of the Tyrone Rebellion in 1603; this was followed by the 'Flight of the Earls' of Ireland and the English plantation of Ulster, the northernmost of the four traditional provinces of the island. Roughly 100 years later, at the end of the 17th century, the interests of Catholic Ireland were crushed by the defeat of James II at the Battle of the Boyne in 1690; the survivors of the amalgamation of Stuart and Irish resisters were then dispersed by the 1691 Treaty of Limerick, which opened the way for repressive anti-Catholic penal laws in 1695. The next century, the 18th, ended in a similar debacle for Ireland. The abortive 1798 Rebellion ended when French support failed, and among the ramifications was abolition of the Irish parliament by the 1800 Act of Union. In the 19th century some promise of progress, epitomized by Catholic Emancipation in 1829, was thwarted by the disastrous Irish potato famine of 1845-48. Despite scattered militancy later in the 19th century, the fortunes of the movement for Irish parliamentary autonomy, or Home Rule, declined to a nadir with the death of the charismatic Irish politician Charles Stewart Parnell in 1891. All these events calamitous for the Irish had an ironical tendency to frustrate English interests as well, and so to create an ongoing 'Irish Problem'. Frustration naturally engenders reassessment, and this briefest survey of pivotal events maps boundaries between phases of English policy toward Ireland and between different perceptions of the Irish.

The earliest of these selections date from the Elizabethan era because it was then that the circumstances essential to these sorts of accounts of Ireland first took shape. Henry VIII had taken the title 'King of Ireland' in 1541, but the full effect of Anglican sovereignty was delayed for a time by the compromise stance of his successor Edward VI and the subsequent toleration of Catholicism under Mary. Confiscation of lands in Leix and Offaly had begun, however, and Elizabeth's 1560 attempt to impose Protestantism on Ireland through the Anglicized 'Reform Parliament' finally brought into direct conflict diametrically opposed interests in sovereignty and property as well as of religion. The Elizabethan conquest of Ireland required overseers, and most of the English visitors to Ireland at this time were civil servants. Confronted with a strange and hostile society, they attempted to render it accurately for purposes of practical politics and profitable commerce. Three writers provided the principal accounts of Ireland for Raphael Holinshed's landmark *Chronicles* in 1587, and they divided the topic with evident efficiency: Campion's focus was on Brehon law, Stanihurst's was on language and local customs, and John Hooker's was on religion. The same three topics provided a general organization for Edmund Spenser, who called the laws, customs, and religion of the country its 'evils'.

In general, the Elizabethans described Ireland as a wilderness and the people as savage participants in bizarre tribal rites and darkly superstitious religion. To Spenser the land and the people were 'untamed', and the Elizabethan visitor to Ireland speaks from a frontier not wholly different from that more distant one to be tamed in North America. The English toehold in the country was limited to the settled region around Dublin known as the 'Pale'. This anthology opens with Edmund Campion's notes on the fragility of the Pale, the English settlement around Dublin, 'whereout', Campion says, 'they durst not peep'. The consciousness of multiple threats to English control of Ireland colors the accounts of all Elizabethan visitors. The threat was not only of native revolt, though there were indeed both Desmond and Tyrone revolts of major proportions and significant duration. Nor was the threat only of foreign attack, though the wreckage of the Spanish Armada in 1588 underscored that possibility. The additional threat felt viscerally by these Elizabethan writers was that of creeping debasement, of assimilation, of the possibility that a visitor might, in Campion's words, 'become degenerate in short space'. As these writers note, the population of Ireland at this time consisted of the native or 'wild' or 'mere' Irish, the loyalist English, and those 'English-Irish' characterized by Spenser as 'degenerated and grown almost mere Irish, yea and more malicious to the English than the very Irish themselves'. The emphasis on this particular threat is suggestive of a network of Elizabethan assumptions about religious, political, and intellectual virtue and its vulnerability to evil forces (i.e the Irish) cast in terms of a kind of malevolent rodent population — pests and threats and addressed with extermination. One of the dramas enacted in these pages is the shift in consciousness that makes it possible for the final, anonymous account writer in this anthology to go to Ireland 300 years after Spenser with the sole purpose of becoming temporarily Irish, of playing out the very scenario so abhorrent to his Elizabethan predecessors.

The 17th century opened with the plantation of Ulster, and before the end of the century there had been two further confiscations of Irish lands.

In mid-century Oliver Cromwell landed in Ireland to squash support for the deposed Stuart monarchy and to retaliate for Irish attacks on Ulster 'planters'. At Drogheda and Wexford in 1649 Cromwell met Irish resistance with notorious savagery, and by the Act of Settlement of 1652 he rewarded his own Protestant supporters and settled his army's debts by allotment of huge parcels of Irish land. The same pattern was repeated at the end of the century, when the Battle of the Boyne in 1690 was followed by Williamite property reapportionment. The Catholic population, deprived of property, was then fully disenfranchised by the penal laws that barred them from government. A final, inestimable loss for Ireland in this century was the flight — early, middle, and again late in the century — of the most ambitious and most rebellious of its young, male, Catholic population.

The English writers of accounts of Ireland in the 17th century roamed the country more freely than their predecessors, and their accounts are identified less often as a 'Description' or a 'View' from a fixed perspective than they are as an 'Itinerary' or as 'Travels'. The progressive subjugation of Ireland encouraged this new kind of visitor to rhapsodize enthusiastically on the great beauty and commercial potential of the confiscated countryside. 'This nymph of Ireland is at all points like a young wench', wrote Luke Gernon in 1620, 'that hath the green sickness for want of occupying'. The emphasis on the barbarism of the people now falls on their localized economy and nomadic culture, as opposed to the English ideal of centralization. The virtue of effective 'industry' and 'husbandry' is the great rising theme of the accounts of all visitors from this era. The corollary theme is the laziness of the Irish, as demonstrated by their evident failure to utilize and commercialize the land according to English ideals. Together, these emphases amount to more of an account of the morality than the economy of Ireland. 'The Irish might in all parts have abundance of excellent sea and fresh-water fish,' wrote Fynes Moryson in the first half of the century, 'if the fisher men were not so possessed with the natural fault of slothfulness.' To writers unsympathetic to the Irish, poverty was proof of moral deficiency rather than economic disadvantage. Even a sympathetic observer, such as John Stevens, writing on the poverty of the people in the second half of the century, concludes that 'the great cause of it, laziness, is most predominant.' This consciousness, too, will undergo its own gradual shift in the chronological course of these selections. In the 17th century a moral fault, sloth, was perceived as the cause of Irish poverty; in the 19th century poverty, and its degrading effects, will be perceived as the cause of moral faults, laziness among them.

The pacification of Ireland effected by the Battle of the Boyne and its aftermath encouraged English travel to Ireland in the 18th century. For the Protestant, Anglo-Irish classes that now dominated the country, the 18th century proved a relatively peaceful period, even a modestly prosperous one. Dublin began to take on something of its present character with the erection of many of its finest public buildings, and the capital's society was notable for luminaries such as Swift. Packet transportation to Dublin from England improved, and so a visitor could conveniently savor the pleasures of 'the empire's second city' before excursions into the countryside. With improved roads, journey by horseback gave way to journey by coach, and as the century progressed the canal system of barge transport fanned out from Dublin. The sense of insecurity endemic to earlier eras did not completely vanish, for there were continuing outbreaks of agrarian violence by 'Whiteboys' and others. But the evidence of these texts suggests that visitors inspected Ireland with some confidence that Irish-Catholic agitators would target particular landowners and middle-men and not just any representative of England at all.

For these reasons the accounts of Ireland from the 18th century are far more congenial than those of earlier eras. 'Travels' and 'Itinerary' were the operative words in the titles of accounts from the 17th century, but in the 18th century these were supplanted by titles suggestive of even more genteel journeys. 'Tour' became the favored title in this age when English writers became prolific literary travelers to distant regions, to the continent, and to the remoter areas of Scotland and Wales. The tour of Ireland could be a fairly comprehensive undertaking by a veteran traveler, such as Arthur Young, or it could be a more modest one, such as Richard Twiss's. The literary products of these visits took on forms suggestive of sociability and domesticity rather than adventure, as in George Cooper's *Letters* and John Bush's *Hibernia Curiosa: A Letter From a Gentleman in Dublin*. The easy accessibility of Ireland in conjunction with the growing appetite of English readers for the reports of compatriot visitors to it produced an enormous proliferation of accounts of Ireland late in the century. By then the mechanics of the genre had become recognizable enough to inspire charade. One of the first was a 1778 *Philosophical Survey of Ireland* notable for its sympathy for the Irish. The writer was an Irish acquaintance of Boswell named Thomas Campbell, a shrewd student of the conventions of accounts of Ireland who adopted the persona necessary to exploit the power of such works over the English reading public. 'A very entertaining book,' reported Boswell in his life of Johnson, 'which has, however, one fault — that it assumes the fictitious character of an Englishman.'

The authentic English visitor to Ireland in the 18th century was confronted with the same images of poverty that run through all of these selections — smoky and overcrowded hovels, disease, rags, dreadful diet, and general malaise worsened by the effects of whiskey. If anything, the distance between the 'lower Irish', as they were now called, and the visitors describing them seems to have grown. For all the revulsion of the earlier visitors, they never quite reached the rhetorical pitch of John Dunton's description of the lower Irish as 'a generation of vermin', Richard Twiss's suggestion that they 'form a distinct race from the rest of mankind' or George Cooper's observation that they are 'miserably destitute of fear, reason, and often of humanity'. The 18th century did, however, produce its own characteristic view of the Irish and their predicament, one that derived more from the English visitor's own general ambience of prosperity, optimism, and benevolence than it did from any significant alteration in the condition of the Irish peasantry. The 18th century visitors concurred with their predecessors that the great problem in Ireland was idleness and lack of industry. Their new conviction was that these flaws could be corrected by instillation of the profit motive, that the problem was one of economics rather than morality. As Young concluded in his tour, 'the villainy of the greatest miscreants is all situation and circumstance: EMPLOY, don't hang them'. On the subject of 'destructive idleness', George Cooper wrote that 'to agriculture and trade and civilization we can alone look for a removal of this defect'. To these visitors the Irish were not so much diabolical, as they were to the Elizabethans, as they were simply backward, as yet unenlightened by the benefits of economic management. To Cooper, 'the polished minority of the nation is one hundred years behind England in refinement, and the rude majority of it is at least five'. Obviously, this characterization of the Irish as backward dovetails nicely with an assumption of English possession of the key to progress in economic management. Together, these entwined assumptions justify, for example, the manipulative trade restrictions on Ireland attacked since the beginning of the 18th century by less disinterested parties such as Swift.

The calendar beginning of the 19th century precisely marked the initiation of a new political era in Ireland. The Act of Union passed in the Irish parliament on June 7, 1800, became law with the royal assent on August 1, 1800, and took effect on January 1, 1801. Thus only 18 years after the Anglo-Irish ascendancy had secured the autonomy of the Irish parliament, the same class surrendered its legislative autonomy for the advantages of being part of the wealthiest and most powerful nation in Europe. The Irish assumed 100 seats in the House of Commons and 32 in the House of Lords, and they also agreed to an oath of office that excluded Roman Catholics from the body of the combined Parliament. There was some resistance to the action, notably the gallant but futile rising inspired by Robert Emmet in 1803. For the most part, however, the transferral of power was taken with a coolness shocking to most in hindsight and incomprehensible to some at the time. 'What madness,' wrote Thomas DeQuincey of his visit to the final session of the Irish parliament, 'has persuaded them to part with their birthright?' The price of submission was a guarantee of protections from foreign invasion like that threatened by the French in 1798, promises of eventual Catholic emancipation, and the prospect of economic revival based on English investment. The protection was provided and the promise of emancipation was kept, but the economic condition of the country continued to slide toward the catastrophic famine of the 1840s. The tenor of DeQuincey's comment, however, remains pertinent nearly two centuries after Union. From the present perspective the act seems most startling for its assumptions that Union could be decreed, that Ireland could be made politically one with England, and that modern politics and economic necessity could override the enduring distinctions between the islands. Subsequent events have proven those assumptions false, and accounts of English visitors to Ireland immediately after Union suggest some of the least statistical, least analytical, and most compelling reasons why.

The distinct variety of account most popular in this era was the 'sketch', like J. Gamble's *Sketches of History, Politics, and Manners Taken in Dublin* (1811), and William Makepeace Thackeray's *Irish Sketch Book* (1842). The form was then popular for other occasions, too, as is evident from Dickens' *Sketches by Boz* (1836). But it is fundamental to the history of these accounts that after Union the 'sketch', with its implication of greater accessibility, would predominate. It is difficult to believe that the dissolution of political borders did not in some small way contribute to the notion that Ireland would surrender its true identity to the jottings and notes of the casual English visitor. Such at least was the assumption of the anonymous *Sportsman in Ireland* who arrived for his holiday swearing that 'ere I revisit the artificial shore of my birth, the Irish as they are, and not as political partisans would paint them, shall be known to me'. Convinced that Union had eradicated a plethora of arbitrary divisions, the English visitor could arrive secure in the knowledge that now, after vestiges of unreasonable suspicion had been shed, Ireland lay before him in its true form for the first time. Henry Inglis remained marginally cognizant of Ireland as 'foreign', but his working assumption was that it would be known to him, too: 'I yet believe that truth may be come at by anyone who seeks it out, and who comes to the search with an unbiassed mind'. Continuing improvement in conveyances no doubt encouraged this notion, for Inglis, among others, felt his search for truth immeasurably enhanced by that 'new race, the drivers of jaunting-cars'. The essential dilettantism of such a 'sketch' writer was recognized immediately by the Irish-born novelist Charles Lever, who contented himself with good-natured burlesques of sketchbook visitors while concocting his own novelistic caricature of the Irish for the delight of a loyal and enormous audience. Others also quickly recognized the rigidity and superficiality of what was a remarkably popular genre; three years after John Carr published *The Stranger in Ireland* in 1805, Edward Dubois ridiculed it in a shrewd burlesque called *My Pocket Book*.

The dominant fact of Irish life that assaulted the best intentions of these visitors was the appalling poverty of the people. Population growth was far in excess of any public assistance, such as the Poor law of 1838. By commonly accepted figures Ireland had 5 million people in 1800, more than 6 million by 1821, and more than 8 million by 1841. The overwhelming majority of this population owned no land, struggled under villainous middlemen to absentee landowners, and lapsed into a subsistence dependence on the potato that would prove disastrous. The palpable result of these conditions was beggary to an extent, these writers assure us, that would never be tolerated in England. As J. C. Curwen wrote with contemptuous sarcasm, 'we were somewhat surprised with the new characters assumed by the mendicants, who travel here *en famille*'. In this particular phase of English reaction to Irish poverty, the shocked condemnations of 'filth' and 'sluttishness' of earlier visitors give way to a surprisingly irritable contempt of the sheer affrontery of paupers. 'They come crawling around you with lying prayers', wrote even as perseveringly jovial a visitor as Thackeray of the beggars and homeless, 'refuse them and the wretches run off with a laugh and a joke, a miserable grinning cynicism'. These are early hints that the curtain of suspicion and difference, ostensibly withdrawn by Union, could be redrawn by intractable deprivation, about to manifest itself in the famine, and the habitual English reaction to it in terms of morality. Even in the age of idealistic abrogation of 'artificial shore[s]', this form of underlying antagonism, Thackeray's concentration on the cynicism of the beggars rather than on their actual poverty, suggests the improbability of any political or commercial elimination of enduring divisions between the two islands.

But those are intimations of developments not foreseen by the early 19th century English visitors to Ireland. What they did see gave them cause for hope, however self-serving that hope seems in retrospect, and they could contain their disgust in peripheral irritation while remaining resolutely optimistic. The new consensus image of the Irish formulated by English visitors between the Act of Union and the famine centered on a sentimental stereotype of a peasantry in unfortunate circumstances soon to be alleviated by the benevolent terms of Union. The stereotype is a familiar one of fetching colleens (as distinct from the aboriginal whores of earlier centuries), servile obedience, harmless superstition (as distinct from Papist blasphemy), childish prevarication ('lying' only in connection with beggary), a charming sense of humor, and a delinquent relish for internecine clubfests. It is in the early 19th century that these visitors begin to attribute belief in fairies to the Irish, who can scarcely have acquired that belief suddenly. It is also in the early 19th century that the term 'Emerald Isle' comes into common usage. The image of the Irish in the era is not one of backwardness but of adolescence. As Inglis observed when confronted with distasteful misbehavior, 'everyone knows how easily a mob, especially an Irish mob, is reduced to obedience by a very trifling display of firmness and force'.

This transformation of the 18th century image implies just that sort of more paternal role for England. The stereotype is also common in the work of Irish writers from this period such as Lever and Samuel Lover and Thomas Moore. Irish writers fueling English stereotypes would not become cause for contempt in Ireland until the end of the century. The possibility of a more complex literary image of the Irish and of an Irish literature in English was just emerging in the work of Maria Edgeworth. From Union to famine there was a period when the fictions of Irish writers and the non-fiction accounts of English visitors came into a brief conjunction, when the innocuous and ostensibly disarming images of the Irish in their own fiction and in the visitor's non-fiction replicated each other. Thus Inglis can at this time cite as a virtually documentary source of information Gerald Griffin's novel *The Collegians* and also describe faction fighting in terms reminiscent of the stories of William Carleton.

Among its many effects, the Great Famine, at its worst from 1846 to 1848, quite suddenly ended frivolous English reportage from Ireland. The cause of the devastation, which fundamentally altered the image of Ireland to other foreigners as well, was a potato blight transported from the U.S. and Canada. This plant disease, in conjunction with poor weather for crops, wiped out almost the entire potato harvest of 1846, forced consumption of seed potatoes ordinarily reserved for sowing, and thus eliminated the bulk of the staple diet of most of the population of Ireland. The consequent misery, progressively exacerbated by typhus, scurvy, and dysentry, has been documented in many works and with special drama in Cecil Woodham-Smith's *The Great Hunger*. The demographic effect on Ireland was a population decline between 1845 and 1851 of 2 million, a loss of almost one-quarter of the population to starvation, disease, and emigration. Although the English poor suffered from the effects of famine at the same time, there was no perception on any part that their suffering was in any way comparable to the national plight of the Irish. Indeed, on visiting post-famine Ireland Harriet Martineau chose Egypt as comparable in widespread misery and visible effects of diseases such as pox and opthalamia.

In such circumstances Ireland quite understandably lost its appeal to ordinary English tourists. It attracted instead politically-motivated visitors: the ones included here are Carlyle, Harriet Martineau, an anonymous correspondent from *The Times*, and an anonymous 'Guardian of the Poor'. They came to Ireland because of its misery rather than despite it, and their surprised emphasis on isolated pockets of moderate prosperity in the country suggests disappointment, not relief. The English visitor to Ireland in this period came prepared to witness deprivation and ready to record in graphic detail the effects of wholesale famine on a population already enured to chronic deprivation. It does not cheapen or distort the actual costs of the famine to note that these English visitors were more ready to stress the effects of deprivation than were their counterparts during earlier famines in Ireland's troubled agricultural history or during other devastating upheavals such as the Cromwellian settlement. Only in the post-famine years, however, did the popular English image of the Irish, to judge at least from these accounts, become one of victimization. In the middle and late 19th century the Irish are consistently treated as guiltless victims, a marked contrast to the earlier sense of their misery as self-inflicted. Thus for Martineau the Irish poor are 'victims of a sudden, sweeping calamity, which bore no relation to vice, folly, laziness, or improvidence' as distinct from the 'degraded order of people' to be found in the English workhouse. To Carlyle the Irish were the victims of both natural calamity and the same forces of pauperism Martineau thought so detrimental to the English poor. To Carlyle the calamity was an irrevocable matter of the past, but Irish victimization continued in the form of English philanthropy, in relief programs and workhouses that were sties for breeding a 'human swinery'. Later in the century, as political tensions mounted with the spread of Irish land league agitation, the image of the Irish as passive victims remained intact. For the correspondent from *The Times*, the peasant population, already victimized by nature, was further victimized in 1886 by their own political organizers. For the anonymous 'Guardian of the Poor', the Irish were victims of poverty and ignorance, and so any militancy on their part is attributed to these doleful burdens, not to any premeditated militancy or justifiable discontent.

There is another significance to Martineau's comparison of the Irish with those geographically and culturally more distant subjects of colonization, the Egyptians. The famine underscored the difference between England and Ireland and gave new finality to the English sense of being a *stranger* in Ireland. The catastrophe of the famine shattered the hope for assimilation epitomized by the Act of Union by demonstrating the government's inability to slow or to counter its devastation. Even if the famine is considered an unforeseeable 'Act of God', it still proved Parliament unable to administer Ireland effectively under the terms of the Union. In the early 19th century, the anonymous 'Sportsman in Ireland' had a sense only of impatience with 'artificial boundaries'. But after the famine this sense gives way to one of implacable divisions between the islands. After the 1840s there is a heightened consciousness of Ireland as foreign to the English visitor, a new awareness of the singular perspective of the English observer of Ireland. This consciousness is expressed, for example, in the frequency with which Martineau's preparatory comments take the form of: 'before entering an Irish workhouse [or cottage, or village], the English visitor is aware that the people to be seen within are altogether a different class or race from those whom he has been accustomed to see in the workhouses [or cottages, or villages] at home'. It was at this time, too, that Matthew Arnold, in *The Study of Celtic Literature* (1861), was promulgating an ostensibly benevolent but ultimately condescending theory of the difference between Celt and Saxon. 'I say this', Arnold wrote, 'what we want is to *know* the Celt and his genius'. Once past his most ethereal formulations, Arnold reported on the current state of that knowledge of the genius of the Celt, 'he loves bright colors, he easily becomes audacious, overcrowing, full of fanfaronade'.

Ironically, this belated English search for the special character of Ireland and simultaneous failure to recognize it seriously takes shape in the midst of the modern erosion of some of the most distinctive features of the culture the writers of these accounts have railed against since Spenser's day. As all histories of modern Ireland concur, among the casualties of the famine was the Irish language, dead with the victims of starvation and dying among the aspirants to emigration. As the language disappeared, so did elements of the cultural heritage residual in it, elements that would have to be reconstructed in the Celtic revival of the late 19th and early 20th centuries, when the Irish formulated images of themselves. Of course, what they formulated was a mythology with its own arbitrary features, ones often influenced by English visions of the Celt and his difference from the Saxon.

But this anthology is a collection of writings about Ireland in which the Irish do not speak. That editorial exclusion focuses attention on the kinds of images of the Irish that persist over centuries and also those that can be invented in particular contexts. The final awareness that emerges from a reading of these works is of the authors' own failures of self-knowledge, their failures to examine their own assumptions in light of the evidence of Ireland. Not that anyone can expect complete self-consciousness or any kind of Olympian perspective on one's own consciousness. But these visitors to Ireland never allow their own assumptions on arrival to be challenged, and so they create images of the Irish in support of those assumptions. In his *Letters on the Irish Nation* of 1800, George Cooper, clearly a well-educated man, wrote as follows:

> The natives of that country [Ireland], the descendants, as it seems probably, of its aborigines, still remain the same rude barbarians that our earliest accounts describe them. I shall have little difficulty in describing this character, as it may be depictured in the same few words with that of all nations who have been seen in a state of ignorance and barbarity.

It is not Cooper's sense of 'barbarity', one supported by his reading of previous accounts of Ireland, that is of greatest interest here. Most interesting of all is the arrogance underlying the assertion that 'I shall have little difficulty in describing this character'. This book is a history of three hundred years of failures to describe the Irish adequately and a history of failures by most of these writers to realize that the task might involve more than a little difficulty.

These writers are not for the most part formidable authorities on the Irish. In the later centuries, especially, their work is part of the popular rather than the specialized English literature on the subject of Ireland. But these authors share the preoccupations of more authoritative ones like J. A. Froude, for example, and precisely because of their popularity they are representative records of a social history. It is also admittedly an anachronistic project to layer the politics of the present day on the experience of, say, an Elizabethan adventurer. But anachronistic or not, the worth of that project is to increase our own awareness of cultural relativity and the ways images of 'them' as opposed to 'us' are invented in defense of aggression or in support of self-congratulation. These kinds of works can serve no better purpose than to help us read our own accounts of the continuing entanglement between Ireland and England and the many others like it.

The Civill Irish Woman   The Civill Irish man

The Wilde Irish man   The Wilde Irish woman

Illustrations from John Speed's *Atlas* (1611), a compilation of histories and maps of Great Britain including Ireland. Speed's text on Ireland was a derivation of Cambrensis's history, one that emphasised the superstitious and the fantastic. This illustration elucidates the Elizabethan distinction between 'English Irish' and 'Wild Irish'.

ELIZABETHAN IRELAND

Elizabethan Ireland, as represented in W. L. Renwick's edition of Edmund Spenser's *View of the Present State of Ireland*. Spenser's residence, Kilcolman, is indicated between Limerick and Cork. The English Pale around Dublin is the most significant border on the map.

Edmund Campion

A HISTORY OF IRELAND
Written in the Year 1571

Edmund Campion (1540-1581), born in London, was a celebrated scholar and orator at Oxford. He took the oath of supremacy on receiving his degree in 1564, but his Catholic sympathies were widely-known and even used against him. Tension between Elizabeth and Pope Pius V, who was about to excommunicate the queen, created a climate for English Catholics that Campion acknowledges below, in reference to fasting, as dangerous. In 1569 he went to Ireland with a pupil, Richard Stanihurst, with the intention of obtaining preferment in the proposed Dublin University (not founded until 1592). Campion was threatened with arrest but protected by the lord deputy, Henry Sidney, and a speaker of the Irish House of Commons, James Stanihurst, his pupil's father. It was under this sponsorship that he wrote his *History of Ireland*. As Elizabeth's persecution of English Catholics grew sterner, Campion fled to the continent. He became a Jesuit in 1573 and returned to England in disguise in 1580. There he was betrayed and arrested in 1581 soon after publication of his *Decem Rationes*, a critique of the Anglican Church. In less than six months there followed a sensational incarceration in the tower, examination before Elizabeth, trial at Westminster, and execution at Tyburn. Campion was beatified by the Catholic Church in 1886.

Given how little of substance had been written about Ireland by this time, it is remarkable how much energy Campion exerts refuting historians of antiquity — Cambrensis, Sylvius, Volateranus, Bede, Solinus, and Strabo. Thus even in the first of these accounts of Ireland a pattern is established of confronting previous descriptions of the country as much as the place itself. Nor is this solely a preoccupation of historians, for the pattern is consistent through other accounts with entirely different purposes.

These selections emphasize Campion's descriptions of the place and the people over his frequently very erratic history proper. His comments on the tenuous status of the Pale and the inexorable degeneration of English into English-Irish savages are especially powerful given his actual refuge in Dublin as he wrote. Campion's descriptions were extremely influential, especially on other Elizabethan commentators such as Spenser. That influence was due in part to his common sense; absurd notions of barnacles hatching into birds, for example, are far outnumbered by more sensible ones such as the geographical explanation for the absence of snakes in Ireland. That influence was also possible because of the fortuitous moderation of his Catholicism, which leaves him free, for example, to make a joke at St. Patrick's expense.

Campion's work was first published, as adapted by Richard Stanihurst, in Holinshed's *Chronicles* in 1577. These selections are modernized versions of the text printed by James Ware in *Ancient Irish Histories* (1633; rpt. Dublin: Hibernia Press, 1809).

THE SITE AND SPECIAL PARTS OF IRELAND

I reland lieth aloof in the West Ocean, and is deemed by the later survey to be in length well-nigh three hundred miles north and south, broad from east to west one hundred and twenty. In proportion it resembleth an egg, blunt and plain on the sides, not reaching forth to the sea in nooks and elbows of land, as Britain doth.

Long since, it was divided into four regions: Leinster, east; Connaught, west; Ulster, north; Munster, south; and into a fifth plot defalked [i.e cut off] from every fourth part, lying together in the heart of the realm, called thereof Media, Meath. . . .

An old distinction there is of Ireland into Irish and English pales, for the Irish had raised continual tumults against the English planted here with the conquest.* At last they coursed [i.e. pursued] them into a narrow circuit of certain shires in Leinster, which the English did choose, as the fattest soil, most defensible, their proper right, and most open to receive help from England. Hereupon it was termed their pale, and whereout they durst not peep. But now both within this pale, uncivil Irish and some rebels do dwell, and without it, countries and cities English are well governed.

* * *

NATURE OF THE SOIL AND OTHER INCIDENTS

The soil is low and waterish and includeth diverse little islands, environed with bogs and marshes: the highest hills have standing pools in their top. Inhabitants (especially new come) are subject to distillations, rhumes and fixes [i.e. colds and dysentery], for remedy whereof they use an ordinary drink of aquavitae, so qualified in the making that it dryeth more, and inflameth less, than other hot confections. The air is wholesome, not altogether so clear and subtle as ours of England. Of bees good store, no vineyards, contrary to the opinion of some writers, who both in this and other errours touching the land may easily be excused as those that wrote of hearsay.

Cambrensis in his time complaineth that Ireland had excess of wood and very little champaigne ground, but now the English pale is too naked. Turf and sea coal [i.e. mineral coal] is their most fuel. It is stored of kyne [i.e. cows], of excellent horses, of hawkes, of fish and fowl. They are not without wolves, and greyhounds to hunt them, bigger of bone and limb than a colt. Their kyne, as also their cattle, and commonly what else soever the country engendereth (except man) is much less in quantity than ours of England. Sheep few and those bearing coarse fleece, whereof they spin

---

*By Henry II in 1171.

notable rug mantles. The country is very fruitful both of corn and grass. The grass, for default of husbandry (not for the cause alleged in *Polychronicon**) groweth so rank in the north parts that oft times it rotteth their kyne. Eagles are well known to breed here, but neither so big nor so many as books tell. Cambrensis reporteth of his own knowledge, and I hear it averred by credible persons, that barnacles, thousands at once, are noted along the shores to hang by the beaks, about the edges of putrified timber, ships, oars, anchor-holds, and such like: which in process taking lively heat of the sun, become water-fouls, and at their time of ripeness either fall into the sea, or fly abroad into the air. Aeneas Sylvius (that after was Pope Pius II) writeth himself to have perceived the like experiment in Scotland, where he learned the truth hereof, to be found in the Orkney Islands.

Horses they have of pace easy, in running wonderful swift. Therefore they make of them great store, as wherein at times of need they repose a great piece of safety. This breed Raphael Volateranus saith to have come at first from Asturia [in] the country of Spain, between Galicia and Portugal, where of they were called Asturcones, a name now properly applied to the Spanish jennet. I heard it verified by honourable to honourable, that a nobleman offered and was refused for one such horse a hundred kyne, five pound of lands, and an aerie of hawks yearly during seven years.

In the plain of Kildare stood that monstrous heap of stones brought thither by giants from Africa and removed thence to the plain of Salisbury at the instance of Ambrose King of Britain.

No venomous creeping beast is brought forth or nourished, or can live here being sent in, and therefore the spider of Ireland is well known not to be venomous. Only because a frog was found living in the meadows of Waterford, somewhat before the conquest, they construed it to import their overthrow. Bede writeth that serpents conveyed hither did presently die being touched with [the] smell of the land, and that whatsoever came hence was then of sovereign virtue against poison. He exemplifieth [this] in certain men stung with adders who drank in water the scrapings of books that had been in Ireland and were cured.

Generally, it is observed, the further West the less annoyance of pestilent creatures. The want whereof is to Ireland so peculiar that whereas it lay long in question, to whither realm (Britain or Ireland) the Isle of Man should pertain, the said controversy was decided, that forsomuch as venomous beasts were known to breed therein, it could not be counted a natural piece of Ireland.

Neither is this property to be ascribed to Saint Patrick's blessing (as they commonly hold) but to the original blessing of God who gave such nature to the situation and soil from the beginning. And though I doubt not but

---

*A history written in Latin by the Benedictine Ranulf Higden (d. 1364), translated into English by John Trevisa in 1387, and printed by Caxton in 1482.

it fared the better in many respects for that holy man's prayer, yet had it this condition notified [i.e. noted] hundreds of years ere he was borne.

* * *

THE DISPOSITIONS OF THE PEOPLE

The people are thus inclined: religious, frank, amorous, ireful, sufferable, of pains infinite, very glorious, many sorcerers, excellent horsemen, delighted with wars, great almsgivers, passing in hospitality. The lewder sort, both clerks and laymen, are sensual and loose to lechery above measure. The same, being virtuously bred up or reformed, are such mirrors of holiness and austerity that other nations retain but a shew or shadow of devotion in comparison of them. As for abstinence and fasting, which these days make so dangerous, this is to them a familiar kind of chastisement. In which virtue and diverse others, how far the best excel, so far in gluttony and other hateful crimes the vicious are worse than too bad. They follow the dead corpses to the grave with howlings and barbarous outcries, pitiful in appearance, whereof grew (as I suppose) the proverb, to weep Irish. The uplandish are lightly abused to believe and avouch idle miracles and revelations vain and childish. Greedy of praise they be, and fearful of dishonour. And to this end they esteem their poets, who write Irish learnedly, and pen their sonnets heroical, for which they are bountifully rewarded. But if they send out libels in dispraise, thereof the gentlemen, especially the mere Irish, stand in great awe. They love tenderly their foster children, and bequeath to them a child's portion, whereby they nourish sure friendship, so beneficial every way, that commonly five hundred kyne and better are given in reward to win a noble man's child to foster. They are sharp-witted, lovers of learning capable of any study whereunto they bend themselves, constant in travail, adventurous, intractable, kind-hearted, secret in displeasure.

Hitherto the Irish of both sorts mere, and English, are affected much indifferently, saving that in these, by good order, and breaking the same, virtues are far more pregnant. In those others, by licentious and evil custom, the same faults are more extreme and odious, I say, by licentious and evil custom, for that there is daily trial of good nature among them. How soon they be reclaimed, and to what rare gifts of grace and wisdom, they do and have aspired. Again, the very English of birth, conversant with the brutish sort of that people, become degenerate in short space, and are quite altered into the worst rank of Irish rogues, such a force hath education to make or mar. It is further to be known that the simple Irish are utterly another people than our English in Ireland, whom they call despitefully *boddai sassoni's*, and *boddai ghalt*, that is, English and Saxon churles [i.e. peasants], because of their English ancestors, planted here with the conquest, and since with descent hath lasted now 400 years. Of this people therefore severally by themselves I must entreat. Yet none otherwise than as they stand, undefiled, and serve their accustomed humours, with whom I join all such as either by living near them, or by liking their trade [i.e. ways], are transformed into them.

OF THE MERE IRISH

Touching the mere Irish, I am to advertise [to] my reader that he impute not to them the faults of their ancestors, which here I have noted for two causes. First, that when the same are read in Cambrensis, Solinus, or others, he confounds not the times, but may be able distinctly to consider their manners then different from these days. Secondly, that it may appear how much Ireland is beholding to God for suffering them to be conquered, whereby many of these enormities were cured, and more might be, would themselves be pliable.

In some corners of the land they used a damnable superstition, leaving the right arms of their infant males unchristened (as they termed it) to the intent it might give a more ungracious and deadly blow.

I found a fragment of an epistle wherein a virtuous monk declareth that to him (travailing in Ulster) came a grave gentleman about Easter, desirous to be confessed and howseled [i.e. given communion], who in all his lifetime had never yet received the Blessed Sacrament. When he had said his mind, the priest demanded [of] him whether he were faultless in the sin of homocide? He answered that he never wist [i.e. knew] the matter to be heinous, but being instructed thereof, he confessed the murder of five, the rest he left wounded, so he knew not whether they lived or no. Then he was taught that both the one and the other were execrable, and very meekly humbled himself to repentence.

Solinus writeth that they woonted [i.e. were accustomed] (because they would seem terrible and martial) to imbrue their faces in the blood of their enemies slain. Strabo, the famous geographer, who flourished under Augustus and Tiberius Caesar more than fifteen hundred years ago, telleth (without asseveration) that the Irish were great gluttons, eaters of man's flesh, and counted it honourable for parents deceased to be eaten up of their children, and that in open sight they meddled with their wives, mothers, and daughters. Which is the less incredible, considering what Saint Jerome avoucheth of the Scots, their offspring and allies, and what all histories do witness of the [Middle Eastern] Scithians, their ancient founders.

Although since the time of Saint Patrick, Christianity was never extinct in Ireland, yet the government being hayled [i.e. forced] into contrary factions, the nobility lawless, the multitude willful, it came to pass that religion waxed with the temporal common sort cold and feeble, until the conquest did settle it, especially in cases of restraint and discipline. The honourable state of marriage they much abused, either in contracts, unlawful meetings, Levitical and canonical degrees of prohibition, or in divorces at pleasure, or in omitting sacramental solemnities, or in retaining either concubines or harlots for wives. Yea even at this day, where the clergy is faint, they can be content to marry for a year and a day of probation, and at the year's end to return her home upon any light quarrels, if the gentlewoman's friends be weak and unable to avenge the injury. Never heard I of so many dispensations for marriage, as those men shew. I pray God grant they be all authentic and built upon sufficient warrant.

Covenant and indent [i.e. legal agreements] with them never so warily, never so precisely, yet they have been found faithless and perjured. Where they are joined in colour of surest amity, there they intend to kill. This ceremony reporteth Cambrensis: the parties to be coupled in league meet at church, become God-septes, or allies, bear each other on their backs certain paces in a ring, kiss together holy relics, take blessing of the bishop, offer each to other a drop of their own blood, and drink it up between them. Even in the doing hereof, they practise mutual destruction.

They have been used in solemn controversies to protest and swear by Saint Patrick's staff, called *Bachal esu*, which oath, because upon breach thereof heavy plagues ensued [upon] them, they feared more to break than if they had sworn by the holy evangelist.

In Ulster thus they used to crown their king. A white cow was brought forth, which the king must kill, and seeth in water whole, and bathe himself therein stark naked. Then sitting in the same caldron, his people about him, together with them he must eat the flesh, and drink the broth wherein he sitteth, without cup or dish or use of his hand.

So much for their old customs. Now a few words of their trade at this present.

Clear men they are of skin and hue, but of themselves careless and bestial. Their women are well favoured, clear coloured, fair handed, big and large, suffered from their infancy to grow at will, nothing curious of their feature and proportion of body.

Their infants of the meaner sort are neither swaddled nor lapped in linen, but folded up stark naked in a blanket till they can go, and then if they get a piece of rug to cover them they are well sped. Linen shirts the rich do wear for wantonness and bravery, with wide hanging sleeves plaited, thirty yards are little enough for one of them. They have now left their saffron and learned to wash their shirts four or five times in a year. Proud they are of long crisped glibs [i.e. forelocks] and do nourish the same with all their cunning. To crop the front thereof they take it for a notable piece of villainy. Shamrocks, watercresses, roots, and other herbs they feed upon. Oatmeal and butter they cram together. They drink whey, milk, and beef broth, flesh they devour without bread, corn such as they have they keep for their horses. In haste and hunger they squeeze out the blood of raw flesh and ask no more dressing thereto, the rest boileth in their stomachs with aquavitae, which they swill in after such a surfeit by quarts and pottles [i.e. half-gallons]. [From] their kyne they let blood, which growen [in]to a jelly they bake and overspread with butter, and so eat it in lumps.

One office in the house of great men is a tale-teller, who bringeth his Lord on to sleep with tales vain and frivolous, [which most] give sooth and credence. So light they are in believing whatsoever is with any countenance of gravity affirmed by their superiors, whom they esteem and honour, that a lewd prelate within these few years, needy of money, was able to persuade his parish that Saint Patrick in striving with Saint Peter to let an Irish gallowglass [i.e. foot soldier] into Heaven had his head broken with the keys, for whose relief he obtained a collation.

Without either precepts or observation of congruity they speak Latin like a vulgar language, learned in their common schools of leach-craft [i.e. medicine] and law, whereat they begin children, and hold on sixteen or twenty years conning by rote the aphorisms of Hypocrates and the Civil Institutions, and a few other pairings of those two faculties. I have seen them where they kept school, ten in some one chamber, groveling upon couches of straw, their books at their noses, themselves lying flat prostrate, and so to chant out their lessons by piecemeal, being the most part lusty fellows of twenty-five years and upwards.

Other lawyers they have, liable to certain families, which after the custom of the country determine and judge cases. These consider of wrongs offered and received among their neighbors, be it murder, or felony, or trespass, all is redeemed by composition [i.e. compensation settlement] (except the grudge of parties seeking revenge). And the time they have to spare from spoiling and proyning [i.e. plundering and preening] they lightly bestow in parling about such matters. The Brehon (so they call this kind of lawyer) sitteth himself down on a bank, the Lords and gentlemen at variance round about him, and then they proceed.

They honour devout friars and pilgrims, suffer them to pass quietly, spare them and their mansions, whatsoever outrage they shew to the country beside them. To rob and prey [upon] their enemies, they deem it no offence, nor seek any means to recover their loss, but even watch them[selves for] the like turn. But if neighbours and friends send their cators [i.e. provisioners] to purloin [from] one another, such actions are judged by the Brehons aforesaid.

Toward the living they are noisome and malicious, the same being dead they labour to avenge eagerly and fiercely. They love and trust their foster brethren more than their own [families]. Turloch Luineach O'Neill, that now usurpeth, is said to repose in them his greatest surety.

Strumpets are there too vile and abominable to write of, which not only without fear, but also without remorse, do advance themselves in numbring [i.e. ascertaining] what noblemen have liking to their bodies. He that can bring most of his name [i.e. clan] into the field, base or other, triumpheth exceedingly. For increase of which name, they allow themselves not only whores, but also choice and store of whores. One I heard named who hath (as he called them) more than ten wives, in twenty places.

There is among them a brotherhood of carrows [i.e. vagrant gamblers] that profess to play at cards all the year long and make it their only occupation. They play away mantle and all to the bare skin, and then truss themselves in straw or in leaves. They wait for passengers on the highway, invite them to a game upon the green, and ask no more but companions to hold them sport. For default of other stuff they pawn portions of their glib, the nails of their fingers and toes, their privy members; which they lose or redeem at the courtesy of the winner.

Where they fancy and favor, they are wonderfully kind. They exchange by commutation of wares for the most part, and have utterly no coin stirring in any great lord's house. Some of them be richly plated [i.e. dressed in armour]. Their ladies are trimmed rather with massy [i.e. weighty] jewels than with garish apparel. It is counted a beauty in them to be tall, round, and fat.

The inheritance descendeth not to the son, but to the brother, nephew, or cousin germaine [i.e. closest], eldest, and most valiant. For the child being oftentimes left in nonage or otherwise young and unskillful, [would] never [be] able to defend his patrimony, being his no longer than he can hold it by force of arms. But by [the] time he grows to a competent age, and has buried an uncle or two, he also taketh his turn, and leaveth it in like order to his posterity. This custom breedeth among them continual wars and treasons.

Woodcut of lice-picking from Andrew Boorde, *The First Book of the Introduction of Knowledge* (1548?). The large scale of the Irish kern's arrow adds a malevolent element to an otherwise domestic and placid scene.

Richard Stanihurst

A Treatise
Containing a Plain and Perfect
DESCRIPTION OF IRELAND

Richard Stanihurst (1547-1618) was born in Dublin, the grandson of a Lord Mayor of Dublin and the son of speaker of the Irish House of Commons. His Irish birth makes him unique in this collection. But his patently 'English' perspective on Irish affairs and his crucial role in the compilation of the Irish sections of Holinshed's *Chronicles* makes his description an essential component of the history of these accounts of Ireland.

Stanihurst entered Oxford in 1563 and studied law immediately after taking his degree in 1568. Far more attractive than the law, however, was the example of Edmund Campion — Stanihurst was presumably among the many Oxford students said to have idolized Campion to the extent of imitating his walk. In 1569 Stanihurst accompanied Campion to Ireland and insured his father's protection against anti-Catholic persecution. It was this connection that led Raphael Holinshed, preparing his *Chronicles* in 1577, to procure 'a learned gentleman master Richard Stanihurst to continue [Campion's *History*] forward as he saw occasion, being furnished with matter to enlarge the work'. For this 1577 edition of the *Chronicles* Stanihurst incorporated Campion's *History* wholesale, adding to it his own continuation of the history through Henry VIII and the description excerpted below. To these were added Hooker's continuation of the history to date for the 1586 edition of the *Chronicles*.

In 1579 Stanihurst left England for the Netherlands, where he converted to Catholicism and eventually took Holy Orders in 1602. His major literary labor in the interim was a translation of the *Aeneid*, inspired by the verse theories of Gabriel Harvey, that has been ridiculed for centuries. In 1812, for example, Robert Southey suggested that 'as Chaucer has been called the well of English undefiled, so might Stanihurst be denominated the common sewer of the language'.

However infelicitous Stanihurst's eccentric and characteristically boorish style was when applied to Virgil, his interest in language and the ramifications of style give his account of Ireland a shrewd and informative emphasis on the language of the country. Indeed, for Stanihurst language — Irish in collision with English — is the key to the fragility of the Dublin Pale and to the Desmond Rebellions erupting in his own time.

These selections are a modernized version of the text printed in the sixth volume of the 1808 edition of Holinshed's *Chronicles*.

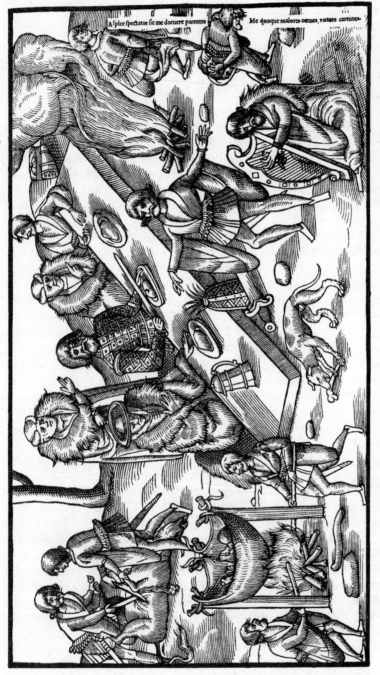

The woodcuts of John Derrick's *Image of Ireland* (1581) are the best-known visual representations of Elizabethan Ireland. This banquet scene is a compendium of what Derrick called 'wild shamrock manners' associated with cooking, eating and dancing.

T here is also another [other than provincial] division of Ireland into the English pale and Irishry. For when Ireland was subdued by the English, diverse of the conquerors planted themselves near to Dublin, and the confines thereto adjoining, and so, as it were enclosing and impaling themselves within certain lists and territories, they feazed [i.e. drove] away the Irish; insomuch as that country became mere English, and thereof it was termed the English pale: which in ancient time stretched from Dundalk to Catherlagh or Kilkenny. But now what for the slackness of the marchours [i.e. border districts], and encroaching of the Irish enemy, the scope of the English pale is greatly impaired and is cramped and couched into an odd corner of the country named Fingal, with a parcel of the king's land, Meath, the counties of Kildare and Louth, which parts are applied chiefly with good husbandry, and taken for the richest and civilest soils in Ireland. But Fingal especially from time to time hath been so addicted to all the points of husbandry, as that they are nicknamed by their neighours, for their continual drudgery, 'collonnes', of the Latin word *Coloni*, whereunto the clipped English word 'clown' seemeth to be answerable.

The word 'Fingal' countervaileth in English the race or sept of the English or strangers, for they were solely seized of that part of the land, gripping with their talons so firmly that warm nest that from the conquest* to this day the Irish enemy could never rouse them from thence. The inhabitants of the English pale have been in old times so much addicted to their civility, and so far sequestered from barbarous savageness, as their only mother tongue was English. And truly, so long as these impaled dwellers did sunder themselves as well in land as in language from the Irish, rudeness was day by day in the country supplanted, civility engrafted, good laws established, loyalty observed, rebellion suppressed, and in fine the coin of a young England was like to shoot in Ireland. But when their posterity became not altogether so wary in keeping, as their ancestors were valiant in conquering, the Irish language was free denizened in the English pale. This canker took such deep root, that the body that before was whole and sound was by little and little festered, and in manner wholly putrified. And not only this parcel of Ireland grew to that civility, but also Ulster and the greater part of Munster, by the sequel of the Irish history, shall plainly appear. But of all other places, Wexford, with the territory bayed and enclosed within the river called the Pill, was so quite estranged from Irishry, that if a traveller of the Irish (which was rare in those days) had pitched his foot within the Pill and spoken Irish, the Wexfordians would command him forthwith to turn the other end of this tongue and speak English, or else bring his trouchman [i.e. interpreter] with him. But in our days they have so acquainted themselves with the

---

*As in Campion, above, the landing of Henry II in 1171.

Irish, that they have made a mingle mangle or gallimaufry of both languages, and have in such medley or checkerwise so crabbedly jumbled them both together that commonly the inhabitants of the meaner sort speak neither good English nor good Irish.

There was of late days one of the peers of England sent to Wexford as commissioner, to decide the controversies of that country. And hearing in affable ways the rude complaints of the country clowns, he conceived here and there sometimes a word, other whiles a sentence. The noble man being very glad that upon his first coming to Ireland he understood so many words, told one of his familiar friends that he stood in very great hope to become shortly a well spoken man in the Irish, supposing that the blunt people had prattled Irish. All the while they jangled English.

To this day, the dregs of the old ancient Chaucer English are kept as well there as in Fingal. They term a spider an 'attercop', a wisp a 'wad', a lump of bread a 'pocket' or a 'pucket', a sillibucke [i.e. curd preparation] a 'copprous', a faggot a 'blease' or a 'blaze" for the short burning of it (as I judge), a physician a 'leech', a gap a 'shard', a base court or quadrangle a 'bawen' or rather (as I do suppose) a 'barton', the household or folks 'many', sharp 'keen', strange 'uncouth', easy 'eeth' or 'effe', a dunghill a 'mizen'. As for the word 'bater', that in Engish purporteth a lane bearing unto a highway, I take it for a mere Irish word that crept unawares into the English through the daily intercourse of the English and Irish inhabitants. And whereas commonly in all countries the women speak most neatly and pertly, which Tully in his third book *De Oratore*, speaking in the person of Crassus, seemed to have observed: yet notwithstanding [that], in Ireland it falleth out contrary. For the women have in their English tongue a harsh and broad kind of pronunciation, uttering their words so peevishly and faintly as though they were half sick and ready to call for a posset [i.e. medicinal drink]. And most commonly in words of two syllables they give the last the accent: as they say, market, basket, gossip, pussoat [plump one], Robert, Nickolas, etc.: which doubltless doth disbeautify their English above measure. And if they could be weaned from that corrupt custom, there is none that could dislike of their English.

Here perchance some snappish carper will take me at rebound, and snuffingly snib me for debasing the Irish language: but truly, whosoever shall be found so overthwartly bent, he takes the matter far awry. For as my skill is very simple therein, so I would be loath to disveil my rashness in giving light verdict in anything to me unknown. My short discourse tendeth to this drift, that it is not expedient that the Irish tongue should be so universally gaggled in the English pale: because that by proof and experience we see that the pale was never in a more flourishing state than when it was wholly English, and never in worse plight than since it hath enfranchised the Irish.

But some will say that I shew myself herein as frivolous as some losing gamesters seem superstitious. When they play themselves dry, they goggle with their eyes hither and thither, and if they can pry out anyone that giveth them the gaze, they stand lumping and lowering, fretting and fuming, for they imagine that all their evil luck proceeded of him. And yet if the standerby depart, the loser may be found as dry shaven as he was before. And even so it fareth with you, because you see all things run to ruin in the English pale, by reason of great enormities in the country, either openly practised or covertly winked at; you glance your eye on that which standeth next you, and by beating Jack for Jill, you impute the fault to that which perhaps would little further the weal public if it were exiled. Now truly you shoot very near the mark. But if I may crave your patience till [the] time you see me shoot my bolt [i.e. arrow], I hope you will not deny, but that as near the prick [i.e. target] as you are, and as very a haggler as I am, yet the scantling [i.e. bull's eye] shall be mine.

First therefore take this with you, that a conquest draweth, or at leastwise ought to draw to it, three things: to wit, law, apparel, and language. For where the country is subdued, there the inhabitants ought to be ruled by the same law that the conqueror is governed [by], to wear the same fashion of attire wherewith the victor is vested, and speak the same language that the vanquisher parleth. And if any of these three lack, doubtless the conquest limpeth. Now whereas Ireland hath been by lawful conquest brought under the subjection of England, not only in King Henry II's reign, but also as well before as after (as by the discourse of this Irish history shall evidently be deciphered), and the conquest hath been so absolute and perfect that all Leinster, Meath, Ulster, the more part of Connaught and Munster, all the cities and boroughs in Ireland have been wholly Englished, and with English conquerors inhabited. Is it decent (think you) that their own ancient native tongue shall be shrouded in oblivion, and suffer the enemy's language, as it were a tettar [i.e. infection] or ringworm, to harbor itself within the jaws of English conquerors? No, truly.

And now that I have fallen unawares into this discourse, it will not be far amiss to stand somewhat roundly upon this point. It is known, and by this history you may in part perceive, how bravely Ulster once flourished. The English families were there implanted, the Irish either utterly expelled or wholly subdued, the laws duly executed, the revenue great, and only English spoken. But what brought it to this present ruin and decay? I doubt not but you guess before I tell you. They were environed and compassed with evil neighbours. Neighbourhood bred acquaintance, acquaintance waffed [i.e. wafted or conveyed] in the Irish tongue, the Irish hooked with it attire, attire haled rudeness, rudeness engendered ignorance, ignorance brought contempt of laws, the contempt of laws bred rebellion, rebellion raked thereto wars, and so consequently the utter decay and desolation of that worthy country. If these chinks, when first they began to chap, had been diligently by the dwellers stopped, her Majesty at this day, to her great charges, should not have been occasioned to dam up with many thousand pounds, yea and with the worthy carcasses of valiant soldiers, the gaps of that rebellious northern country.

*   *   *

As the whole realm of Ireland is sundered into four principal parts, as before was said, so each parcel differeth very much in the Irish tongue, every country having its dialect, or peculiar manner in speaking the language. Therefore commonly in Ireland they ascribe a property to each of the four countries in this sort. Ulster hath the right Irish phrase, but not the true pronunciation. Munster hath the true pronunciation, but not the phrase. Leinster is devoid of the right phrase and true pronunciation. Connaught hath both the right phrase and true pronunciation.

There is a choleric or disdainful interjection used in the Irish language called 'boagh', which is as much in English as 'twish'. The Irish both in ancient times and to this day commonly use it, and therefore the English conquerors called them 'Irish poghes', or 'pogh Morice'. Which taunting term is at this day very wrongfully ascribed to them of the English pale. The English interjection, 'fough', which is used in loathing a rank or strong savour, seemeth to be sib [i.e. akin] to the other.

John Hooker

THE CHRONICLES OF IRELAND

In 1569, Edmund Campion and Richard Stanihurst were in Dublin to enjoy the hospitality of Stanihurst's father, speaker of the House of Commons, and to avoid Elizabethan interdictions against English Catholics. By coincidence, that same year John Hooker so truculently lectured that same house on Elizabeth's prerogatives and so imperiously denounced the papal antichrist that the session was suspended and Hooker spirited away for his own protection. The only other link between all three is their presence as an odd trio of collaborators on the chronicles of Ireland for the premier English history of their time.

John Hooker, alias Vowell, (1526-1601) was born in Exeter, son of a mayor of the town. His 'alias' commemorates a pre-15th century family name. Left without parents at an early age, he attended Oxford and wandered leisurely around the continent. By 1555 he appears as the first chamberlain of his native Exeter. He came to Ireland in 1568 as Sir Peter Carew's solicitor, a role demanding an audacity Hooker apparently possessed. Carew, an adventurous Elizabethan entrepreneur, lodged absurd claims to enormous land holdings from Meath to Kerry. These were actually recognized by the Irish Council in the year of Hooker's arrival. As a fillip Hooker managed to obtain the license for printing the acts of the Irish parliament.

For the second, enlarged edition of Holinshed's *Chronicles* Hooker added to the Campion-Stanihurst materials a translation of Gerald Cambrensis's Irish history and his own 'chronicles' from the death of Henry VIII to date, 1586, as 'a witness of sundry things as yet fresh in memory'. The conclusion of these chronicles is excerpted below. Clearly, his primary concerns were to excoriate the recent Desmond Rebellions and to laud John Perrot's 1585 composition of Connaught, by which Irish land titles were formalized in partisan fashion in exchange for quitrents to the queen.

Hooker writes in the context of the very nadir of English relations with Rome. Pius V excommunicated Elizabeth in 1570, and soon after Gregory XIII by Papal bull withdrew recognition of Elizabeth's secular authority. Therein lies the basis for Hooker's claims of papal bloodthirstiness in an ostensibly peaceful Ireland. There are, too, apparent economic considerations embedded in his nearly hysterical religious rhetoric. But the most revealing dimension of this frequently revolting litany of brutal executions is the apparent hypocrisy in the strategy of mercilessly dismembering the Irish for the offense of being violent. The selection printed here is a modernized version of the text of the 1808 edition of Holinshed's *Chronicles*.

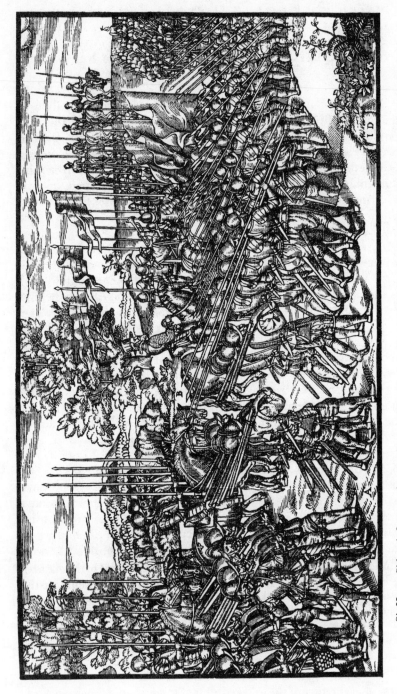

Sir Henry Sidney's force on the march, as rendered in John Derrick's *Image of Ireland.* Sidney (1529-1586) commanded the English pursuit of Shane O'Neill, a campaign that matched contrasting English and Irish leaders, troops, and tactics.

W hen he [John Perrot] had performed this [the composition of Connaught], and established the same by act of parliament, then Her Majesty's writs and process had a free passage and were current throughout the whole land, and Her Majesty known to be sovereign lady and queen of the same. Then the Irishry by little and little gave over their Brehon laws, and their Irish usage, and became obedient unto the English laws, unto which they referred themselves to be tried, and to have all their quarrels to be decided and determined. Whereof at present is extant a very notable precedent and example between two of the most principal and chief personages in the province of Ulster. The one is he, who nameth himself O'Neill, and the other is the Earl of Tyrone, the heir to the great Conn O'Neill.* These two and their ancestors, and all other noble men in that province, when soever any discord or enmity did fall out among them, they had no peacemaker but the sword, and by wars and bloodshed was the same decided. Nevertheless, these two noble men leaving to pursue their quarrels, as in times past with the sword and in hostile manner, do refer themselves to the trial of the laws; and each one of them sueth the other at the common laws, and in the chancery in Her Majesty's court at Dublin, and there as dutiful subjects do abide the trial of their cause. A thing so much the more to be considered, as the parties be of that nobility and stoutness, and a thing so rare, as heretofore not heard nor known. Which course, if it have so happy a progress and success as it hath a good entrance and beginning, no doubt but that partly by the laws, and partly by the sword, a universal obedience shall through that land be established, the common society shall be preserved, the whole realm shall flourish and prosper, Her Majesty shall be obeyed, the revenues shall be increased, and in the end peace shall be upon Israel. And as this example giveth some manifest good hope thereof, so the same is confirmed and increased by the happy victory of late in Connaught, where a number of Scots, having made an invasion, were met and encountered withall by the right worthy Sir Richard Bingham, Knight, chief commissioner of that province, and by him they were vanquished and overthrown, to the number of fifteen hundred persons; so that very few or none escaped the sword, to return home with news of their success, but were either killed or drowned.†

Thus much hitherto generally concerning the government of that land of Ireland, since the death of King Henry VIII until the present. In the

---

*The Ulster chief Conn O'Neill died in 1559, leaving rival claims based on Brehon and common law. Hooker speaks here of the rivals a generation later, Turlough Lineach, 'The O'Neill', and Hugh O'Neill, Earl of Tyrone, both of whom acceded to Perrot's Dublin Parliament of 1585. Hugh reunited the titles in 1593.

†In 1586 Richard Bingham, President of Connaught, routed a force of Scots invading to aid rebels in Mayo.

course of which time, many more notable things have been done worthy to be registered in the chronicles of perpetual fame and memory. For the attaining to the knowledge whereof, though John Hooker the writer hereof has been a diligent traveller and a searcher for the same, yet he wanted that good success, as both the history itself requireth and he himself wisheth. And yet the most part of all the actions in that age consisted most in continual wars, rebellions, and hostility, either against their most sacred kings and queens, or amongst themselves. But whatsoever hithertofore hath been done, none were so tragical, impious, and unnatural as were the last wars of the Geralds of Desmond in Munster. For of the Geralds of Kildare, who were not acquainted, nor consenting to these wicked actions, nothing is meant. Whereinto who so listeth to look, and well to consider, he shall find and see most evident and apparent examples of God's justice and judgement against such as do rebel against the Lord's annointed; whom the Lord by his express word hath commanded to be honoured and obeyed in all humbleness and duty, because they are his vicars, substitutes, and vice-regents upon the earth, to defend the good, and to punish the evil. And who so resisteth them, do resist his ordinances, and shall receive hard judgement, as most manifestly it do appear in this the Earl of Desmond's rebellion. All which if it should be set down particularly, as in course it fell out, it would be very tedious, but much more lamentable and doleful, to be read.*

And therefore leaving the large discourse, it shall suffice to shut and conclude this history with the brief recital of the most special points, to move each man to consider the mighty hand of God against traitors and rebels, and his loving mercy and kindness upon the dutiful and obedient. First, therefore, James Fitzmaurice, the first ringleader in this pageant, and who most unnaturally had flocked in strangers and foreigners to invade the land, for establishing the antichristian religion, and the depriving of Her Majesty from her imperial crown of the realm of Ireland. This man (I say) was he who yielded the first fruits of this rebellion. For in his idolatrous pilgrimage to the holy cross, and his traitorous journey to practice with all the rebels and inhabitants in Connaught and Ulster to join with him, he did commit a robbery; and being pursued for the same, he was slain by a gentleman, and one of his own kinsmen, Theobald Burke, and his head and quarters set upon the gates of the town of Kilmallock.

Then James of Desmond, brother to the earl, having done a robbery upon Sir Corman MacTeige, was likewise taken and carried to Cork,

---

*The First (1569-1573) and Second (1579-1583) Desmond Rebellions were suppressed brutally. The executions described in the next paragraphs concern the second. It was initiated when James Fitzmaurice returned from Rome, accompanied by the papal emissaries Saunders and Allen, with assurances of not just papal but also Spanish support. For another description of the post-rebellion famine, see Edmund Spenser, below.

where he was drawn, hanged, and quartered, and his head and quarters set upon the gates and walls of the city of Cork. After him, Sir John of Desmond, one other brother to the said earl, who was a special champion of the Pope, from whom he had received many blessings, bulls, and *Agnos dei*, which should keep and preserve him from all harm. Yet for all this, his holy coat of armour, he was met withall by Captain Zouch and Captain Dowdall, and by them he received his just reward of a bloody traitor and a friendkiller, being killed and then carried dead to Cork, where his body was hanged by the heels, and his head sent to Dublin, and there set upon the top of the castle. And in the end, the earl himself was also taken, and with the sword the head was divided from the body: the one was sent to London, and there set upon London Bridge, and his body [it is] uncertain whether it were buried or devoured by the wild beasts.

And thus a noble race and ancient family, descended from out of the loins of princes, is now for treasons and rebellions utterly extinguished and overthrown. Only one son of the said earls is left, and yet prisoner in the Tower of London. The two doctors, Allen and Sanders, who were the Holy Father's legats and nuncios, and in their foolish fantasies dreamed that they had the Holy Ghost at commandment, and yet most errant traitors against the Lord's annointed: the one of them lifting up his sword against Her sacred Majesty, under the Pope's banner at Munster, 1579, was slain and killed. The other after he had followed the heels of the Desmonds almost four years, wandering to and fro in the woods and bogs, died most miserably in the wood of Cleneles, in such diseases as famine and penury use to bring. [As for] the Romans and Spaniards, and the strangers which were sent from the Pope and King Philip, with all their consorts and companies, very few [were] left of them to return home, and to carry news of their success, but were all put to the sword.

And as for the great companies of soldiers, gallowglasses, kern, and the common people who followed this rebellion, the numbers of them are infinite whose blood the earth drank up and whose carcasses the fowls of the air and the ravening beasts of the field did consume and devour. After this followed an extreme famine, and such as whom the sword did not destroy, the same did consume and eat out. Very few or none remained alive, saving such as dwelled in cities and towns, and such as were fed over into England. And yet the store in the towns was very far spent, and they in distress, albeit nothing like in comparison to them who lived at large. For they were not only driven to eat horses, dogs, and dead carrion, but also did devour the carcasses of dead men. Whereof there be sundry examples. Namely, one in the county of Cork, where when a malefactor was executed to death, and his body left upon the gallows, certain poor people secretly came, took him down, and did eat him. Likewise in the bay of Smerwick, or Saint Marie Wick, the place which was first seasoned with this rebellion, there happened a ship to be there, lost through foul weather, and all the men being drowned were there cast on land. The common people, who had a long time lived on limpets, orewads [i.e. seaweed], and such shellfish as they could find, and which were now spent, as soon as they saw these dead bodies, they took them up, and most greedily did eat and devour them. And not long after, death and famine did eat and consume them.

The land itself, which before those wars was populous, well inhabited, and rich in all the good blessings of God, being plentious of corn, full of cattle, well stored with fish and sundry other good commodities, is now become waste and barren, yielding no fruits, the pastures no cattle, the fields no corn, the air no birds, the seas (though full of fish) yet to them yielding nothing. Finally, every way the curse of God was so great, and the land so barren both of man and beast, that whosoever did travel from the one end unto the other of all Munster, even from Waterford to the head of Smerwick, which is about six score miles, he should not meet any man, woman, or child, saving in towns and cities; nor yet see any beast, but the very wolves, the foxes, and other like ravening beasts, many of them lay dead, being famished, and the residue gone elsewhere.

A heavy, but a just judgement of God upon such a Pharoical and stiffnecked people, who by no persuasions, no counsels, and no reasons, would be reclaimed and reduced to serve God in true religion, and to obey their most lawful prince in dutiful obedience. But [they] made choice of a wicked idol, the god Mazin to honour, and of that wicked antichrist of Rome to obey, unto the utter overthrow of themselves and of their posterity. This is the goodness that cometh from that great city upon the seven hills, and that mighty Babylon, the mother of all wickedness and abominations upon the earth. These be the fruits which come from that holy father, master Pope, the son of satan, and the man of sin, and the enemy unto the cross of Christ, whose bloodthirstiness will never be quenched, but in the blood of the saints, and the servants of God; and whose ravening guts be never satisfied, but with the death of such as do serve the Lord in all godliness, and who will not be drunk in the cup of his fornications: as it doth appear by the infinite and most horrible massacres, and bloody persecutions, which he daily exerciseth throughout all Christian lands. Which, because he cannot perform also within the realms of England and Ireland, what practises hath he made by enchantments, sorceries, witchcrafts, and treasons to bereave Her Majesty of her life? What devices hath he used to raise up her own subjects to rebellions and commotions, to supplant her of her royal estate and government? What practises hath he used with foreign princes and potentates, to seek occasions of breaches of peace and raisings of wars? And how craftily hath he suborned [i.e. bribed and procured] his unholy and traitorous Jesuits, under colour of holiness, to range from place to place through Her Majesty's realms, and to move and persuade her people from dutiful obedience unto Her Highness, and to deny her supreme authority and government? Finally, how doth he from time to time like a ravening wolf seek to devouring of her, and of all her good subjects, which live in the fear of God, and in the religion established upon his holy word and gospel?

Whereof hath ensued the loss of infinite thousands of people, as whereof many apparent examples are set down and recorded in the histories of England. But of them all, none more lamentable than this history of Ireland, and especially this tragedy of Munster. In which it doth appear, how for the maintenance of the Pope's quarrels, the earth hath drunk up the blood, the fouls of the air have preyed, and the beasts of the field have devoured the carcasses of infinite multitudes and numbers of people. Which if every man would well look into and consider the ungodly shall see the great judgements of God, and his severe justice against all such as shall dishonour his holy name; and against such as shall rebel and resist against his annointed: that thereby they may repent, amend their lives, and be converted unto the Lord, both in true religion towards Him, and in all dutiful obedience to his annointed. And the good and Godly shall see, and thereby consider, the great good mercies shewed upon them, in that He hath and continually doth preserve and keep them from out of the jaws of the lion in all safety, that they should daily more and more grow from grace to grace, and live in all holiness and virtue toward him, and persist in all dutiful obedience unto Her Majesty our sovereign lady and queen, whose days the Lord God continue and prolong to reign over us to his good will and pleasure. And so shall we her people see good days, live in security, and the peace of Israel shall be upon us.

Irish kern, artist unknown, in a mid-16th century woodcut. The kern was drawn from the poor, 'wild Irish' class, indicated here by bare feet. Ruder images of them reached Shakespeare, whose Richard II vows to 'supplant those rough, rug-headed kerns'.

Albrecht Durer's drawing of Irish gallowglasses, highly specialized and usually mercenary soldiers retained by Irish chieftains. The term derives from *gall*, or stranger, and those pictured on the left clearly differ from the Irish on the right in armour, footgear, and weaponry.

Robert Payne

A BRIEF DESCRIPTION OF IRELAND
Made in This Year 1589

One outcome of the Desmond Rebellion described above by John Hooker was the Act of Attainder of 1586. By this Gerald Fitzgerald, Earl of Desmond, forfeited his land, and it was 'planted' with English settlers called 'undertakers' for their agreement to modest conditions in exchange for major economic incentives. Robert Payne, of whom little is known other than his authorship of this description, was one such undertaker. His purpose in this brief tract, which was published in Nottinghamshire in 1589, was to correct rumors spread by failed English settlers and to encourage others to take advantage of the attractive terms of the English plantation of Munster. Payne thus provides the first patently merchantile account of Ireland as a commercial endeavor and English resource.

For Payne the obstacles to successful possession of Ireland are not cultural, linguistic, or religious. In his account the only obstacle is economic, a lack of industry. This is a commercial interpretation of affairs that grows increasingly prominent in the sequence of these accounts of Ireland. What follows from Payne's premise is a remarkably benevolent portait of the Irish, one that effectively qualifies other contemporary images of the Irish as diabolical savages. Payne's description is a call to pioneers, and of course it is suspect for advertising hyperbole. But as an alternative image of the Irish it serves as a useful reminder of the profound impact of personal interests and motivations on the reports of these visitors to Ireland. Certainly, Payne's equation of the Irish with the West Indians suggests that his own empiricism may be as limited as that of other writers who produced far more fantastical versions. These selections are modernized versions of the text printed by the Irish Archeological Society in 1841. That text was ably edited by Aquilla Smith, and two of his notes are retained here.

John Derrick's *Images of Ireland* woodcut of a more humble Irish kern than those in the anonymous woodcut on page 50. Derrick's text urges that his images are accurate and not disdainful.

L et not the reports of those that have spent all their own and what they could by any means get from others in England, discourage you from Ireland, although they and such others by bad dealings have wrought a general discredit to all English men in that country which are to the Irish unknown.

These men will say there is great danger in traveling the country, and much more to dwell or inhabit there. Yet are they freed from three of the greatest dangers. First, they cannot meet in all that land any worse than themselves. Secondly, they need not fear robbery, for they have not anything to lose. Lastly, they are not likely to run into debt, for there is no one will trust them. The greatest matter which troubleth them is, they cannot get anything there but by honest travail, which they are altogether ignorant of. These men cannot tell what good fruits England hath, which Ireland wanteth. Neither can they justly say but that it lieth better for the vent [i.e. sale] of all commodities than England doeth.

What these men have reported, or what the simple have credited, that would rather believe a renegade than travel to see, I care not. But what I have discovered or learned in that country, I will herein recite unto you.

First, the people are of three sorts. The better sort are very civil and honestly given: the most of them greatly inclined to husbandry, although as yet unskillful. Notwithstanding [this], through their great travail many of them are rich in cattle. Some one man there milketh one hundred kyne [i.e. cows] and two or three hundred ewes and goats, and reareth yearly most of their brood.

Their entertainment for your diet shall be more welcome and plentiful than clean and handsome. For although they did never see you before, they will make you the best cheer their country yieldeth, for two or three days, and take not anything therefore. Most of them speak good English and bring up their children to learning. I saw, in a grammar school in Limerick, one hundred and three score scholars, most of them speaking good and perfect English, for they are used to construe Latin into English. They keep their promise faithfully, and are more desirous of peace than our Englishmen; for that, in time of war they are more charged [i.e. attacked], and also they are fatter prey for the enemy who respecteth no person. They are quick-witted and of good constitution of body. They reform themselves daily more and more after English manners. Nothing is more pleasing unto them than to hear of good Justices placed amongst them. They have a common saying which I am persuaded they speak unfeignedly, which is, *Defend me and spend me*, meaning from the oppression of the worse sort of their countrymen. They are obedient to the laws, so that you may travel through all the land without any danger or injury offered by the very worst Irish, and be greatly relieved by the best.

The second sort, being least in number, are called Kernes [i.e. foot soldiers]. They are warlike men. Most of that sort were slain in the late wars.

The third sort are a very idle people, not unlike our English beggars, yet for the most part of pure complexion and good constitution of body. One of the greatest oversights in the better sort is that they make not that idle sort give account of their life.

* * *

The country is situated somewhat nearer the equinoctial line than England. But yet, for that, it lieth more upon the ocean seas and is full of rivers and small brooks. It is not so hot in summer as England. Neither is it so cold in winter, for the seas fretteth away the ice and snow there much more than in England.

The general map of Ireland, which is joined with the old map of England, is most false.* The author (as it seemeth) drew them both by report and common computation of miles, and made his scale after the English measure, that is, one thousand paces, or five thousand feet, to the mile. But herein he greatly deceived himself, for the shortest miles in England are much longer than that measure, and an Irish mile is longer than two of those miles. By these means he hath made the map of England less by half than it should be. Notwithstanding, he hath overreached in his number of parish churches, and [made] the map of Ireland little more than one-fourth of what it should be if truly drawn. This seemeth strange, and hath deceived many ignorant in geometry. Always take this for a principle: the square of two miles containeth just four times so much as the square of one mile, and so all proportions from the greatest to the least. As much may be said of the long mile which containeth two short miles.

Some mistrust that the Spaniards will enter the land and that the Irish will relieve [i.e. assist] them. No doubt there are some traitors in Ireland. I wish I could truly say there were none in England. But this I dare assure you: the greater number, and all the better sort, do deadly hate the Spaniards. And yet I think they bear them fair weather because they are the Pope's champions, and a great part of the Irish (for want of good preaching and discipline) are greatly inclined to papistry.

But their entertainment this last year amongst the Irish (notwithstanding they brought the Pope's holy candles and pardons) sheweth how they affect [i.e. take to] Spanish government.† Most of the better sort of the Irish have read of their monstrous cruelties in the West Indies, where they

---

*'The author's remarks appear to have reference to the map of England and Ireland published by Gerald Mercator in 1584, in his edition of Ptolemy's Geography' [Smith's note].

†Survivors of the Spanish Armada were slaughtered on the coasts of Ireland in 1588; in the west the killing was indeed by the Irish, though under threat of reprisal by the English.

most tyrannously have murdered many millions more of those simple creatures than now live in Ireland, even such as sought their favors by offering unto them all that they had, never resisting nor offering them any harm. Wherefore I doubt that the Irish are so foolish [as] to entertain such proud guests knowing their tyranny and having not so well deserved [as much] at their hands as those simple souls whom they so cruelly murdered. Neither are the Spaniards so unwise [as] to trust those Irish who so lately embued their hands in their blood, slaying them like dogs in such plentiful manner that their garments went about the country to be sold as cheap as beast's skins. If you have not the so-called book of the Spanish cruelties, I pray you buy it [for] it is well worth reading. I have forgotten the title, but it is a small volume in quarto. It is written by a learned bishop of their own country, about forty years ago, in the Castilian tongue, and dedicated to their King for reformation of those cruelties. Afterwards [it was] translated into English and diverse other languages to make their monstrous tyranny known to the world.* When you have read the same, commend it to our Catholics that would be swayed by their works, and yet will not give God thanks at their meat, for they will not once have in their mouth the prayer for our Queen annexed to our usual thanksgiving at meat. I pray God open the eyes of their upholders, and let them see what these men gape [i.e. yearn] for, which is (no doubt) the ruin and overthrow of her highness, whom I pray God preserve. But none are so blind as those that will not see. The Catholics are borne with [i.e. suffered] for their conscience sake, yet from such consciences spring all the traitorous practices against her Majesty.

Although some of small judgement (which think every soil good that beareth long grass) have failed in their expected woad [i.e. blue dye] crops, by means of their unskillful choice of ground, yet assuredly the commodities of the country are many more than either the people can well use or I recite. Their soil for the most part is very fertile and apt for wheat, rye, barley, peas, beans, oats, woad, mather [i.e. chamomile], rape [i.e. turnip], hops, hemp, flax, and all other grains and fruits that England anywhere doth yield. There is much good timber in many places, and that of straightness so good to reave [i.e. split] that a simple workman with a brake axe will cleave a great oak to boards of less than one inch thick, thirteen inches broad, and fifteen feet in length. Such a board, there, is usually sold for two pence halfpenny. There is very rich and plentiful iron stone, and one sort more than we have in England, which they call bog mine, of which a smith there will make at his forge iron presently. Also there is great store of lead ore and wood sufficient to maintain divers iron and lead works (with good husbandry) forever.

---

*'The work referred to is "The Spanish Colonie, or Briefe Chronicle of the Acts and Gestes of the Spaniards in the West Indies" . . . Quarto 1583' [Smith's note].

*   *   *

Although the name of the Irish amongst the ignorant is odious, yet how many have any of you seen executed in England for treason, murder, or felonies? Their cases are scarcely so well favored [i.e. so plentiful] as others [of] our nearer neighbors which daily pester our prisons and monthly deck our gallows. I cannot deny but in the Desmond wars [there] were many Irish traitors. Yet herein judge charitably, for such was the misery of that time that many were driven to this bad choice: whether they would be spoiled as well by the enemy as the worse sort of soldiers at home, or go out to the rebels and be hanged, which is the fairest end of a traitor. But as touching their government in their corporations where they bear rule, [it] is done with such wisdom, equity, and justice, as merits worthy commendations. For I myself divers times have seen in several places within their jurisdictions well near twenty causes [i.e. cases] decided at one sitting, with such indifference [i.e. objectivity] that for the most part both plaintiff and defendant departed contented. Yet many that make show of peace and desire to live by blood do utterly dislike this or any good thing that the poor Irishmen do. Wherefore let us daily pray unto almighty God to put into the heart of our dread sovereign Elizabeth, that as her highness is queen of so great and fruitful a country, wherein her majesty hath a great number of loyal and dutiful subjects, to have especial care that they be not numbered nor gathered up with traitorous rebels. Neither that her Majesty will vouchsafe to tolerate traitorous subjects to stand upon any condition but only her gracious mercy. Then would the hope of the rebels soon be cut off, and the good subjects emboldened to fetch them in, which [they] now dare not so to do for fear of after harms [i.e. reprisals].

With the eye of your mind you cannot view her Majesty's able subjects [at] less than six million men.* One of them in this country is good enough for three weatherbeaten Spaniards, whom a few of our frosty nights will make shrink like rotten sheep. Yet this much I must say for them. If almighty God for our contempt of his holy word hath given them power against us, as he did the frogs against the Egyptians, then there is no force able to resist them. (Without that) I see no cause why we either in England or in Ireland should fear them. Yet there is a foolish rumour that Sir William Standley† with the Spanish King's force, will enter Ireland, and that the Irish people who loved him will take his part. No doubt he was well beloved there, but I think rather for his justice and good dealings amongst

---

*A grossly inflated estimate, perhaps six times the fact.
†Sir William Standley, sheriff of Cork, left Ireland in 1587 for Holland, where he surrendered Deventer to the Spanish; his threat to Ireland never materialized, but he is compared here to the Earl of Desmond, Gerald Fitzgerald, whose death in 1583, in a rebellion aided by Spain, is described above by Hooker.

them before he was suspected of treachery than for any matter of false conspiracy either to prince or country. I do think that Sir William then knew not ten traitors in all Ireland, for how does any rebel make his villianous intent known to a man so famous for true service, as in those days he was accounted [to be]? But suppose that he does come. What is he to the last great Earl of Desmond, who had more followers than Sir William has, and the King of Spain's purse more plentiful then he can have it? Yet did not the said Desmond bring his country to such misery that one did eat another for hunger, and himself with all his posterity and followers [did fall] to utter ruin? Can the Irish so soon forget such great distress and be drawn into the like action with a meaner man? Surely no. For the better sort will bring in their own brothers if they be traitorous, and [are] therefore unlikely to join with a stranger, although they loved him for his virtues. He is a simple Irish man that cannot tell you that the Spaniards love treason, but deadly hateth traitors. I think it true the Irish would gladly have their public masses again, but they had rather continue it in corners than to hear it openly in fetters and chains as the poor [West] Indians do. The Irish are as wise as the Spaniard is proud, and there is no grief greater to the wise man than to live in bondage to a proud man. The very name of the Spaniard, in respect to his pride and tyranny, is odious to many nations whom they never hurt. But in Ireland they seemed to do some harm, or else the Irish did them wrong to take so many of their heads for recompence. A humbler nation than the Spaniards would not so quickly forget such measure as they received this other year in Ireland, and that the Irish (who can be warned by other men's harm) know right well. For until the Spaniard's tyranny in the West Indies be wrapped up in oblivion, the Irish will speak [of] them fairly, but trust them nothing at all, until their heads be off.

Edmund Spenser in poet-statesman iconography with altered spelling of his name.

Edmund Spenser

A View of
THE PRESENT STATE
OF IRELAND

Edmund Spenser (1552-1599) lived a substantial portion of his creative life in Ireland, and it was there that he wrote most of *The Faerie Queene*. All that time, though, he viewed Ireland from the rather elevated perspective of a true humanism. That is most apparent here in the lovely rhetorical conceit of a Ciceronian dialogue between Eudox, interested in Ireland but uninformed about it, and Iren, the experienced traveller in the country come home to make the case for a particular state policy. Spenser was especially well-informed about Ireland, but never any less than a stranger in it.

In 1580, having established some reputation with his poems and having begun *The Faerie Queene*, Spenser was appointed secretary to Lord Gray of Wilton, new Lord Deputy of Ireland. His subsequent state career was a series of minor clerkships. The *View* may itself have been a rather late application of sorts for the preferment to the London court that Spenser continually sought and never received. In Ireland he lived first at New Abbey, in Kildare, and then, from 1588, at Kilcolman on the Munster route between Limerick and Cork cities. With 3,000 acres, a stone mansion house, and a 14th century Desmond castle, Kilcolman might seem rather grand. But the necessary scale must be in reference to his neighbor Sir Walter Raleigh's 42,000 acres around Youghal, and that obtained during one of the dips in Raleigh's career.

With Lord Grey, Spenser was witness to the surrender and massacre of the Spanish and Italian garrison at Smerwick in 1580. Gray lasted only two years in Ireland, defeated by the persistent Desmond Rebellions described by Spenser in terrifying detail at the end of these selections. The *View* consistently defends Gray's policies, and Gray appears as the embodiment of justice, Sir Artegall, in *The Faerie Queene*. In 1590 Spenser was in London with the first three books of the poem and futile hopes for a position in the court. In 1596 he was in London again with the second three books of the poem and *A View of the Present State of Ireland*. Two years later, back in Ireland, Spenser may have enjoyed some very bitter consolation in the knowledge that the *View* urged the immediate necessity of economic and social conquest of Ireland as an imperative corollary to its military occupation. For in 1598 Hugh Tyrone battered the English from the north to the south of Ireland. When the insurrection spread through Munster, Kilcolman was sacked. Spenser fled to Cork, according to legend having seen his child tossed into the flames of the burning mansion house. Then he undertook a final, crucial mission to carry letters to the Privy Council in London. He arrived there on Christmas Eve, 1598, and he died suddenly at Westminster on the following January 13.

A View of the Present State of Ireland was not published until 1633, and then in Dublin by Sir James Ware. These selections are taken from W. L. Renwick's modern edition (Oxford: Clarendon Press, 1970), with some bracketed insertions and further regularization of spelling and punctuation. The selections attempt to reflect the principal focuses of Spenser's work: on the laws, the customs, and the religion of Ireland. He is of his time and background in his contempt for the less than pacific machinations of Brehon Law, and he is perhaps more tolerant than most of his time and background in his attitude toward Catholicism. But it is on the customs, such as the dress and appearance of the people, that Spenser shows the fruit of his long residence in Ireland. There is an almost anthropological level of detail to his descriptions of the glib, or forelock, for example. And there are sinister implications in his presentation of those details that suggest how the allegories of kinds of good and evil in *The Faerie Queene* could be projected from his experience as a stranger in Ireland.

I *ren:* I will then according to your advisement begin to declare the evils which seem to be most hurtful to the common weale of that land, and first those which I said were most ancient and long grown; and they are also of three kinds: the first in the laws, the second in customs, and last in religion.

Eudox: Why, Irenius, can there be any evil in the laws? Can the things which are ordained for the safety and good of all turn to the evil and hurt of them? This well I wot [i.e. know] both in that state and in all other, that were they not contained in duty with fear of law which restraineth offences, and inflicteth sharp punishment to misdoers, no man should enjoy anything; every man's hand would be against another. Therefore in finding fault with the laws I doubt me you shall much overshoot yourself, and make me the more dislike your other dislikes of that government.

Iren: The laws, Eudoxus, I do not blame for themselves, knowing right well that all laws are ordained for the good of the commonwealth, and for repressing of licentiousness and vice: but it falleth out in laws no otherwise than it doth in physic, which was at first devised and is yet daily meant and ministered for the health of the patient, but nevertheless we often see that either through ignorance of the disease, or unseasonableness of the time, or other accidents coming between, instead of good it worketh hurt, and out of one evil, throweth the patient into many miseries. So the laws were at first intended for the formation of abuses and peaceable continuance of the subjects, but are since either disannulled or quite prevaricated through change and alteration of times; yet are they good still in themselves, but to that Commonwealth which is ruled by them they work not that good which they should, and sometimes also perhaps that evil which they would not.

Eudox: Whether do you mean this by the Common Law of the realm, or by the statute laws and acts of Parliaments?

Iren: Surely by them both. For even the Common Law, being that which William of Normandy brought in with his conquest and laid upon the neck of England, though it perhaps fitted well with the state of England then being, and was readily obeyed through the power of the commander which had before subdued the people to him and made easy way to the settling of his will; yet with the state of Ireland peradventure it doth not so well agree, being a people altogether stubborn and untamed, and if it were once tamed, yet now lately having quite shaken off their yoke and broken the bands of their obedience. For England before the entrance of the Conqueror was a peaceable kingdom, and but lately enured to the mild and godly government of King Edward surnamed the Confessor, besides now lately grown unto a loathing and detestation of the unjust and tyrannous rule of Harold, an usurper, which made them the more willing to accept of any reasonable conditions and order of the new victor, thinking surely it could be no worse than the latter, and hoping well it would be as good as the former; yet what the proof of the first bringing in and establishing of those laws was, was to many full bitterly made known. But with Ireland it is far otherwise. For it is a nation ever acquainted with wars though but amongst themselves, and in their own kind of military discipline trained up even from their youths, which they have never yet been taught to lay aside, nor made to learn obedience unto the law, scarcely to know the name of law, but instead thereof have always preserved and kept their own law which is the Brehon law.

Eudox: What is that which you call the Brehon law? It is a word to us altogether unknown.

Iren: It is a certain rule of right unwritten, but delivered by tradition from one point to another, in which often there appeareth great show of equity in determining the right between party and party, but in many things repugning [i.e., contradicting] quite both to God's law and man's, as for example, in the case of murder, the Brehon that is their judge will compound between the murderer and the friends of the party murdered which prosecute the action, that the malefactor shall give unto them, or to the child or wife of him that is slain, a recompense which they call an Iriach, by which vile law of theirs many murders are amongst them made up and smothered. And this judge, being as he is called the Lord's Brehon, adjudgeth for the most part a better share unto his Lord, that is the lord of the soil or the head of that sept, and also unto himself for his judgement a greater portion than unto the plaintiffs or parties grieved.

Eudox: This is a most wicked law indeed, but I trust it is not now used in Ireland, since the kings of England have had the absolute dominion thereof and established their own laws there.

Iren: Yes, truly, for there are many wide countries in Ireland in which the laws of England were never established, nor any acknowledgement of subjection made, and also even in those which are subdued, and seem to acknowledge subjection, yet the same Brehon law is privily practised amongst themselves, by reason that dwelling as they do whole nations and septs of the Irish together without any Englishman amongst them, they may do what they list, and compound or altogether conceal amongst themselves their own crimes, of which no notice can be had by them which would and might amend the same by the rule of the laws of England.

*   *   *

Iren: I will then begin to count down their customs in the same order that I counted their nations, and first with the Scythian, or Scottish manners, of the which there is one use amongst them to keep their cattle and to live themselves the most part of the year in Bollies [i.e. cattle-folds], pasturing upon the mountain and waste wild places, and removing still to fresh land as they have depastured the former days; the which appeareth plain to be the manner of the Scythians as ye may read in Olaus Magnus et Johannes

Boemus, and yet is used amongst all the Tartarians and the people about the Caspian Sea which are naturally Scythians, to live in herds as they call them, being the very same that the Irish Bollies are, driving their cattle continually with them and feeding only on their milk and white meats.

Eudox: What fault can ye find with this custom, for though it be an old Scythian use, yet it is very behoveful in this country of Ireland where there are great mountains and waste deserts full of grass, that the same should be eaten down and nourish many thousand of cattle, for the good of the whole realm, which cannot, methinks, well be any other way than by keeping those Bollies as there ye have showed?

Iren: But by this custom of Bollyng there grow in the meantime many great enormities unto that commonwealth. For, first, if there be any outlaws or loose people, as they are never without some which live upon stealths and spoils, they are ever more succoured and find relief only in these Bollies being upon the waste places; where else they should be driven shortly to starve, or to come down to the towns to seek relief, where by one means or another they would soon be caught. Besides, such stealths of cattle as they make they bring commonly to those Bollies where they are received readily, and the thief harboured from danger of law or such officers as might light upon him. Moreover, the people that live thus in these Bollies grow thereby the more barbarous and live more licentiously than they could in towns, using what means they list, and practising what mischiefs and villainies they will, either against the government there generally by their combinations, or against private men, whom they malign by stealing their goods or murdering themselves; for there they think themselves half exempted from law and obedience, and having once tasted freedom do, like a steer that hath been long out of his yoke, grudge and repine ever after to come under rule again.

Eudox: By your speech, Irenius, I perceive more evil come by these Bollies than good by their grazing, and therefore it may well be reformed, but that must be in his due course. Do you proceed to the next.

Iren: They have another custom from the Scythians, that is the wearing of mantles and long glibs, which is a thick curled bush of hair hanging down over their eyes, and monstrously disguising them, which are both very bad and hurtful.

Eudox: Do ye think that the mantle cometh from the Scythians? I would surely think otherwise, for by that which I have read it appeareth that most nations in the world anciently used the mantle, for the Jews used it as ye may read of Elias' mantle.*

The Caldees also used it, as ye may read in Diodorus, the Egyptians likewise used it, as ye may read in Herodotus and may be gathered by the description of Berenice in the Greek commentaries upon Callimachus. The

*Elijah's mantle: see 1 Kings 19: 13 and 2 Kings 2: 13-14.

Greeks also used it anciently, as appeareth by Venus' mantle lined with stars, though afterwards they changed the form thereof into their cloaks called *pallia*, as some of the Irish also use. And the ancient Latins and Romans also used it, as ye may read in Virgil who was a very great antiquary, that Evander, when Aeneas came to him at his feast, did entertain and feast him sitting on the ground, and lying on mantles. Insomuch as he useth the very word *mantile* for a mantle, *mentilia humi sternunt*, so that it seemeth that the mantle was a general habit to most nations, and not proper to the Scythians only as ye suppose.

Iren: I cannot deny but anciently it was common to most and yet Sithence disused and laid away. But in this latter age of the world since the decay of the Roman Empire, it was renewed and brought in again by those northern nations, when breaking out of their cold caves and frozen habitation into the sweet soil of Europe, they brought with them their usual weeds, fit to shield the cold and that continual frost to which they had at home been enured; the which yet they left not off, by reason that they were in perpetual wars with the nations where they had invaded, but still removing from place to place carried always with them that weed as their house, their bed and their garment, and coming lastly into Ireland they found there more special use thereof, by reason of the raw cold climate, from whom it is now grown into that general use in which that people now have it; afterward the Africans succeeding, yet finding the like necessity of that garment, continued the like use thereof.

Eudox: Since then the necessity thereof is so commodious as ye allege, that it is instead of housing, bedding, and clothing, what reason have you then to wish so necessary a thing cast off?

Iren: Because the commodity doth not countervail the discommodity. For the inconveniences which thereby do arise are much more many, for it is a fit house for an outlaw, a meet bed for a rebel, and an apt cloak for a thief. First the outlaw being for his many crimes and villainies banished from the towns and houses of honest men, and wandering in waste places far from danger of law, maketh his mantle his house, and under it covereth himself from the wrath of heaven, from the offence of the earth, and from the sight of men: when it raineth it is his pentice [i.e. cover], when it bloweth it is his tent, when it freezeth it is his tabernacle; in summer he can wear it loose, in winter he can wrap it close; at all times he can use it, never heavy, never cumbersome. Likewise for a rebel it is as serviceable: for in his war that he maketh (if at least it deserve the name of war) when he still flyeth from his foe and lurketh in the thick woods and straight passages waiting for advantages, it is his bed, yea and almost all his household stuff. For the wood is his house against all weathers, and his mantle is his cave to sleep in. There he wrappeth his self round and ensconceth himself strongly against the gnats, which in the country do more annoy the naked rebels whilst they keep the woods, and do more sharply wound them than all their enemies' swords or spears which can seldom come nigh them; yea and oftentimes their mantle serveth them when they are near driven, being wrapped about their left arm instead of a target, for it is hard to cut through it with a sword; besides, it is light to bear, light to throw away, and being as they then commonly are naked, it is to them all in all. Lastly, for a thief it is so handsome, as it may seem it was first invented for him, for under it he can cleanly convey any fit pillage that cometh handsomely in his way, and when he goeth abroad in the night on freebooting [i.e., plundering] it is his best and surest friend, for lying as they often do, two or three nights together abroad to watch for their booty, with that they can prettily shroud themselves under a bush or a bankside till they may conveniently do their errand. And when all is done he can, in his mantle, pass through any town or company, being close hooded over his head as he useth from knowledge of any to whom he is endangered. Besides all this he or any man else that is disposed to mischief or villainy may, under his mantle, go privily, armed without suspicion of any, carry his headpiece, his skene [i.e. dagger] or pistol, if he please to be always in a readiness. Thus necessary and fitting is a mantle for a bad man. And surely for a bad housewife it is no less convenient. For some of them that be these wandering women, called of them *Monashut*, it is half a wardrobe, for in summer ye shall find her arrayed commonly but in her smock and mantle to be more ready for her light services; and in her travel it is her cloak and safeguard, and also a coverlet for her lewd exercise, and when she hath filled her vessel, under it she can hide both her burden and her blame; yea, and when her bastard is born it serves instead of all her swaddling clothes, her mantles, her cradles with which others are vainly cumbered, and as for all other good women which love to do but little work, how handsome it is to lie in and sleep, or to louse themselves [i.e., *de*-louse themselves] in the sunshine, they that have been but a while in Ireland can well witness. Sure I am that ye will think it very unfit for good housewives to stir in or to busy herself about her housewifery in sort as they should. These be some of the abuses for which I would think it meet to forbid all mantles.

Eudox: O evil minded man, that having reckoned up so many uses of mantles, will yet wish it to be abandoned. Sure I think Diogenes' dish did never serve his master more turns, notwithstanding that he made his dish his cup, his measure, his waterpot, than a mantle doth an Irishman, but I see they be all so bad intents, and therefore I will join with you in abolishing it. But what blame lay you then to glib? Take heed, I pray you, that you be not too busy therewith, for fear of your own blame, seeing our Englishmen take it up in such a general fashion, to wear their hair so unmeasurably long that some of them exceed the longest Irish glibs.

Iren: I fear not the blame of any undeserved mislikes, but for the Irish glibs I say that besides their savage brutishness and loathly filthiness, which is not to be named, they are fit masks as a mantle is for a thief, for whensoever he hath run himself into that peril of law that he will not be known, he either cutteth off his glib quite, by which he becometh nothing like himself, or pulleth it so low down over his eyes that it is very hard to discern his thievish countenance, and therefore fit to be trussed up with the mantle.

* * *

Eudox: Surely ye have very well handled these two former, and if you shall as well go through the third likewise ye shall merit a very good meed. [i.e. reward]

Iren: Little have I to say of religion, both because the parts thereof be not many, itself being but one, and myself have not been much conversant in that calling, but as lightly passing by I have seen or heard. Therefore the fault which I find in religion is but one, but the same universal throughout all that country, that is that they are all Papists by their profession, but in the same so blindly and brutishly informed, for the most part as that you would rather think them atheists or infidels; but not one amongst an hundred knoweth any ground of religion and article of his faith, but can perhaps say his pater noster or his Ave Maria, without any knowledge or understanding what one word thereof meaneth.

Eudox: This is truly a most pitiful hearing, that so many souls should fall into the Devil's hands at once, and lack the blessed comfort of the sweet Gospel and Christ's dear passion. Aye me, how cometh it to pass that being a people as they are trading with so many nations, and frequented of so many, yet they have not tasted any part of those happy joys, nor once been lightened with the morning star of truth, but lie weltering in such spiritual darkness, hard by hell mouth, even ready to fall in, if God haply help not.

Iren: The general fault cometh not of any late abuse either in the people or their priests, who can teach no better than they know, nor show no more light than they have seen but in the first institution and planting of religion in all that realm, which was, (as I read) in the time of Pope Celestine; who, as it is written, did first send over thither Palladius, who there deceasing, he afterwards sent over St. Patrick, being by nation a Briton, who converted the people, being then infidels, from paganism, and christened them; in which Pope's time and long before, it is certain that religion was generally corrupted with their Popish trumpery. Therefore, what other could they learn than such trash as was taught them, and drink of that cup of fornication, with which the purple harlot had then made all nations drunken?

Eudox: What? Do you then blame and find fault with so good an act in that good Pope as the reducing of such a great people to Christendom, bringing so many souls to Christ, if that were ill what is good?

Iren: I do not blame the christening of them, for to be sealed with the mark of the Lamb, by what hand soever it be done rightly, I hold it a good and gracious work; for the general profession which they then take upon them of the Cross and faith in Christ, I nothing doubt but through the powerful grace of that mighty Saviour, will work salvation in many of them. But nevertheless, since they drunk not of the pure spring of life, but only tasted of such troubled waters as were brought unto them, the dregs thereof have brought great contagion in their souls, the which daily increasing and being still more augmented with their own lewd lives and filthy conversation, hath now bred in them this general disease, that cannot but only with very strong purgations be cleansed and carried away.

Eudox: Then for this defect ye find no fault with the people themselves nor with the priests which take the charge of souls, but with the first ordinance and institution thereof?

Iren: Not so, Eudoxius, for the sin of ignorance of the priest shall not excuse the people, nor the authority of their great pastor, Peter's successor, shall not excuse the priest, but they all shall die in their sins, for they have all erred and gone out of the way together.

Eudox: But if this ignorance of the people be such a burden unto the Pope, is it not a like blot to them that now hold that place, in that they which now are in the light themselves, suffer a people under their charge to wallow in such deadly darkness, for I do not see that the fault is changed but the fault's master?

Iren: That which you blame, Eudoxius, is not, I suppose, any fault of will in these godly Fathers which have charge thereof, nor any defect of zeal for reformation hereof, but the inconvenience of the time and troublous occasions wherewith that wretched realm hath been continually turmoiled. For instruction in religion needeth quiet times, and ere we seek to settle a sound discipline in the clergy, we must purchase peace unto the laity; for it is ill time to preach amongst swords, and most hard or rather impossible it is to settle a good opinion in the minds of men, for matters of religion doubtful, which have a doubtless evil opinion of ourselves; for ere a new be brought in, the old must be removed.

Eudox: Then belike it is meet that some fitter time be attended, that God send peace and quietness there in civil matters, before it be attempted in ecclesiastical, I would rather have thought that, as it is said, correction should begin at the House of God, and that the care of the soul should have been preferred before the care of the body.

Iren: Most true, Eudoxius. The care of the soul and soul matters are to be preferred before the care of the body, in consideration of the worthiness thereof, but not in the time of reformation. For if you should know a wicked person dangerously sick, having now both soul and body greatly diseased, yet both recoverable, would ye not think it ill advisement to bring the preacher before the physician? For if his body were neglected, it is like that his languishing soul, being disquieted by his diseaseful body, would utterly refuse and loath all spiritual comfort. But if his body were first recured and brought to good frame, should there not then be found best time to recure his soul also? So it is in the state of the realm. Therefore, as I said, it is expedient first to settle such a course of government there, as thereby both civil disorders and ecclesiastical abuses may be reformed and amended whereto needeth not any such great distance of times as ye suppose I require, but one joint resolution for both that each might second and confirm the other.

Eudox: That we shall see when we come thereto. In the meantime I consider thus much as you have delivered touching the general fault which ye suppose in religion, to weet that it is Popish, but do you find no particular abuses therein, nor in the ministers thereof?

Iren: Yes, verily, for whatever disorders ye see in the Church of England ye may find there, and many, many more, namely, gross simony, greedy covetousness, fleshly incontinence, careless sloth, and generally all disordered life in the common clergymen, and besides all these, they have their own particular enormities, for all the Irish priests which now enjoy the church livings there, are in manner mere laymen, saving that they have taken holy orders, but otherwise they do like laymen, go like laymen, live like laymen, follow all kind of husbandry and other worldly affairs, as the other Irish laymen do. They neither read scriptures nor preach to the people, nor minister the sacrament of Communion, but the Baptism they do, for they christen yet after the Popish fashion, and with the Popish Latin ministration; only they take the tithes and offerings, and gather what fruits else they may of their livings, the which they convert as badly. And some of them, they say, pay as due tributes and shares of their livings to their Bishops, (I speak of those which are Irish) as they receive them duly.

*   *   *

Eudox: Surely of such desperate persons as wilfully follow the course of their own folly, there is no compassion to be had, and for the others ye have proposed a merciful means, much more than they have deserved. But what then shall be the conclusion of this war,* for you have prefixed a short time of his continuance?

Iren: The end I assure me will be very short and much sooner than can be in so great a trouble (as it seemeth) hoped for. Although there should none of them fall by the sword, nor be slain by the soldier, yet thus being kept from manurance, and their cattle from running abroad by this hard restraint, they would quickly consume themselves and devour one another. The proof whereof I saw sufficiently ensampled in those late wars

---

*The Desmond Wars, as described by Hooker, above. Spenser disregards the length of the Desmond feud for the purpose of his argument. [Renwick's note].

in Munster, for notwithstanding that the same was a most rich and plentiful country, full of corn and cattle, that you would have thought they would have been able to stand long, yet ere one year and a half they were brought to such wretchedness, as that any stony heart would have rued the same. Out of every corner of the woods and glens they came creeping forth upon their hands, for their legs could not bear them. They looked anatomies of death, they spake like ghosts crying out of their graves, they did eat of the dead carrions, happy were they could find them, yea and one another soon after in so much as the very carcasses they spared not to scrape out of their graves, and if they found a plot of water cress or shamrocks, there they flocked as to a feast for the time, yet not able long to continue therewithal, that in short space there were none almost left and a most populous and plentiful country suddenly left void of man or beast. Yet sure in all that war there perished not many by the sword, but all by the extremity of famine, which they themselves had wrought.

Eudox: It is wonder that you tell, and more to be wondered how it should so shortly come to pass.

Iren: It is most true, and the reason also very ready; for ye must conceive that the strength of all that nation is the kern, gallowglass, stocagh, horseman and horseboy, the which having been never used to have anything of their own, and now living upon spoil of others, make no spare of anything, but havoc and confusion of all they meet with, whether it be their own friends' goods or their foes', and if they happen to get never so great spoils at any time the same they waste and consume in a trice, as naturally delighting in spoil, though it do themselves no good. And on the other side whatsoever they leave unspent, the soldier, when he cometh there, he havocketh [i.e., makes havoc] and spoileth likewise, so that between them both nothing is very shortly left. And yet this is very necessary to be done, for the soon finishing of the war. And not only this in this wise, but also all those subjects which border upon those parts are either to be removed and drawn away or likewise to be spoiled, that the enemy may find no succour thereby, for what the soldier spares the rebel will surely spoil.

The submission of Turlough O'Neill to Sir Henry Sidney after the death of Shane O'Neill in 1567, as illustrated in John Derrick's *The Image of Ireland*. Sidney oversaw Anglicisation of Ulster, a matter of contrasting cultures, one in ascent, one in descent, as represented here.

James Perrott

THE CHRONICLE OF IRELAND
1584-1608

Sir James Perrott (1571-1637) was the illegitimate son of Sir John Perrott, Lord Deputy of Ireland from 1584 to 1588. It is not known if the younger Perrott visited Ireland during his father's term in that office or his several others in Ireland. However, it is known, from the work excerpted here, that James had no illusions about his alternatively charismatic and contentious father's failures of policy in Ireland. Knighted during the procession of James I to London in 1603, James Perrot was effectively indoctrinated into Irish affairs during Sir Arthur Chichester's term as lord deputy from 1604 to 1614. Chichester, too, was a relative of sorts, having married John Perrott's legitimate daughter Lettice.

In Chichester's service Perrott enjoyed significant responsibility, distinction, and remuneration. He became an important member of Parliament on his return to London in 1614. In fact, his next term of residence in Ireland, beginning in 1621, was a kind of honorable banishment for his parliamentary denunciations of the king's policies with Catholic Spain. That position is consistent with his discussion of Catholicism in Ireland here: he objects not to Catholicism itself so much as official recognition of its practice in Ireland.

Perrott was an educated man with some literary aspirations. This chronicle of Ireland was apparently intended as a continuation of John Hooker's, which stopped in about 1586. Perrott seems to have abandoned the chronicle at the year 1608 because of rumors of the work of Fynes Moryson (see below). The work opens with an ample discussion of historiography itself and continues through the section presented here, 'A Brief Discourse of the Ancient conditions, Customs, and Government of the Irish Nation', before beginning its historical chronicle. In this selection his intellectual character is evident. In particular, his discussion of nature and art seems indebted to Montaigne, also an influence on Shakespeare's *The Tempest*. Perrott, though, seems unable or unwilling to emulate the spirit of Montaigne's critique of xenophobic assumptions about barbarism. Perrott describes the customs of the people, for example, less for what they are than for what they lack in relation to English 'civility'. He is ambiguous as well on whether English 'constraints' on the Irish encourage either civility or rebellion. Perhaps most intriguing of all is Perrott's condemnation of the Irish as 'no just observers of matrimony'. For in addition to being illegitimate himself, his father was illegitimate, almost certainly a son of Henry VIII, his father married twice himself, and Lettice Perrott's marriage to Chichester was her third.

The Chronicle of Ireland 1584-1608 was edited by Herbert Wood and published in Dublin by the Stationery Office in 1933. This selection further modernizes the spelling and syntax of Wood's edition.

Boy and girl at Cahera.

N othing can be said so general and universal of the qualities of any nation but in particular may be subject to exceptions, for men's dispositions in all places do differ, and as the common saying is: 'so many men, so many minds'. Yet do we find that men do much incline both in the constitution of their bodies and condition of their minds according to the natural habit of their parents: diet, air, and exercise they use for the one, faculties, organs, education, and conversation they receive of the other. Both these, the soil and situation of the country, [and] the example of the countrymen where any persons have their birth and breeding, hath a great stroke to frame men's minds unto virtue or vice, boldness or bashfulness, moderation or extremity. So we see in the cold climates, where the airs are sharp and the soil most barren, the people are for the most part quick-witted, nimble in body, ready to undertake, and active in spirit; where on the other side we see, for the most part, such as have their birth and being in deep and fertile soils (the air being there foggy) they are commonly of a braver temper and duller conceit [i.e. conception], sluggish and slow in action or invention. This for the temperature, which follows the native soil and situation; so likewise education and example are great motives to make men either rude, rash, well-governed, gentle and gener-ous. Though nature hath either a sway, or at least some sympathy, to produce similitude or antipathy in dissimilitude of manner and conditions, yet surely education, example, and use [i.e. custom] brings forth great effects of perfection and imperfection in men. It is not unknown but a courtier's son, brought up from his cradle and so continuing for a long time with a clown, may perchance retain some kind of his native vivacity and valour of mind, but for the most part his manners and behavior will be framed according to the external fashion and representation of the persons with whom he converseth. The like may be said of a clown's son living from his childhood at court; he will somewhat alter nature by art, and sight shall teach him by others' example to supply or correct his own primary defects.

This much we speak to shew that nations are not all of one nature, though they have an aptness to concur in conditions suitable to the places and persons where and with whom they have their birth and bringing up. It is true that in ancient times they made observation that such people inhabiting in such countries and climates had such faults, as the Carthaginians were said to be perfidious. But of these and other nations I think, as I may say truly, as it is said by judicious astrologers in the question whither the infuence of the stars and the celestial bodies in the superior orbs do help dispose these our terrestrial and inferior bodies, it is held that they do rather incline than necessitate. So may I (as I think) say the like of the qualities and conditions of men; they are more moved and instigated than altogether compelled by the climates wherein they live. Though first natural constitution, [rather] than nature or usual habita-tion, do prevail much, the one in the direction of men's minds, the other of

their manners, yet education and conversation being secondary and subordinate causes of their external behavior, or else of their internal conditions
good or evil, we may then conclude that though the soil breed some operation, yet education, custom, and conversation work the greatest effects in
disposing of their minds and manners.

This may be said not only of Ireland but of all other countries. The
people participate [i.e. share] most of the properties wherein they do
communicate with nature, the first mover, and instruction and education,
the second; or else (amongst men merely rude and illiterate) company and
conversation, a chief conductor of the multitude and vulgar sort of men. No
marvel then if [in] this conquered island of Ireland, where men subjected
are kept in order by constraint rather than by moderation in themselves,
their manners should be such as could not answer the strict rules of civility
and sovereignty.

The customs of Ireland were anciently of two kinds; the one concerning
their behavior, breeding, and manner of life, the other touching their
government in war and in peace. For the first, their breeding (I mean the
mere Irish) could be but mean, for they had little, and in a manner no
commerce with foreign nations, which is commonly the chief means to
beget civilization. Their diet was but mean, feeding more on milk scarcely
strained, and therefore usually stuffed with that which is not fit to be
named, much less to be used, and with butter neither cleanly made nor
handsomely kept, diversely coloured and as evilly [i.e. badly] savored. The
flesh they used, being for the most part pork and beef, both fresh and not
salted, neither was well dressed. Answerable to their diet was their
lodging: [they had] no beds but rushes or straw under them, nor sheets to
set about them, nor coverlets to put upon them but rugs and mantles. For
clothes it was somewhat like their fare: the chiefest sort wearing trowses
[i.e. loose pants] and mantles of frieze or very coarsely made cloth. Their
breeches were close stockings of the same called trewses, their other coverings but mantles, and their heads many times bare (except some of the
best) and no hat or shelter from foul weather but their long hair called
glibs. [There was] no drink usually in their houses but milk and water; if
they had wine or aquavitae, termed there *uscubage*, it was not ready in the
best men's houses at all times but must be sent for when strangers should
come. Then scarcely any linen to lay before their guests; none at all for
themselves. This being the manner of diet and attire amongst most of the
better sort.

For their behavior, that could not be much better than their diet, except
they were brought up abroad. Bold they were for the most part, rude
without reverence, or scarcely any civil respect for their superiors. In
former times [they were] no just observers of matrimony, but apt to put
away their wives upon any slight occasion without lawful cause, and more
ready to take on any new [one] than to be constant in their old choice. This

proceedeth of evil example allowed by custom and sufferance, being not restrained by law and justice, begun by the great ones who had no governors to regulate them, nor no laws to guide them but their own lust and licentious liberty.

For the laws and judges they had, I mean the mere Irish laws, were as different in the several provinces and parts of the kingdom as the places and persons were divided in countries and conditions. For each lord made several orders which once continuing and confirmed by custom were held for laws, as was most agreeable to the wills of the chieftains and their governors. So were their judges called Brehons; as simple in judgement as they were subject to those persons who had power over them; being men for the most part illiterate and not furnished with any knowledge but what concerned the customs of the country and constitutions of their chieftains.

For their management of war and use of arms in ancient times, and even until this late age, they neither had skillful commanders to conduct them nor good arms to use in defence of themselves or offence to their enemies. For the first, their leaders were themselves, until of late, neither able to embattle and put their men in order, or to bring them, after an onset, into any order or safety. Neither were their arms such as might well guard themselves or much hurt others who were better provided; for in former times the chief guard of their greatest lords consisted of gallowglasses, which were their lustiest men, armed chiefy with staves headed somewhat like battle-axes. Their light throwing weapons were but darts, much lesser and lighter than our javelins, which they could nimbly handle and throw steadily, but they could not pierce far or have any great power against armed men. Chiefly they could annoy horsemen, and sometimes kill or wound such as were unarmed. For their horsemen, they were more ready to turn upon the hand [i.e. rein aside], to shake and sometimes to charge with their spears above hand, than to come close to the charge, or strong to endure shock when they were charged. This was the manner of their force, arms, and fight in former times, but of late (especially since they were trained as soldiers under Queen Elizabeth to be sent abroad and to serve at home) they grew to another kind of skill and strength. For in this late revolt* and almost general rebellion of the evilly affected Irish and much degenerate old English race in that realm, they grew to have perfect use of arms for the service of that country. And within four or five years after their combinations [i.e. alliances] grew common, our truces and treaties made them so to multiply arms that in the end they provided themselves of a competent proportion of arms for pike and shot that came as little short of the English for proportion and provision as they were for the skill and use of arms. This difference could ten or twelve years at the most [make] betwixt the English and Irish for the possession, proportion, and exercise of armies.

---

*The Tyrone Rebellion (1595-1603) of Hugh O'Neill.

Now for the alteration of their ancient customs in matters of civility or incivility. It is true that travel abroad, to which they have been lately much addicted and overmuch permitted in this time of peace, hath wrought in many of them more abilities to annoy the state, here at home, than will to do service, if they be evil minded. First for religion. We all know there is engrafted in them by education, custom, and company nothing but the Roman character. Next for the disposition of their minds. An averseness in religion is sufficient (if there were no other cause) to make them mislike the present government and to desire the alteration of that which is, though it be a change and commutation of they know not what, and in a manner they know not what, and though it tend to their own prejudice and destruction. Besides this, [there is] the alteration of their late possessions and the plantation of others, in some places of their own septs and kindreds, from other parts of the English and Scottish nations. How much hatred and heartburning this breeds in their breasts, they that do live amongst them can well witness. What then, are their conditions changed by education? No, for the mere Irish remaining at home and not bred up in learning have only the same knowledge, customs, and conditions they had in former times. Those that travel or are brought up in our Universities and Inns of Court at home, though they have better breeding and learn more wit and experience, yet retain the religion which at first they received, and with it desire to enjoy the exercise thereof, though against the allowance of the state, or else to receive that which their parents or progenitors had and have lost. The want of both breeds in many of them a desire of alteration, and an aberration from forms of amity and affection to the state.

In these long times of peace, when open hostility is not proclaimed nor arms used, the diversity of religion breeds evil disposition in the most part of them who do not so freely enjoy the use of what they desire (though they have it in great measure). [This] doth but beget discontent and distemper in their minds. The travels of such discontented persons doth but make them presume that they know more than other men, and that they can kindle more coals (when they see time and opportunity serves their turns) than any of their predecessors had skill and experience to perform. It were a work worthy of consideration in the comparison of the ancient and modern condition touching people of that kingdom, with their present conditions power and property, how far it differs from the former, and of their strength and state compared with that which lately it was. That will require a more large but withall a more private discovery than here may be published.

Their language is significant. It hath in many words much affinity with the Welsh or British, for the proper and particular parts of the body, and some other things, are in both the same or very like, [such] as nose, hand, eye, leg, and the like. So the name of a house, fire, a church, to burn, to run, and many more. This makes some shew that the nations were originally

Their language is significant. It hath in many words much affinity with the Welsh or British, for the proper and particular parts of the body, and some other things, are in both the same or very like, [such] as nose, hand, eye, leg, and the like. So the name of a house, fire, a church, to burn, to run, and many more. This makes some shew that the nations were originally the same, or else had much commixture by commerce, marriage, or mutual aid in times of danger.

They are very apt to give entertainment according to their ability and manner of living in their houses, not denying such as they have unto travellers. In apparel they keep the same fashion still; in diet little choice, no dainties; and their dressing [is] as far from effeminateness as from curiosity or from cleanliness. [They are] more tied to custom than to observation of civility; the best servants, but not the best subjects; the sharpest revengers, and suddenest executioners. In body for the most part [they are] strong and nimble; in wit very acute; and yet in that which is said must be understood the greater part [is] not at all. For no nation hath all things and all conditions of men alike.

It sufficeth [to say] that for execution of justice the mere Irish had no set or settled form of judiciary, neither were those they accounted for their judges learned in civil, canon, or municipal laws of that kingdom. But every lord of a seigniory had one commonly called a Brehon, supplying the place of a judge, yet skilled in nothing but in the customs of that part of the coury wherein he lived, which were usually as different one from the other as could be devised, and those either made or interpreted according to the will and the pleasures of the chief lords, who did ordain those orders as they authorized such as adjudged them.

*   *   *

The Brehons were men nearly unlearned and barbarous. They kept commonly their consistories and kinds of courts on the tops of hills, where they called such as had any controversies to be determined before them. They dealt as much in divorces of man and wife as in other matters merely lay. But of late times, since the Roman conventicles had greater force than in former times they had, the clergymen took that matter more in hand. Yet these supposed ecclesiastical judges allow divorces upon small and unwarrantable causes, [such] as for carnal copulation and knowledge of one another before marriage, which they do not make known til they grow weary of one another, [or] for being gossips or baptising one another's children. [There are] many of these allowed exceptions [but far] more allowable lay hidden, not at first known, and so easy to be made known and quarrelled [about] as they grow unkind. So were their Brehons ready to dissolve marriage.

The lords of countries had their several and slight officers and servants as their physicians, which made their practice and profession more by septs and kindreds than by knowledge. Their rhymers, who with setting forth the praise of their progenitors and the dispraise of their adversaries, stirred up much passion and had great power over the people and chiefest persons amongst those parts where they lived.

17TH CENTURY IRELAND

View of Cahir Castle on the River Suir, from Thomas Stafford's *Pacata Hibernia, Or A History of the Wars in Ireland During the Reign of Elizabeth* (1633). The image is Elizabethan for its central fortress, but the outlying farmland of economic potential suggests the shift in English views of Ireland in the 17th century.

Barnaby Rich

A NEW DESCRIPTION OF IRELAND
Wherein is Described the
Disposition of the Irish and Whereunto
They Are Inclined

Barnaby Rich (1540?-1617) was the most prolific of all writers of accounts of Ireland, as well as one of the fascinating major-minor jacks of several literary trades abundant in Tudor-Stuart England.

His career began as a military one in the campaigns against the Spanish in the low countries, where Rich formed his life-long loathing of the Papacy. He came to Ireland with the first Earl of Essex in 1573, after which he capped his initial literary career as a writer of soldierly tracts with *Rich His Farewell to Militarie Profession* (1581), from which Shakespeare and other dramatists borrowed freely. He was nevertheless back in the field in Ireland in 1585, when his troops were slaughtered at Coleraine while he was on a junket to Dublin. He returned again with the second Earl of Essex's campaign against Tyrone in 1599, and he remained there with Mountjoy's subsequent and successful campaign. By then his literary endeavors had taken a fashionable turn toward romance.

After 1607 and the flight of the Earls of Ireland there was a flurry of applications for escheated lands in Ulster. As opportunist as ever, Rich then turned his hand to Irish polemics, completing six between *A Short Survey of Ireland* in 1609 and *The Irish Hubbub* in 1617. One, *The Anothomy of Ireland* (1615), borrowed Spenser's dialogue form to far less felicitous effect.

Rich's productions on Ireland are all driven by the double urgency of petition for reward and of fervent admonition of the Papal threat. One effect of these circumstances is the tenacity with which he derogates competitors, usually for perceived Catholic biases. This *New Description of Ireland* (1610), for example, opens with a diatribe against 'other collections drawn from unworthy authors'. It heaps special abuse on Richard Stanihurst for being an alchemist, a Papist, and, for good measure, a translator of Virgil who 'stripped him . . . out of Latin herocial verse into an English riff-raff'. Here again, then, is the consistent tendency of these writers to address themselves to previous accounts of Ireland as much as to the place itself.

Apparent self-contradictions are a further effect of Rich's program to describe Ireland, but to do so in a manner to please the court. Given different rhetorical occasions, he may claim that the Irish are naturally inclined to cruelty or that they are educated to it by enemies of the crown. Given different political goals on different occasion, he may characterize the Irish as revolting or as merely naive. There is as well a persistent self-contradiction in these selections that exposes the workings of ideology in ostensibly scientific and factual reportage. Rich virulently denounces the Irish adherence to custom, but he does so with such a heavy reliance of his own on proverb and scripture that he indicts himself of the same offense. In these ways the benefit of historical hindsight reveals the failure in these accounts to see the Irish truly and also the compound failure to see oneself truly.

The text is a new modernization of the first edition of *A New Description of Ireland* printed in London in 1610.

FROM WHENCE IT PROCEEDETH THAT THE IRISH ARE SO
REPUGNANT TO THE ENGLISH

I remember there was sometime one Alan Cope*, who hath written of many matters, who, if a man might judge of, (but as he hath testified of himself) was a most arrogant and superstitious Papist. Yet, writing against that foolish conceit held by the Irish, that Ireland was purged from venomous worms by the only prayers of St. Patrick, [Cope] was therefore complained of and accused by M. Stanihurst [for having] wronged and slandered the whole Irish nation.

I hope I shall not be so dealt with because I have detected and reproved the uncivil demeanors of those that be blameworthy. [I hope] I shall not therefore be exclaimed to be an open depraver of all that whole nation.

I protest, I do know never a man in Ireland that I do hate, or that I do wish any harm unto. Therefore, if I happen to glance at the abuses of those that be ill, let not those that be good think themselves thereby to be detected, or so much as touched. But as the throng of fools doth evermore exceed the number of the wise, so the multitude of the rude and ignorant among the Irish do far pass the number either of the religious, or civilly reformed. I do not hold that every citizen or townsman that liveth in common society is therefore to be accounted civil; neither doth it follow, that every man inhabiting the country is therefore to be called uncivil; for civility and uncivility hath no relation to the city or country, but it hath consideration to the manners and conditions of men, that are therefore to be accounted civil or uncivil according to the dispositions of the mind.

All the countries that are known (especially in Europe) have their several inclinations as well to virtue as to vice. We say, the Frenchmen are politic and deceitful, and not so valiant in conquering as provident in keeping. The Spaniard is said to be proud and tyrannous. The Italian full of courtesy and full of craft. The Dutch are more wise when they be in their cups than when they be in their closets [i.e. at study]. The English are reputed to be more wise to look after than they are to foresee; and the Englishman (indeed) doth then think himself to be best in fashion, when he is most out of fashion.

To speak now of the Irish more at large, for to them my talk doth especially belong, I say they are beholding [i.e. indebted] to nature, that hath framed them comely personages, of good proportion, very well limbed. To speak truly, the English, Scottish, and Irish are easy to be discerned from all the nations of the world as well by the excellency of their complexions as by all the rest of their lineaments, from the crown of the head, to the sole of the foot. And although that in the remote places the uncivil sort so disfigure themselves with their glibs, their trousers, and

*Alan Cope (d. 1578), an English Catholic who published theological tracts by himself and others from the safety of the continent.

their mishapen attire, yet they appear to every man's eye to be men of good proportion, of comely stature, and of able body.

Now to speak of their dispositions, whereunto they are addicted and inclined. I say, not only are they rude, uncleanly, and uncivil, they are very cruel, bloody minded, apt and ready to commit any kind of mischief. I do not impute this so much to their natural inclination, as I do to their education. They are trained up in treason, in rebellion, in theft, in robbery, in superstition, in idolatry, and nuzzled from their cradles in the very puddle of Popery.

This is the fruit of the Pope's doctrine, that doth preach cruelty, that doth admit murderers and bloody executions by poisoning, stabbing, or by any other manner of practice howsoever. The Pope teacheth subjects to resist, to mutiny, and to rebel against their princes.

From hence it proceedeth, that the Irish have ever been, and still are, desirous to shake off the English government.

From hence it doth proceed, that the Irish cannot endure to love the English, because they differ so much in religion.

From hence it proceedeth, that as they cannot endure to love the English, so they cannot be induced to love anything that doth come from the English. According to the proverb, 'Love me and love my dog', so, contrariwise, he that hateth me, hateth in like manner all that cometh from me.

From hence it is, that the Irish had rather still retain themselves in their sluttishness, in their inhumane loathsomeness, than they would take any example from the English, either of civility, humanity, or any manner of decency.

We see now the author of this enmity is he that never did any good where he had to do with men's consciences.

There is yet a difference to be made between those faults that do grow from our weakness and those that do proceed from our malice. And the Irish, in this, are the more to be pitied that [they] are no better taught. As they are rude, so they are blinded with ignorance, and I think for devotion's sake they have made a vow to be ignorant.

But although the vulgar sort, through their dull wits, and their brutish education, cannot conceive what is profitable for themselves, and good for their country, yet there be some other of the country birth whose thoughts and minds being enriched with knowledge and understanding, that have done good in the country, and whose example hereafter may give light to many others; for I think that if these people did once understand the preciousness of virtue, they would far exceed us, not withstanding our long experience in the sovereignty of virtue.

THAT THE IRISH BY NATURE ARE INCLINED UNTO CRUELTY

It cannot be denied, but that the Irish are very cruel in their executions, and no less bloody in their dispositions. The examples are too many, and too manifest, to be by any means contradicted.

But some will say, their cruelty doth not so much proceed from that natural inclination that is in themselves, as from the malice and hatred they bear to the English government, which they have always spurned at, and are still desirous to shake off. But their rebellious dispositions are thereby made the more apparent, and they ought therefore to be so much the more restrained. For there is not a more dangerous thing [than] to rely either on the promises, or many other assurances, of those men, that are by nature ambitious, disloyal, cruel, and accustomed to shed blood.

But let us make a short survey [of] what they are in behaviour amongst themselves, and we shall find that it is the English government that stayeth them from their bloody executions, the one of them against the other, and that our late gracious queen was in nothing more troubled than in keeping them from persecuting and prosecuting one another, with fire, with sword, and with such raging fury that the most barbarous savages that never knew civility are not more tragical in their executions than are the Irish.

The time hath been, when they lived like barbarians, in woods, in bogs, and in desolate places, without political law, or civil government, neither embracing religion, law, nor mutual love.

That which is hateful to all the world besides, is only beloved and embraced by the Irish. I mean civil wars and domestic dissension.

The wild uncivil Scythians do forebear to be cruel to one another. The cannibals, devourers of men's flesh, do leave [i.e. cease] to be fierce amongst themselves. But the Irish, without all respect, are ever most cruel to their very next neighbours.

In civil broils, every base rascal is an equal companion with the greatest commander, and their liberty to do wrong is no less for the one than the other. They know they are the more willingly drawn to undertake commotions and rebellions for the aid and assistance of the licentious routs that follow them. They therefore forebear no mischief, abstaining no more from that which is holy, than from that which is profane. Neither marriage nor honour so protect any that rape be not mingled with murder, nor murder with rape.

All things are full of misery in civil wars. In foreign encounters, there is nothing more honourable than conquest. So in civil and domestic conflicts there is nothing more miserable than victory: for the rebellious that are led by cruelty first to undertake [i.e. attack], can use no moderation when they become victors.

These civil furies are by several means engendered. Many take arms oppressed by the tyranny of princes, but these through sufferance and overmuch liberty. Some others, having been offered wrongs and injuries, have therefore betaken themselves to actions of rebellion; but these, fearing to be punished for wrongs by themselves committed, do therefore seek to prevent it by playing the rebels. Some to free themselves from thraldom (as they pretend) have opposed themselves against their princes (as they say) to purchase liberty. But what subjects in Europe do live so lawlessly as the Irish, when the lords and great men throughout the country, do rather seem to be absolute, than to live within the compass of subjection? Neither have I known any amongst the Irish who have stood upon those terms of liberty, for who they would set free from the prince they would enthrall to the Pope. I neither yet heard of any man who was an enemy to the common quiet of a realm, but he was likewise an enemy to the commonwealth.

Alexander was wont to say that the clemency of kings and princes consisted not so much in themselves that were to command, as in the disposition of their subjects, that were to obey. [Also, some]one attributed the flourishing estate of Sparta to the government of the kings that knew how to rule well; nay, answered another, it is to be imputed to the virtue of the citizens, that know how to obey well.

Alas poor Ireland, what safety may be hoped for thee, that are still so addicted to disobedience, to contempt, to sedition, to rebellion, that thy wounds are no sooner closed up but thou thyself goest about to open them again? Your grandfathers have felt the smart of disobedience, your fathers have complained of it, yourselves have seen the calamities of contempt, and God grant that your children's children have not just cause to curse the miseries that are raised up by rebellion.

The extremest point whereunto the cruelty of man may stretch is for one man to kill another. Yea, divinity itself willeth us to shew favor, and not to be cruelly inclined, no not [even] to brute beasts, which the Almighty hath created and placed amongst his other creatures, as well for his glory as for his service. He hath himself had merciful respect unto them: as when he said to Jonas, 'Should not I spare Nineveh, that great city, wherein are six score thousand persons who cannot discern between the right hand and the left, and also much cattle'. We see here God himself had some commiseration with the poor cattle, and it was not without respect that he prescribed to Moses in the first Table of the Commandments that 'as well the cattle as the stranger within thy gates should cease from their labour and rest on the Sabbath day'.

If it hath pleased God, the creator of all things, to be thus regardful to the work of his hands, I am fully persuaded that such as by nature do shew themselves to be no less bloody minded towards men, than towards beasts, do shew themselves to be naturally inclined to cruelty, the ugliness thereof, is to be abhorred and detested amongst men.

OF THE INGRATITUDE OF THE IRISH

The Irish, as they are naturally inclined to cruelty, so there is neither lenity [i.e. mercy], love, nor liberality, whereby to confirm them in their duty and allegiance to their prince.

Some will say that there is not a readier means whereby to draw subjects to a settled love than a gracious clemency to be used by the prince. But in times past it would not serve, and I shall not need any far-fetched precedents. Let us but remember our late gracious queen, with what mildness and with what mercy she ruled and governed forty odd years, and with what disloyalty was she still requited.

Her Majesty thought in being gracious she might thereby have won their hearts to a more loving and willing obedience, and to this end, to draw them to a more dutiful regard, what did she neglect that was either befitting for a prince to grant amongst subjects or behoveful for subjects to receive from their prince? If clemency might have mitigated the rigor of cruelty, what pardoning, what protecting, and what tolerating of offences that were daily and continually committed against her?

But for the better discovery of their ingratitude towards Her Majesty, how did she continually grace and countenance the nobility of that realm, not only suffering them to triumph and tyrannize over their tenants and followers, with such privileges and prerogatives as were more befitting kings than behoveful for subjects. But also she bountifully bestowed on them contributions, stipends, pensions, and other daily pay out of her coffers, for the better upholding of their decayed estates and to have won them (if it had been profitable) to her love and their allegiance. And how some of them requited her is so manifestly known as it were but lost labour any further to rehearse.

How many gentlemen of that country's birth came daily into England about suits, that were still begging and craving, and were continually returned from Her Majesty's court back again into Ireland laden with gifts and preferments that she graciously and liberally bestowed on them? After they had passed and possessed their grants [they] would never come in place to say Amen when they heard Her Majesty prayed for; but rather by their ill example of contempt made some others more obstinate and stubborn than otherwise they would be.

I think the ingratitude of the Irish (considering how mildly they have been and are yet governed) deserveth no less to be condemned than their treasons and rebellions, and there is nothing so much detested amongst the Irish themselves as this vice of ingratitude.

Ingratitude is no way to be excused nor coloured. Theft, robbery, murder, yea treason itself may be a little flourished over with some blind excuse, but ingratitude can neither be covered nor shadowed by any means, but remaining naked, must manifest itself everywhere with shame and dishonour.

Not to requite a benefit received is ill, but this may be said to be the frailty of man: but to render and requite evil for good is most pernicious, and this malignity hath evermore proceeded from detestable creatures, denounced and abhorred by God and all good men.

The Egyptians used to geld such persons as were detected with this vice of ingratitude, to the end that there might be no further procreation of so viperous a brood. If this severity were used to those of the Irish that have tasted the bounty, liberality, and mercy of their princes, and have repaid them again with grudge, murmur, disobedience, contempt, and sometimes with treason itself, I say the eunuchs of Ireland would far exceed in number over and above all the rest that were fit for propagation.

They have been governed by such princes, who, shunning the severity of laws, have conformed themselves to divine mercy rather than to due justice. They have been and still are governed by Christian princes, endowed with the knowledge of the truth, that have ruled and do rule with courtesy and clemency. But it is the imperfections of their judgements that maketh them mistake the perfection of their princes.

OF THE INCIVILITY, BOTH OF MANNERS AND CONDITIONS, USED BY THE IRISH

If I should set down the sluttish and uncleanly observations of the Irish, as well of the men as the women, but especially of those manners and conditions whereunto they have inured themselves in the remote places of the country, I might set down such unreverent and loathsome matter as were unfit for every queasy stomach to understand of.

I will not speak of those affairs belonging to childbearing women, that are no less uncivil than uncleanly in many of their demeanors belonging to those businesses. Neither will I speak of their unmannerly manners in making of their butter, nor of the beastly physic they have used to apply to a cow when she will not give down her milk.

I might speak here what I myself have seen in the north parts of Ireland, how unhandsomely the women do use to grind their oatmeal.

But to speak generally, throughout the whole realm of Ireland, in those things wherein they should be most neat and cleanly, they do shew themselves to be most sluttish and filthy; namely, in making of their butter and washing of their linen.

First, they do abuse one of the greatest blessings of God bestowed upon that country, for as God promised the children of Israel to transport them into a land that flowed with milk and honey, so the plenty of milk throughout all the parts of Ireland doth so abound that the greatest part of the people (of the poorest sort) are especially relieved and sustained (both summer and winter) with milk and butter. But according to the proverb,

God sends meat and the devil sends cooks. So, it pleaseth God to send them plenty of milk, but as they behave themselves in the using of it, it is fit for nobody but for themselves, that are of the uncleanly diet, not only in their milk and butter but in many other unsavoury dishes besides.

It is holden [i.e. believed] among the Irish to be a presagement of some misfortune to keep their milking vessels cleanly, and that if they should either scald or wash them, some unlucky misadventure would surely betide them. Upon this conceit, all the vessels that they use about their milk are most filthily kept: and I myself have seen, that vessel which they hold under the cow whilst they are in milking, to be furred half an inch thick with filth, so that Dublin itself is served every market day with such butter as I am sure is much more loathsome than toothsome.

Now, in the manner of their washing, they are yet more filthy than in any other of their exercises, wherein they are most uncleanly, and I do almost loath but to think of the scouring stuff which they do use instead of soap. He that came in place when they were in their laundry, in their "netting" (as they call it), would never after stop his nose if he chanced to go by where they were scouring a privy.

These and many other loathsome observations are used by the Irish, from the which they will not be disuaded, but the unnurtured sort among them are no less admiring [i.e. surprised by] our decency than we their rudeness and incivility. And as I have said elsewhere, they will not take any precedents from the English, and long it was before they could be brought to imitate our English manner in divers points of husbandry, but especially in the ploughing of their land. In the performing whereof, they used the labour of five persons to every plough, and their team of cattle, which commonly consisted of five or six horses, were placed all in front, having neither cords, chains, nor lines, whereby to draw, but every horse by his own tail. This was the manner of ploughing when I knew Ireland first, and is used still at this day in many places of the country.

Demand of them why they should be so much addicted to their own dirty demeanours and why they should not conform themselves to those civil courses which they see are to be performed with less pain and more profit. They can satisfy us with no other reason but custom: 'thus did our ancestors'.

Custom is a metal amongst them that standeth which way soever it be bent. Charge them for their uncleanliness, and they plead custom; reprehend them for their idolatry, and they say thus did our fathers before us; and I think it be custom that draweth them so often into rebellion, because they would do as their fathers have done before them.

But alas their judgements are both blind and lame, and they are deaf to all good counsel. They are fallen into a blind arrogance, and they are so generally bewitched with Popery that they will neither draw example nor precept from the English.

I hope my general speeches will breed no general offence. The Irish are generally addicted to Popery, and it would argue but a quarrelsome disposition, to deny that truth, which we see in daily example before our eyes. The Irish themselves (I am sure) would be much offended if they were not able to drop ten Papists for one Protestant throughout the whole realm. Themselves are neither ashamed, nor afraid to confess it, and I would we might as well trust them in their fidelity to the king as we may believe them in that. But they all speak fair, and they say they love the king, and without doubt there are some small number to whom it hath pleased God to open their eyes, and that do stand assured to His Majesty. But for the greatest number of those that be Papists, what fair semblance soever they make, His Majesty may well say with our Saviour, 'This people honoureth me with their lips, but their hearts are far from me.' And for these, whatsoever they speak with their lips, their hearts are at Rome. Do they not shew it through every part of the realm, in city, town, and country, in their receiving and entertaining of Jesuits, seminarians, and Popish priests, the protested enemies to His Majesty?

With what face may they then avouch themselves to love the king, that doeth with such fervour embrace His Majesty's deadly enemies? I will never believe them. Neither can it sink into my head that an honest man may be brought to be in league with God and devil, and to be in perfect love and charity with them both together.

The vulgar sort of the Irish, wanting faculty to judge of things truely as they are, and suffering themselves to be led and carried away with outward apparitions, are not only possessed with boldness to despise, but likewise with impertinence to impugn those means that should as well induce them to the love and obedience of their prince as to the true knowledge of their God, wherein consisteth the state of their salvation.

It is ignorance that hunteth after light in darkness, that believes shadows to be substantial. But divine knowledge, from whence proceedeth all blessings, it is the parent of peace, of wisdom, of obedience, and it is the light of reason that discovereth truth from falsehood, and therefore the most resplendent ornament of man.

Fynes Moryson

AN ITINERARY:
Containing His Ten Years Travel through the Twelve Dominions of Germany, Bohmerland, Switzerland, Netherland, Denmark, Poland, Italy, Turkey, France, England, Scotland, and Ireland

One of the great world travellers of his time, Fynes Moryson (1566-1617) was the son of an M.P. from Lincolnshire. After graduation from Cambridge in 1580, he became a Fellow of Peterhouse in 1584 and the recipient of its travel allowances in 1591. His principle 'tour' through Europe took place from 1591 to 1595 and from 1596 to 1597.

Moryson's brother Richard had gone to Ireland with Essex and risen to the post of Governor of Dundalk. In 1600 Fynes Moryson resigned from Cambridge to join his brother in Ireland, where he became secretary to the new Lord Deputy of Ireland, Mountjoy. In Mountjoy's company Moryson witnessed the campaign against Hugh O'Neill, Earl of Tyrone. Mountjoy succeeded where Essex had failed: he accepted the surrender of Tyrone on March 30, 1603, thus fulfilling Elizabeth's wishes six days after her death.

Moryson stayed in Ireland to witness the beginnings of the post-Elizabethan plantation. Only then, after the death of Mountjoy in 1606 relieved him of other duties, did he begin to write his *Itinerary* in England. He worked on the lengthy manuscript, written in both Latin and English, for the rest of his life. The first, ample selections from it were published in the year of his death. Most of his Irish materials, however, were published much later, notably in a Dublin edition of 1735. Moryson's work has been valued especially as an essential sourcebook on the Elizabethan age; for example, important parts of it, some from manuscript, were edited by Charles Hughes and published in 1903 under the title *Shakespeare's Europe*. The text reprinted here is a modernization of the four-volume Glasgow edition of 1908.

Moryson's comments display some of the subtle changes in English perceptions of the Irish in the midst of the shift from 16th to 17th centuries and from Tudor to Stuart monarchies. He concurs with his predecessors in his revulsion at nomadic culture, in his apparent fear of English-Irish degeneration, and in his audit of the natural, exploitable resources of the country. But here there are as well the beginnings of English charges of Irish sloth, charges that continue through these accounts into Victorian times and beyond them in more oblique forms into our own century. The charge, in any colonial context, is a significant juncture of assumptions and revelations. One dynamic in it is a failure of self-perception, for the manners of the Irish as described here engender no corresponding examination of English industry, husbandry, or general ideology of 'great gain', in Moryson's phrase. Another is that perceived laziness justifies enlightened intervention, here a kind of early 17th century economic development. Above all, Moryson's ideology of 'great gain' is erected on the paradox that the Irish are naturally lazy but laziness is not natural. In Moryson's own account here of a telling incident it is in fact Lord Mountjoy himself, and not the author, who proves to be the shrewder and more provocative commentator on what is 'contrary to nature'.

T he land of Ireland is uneven, mountainous, soft, watery, woody, and open to winds and floods of rain, and so fenny, as it hath bogs upon the very tops of mountains, not bearing man or beast, but dangerous to pass, and such bogs are frequent over all Ireland. Our mariners observe sailing into Ireland to be more dangerous, not only because many tides meeting makes the sea apt to swell upon any storm, but especially because they ever find the coast of Ireland covered with mists, whereas the coast of England is commonly clear, and to be seen far off. The air of Ireland is unapt to ripen seeds, yet (as Mela* witnesseth) the earth is luxurious in yielding fair and sweet herbs. Ireland is little troubled with thunders, lightnings, or earthquakes, yet (I know not upon what presage) in the year 1601, and in the month of November almost ended, at the siege of Kinsale, and a few days before the famous battle in which the rebels were happily overthrown, we did nightly hear and see great thundrings and lightnings, not without some astonishment what they should presage.

The fields are not only most apt to feed cattle, but yield also great increase of corn. I will freely say, that I observed the winter's cold to be far more mild than it is in England. So the Irish pastures are more green, and likewise the gardens all winter time. But in summer, by reason of the cloudy air and watery soil, the heat of the sun hath not such power to ripen corn and fruits, so their harvest is much later than in England. Also, I observed that the best sorts of flowers and fruits are much rarer in Ireland than in England, which notwithstanding is more to be attributed to the inhabitants than to the air. For Ireland being oft troubled with rebellions, and the rebels not only being idle themselves, but in natural malice destroying the labours of other men, and cutting up the very trees of fruits for the same cause, or else to burn them. For these reasons the inhabitants take less pleasure to till their grounds, or plant trees, content to live for the day in continual fear of like mischiefs. Yet Ireland is not altogether destitute of these flowers and fruits, wherewith the county of Kilkenny seems to abound more than any other part. And the said humidity of air and land, making the fruits for food more raw and moist: hereupon the inhabitants and strangers are troubled with looseness of body, the country disease. Yet for this rawness they have an excellent remedy in their aquavitae, vulgarly called usquebagh, which binds the belly, and drieth up moisture, more than our aquavitae, yet inflameth not so much. Also, inhabitants as well as strangers are troubled there with an ague, which they call the Irish ague, and they who are sick thereof, upon a received custom, do not use the help of the physician, but give themselves to the keeping of Irish women, who starve the ague, giving the sick man no meat, nothing but milk and some vulgarly known remedies at hand.

Ireland, after much blood spilt in the civil wars, became less populous,

---

*Pomponius Mela, known for the geographical treatise *De Situ Orbis* (c. A.D. 43).

and great lords of countries as well as other inferior gentlemen laboured more to get new possessions for inheritance than by husbandry and peopling of their old lands to increase their revenues. So I observed much grass (wherewith the land so much abounds) to have perished without use, and either to have rotted or in the next spring time to be burnt lest it should hinder the coming of new grass. This plenty of grass makes the Irish have infinite multitudes of cattle, and in the heat of the last rebellion the very vagabond rebels had multitudes of cows, which they still (like the nomads) drove with them, wherever themselves were driven, and fought for them as for their altars and families.

By this abundance of cattle, the Irish have a frequent, though somewhat poor, traffic for their hides, the cattle being very little, and only the men and the greyhounds of great stature. Neither can the cattle possibly be great, since they eat only by day, and then are brought at evening within the bawnes [i.e. courtyards] of castles, where they stand or lie all night in a dirty yard, without so much as a lock of hay, whereof they make little for sluggishness, and that little they altogether keep for their horses. And they are thus brought in by night for fear of thieves, the Irish using almost no other kind of theft, or else for fear of wolves, the destruction whereof being neglected by the inhabitants, oppressed with greater mischief. [The wolves] are so much grown in number as sometimes on winter nights they will come to prey in villages and the suburbs of cities.

The Earl of Ormond in Munster, and the Earl of Kildare in Leinster, had each of them a small park enclosed for fallow deer, and I have not seen any other park in Ireland, nor have I heard that they had any other at that time. Yet in many woods they have many red deer, loosely scattered, which seem more plentiful because the inhabitants used not then to hunt them, but only the governors and commanders had them sometimes killed with the piece [i.e. a firearm]. They have also about Ophalia and Wexford, and in some parts of Munster, some fallow deer scattered in the woods. Yet in the time of the war I did never see any venison served at the table, but only in the houses of the said earls and of the English commanders.

Ireland hath great plenty of birds and fowls, but by reason of their natural sloth they had little delight or skill in birding or fowling. But Ireland hath neither singing nightingale nor chattering pie [i.e. magpie], nor undermining mole, nor black crow, but only crows of mingled colour, such as we call royston crows. They have such plenty of pheasants, as I have known sixty served at one feast, and abound much more with rayles [i.e. rails, a wading bird], but partridges are somewhat rare. There be very many eagles, and great plenty of hares, conies [i.e. rabbits], hawks called goshawks, much esteemed with us, and also of bees, in hives at home as well as in hollow trees abroad and in caves of the earth. They abound in flocks of sheep, which they shear twice in the year, but the wool is coarse and merchants may not export it, forbidden by a law made on behalf of the poor, that they may be nourished by working it into cloth, namely rugs (whereof the best are made at Waterford), and [the] mantles generally worn by men and women and exported in great quantity.

Ireland yields much flax, which the inhabitants work into yarn and export the same in great quantity. And of old they had such plenty of linen cloth, as the wild Irish used to wear 30 or 40 ells [i.e. units 45 inches in length] in a shirt, all gathered and wrinkled, and washed [i.e. dyed] in saffron, because they never put them off till they were worn out. Their horses, called hobbies, are much commended for their ambling pace and beauty, but Ireland yields few horses good for service in war. The said hobbies are much inferior to our geldings in strength to endure long journeys, and being bred in the fenny soft ground of Ireland are soon lamed when they are brought into England. The hawks of Ireland, called goshawks, are (as I said) much esteemed in England, and they are sought out by many and all means to be transported thither. Ireland yields excellent marble near Dublin, Kilkenny, and Cork, and I am of their opinion who dare venture all they are worth that the mountains would yield abundance of metals if this public good were not hindered by the inhabitant's barbarousness, making them apt to sedition and so unwilling to enrich their prince and country, and by their slothfulness, which is so singular as they hold it base to labour, and by their poverty, not able to bear the charge of [i.e. responsibility for] such works. Besides that, the wiser sort think their poverty best for public good, making them peaceable, as nothing makes them sooner kick against authority than riches.

Ireland hath in all parts pleasant rivers, safe and long havens, and no less frequent lakes of great circuit, yielding great plenty of fish. And the sea on all sides yields like plenty of excellent fish, as salmon, oysters (which are preferred before the English), and shellfish with all other kinds of sea fish. So as the Irish might in all parts have abundance of excellent sea and freshwater fish, if the fishermen were not so possessed with the natural fault of slothfulness [that] no hope of gain [and] scarcely any fear of authority can in many places make them come out of their houses and put to sea. Hence it is that in many places they use Scots for fishermen, and they, together with the English, make profit of the inhabitants' sluggishness. And no doubt if the Irish were industrious in fishing they might export salted and dried fish with great gain. In time of peace the Irish transport good quantity of corn, yet they may not transport it without licence, lest upon any sudden rebellion the king's forces and his good subjects should want corn.

Ulster and the western parts of Munster yield vast woods in which rebels cutting up trees and casting them in heaps used to stop the passages and therein, as also upon fenny and boggy places, to fight with the English. But I confess myself to have been deceived in the common fame [i.e. report] that all Ireland is woody, having found in my long journey from Armagh to Kinsale few or no woods by the way, excepting the great woods of Ophalia and some low shrubby places, which they call glens. Also I did observe many boggy and fenny places, whereof a great part might be dried by good and painful husbandry.

I may not omit the opinion commonly received that the earth of Ireland will not suffer a snake or venomous beast to live, and that the Irish wood transported for building is free of spiders and their webs. Myself have seen some (but very few) spiders, which the inhabitants deny have any poison. But I have heard some English of good credit affirm by experience the contrary.

The Irish, having in most parts great woods or low shrubs and thickets, do use the same for fire, but in other parts they burn turf and sea coal brought out of England. They export great quantity of wood to make barrels, called pipe-staves, and make great gain thereby. They are not permitted to build great ships for war, but they have small ships in some sort armed to resist pirates, [when] transporting commodities into Spain and France, yet no great number of them. Therefore, since the Irish have small skill in navigation, I cannot praise them for this art; [but] I am confident that, the nation being bold and warlike, would no doubt prove brave seamen if they shall practice navigation, and could possibly be industrious therein. I freely profess that Ireland in general would yield abundance of all things to civil and industrious inhabitants. And when it lay wasted by the late rebellion, I did see it after the coming of the Lord Mountjoy daily more and more to flourish, and in short time after the rebellion appeased, like the new Spring to put on the wonted beauty.

Touching the Irish diet, some lords and knights and gentlemen of the English-Irish, and all the English there abiding, having competent means, use the English diet. But some [use it] more, some less cleanly, few or none curiously, and no doubt they have as great and for their part greater plenty than the English of flesh, fowl, fish, and all things for food, if they will use like art of cookery. Always I except the fruits, venison, and some dainties proper to England and rare in Ireland. And we must conceive that venison and fowl seem to be more plentiful in Ireland, because [the Irish] neither so generally affect dainty food, nor so diligently search [for] it as the English do. Many of the English-Irish have by little and little been infected with the Irish filthiness, and that in the very cities, excepting Dublin and some of the better sort in Waterford, where the English continually lodge in their houses [and] they more retain the English diet. The English-Irish after our manner serve to the table joints of flesh cut after our fashion, with geese, pullets, pigs and like roasted meats, but the ordinary food for the common sort is of whitemeats [i.e. dairy products], and they eat cakes of oat for bread and drink not English beer made of malt and hops but ale. At Cork I have seen, with these eyes, young maids stark naked grinding corn with certain stones to make cakes thereof, and striking into the tub of meal such relics thereof as stuck to their belly, thighs, and more unseemly parts.

And [as] for the cheese or butter commonly made by the English-Irish, an English man would not touch it with his lips though he were half starved. Yet many English inhabitants make very good of both kinds. In cities they have such bread as ours, but of a sharp savour, and some mingled with anise and baked like cakes, and that only in the houses of the better sort.

At Dublin and in some other cities, they have taverns wherein Spanish and French wines are sold, but more commonly the merchants sell them by pints and quarts in their own cellars. The Irish aquavitae, vulgarly called usquebagh, is held the best in the world of that kind; [it] is made also in England, but nothing so good as that which is brought out of Ireland. And the usquebagh is preferred before our aquavitae, because the mingling of raisins, fennel seed, and other things, mitigating the heat, and making the taste pleasant, makes it inflame less and yet refresh the weak stomach with moderate heat and a good relish. These drinks the English-Irish drink largely, and in many families (especially at feasts) both men and women use excess therein. And I have in part seen, and often heard from others' experience, that some gentlewomen were so free in this excess as they would kneel upon the knee and otherwise carouse health after health with men. Not to speak of the wives of the Irish lords, or to defer it to the due place, who often drink till they be drunken, or at least till they void urine in full assemblies of men. I cannot (though unwilling) but note the Irish women more specially with this fault, which I have observed in no other parts to be a women's vice, but only in Bohemia. Yet so accusing them, I mean not to excuse the men. And [I] will also confess that I have seen virgins, gentlewomen as well as citizens, commanded by their mothers to retire after they had in courtesy pledged one or two healths.

In cities passengers may have featherbeds, soft and good, but most commonly lousy, especially on the highways; either that came by their being forced to lodge common soldiers, or from the nasty filthiness of the nation in general. For even in the best city, as at Cork, I have observed that my own and other Englishmen's chambers hired from the citizens were scarcely swept once in the week, and then the dust laid in a corner was perhaps cast out once in a month or two. I did never see any public inns with signs hung out among the English or English-Irish, but the officers of cities and villages appoint lodgings to the passengers. And perhaps in each city they shall find one or two houses where they will dress meat, and these commonly houses of Englishmen. [But] as these houses have no sign hung out, a passenger cannot challenge [i.e. demand his] right to be entertained in them, but must have it of courtesy or by entreaty.

The wild and (as I may say) mere Irish, inhabiting many and large provinces, are barbarous and most filthy in their diet. They skim the seething pot with a handful of straw and strain their milk taken from the cow through a like handful of straw, none of the cleanest, and so cleanse, or rather more defile, the pot and the milk. They devour great morsels of beef unsalted, and they eat commonly swine flesh, seldom mutton. And all these pieces of flesh, and also the entrails of beasts unwashed, they seeth in a hollow tree lapped [i.e. lined] in a raw cow's hide and so set over the fire, and [they] therewith swallow hole lumps of filthy butter. Yea (which is more contrary to nature) they will feed on horses dying of themselves, not only upon small want of flesh but even for pleasure. For I remember an accident in the army, when Lord Mountjoy, the Lord Deputy, riding to take the air out[side] of the camp, found the buttocks of dead horses cut off, and suspecting that some soldiers had eaten that flesh out of necessity, being defrauded of the victuals allowed them, commanded the men to be searched out. Among whom a common soldier, and that of the English-Irish, not of the mere Irish, being brought to the Lord Deputy, and asked why he had eaten the flesh of dead horses, thus freely answered: 'lordship may please to eat pheasant and partridge, and much good do it you that best likes your taste; and I hope it is lawful for me without offence to eat this flesh that likes me better than beef'. Whereupon my Lord Deputy perceiving himself to be deceived, and further understanding that [the soldier] had received his ordinary victuals (the detaining whereof he suspected and proposed to punish for example) gave the soldier a piece of gold to drink in usquebagh for better digestion, and so dismissed him.

The foresaid wild Irish do not thresh their oats, but burn them from the straw, and so make cakes thereof. Yet they seldom eat this bread, much less any better kind, especially in time of war. Whereof a Bohemian baron complained, who, having seen the courts of England and Scotland, would need out of his curiosity [to] return through Ireland in the heat of the rebellion. Having letters from the King of Scots to the Irish lords then in rebellion, [he] first landed among them in the furthest north, where for eight days' space he had found no bread, not so much as a cake of oats till he came to eat with the Earl of Tyrone. After obtaining the Lord Deputy's pass to come into our army, [he] related this want of bread to us for a miracle, [but we] nothing wondered thereat. Yea, the wild Irish in time of greatest peace imput covetousness and base birth to him that hath any corn after Christmas, as if it were a point of nobility to consume all within those festival days. They willingly eat the herb shamrock, being of a sharp taste, which as they run and are chased to and fro they snatch like beasts out of the ditches.

Neither have they any beer made of malt and hops, nor yet any ale, no, not the chief lords except it be very rarely. But they drink milk like nectar, warmed with a stone first cast into the fire, or else beef broth mingled with milk. When they come to any market town, to sell a cow or a horse, they never return home till they have outslept two or three days drunkenness. And not only the common sort, but even the lords and their wives. The more they want this drink at home, the more they swallow it when they come to it, till they be as drunk as beggars.

Many of these wild Irish eat no flesh, but that which dies of disease or otherwise of itself. Neither can it [e]scape them for stinking. They desire no broth, nor have any use of a spoon. They can neither seeth artichokes nor eat them when they are sodden. It is strange and ridiculous, but most true, that some of our carriage horses, falling into their hands, when they found soap and starch, carried for the use of our laundresses, they, thinking them to be some dainty meats, did eat them greedily. And when they stuck in their teeth, cursed bitterly the gluttony of us English churles, for so they term us. They feed most on whitemeats, and esteem for a great dainty sour curds, vulgarly called by them bonaclabba. And for this cause they watchfully keep their cows, and fight for them as for religion and life; and when they are almost starved, yet they will not kill a cow, except it be old and yield no milk. Yet will they upon hunger in time of war open a vein of the cow, and drink the blood, but in no case kill or much weaken it. A man would think these men to be Scythians, who let their horses' blood under the ears, and for nourishment drink their blood, and indeed (as I have formerly said), some of the Irish are of the race of Scythians, coming into Spain and from thence into Ireland. The wild Irish (as I said) seldom kill a cow to eat, and if perhaps they kill one for that purpose, they distribute it all to be devoured at one time. For they approve not the orderly eating at meals, but so they may eat enough when they are hungry, they care not to fast long. And I have known some of these Irish footmen serving in England (where they are nothing less than sparing in the food of their families) to lay meat aside for many meals, to devour it all at one time.

These wild Irish, as soon as their cows have calved, take the calves from them, and thereof feed some with milk to rear for breed. Some of the rest they flay, and seeth them in a filthy poke, and so eat them, being nothing but froth, and send them for a present one to another. But the greatest part of these calves they cast out to be eaten by crows and wolves, that themselves may have more abundance of milk. And the calves being taken away, the cows are so mad among them as they will give no milk till the skin of the calf be stuffed and set before them, that they may smell the odor of their own bellies. Yea when these cows thus madly deny their milk, the women wash their hands in cow's dung, and so gently stroke their dugs, yea, put their hands into the cow's tail, and with their mouths blow into their tails, that with this manner (as it were) of enchantment they may draw milk from them. Yea, these cows seem as rebellious to their owners as the people are to their kings, for many times they will not be milked but of some one old woman only, and of no other.

These wild Irish never set any candles upon tables. What do I speak of tables? Since indeed they have no tables, but set their meat upon a bundle of grass and use the same grass for napkins to wipe their hands. But I mean that they do not set candles upon any high place to give light to the house, but place a great candle made of reeds and butter upon the floor in the midst to a great room. And in like sort the chief men in their houses make fires in the midst of the room, the smoke thereof goeth out at a hole in the top thereof.

An Italian Friar, coming of old into Ireland, and seeing at Armagh this their diet and nakedness of the women (whereof I shall speak in the next book of this Part, and the second Chapter thereof) is said to have cried out:

> *Civitas Armachana, Civitas vana*
> *Carnes curdae, mulieres nudae.*

> Vain Armagh City, I did thee pity,
> Thy meats' rawness, and women's nakedness.

I trust no man expects among these gallants any beds, much less feather-beds and sheets, who, like the nomads removing their dwellings, according to the commodity of pastures for their cows, sleep under the canopy of heaven, or in a poor house of clay, or in a cabin made of the boughs of trees, and covered with turf, for such are the dwellings of the very lords among them. And in such places they make a fire in the midst of the room, and round about it they sleep upon the ground without straw or other thing under them, lying all in a circle about the fire, with their feet towards it. And their bodies being naked, they cover their heads and upper parts with their mantles, which they first make very wet, steeping them in water on purpose. For they find that when their bodies have once warmed the wet mantles the smoke of them keeps their bodies in temperate heat all the night following. And in this manner of lodging, not only the mere Irish lords, and their followers, but even some of the English-Irish lords and their followers, when after the old but tyrannical and prohibited manner vulgarly called coshering, they go (as it were) on progress, to live upon their tenants, till they have consumed all the victuals that the poor men have or can get.

To conclude, not only in lodging passengers, not at all or most rudely, but even in their inhospitality towards them, these wild Irish are not much unlike to wild beasts, in whose caves a beast passing that way might perhaps find meat, but not without danger to be ill entertained, perhaps devoured by his insatiable host.

Luke Gernon

A DISCOURSE OF IRELAND
ANNO 1620

Luke Gernon is one of the most shadowy authors of signed accounts of
Ireland, and his *Discourse of Ireland* is one of the most vivid and startling of
them. His date of birth is unknown. It seems probable that he was admitted to the bar at Lincoln's Inn in 1604. Possibly on the basis of a wife's
infuential family, he became Second Justice of Munster in 1619, serving, as
he notes in this selection, in Limerick. Perhaps a combination of family
relations and personal guile explain his resourceful survival in an Ireland
in turmoil: cast out of office and onto the roads in the rebellion of 1641, he
managed to obtain a pension from Cromwell, and then a continuation of
that pension after the Restoration. His date of death, too, is unknown,
though a will was probated in 1673.

Most of this information comes from notes attached to the first publication of the *Discourse*, by C. Litton Falkiner in his *Illustrations of Irish History*
in 1904. It was Falkiner, a superb Irish historian, who dated the manuscript in accord with internal references reproduced here to Tyrone's
Rebellion and a great fire in Galway. The dating is more generally
corroborated by Gernon's references to 'the new plantation in the north'
and to Waterford under military government. In Falkiner's opinion,
Gernon 'expresses himself with a freedom not quite appropriate to the
social amenities of the twentieth century'. So, to make this freedom seem
less 'jarring', Falkiner retained 17th century orthography in his edition.
Social amenities being what they are at this later date in the twentieth
century, modernized spelling and syntax have been adopted for this
edition based on Falkiner's printing.

Gernon wrote as he assumed his judgeship in Limerick. The *Discourse*
thus stands as a kind of prurient prothalamion. Gernon's is a rhetoric of
possession that exhuberantly delineates some of the infrequently acknowledged dimensions of colonialism. Beyond the salacious opening passage,
this is apparent too in his undisguised fondness for details of public
ceremony and arrogant condescension toward the Irish. There are few
more chilling images in this collection than Gernon's extended simile of
ravaged Irish settlements as like the remnants of finished meals.

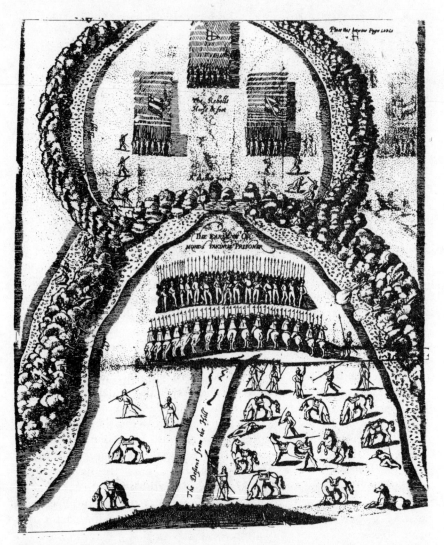

The army of the Earl of Ormond, led by and comprised of 'English-Irish', as pictured in Thomas Stafford's *Pacata Hibernia*. In the last years of Elizabeth, Ormond, with Sir George Carew, attempted pacification of the south of Ireland while Lord Mountjoy subdued the north. Prepared in Stuart years, Stafford's image of an organised Irish army in support of England coalesces with the 17th-century sense of Ireland as assimilable. That sense of Ireland is also apparent in writers such as Fynes Moryson and Luke Gernon.

T his Nymph of Ireland is at all points like a young wench that hath the green sickness for want of occupying. She is very fair of visage, and hath a smooth skin of tender grass. Indeed she is somewhat freckled (as the Irish are), some parts darker than others. Her flesh is of a soft and delicate mould of earth, and her blue veins trailing through every part of her like rivulets. She hath one master vein called the Shannon, which passeth quite through her, and if it were not for one knot (one main rock) it [would be] navigable from head to foot. She hath three other veins called the sisters, the Suir, the Nore, and the Barrow, which rising at one spring trail through her middle parts and join together in their going out. Her bones are of polished marble, the grey marble, the black, the red, and the speckled, so fair for building that their houses shew [forth] like colleges, and being polished [are] most rarely embellished. Her breasts are round hillocks of milk-yielding grass, and that so fertile that they contend with the valleys. And betwix her legs (for Ireland is full of havens), she hath an open harbor, but [one] not much frequented. She hath had goodly tresses of hair *arboribusque comae*, but the iron mills, like a sharp-toothed comb, have knotted and poled her much, and in her champion parts she hath not so much as will cover her nakedness. Of complexion she is very temperate, never too hot, nor too cold, and hath a sweet breath of favonian [i.e. west] wind. She is of a gentle nature. If the anger of heaven be against her, she will not bluster and storm, but she will weep many days together, and (alas) this last summer she did so water her plants that the grass and blade was so bedewed that it became unprofitable, and threatens a scarcity. Neither is she frozen-hearted; the last frost was not so extreme here as it was reported to be in England. It is now since she was drawn out of the womb of rebellion about sixteen years, by'rlady [i.e. 'by our lady', an expletive] nineteen, and yet she wants a husband. She is not embraced, she is not hedged and ditched, [and] there is no quicksett [i.e. plant cuttings] put into her.

How shall I describe her towns, her people, her flocks? Her towns shall be her palaces. I have sacred warrant. The daughter of Zion is all desolate, her palaces are destroyed. Those which are called by the name of cities are Dublin, Waterford, Cork, Limerick, Galway, Kilkenny, the Derry, and Coleraine. A point must serve for a description, but I will place it in that part which is most worthy of your apprehension.

Dublin is the most frequented, more for convenience than for majesty. There reside the Deputy and the Council; there she receives intelligences, advertisements, instructions. The buildings are of timber, and of the English form, and it is resembled [i.e. compared] to Bristol, but falleth short. The circuit of the castle is a huge and mighty wall, foursquare and of incredible thickness, built by King John. Within it are many fair buildings, and there the Deputy keeps his court. There are two cathedrals under one Archbishop, St. Patrick's and Christ Church. St. Patrick's is more vast and ancient, the other is in better repair*. The courts of justice (the same as in England) are kept in a large stone building of Christ Church, which is built in [the] form of a cross; at the four ends are the four courts well adorned, the middle is to walk in. There is a house of court where the judges and other lawyers have chambers, and a common hall to dine in, and it is called the Inns. The judges and the King's Council make the bench, in which number I am. The rest are barristers and attorneys. Further, there is a college which is also a university. You will expect to know the state of our state. It is not very magnificent, nor to be disregarded. There is a presence where they stand at all times uncovered, and a cloth of state under which the [Lord] Deputy sitteth. When he sitteth at meat, there sit [with him] men of quality, as many as the table will contain. When he goeth abroad in solemn manner, all whom it concerns do attend him. Before him go the gentlemen captains, knights, and officers, all on foot. Then cometh the Deputy riding in state, and before him a knight bareheaded carrying the sword. After the Deputy, the nobles, the Council, and the judges, all in footeclothes [i.e. on horseback, in regalia]. His guard consists of fifty tall men. They wear not red coats, but soldiers' cassocks, and halberts [i.e. battle-axes] in their hands. On principal festivals, the herald goes before him in a coat of arms. So much for Dublin. I may call her Whitehall. Let us take our journey to Waterford.

Waterford is situated on the best harbor, and in a pleasant and temperate air. The buildings are of English form, and well compact. There is a fair cathedral, but her beauty is in the quay, for the wall of the town extending for near half a mile along the water, between that and the water there is a broad quay mainly fortified with stone and strong piles of timber, where a ship of the burden of 1000 tons may ride at anchor. It was famous for merchandise, but her high stomach [i.e. spirit] in disobeying the state deprived her of her magistrate, and now she is in the government of a soldier. In her prosperity, there was a league between her and Bristol that their merchants respectively should be exempted of customs, but now she complains that Bristol refuseth her. Our next journey is to Cork.

Cork is a port of the sea also, but stands in a very bog and is unhealthy. The building is of stone, and built after the Irish form, which is castlewise and with narrow windows more for strength than for beauty, but they begin to beautify it in better form. There is [a] quarry of red marble, which maketh the town appear of a ruddy colour. There is also a cathedral, but in decay. It is a populous town and well compact, but there is nothing in it remarkable. There is nothing to commend it but the antiquity, and nothing doth disgrace it so much as their obstinacy in the antic religion. Pass on to Limerick.

---

*"This is incorrect as to the relative antiquity of the two cathedrals. St. Patrick's Cathedral was consecrated in 1191, Christ Church in 1038'. [Falkiner's note].

Limerick is the place of my commerce. Let me entertain you with a broad cake and a cup of sack, as the manner is. You will be the less sensible of my tediousness. Limerick divides itself into two parts, the high town, which is compassed with the Shannon, and the base town, and in form it doth perforce resemble an hour glass, being bound together by that bridge which divides the two parts. A philosopher saw a little town with a wide open gate, gave warning to the citizens to shut up their gate lest the town should run out. The founders of this city were more considerate, for they have fenced the base town with such a huge strong wall that travellers affirm they have not seen the like in Europe. It is a mile in compass, and three men abreast may walk the round. Notwithstanding their providence, I am of the opinion that that part hath crept over the bridge into the high town, for now there is nothing remaining in that part but a street of decayed houses, saving a church and a storehouse, monuments to former habitation. The other part is a lofty building of marble. The high street is built from one gate to the other in one form, like the colleges in Oxford, so magnificent that at my first entrance it did amaze me [to see], *sed intus cadavera*, noxious and stinking houses. The cathedral is not large but very lightsome [i.e. graceful and well-lighted], and by the providence of the Bishop fairly beautified within, and as gloriously served with singing and organs. There is in this city an ancient castle, the Bishop's palace, and a stone bridge of fourteen arches. But that which is most notorious to my judgement is the quay wall. This wall is extended from the town wall into the middle of the river and was made for a defense and harbor for the shipping. It is in length about 200 paces, and it is a double wall. In the bottom it is a mayne [i.e. remarkable] thickness, and so continueth until it be raised above high water. Then there is within it a long gallery arched overhead, and with windows most pleasant to walk in, and above that a terrace to walk upon with fair battlements. At the end of it there is a round tower with two or three chambers, one above the other, and a battlement above. This town now rejoiceth in the residence of the president. The presidency is kept in the form as it is in Wales: a president, two justices, and a council. We sit in council at a table. When the president goeth forth, he is attended in military form: when he rideth, with a troupe of horse; when he walketh, with a company of foot[soldiers] with pikes and muskets in hand. I have kept you too long at Limerick, let me conduct you towards Galway.

I was never there myself, but it is reported to be the Windsor of Ireland. It hath been praised for the magnificent building and a stately abbey there, used for a parish church. But a great fire which happened in May twelvemonth did consume 400 houses, and utterly defaced the abbey, being so vehement that the bodies of the dead lying in vaults were consumed to ashes. They begin to re-edify. Let us return by Kilkenny.

Kilkenny is an inland town situated in a pleasant valley and upon a fresh river. It is praised for the wholesome air, and delightful orchards and gardens, which are somewhat rare in Ireland. The houses are of grey marble fairly built, the fronts of their houses are supported (most of them) with pillars, or arches under which there is an open pavement to walk on. At the one end of the town is a large cathedral, at the other end a high mounted castle appertaining to the Earls of Ormond, but now it is allotted to the portion of the Countess of Desmond.

The other two cities, the Derry and Coleraine, are of the new plantation in the north. They are reported to be fairly built, but they are like new palaces. They are not slated, nor [are] the flowers laid yet. Let them alone till they be finished.

To the inferior places I will not invite you, only cast your regard upon Youghal and Bandonbridge.

Youghal is a sea town and little inferior to the cities. It is situated between Waterford and Cork and is a lurcher [i.e. pilferer in advance of others], for it hath gotten the traffic from them both, especially for transporting of cattle.

Bandonbridge is a new plantation begun within these fifteen years and is increased to be near as large as Leicester. It rejoiceth in the patronage of that happy man Richard Boyle, now Earl of Cork, by whose procurement it is now engirting with a new wall for which the province is taxed at 5 shillings the plowland. It is estimated that the charge will amount to 4,000 pounds.

In this peregrination you have viewed the country in passing. The villages are distant each from the other about two miles. In every village is a castle and a church, but both in ruin. The baser cottages are built of underwood, called wattle, and covered some with thatch and some with green sedge, of a round form and without chimneys, and to my imagination resemble so many hives of bees about a country farm. In the end of harvest the villages seem as big again as in the spring, their corn being brought into their haggards [i.e. stack-yards] and being laid up in round cocks, in [the] form of their houses. And by the way, there is no meat so dainty as a haggard pig, a pig that hath been fed at the reeke [i.e. stack]. Take him at a quarter[year] old, and use him like a roasting pig. Because his bigness should not be offensive, they serve him up by quarters. Here I would conclude with our buildings, but when I look about I cannot but bewail the desolation which civil rebellion hath procured. It looks like the later end of a feast. Here lieth an old ruined castle like the remainder of a venison pasty [i.e. pie], there a broken fort like a mince pie half subjected, and in another place an old abbey with some turrets standing like the carcass of a goose broken up. It makes me remember the old proverb — it is better to come to the end of a feast, than the beginning of a fray. But I have held you too long among this rubbish.

Let us converse with the people. Lord, what makes you so squeamish — be not afraid. The Irishman is no cannibal to eat you up nor no lousy Jack to offend you. The man of Ireland is of a strong constitution, tall and big limbed but seldom fat, patient of heat and cold, but impatient of labour. Of nature he is prompt and ingenious, but servile, crafty, and inquisitive after news, the symptoms of a conquered nation. Their speech hath been accused to be a whining language, but that is among the beggars. I take it to be a smooth language well commixed of vowels and of consonants, and hath a pleasing cadence.

The better sort are apparelled at all points like the English, only they retain their mantle, which is a garment not indecent. It differs nothing from a long cloak, but in the fringe at the upper end, which in cold weather they wear over their heads for warmth. Because they are commanded at public assemblies to come in English habit, they have a trick against those times, to take off the fringe, and to put on a cape, and after the assembly passed to resume it again. If you ask an Irishman for his cloak, he will tell you it is in his pocket and show you his cape. The churl is apparelled in this manner. His doublet is a pack saddle of canvas, or coarse cloth without skirts, but in winter he wears a frieze coat. The trowser is a long stock of frieze, close to his thighs, and drawn on almost to his waist, but very scant, and the pride of it is to wear it so in suspense that the beholder may still suspect it to be falling from his arse. It is cut with a pouch before [i.e. in front], which is drawn together with a string. He that will be counted a spruce lad ties it up with a twisted band of two colours like the string of a cloakbag. An Irishman [was] walking in London [and] a cutpurse took it for a cheate [i.e. thing to steal] and gave him a slash.

His brogues are single soled, more rudely sewn than a shoe but more strong, sharp at the toe, and a flap of leather left at the heel to pull them on. His hat is a frieze cap close to his head, with two lappets to button under his chin. And for his weapon he wears a skeyne, which is a knife, three fingers broad, of the length of a dagger, sharpening towards the point, with a rude wooden handle. He wears it point blank at his codpiece. The ordinary kerne seldom wears a sword. They are also wedded to their mantle. They plow, they ditch, they thresh with their mantles on. But you look after the wenches.

The women of Ireland are very comely creatures, tall, slender, and upright. Of complexion very fair and clear-skinned (but freckled), with tresses of bright yellow hair, which they chain up in curious knots and devices. They are not strait-laced nor plated [i.e. girdled] in their youth, but suffered to grow at liberty, so that you shall hardly see one crooked or deformed. But yet as the proverb is, soon ripe soon rotten. Their propensity to generation causeth that [which] they cannot endure. They are women at thirteen, and old wives at thirty. I never saw fairer wenches nor fouler callets [i.e. scolds], [as] we call the old women. Of nature they are very kind and tractable. At meetings they offer themselves to be kissed, with the hand extended to embrace you. The young wenches salute you, confer with you, drink with you without control. They are not so reserved as the English, yet very honest. Cuckoldry is a thing almost unknown among the Irish. At solemn invitations, the 'benytee', so we call the goodwife of the house, meets at the hall door with as many of her female kindred as are about her, all on a row; to leave any of them unkissed [would be] an indignity though it were done by the lord president.

I come to their apparel. About Dublin they wear the English habit, mantles only added thereunto, and they that go in silks will wear a mantle of country making. In the country even among their Irish habits they have sundry fashions. I will begin with the ornament of their heads. At Kilkenny they wear broad beaver hats, coloured, edged with a gold lace, and faced with velvet, with a broad gold hatband. At Waterford they wear caps, turned up with fur and laced with gold lace. At Limerick they wear rolls of linen, each roll containing twenty bandles of fine linen cloth (a bandle is half an ell) [i.e. an ell = 45 inches], and made up in the form of a mitre. To this if it be cold weather, there is added a muffler over their neck and chin of like quantity of linen; being so muffled, over all they will pin on an English mask of black taffeta, which is most rarely ridiculous to behold. In Connaught they wear rolls in [the cylindrical] form of cheese. In Thomond they wear kerchiefs hanging down to the middle of their back. The maids wear on the forepart of their head about four yards of coloured ribbon smoothly laid, and their own hair plaited behind. In other places they wear their hair loose and cast behind. They wear no bands, but the ornament of their necks is a carcanet [i.e. necklace] of goldsmith's work beset with precious stones, some of them very rich but most of them gaudy and made of painted glass, and at the end of them a crucifix. They wear also bracelets, and many rings.

I proceed to their gowns. Lend me your imagination and I will cut it out as well as the tailor. They have straight bodies, and long waists, but their bodies come no closer but to the middle of the rib. The rest is supplied with lacing, from the top of their breasts to the bottom of their placket. The ordinary sort have only their smocks between, but the better sort have a silk scarf about their neck, which they spread and pin over their breasts. On the forepart of those bodies they have a set of broad silver buttons of goldsmith's work set round about. A set of those buttons will be worth forty shillings, some are worth five pounds. They have hanging sleeves, very narrow, but no arming sleeves other than their smock sleeves or a waistcoat of striped stuff, only they have a wristband of the same cloth, and a list [i.e. strip] of the same to join it to their wing, but nothing on the hinder part of the arm lest they should wear out their elbows. The better sort have sleeves of satin. The skirt is a piece of rare artifice. At every breadth of three fingers they sew it quite through with a welt, so that it seemeth so many lists put together. That they do for strength. They gird their gown with a silk girdle, the tassel whereof must hang down point blank before to the fringe of their petticoats. But I will not descend to their petticoats, lest you should think that I have been under them. They begin to wear knit stockings coloured, but they have not distained to wear stocking of raw white frieze, and brogues. They wear their mantles also within doors as well as without. Their mantles are commonly of a brown-blue colour with fringe alike, but those that love to be gallant wear them of green, red, yellow, and other light colours, with fringes diversified. An ordinary mantle is worth four pounds. Those in the country which cannot go to the price wear white sheets mantlewise. I would not have you suppose that all the Irish are thus strangely attired as I have described. The old women are loath to be shifted out of their ancient habits, but the younger sort, especially in gentlemen's houses are brought up to resemble the English, so that it is to be hoped that the next age will wear out these disguises. Of their cleanliness I will not speak.

Let us not pass by their entertainment. I will not lead you to the baser cabins, where you shall have no drink but bonnaclabba, milk that is soured to the condition of buttermilk, nor meat but mullagham (mullabanne), a kind of choke-daw cheese, and blue butter and no bread at your first coming in. But if you stay half an hour you shall have a cake of meal unboulted [i.e. unsifted], and mingled with butter, baked on an iron called a griddle, like a pudding cake. But we will go to the gentleman that dwells in the castle. See the company yonder, they are riding to a coshering, let us strike in among them. (Cosherings are public invitations, by occasion of marriages, neighbourhood or the like, and for the present open house). Mark how they be mounted, some upon sidesaddles, and some upon pillions. The Irish saddle is called a pillion, and it is made on this form. The tree is as of an ordinary saddle, but the seat is a plain table of two foot long and a foot broad or larger, high mounted, and covered with a piece of checkered blanket. It is not tied with girths, but it is fastened with a breast plate before, a crupper behind, and a surcingle in the middle. The men ride upon it astride, with their legs very far extended, and towards the horse's neck. If the horse be dull, they spur him in the shoulder. It seemeth very uneasy to us, but they affirm it to be an easy kind of riding. If it be, it is very useful, for a man may ride astride, a woman may ride a side [i.e. sidesaddle], and a man may ride with a woman behind him, all upon the like saddle. It is an excellent fashion to steal a wench and to carry her away.

We are come to the castle already. The castles are built very strong, and with narrow stairs, for security. The hall is the uppermost room. Let us go up, you shall not come down again till tomorrow. Take no care of your horses, they shall be sessed [i.e. imposed] among the tenants. The lady of the house meets you with her train. I have instructed you before how to accost them. Salutations past, you shall be presented with all the drinks in the house, first the ordinary beer, then aquavitae, then sack, then old ale. The lady tastes it, you must not refuse. The fire is prepared in the middle of the hall, where you may solace yourself till supper time. You shall not want sack and tobacco. By this time the table is spread and plentifully furnished with [a] variety of meats, but ill cooked and without sauce. Neither shall there be wanting a pasty or two of red deer (that is more common with us than the fallow). The dish which I make choice of is the swelled mutton, and it is prepared thus. They take a principal wether [i.e. ram], and before they kill him it is fit that he be shorn. Being killed they singe him in his woolly skin like a bacon and roast him by joints with the skin on, and so serve it to the table. They say that it makes the flesh more firm and preserves the fat. I make choice of it to avoid uncleanly dressing.

They feast together with great jollity and healths around. Toward the middle of supper, the harper begins to tune and singeth Irish rhymes of ancient making. If he be a good rhymer, he will make one song to the present occasion. Supper being ended, it is at your liberty to sit up or to depart to your lodging. You shall have company in both kind. When you come to your chamber, do not expect canopy and curtains. It is very well if your bed content you, and if the company be great, you may happen to be bodkin in the middle [i.e. squeezed between two others]. In the morning there will be brought unto you a cup of aquavitae. The aquavitae or usquebagh of Ireland is not such an extraction as is made in England, but far more qualified and sweetened with licorice. It is made potable and is of the colour of Muscadine. It is a very wholesome drink and natural to digest the crudities of the Irish feeding. You may drink a noggin without offense, that is the fourth part of a pint. Breakfast is but the repetition of supper. When you are disposing of yourself to depart, they call for *deoch a' dorais*, that is, to drink at the door. There you are presented again with all the drinks in the house, as at your first entrance. Smack them over, and let us depart.

Wiliam Brereton

TRAVELS
In Holland, The United Provinces, England,
Scotland, and Ireland, 1634-1635

Though he was later to distinguish himself as a parliamentary commander in the English civil wars, William Brereton (1606-1661) came to Ireland as one of the first true English travellers in the country. His visit in 1635 was the finale of a 'Grand Tour' begun a year earlier and extended as far as Holland. In Ireland, as this diary suggests, Brereton was a fairly disinterested observer, with none of practical concern for the immediate gain evident in the reports of some of his predecessors. The names he mentions indicate some prestigious connections in Ireland even at this early stage of his career. But his battles with the dread Irish digestive diseases, his persistent frustration with canny Irish guides, and his paranoid obsession with being overcharged by innkeepers all give his written account characteristics of the travelogues of Ireland not common until the following century.

Among the effects of Brereton's rather leisurely circumstances are the leniency and even liberality of his comments on Irish Catholics and Irish rebels. In regard to Catholics, he expresses only mild surprise that they practice openly and that 'they are not ashamed of their religion'. The rebel presence he seems scarcely to fear — indeed, his anecdote of the three rebels and the mayor of Ross seems told at the expense of the latter. In addition, Brereton presents the Wexford assizes as an almost gay affair for all involved. Yet this is the man who, a decade later, would seize leadership of the Cheshire Puritan forces, rout the loyalists and Irish supporters at Nantwich, and go on to capture Liverpool. Even allowing for a decade of personal evolution and the exigencies of civil militia command, that is enough at variance with his comments here to suggest some of the effects of immediate political pressure on ordinary behavior and perception of the enemy. This selection is adapted from the first full publication of Brereton's *Travels*, in 1844 by the Chetham Society, as edited by Edward Hawkins. Place names, in particular, have been standardized and interpolations inserted in brackets.

Mount Ivers Castle, Co. Clare, by Thomas Dineley. Like many English travellers to Ireland in the 17th century, Dineley was antiquarian in taste and reformist in intention. He wrote *Observations in a Voyage Through the Kingdom of Ireland* in 1680, but the work was not published until nearly two centuries after his death in 1695. This formidable castle, near Limerick, was owned by the High Sheriff in Co. Clare.

A t my coming to Carrickfergus, and being troubled with an extreme flux, not as yet come to so great height as a bloody flux, my hostess, Mrs. Wharton, directed me the use of cinnamon in burnt claret wine, or rather red wine, and also the syrup and conserve of sloes well boiled, after they have been strained and mingled according to discretion with sugar; they are to be boiled with sugar until they be cleared, having been first boiled in water until they be softened, and then strained.

But a more effectual strong medicine, which is to be used with discretion and caution, lest it beget a contrary distemper: take three or four ounces of the bark of oak, the outside being scraped clean, and boil the same in spring water until half be consumed; then strain it through a fine cloth, then add to that quart another quart of red wine, and add thereunto one ounce of cinnamon punned [i.e. pounded in] to powder and half a pound of sugar. Boil all these together until half be consumed, then put this liquor into a stone-bottle, wherein it may be kept close so as to take no wind, nor lose not its strength, and take evening and morning about four or five spoonfuls; if you be in extremity, then it must be taken the oftener, two or three times a day.

I found by my own experience burnt aquavitae and papes-milk,* well sodden with wheat flour, three or four eggs, and cinnamon; these did me much good, but by reason of taking too liberally of burnt usquebaugh, here called aquavitae, which was but twice, and not above the half of a gill at either time, there was occasioned unto me, for two or three days after, great pain and torment in parting with my urine. To cure this I found new milk the best medicine I used. This flux, though it did not hold me above three days at first when I landed, yet it brought a great weakness and indisposition upon me, the rather the more by reason my body was sufficiently purged by vomit at sea, which wrought with me more effectually than it ever did formerly in my whole life. During my stay in this kingdom my body was always disposed and inclined to be laxative and soluble, so as always every night it caused me to rise once about three hour. But all these formerly prescribed medicines did but a little avail me when it seized upon me the second time, which was upon Friday last; and, as I conceived, it was occasioned by reason of drinking milk over-liberally at Ermerscorffie and at Mr. Hardye's at Parke; I purged exceedingly at Sir Adam Cocliffe's, more than two parts of a close stoolful of thin watery stuff, which came from me like a stream gushing; this continued with me two or three days, and although I used all the medicines I could learn, as claret wine well burnt with cinnamon, milk well boiled with rice, cinnamon and eggs, yet all these did nothing help to stay it; I did forbear all drink save claret wine, and was as curious in my diet as was possible.

These things by experience I found hurtful: fruit, gross or raw meat,

*'By this is probably meant white juice of poppies, whose narcotic qualities might be beneficial'. [Hawkins' note].

milk, drink, especially Irish, cold, any violent exercise or motion; riding moderately is good, but when the body is weakened, I found nothing more hurtful unto me than going on foot from the ferry to Waterford, which did me much hurt, and weakened me exceedingly; wineberries made me subject to fainting also, and are churlish things for the stomach.

The best things I found were these: usquebaugh with the yolk of an egg first and last, fast two hours after it; cinnamon water is also good and diacinamomum [i.e. medicinal cinnamon]; but I found cinnamon water did so distemper me in parting with my water as put me to much pain and torment. The best thing to drink is French barley boiled in spring water; to every pottle [i.e. two quarts] of water there being put one ounce of the powder of cinnamon, this an excellent drink; hereof you may drink sufficient, as much as you please; you may add some sugar to relish it, and the juice of almonds bruised. Sr. Marmaduke Lloyde prescribed barley boiled in a bag as hot as may be to be placed in your close stool or under you when you go to stool, the fume hereof hath an excellent virtue; this was old Dr. [William] Butler's direction to him, and to ride as far and as fast as he possibly could endure for a whole day. Sr. Urian Leigh affirmed the fume of sage burnt upon a chafing-dish of coals often renewed placed in the close stool to have cured many.

Jul. 7. – We left Dromore and went to the Newry, which is sixteen miles. This is a most difficult way for a stranger to find out. Herein we wandered, and being lost, fell amongst the Irish towns. The Irish houses are the poorest cabins I have seen, erected in the middle of the fields and grounds, which they farm and rent. This is a wild country, not inhabited, planted, nor enclosed, yet it would be good corn if it were husbanded. I gave an Irishman to bring us into the way a groat, who led us like a villain directly out of the way and so left us, so as by this deviation it was three hour before we came to the Newry. Much land there is about this town belonging to Mr. [Arthur] Bagnall, nothing well planted. He hath a castle in this town, but is for most part resident at Green Castle; a great part of this town is his, and it is reported that he hath a £1,000 or £1,500 per annum in this country. This is but a poor town, and is much Irish, and is navigable for boats to come up unto with the tide. Here we waited at a good inn, the sign of the Prince's Arms. Hence to Dundalk is eight mile; stony, craggy, hilly, and uneven, but a way it is nothing difficult to find. Before you come to Dundalk you may discern four or five towers or castles seated upon the sea side.

This town of Dundalk hath been a town of strength, and is still a walled town, and a company of fifty soldiers are here in garrison under the command of Sir Faithfull Fortescue. This town is governed by two bailiffs, sheriffs, and aldermen; the greatest part of the inhabitants of the town are popishly affected, and although my Lord Deputy, at the last election of burgesses for the Parliament, commended unto them Sir Faithfull Fortescue and Sir Arthur Teringham, yet they rejected both, and elected a couple of recusants. One of the present bailiffs is popish. Abundance of Irish, both gentlemen and others, dwell in this town, wherein they dare to take the boldness to go to mass openly. This town [is] seated upon the sea so as barks may come within a convenient distance with the flood; much low, level, flat land hereabouts, which is often overflowed in the winter, and here is abundance of fowl, and a convenient seat. Here we lodged at one Mrs. Veasie's house, a most mighty fat woman; she saith she is a Cheshire woman, near related in blood to the Breretons; desired much to see me; so fat she is, as she is so unwieldy, she can scarce stand or go without crutches. This reported one of the best inns in north of Ireland; ordinary 8*d.* and 6*d.*, only the knave tapster over-reckoned us in drink.

* * *

Jul. 18. – This day I went to the court (the assizes being now here held for this county of Wexford, which began on Wednesday last, and ended this day) where is their shire hall. The judges that ride this circuit are Sir George Shirley, Lord Chief-Justice of Ireland, and Sir John Philpot, one of the Judges in the Common Pleas, a little, black, temperate man. The one, viz. my Lord Chief-Justice, sits upon *nisi prius*, the other upon matters of misdemeanours and trials for life and death. Here I saw four justices of peace sit upon the bench with Sir John Philpot, amongst which was one Nicholaus Devereux and my cousin Mainwaring, uncle to Mr. Mainwaring of Caringham that now is, a courteous, grave, civil gentleman, who came from the bench, and saluted me in the hall, and accompanied me to the tavern, and bestowed wine upon me. He is agent unto Sir Henry Wallopp, and is a justice of peace of this county, and was a burgess for the parliament. He told me there were three rebels condemned, as also he advised me rather to go by Ballyhack and by the way of the Passage than by Ross, because of the rebels which frequent thereabouts; hereof, he said there were about six or eight, and these furnished with some pieces, pistols, darts, and skenes [i.e. daggers], and some of them most desperate spirits, and so cruel, that the inhabitants of the country dare scarce travel that way; these are proclaimed rebels, and such as are to be hanged, drawn and quartered, so soon as they are apprehended. So also are those to be dealt withal, who are now to be executed. One of them I saw in the streets returning towards the castle, and the women and some other following making lamentation, sometimes so violent as though they were distracted, sometimes as it were in a kind of tune singing; one of these ('twas said) was his wife. This is the Irish garb [i.e. custom]. This town is governed by a mayor and two bailiffs or sheriffs, and ten or twelve aldermen.

Beyond the bar also, it hath a very safe harbour and shelter for ships to ride at anchor in, who want tide to bring them into the haven. Sir Adam

Colclough told me that he had dined at Milford in Wales and supped in this town, which is about twenty-four hours' sail from Bristol, and as much to Dublin. By reason of the assizes here, the inhabitants of the country resorted hither in greater numbers and better habits (Irish garments I mean) than I have yet seen. Some gentlewomen of good quality here I observed clothed in good handsome gowns, petticoats and hats, who wore Irish rugs, which have handsome, comely, large fringes, which go about their necks, and serve instead of bands. This ruggy fringe is joined to a garment which comes round about them, and reacheth to the very ground, and this is an handsome, comely vestment, much more comely as they are used than the rug short cloaks used by the women upon festival days in Abbeyville, Bullein, and the nearer parts of Picardy in France. The most of the women are bare-necked, and clean-skinned, and wear a crucifix, tied in a black necklace, hanging betwixt their breasts. It seems they are not ashamed of their religion, nor desire to conceal themselves; and indeed in this town are many papists.

Jul. 19. – The present mayor, Mr. Mark Cheveu, attended the judges to the church door, and so did the sheriff of the shire, both which left them there, and went to mass, which is here tolerated, and publicly resorted unto in two or three houses in this town, wherein are very few Protestants, as appeared by that slender congregation at church where the judges were. This morning I went unto and visited both the judges, and was respectively used by them; the mayor, a well-bred gentleman, an inns-of-court man, who is a counsellor, a gentleman that hath an estate in the country, and was knight of this shire for last parliament, invited me to dinner, as also to supper, with the judges. He is an Irishman, and his wife Irish, in a strange habit, a threadbare short coat with sleeves, made like my green coat of stuff, reaching to her middle; she knew not how to carve, look, entertain, or demean herself. Here was a kind of beer (which I durst not taste) called Charter beer, mighty thick, muddy stuff, the meat nothing well cooked nor ordered. Much discourse here, complaint and information given against the rebels, the captain whereof is called Simon Prendergrass, whose brother also will be brought in trouble for relieving, &c. Three carriers were robbed betwixt Ross and this town on Friday last, and two other travellers, and one in his lodging, by three of these rebels well appointed, who said if they could have taken my Lord of Kildare, who passed through them nakedly attended, he should have procured their pardon. There was a letter sent and read this night at supper, advertising a gentleman in town that last night they came to his house with a purpose to take away his life, because he prosecuted against them, and informed that they had taken from him to the value of £200. The judge here said, if all the justices of peace did not wait upon them to Ross to guard them from the rebels, he would fine them deeply. The junior judge told me of a very wise demeanour of the now mayor Ross, who being informed that three of these rebels lay asleep near the town, and being required to send out some ten or twelve with him to apprehend them, he answered that he would provide for the safety of his town, commanded the gates to be shut, the drum to be beat, and pieces, warning-pieces, to be discharged, whereby they awaked, and took notice thereof and escaped.

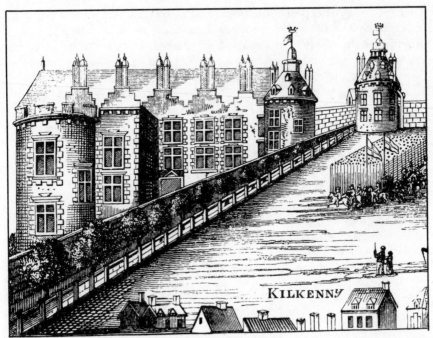

Thomas Dineley's illustration of Kilkenny in 1680. Its odd perspective joins suggestions of impressive architecture, peaceful town life, and organised leisure, all distinctly positive in comparison with Elizabethan images of Irish life.

Limerick, also by Thomas Dineley, for his *Observations*. Such images of a peaceful Ireland helped fuel indignation at the idea of a Catholic rebellion under James II. Dineley's illustration bears comparison with the account of Limerick written by Luke Gernon (pages 104-105).

William Petty

THE POLITICAL ANATOMY OF
IRELAND 1672

William Petty (1623-1687), son of a clothier, became one of the celebrated political economists in the early evolution of the science. However, his interests and accomplishments were far broader than that principal preoccupation might suggest. He was a seaman deserted by his crew in France, a student of medicine at Leyden, an industrialist, a founding member of the Royal Society, and a widely admired composer of Latin verse. Terribly nearsighted, he had the wit on being challenged to a duel to name as the place a dark cellar and as the weapons axes. Devoted to mechanical inventions, he labored for years on a kind of Irish Channel catamaran, each prototype of which proved less successful than its predecessor. The great diarists of the 17th century, Samuel Pepys and John Evelyn, both prized Petty's coffeehouse company and wrote laudatory portraits of him.

Petty became physician general of the British troops in Ireland in 1652. That was the year of the Cromwellian Act of Settlement, which involved repaying soldiers and creditors of the Commonwealth with confiscated lands amounting to all of Ireland but Connaught. To this end, though apparently with only practical mechanical problems in mind, Petty completed the first scientific map survey, called The Down Survey because it set topographical measurements of land 'down' on a map rather than in a table. He then busied himself with a survey of all of Ireland that was not completed until 1673, when the project initiated by Cromwell was presented to Charles II.

At the end of the great map project, Petty completed his *Political Anatomy of Ireland 1672*; it circulated in manuscript but was not published until 1691. In it he writes as a proto-economist and statistician, and with a scientific disinterest that thoroughly obscures his own interest as owner of extensive and valuable Limerick lands awarded him for The Down Survey. Throughout, and especially in the opening passage presented here, he accounts for Ireland on the quantitative grounds he formalized in *Political Arithmetic*, a landmark work not published until 1690. In this view of the country the poor are 'impotents' and the rich are 'optimates'. Rebels, because they harm the gross national product, are thieves. Since trade and commerce are the supreme goals, Petty can dismiss as 'frivolous' early intimations of the eventually catastrophic economic drain on Ireland of absentee landlords. In fact, trade is such an unexamined ideal for Petty that he seems unaware of his own description's suggestion of the sturdy self-sufficiency of the Irish. These selections, chapters XI and XII of *The Political Anatomy* are edited versions of the texts printed in *A Collection of Tracts and Treatises* (Dublin, 1861).

OF THE TRADE OF IRELAND.

I f it be true, that there are but about 16,000 families in Ireland, who have above one chimney in their houses; and above 160,000 others; it will be easily understood what the trade of this latter sort can be, who use few commodities; and those such as almost every one can make and produce. That is to say, men live in such cottages as themselves can make in 3 or 4 days; eat such food (tobacco excepted) as they buy not from others; wear such clothes as the wool of their own sheep, spun into yarn by themselves, doth make; their shoes, called brogues, are but a quarter so much worth as a pair of English shoes; nor of more than a quarter in real use and value. A hat costs 20d.; a pair of stockings 6d.; but a good shirt near 3s. The tailor's work of a doublet, breeches and coat about 2s. 6d. In brief, the victuals of a man, his wife, three children, and servant, resolved into money, may be estimated 3s. 6d. per week, or 1d. *per diem*. The clothes of a man 30s. *per ann.*; of children under 16, one with another, 15s.; the house not worth 5s. the building; fuel costs nothing but fetching. So as the whole annual expense of such a family, consisting of 6 in number, seems to be but about 52s. *per ann.*, each head one with another. So as 950,000 inhabitants of these edifices, may spend 2,375,000*l. per ann.* And the 150,000 who inhabit the 16,000 other houses, may spend 10*l. per ann.* each one with another, viz., one million and half. So as the whole people of both sorts spend under 4 million, whereof the 10th part, viz., 400,000 *l.* is for foreign commodities, tobacco included, whereof every 1,000 souls spends one tun [i.e. 100,000 florins] *per ann.*, or every 1,000 tobacco-takers, viz., people above 15 years old, spend two tuns one with another: for it appears by the latest account of importance, that what is here said, is true to a trifle. From whence I observe by the way, that the King's revenue, *viis et modis*, being about 200,000*l. per ann.*, that it is the 20th part of the whole expense; which in some of the Grecian common-wealths was thought too much, although the Israelites allowed the tenth to the Levites only, though perhaps to defray the whole charge of the Government, the supremacy amongst that people being then sacerdotal.

I observe also by the way, that the lands and housing of Ireland being worth about one million *per ann.*, which is earned by about 750,000 (of the 1,100,000) who by their age and quality are fit and applicable to corporal labours, and consequently each labouring person earns but 4s. *per ann.* if all work. Or if each earns 8*l.* then but half of them work, or all but half their full time, or otherwise in other proportions. But be it one way or the other; I am as certain that the hands of Ireland may earn a million *per ann.* more than they now do, as I am certain that there are 750,000 in Ireland who could earn 2s. a week or 5*l. per ann.* one with another, if they had suitable employment, and were kept to their labour.

I further observe, that if there be naturally but 2,000 impotents in

Ireland, and that 50 shillings *per ann.* doth maintain the poorer sort of people; it follows, that 8,000*l. per ann.* would amply maintain all the impotents of Ireland, if well applied. For other beggars, as also thieves, and rebels, which are but bigger thieves, are probably but the faults and defects of government and discipline.

As for the fitness of Ireland for trade, we say as followeth.

First. That Ireland consisting of above 18,000 square miles, it is not one place with another above 24 miles from the sea, because it is 750 miles about:* wherefore forasmuch as the land-carriage of gross that will be easy in such a country, it is fit for trade, because the greatest and most profitable part of trade, and the employment of shipping, depends upon such goods, viz. metals, stones, timber, grain, wood, salt, etc.

Second, Ireland lieth commodiously for the trade of the new American world; which we see every day to grow and flourish.

It lieth well for sending butter, cheese, beef, fish, to their proper markets, which are to the southward, and the plantations of America.

Thus is Ireland by nature fit for trade, but otherwise very much unprepared for the same; for as hath been often said, the housing thereof consists of 160,000 nasty cabins, in which neither butter nor cheese, nor linen, yarn nor worsted; and I think no other, can be made to the best advantage; chiefly by reason of the soot and smoke annoying the same; as also for the narrowness and nastiness of the place; which cannot be kept clean nor safe from beasts and vermin, nor from damps and musty stenches, of which all the eggs laid or kept in those cabins do partake. Wherefore to the advancement of trade, the reformation of these cabins is necessary.

It may also be considered, whether the institution of these following corporations would not be expedient, viz. 1. of cattle, 2. of corn, 3. of fish, 4. of leather, 5. of wool, 6. of linen, 7. of butter and cheese, 8. of metals and minerals: for unto these, almost all the commodities exportable out of Ireland, may be referred.

It may also be considered, whether the taxing of those cabins with hearth-money be proper, but rather with days labour; the former being scarce possible for them to have, but the latter most easy. Insomuch as 'tis more easy for them to give 40 days labour *per ann.* at seasonable times, than to pay 2s. in silver at a pinch, and just when the collectors call for it.

The diet, housing and clothing of the 16,000 families above-mentioned, is much the same as in England: nor is the French elegance unknown in many of them, nor the French and Latin tongues. The latter whereof is very frequent among the poorest Irish, and chiefly in Kerry, most remote from Dublin.

The housing of 160,000 families, is, as hath been often said, very wretched. But their clothing is far better than that of the French peasants,

---

*All extreme underestimates, of course.

or the poor of most other countries; which advantage they have from their wool, whereof 12 sleep furnisheth a competency to one of these families. Which wool, and the cloth made of it, doth cost these poor people no less than 50,000*l. per ann.* for the dying it; a trade exercised by the women of the country. Madder, allum, and indigo, are imported, but the other dying stuffs they find nearer home, a certain mud taken out of the bogs serving them for copperas, the rind of several trees, and saw-dust, for galls; as for wild and green weeds, they find enough, as also of Rhannus-berries.

The diet of these people is milk, sweet and sour, thick and thin, which also is their drink in summer-time, in winter small-beer or water. But tobacco taken in short pipes seldom burnt, seems the pleasure of their lives, together with sneezing: insomuch, that two-sevenths of their expense in food is tobacco. Their food is bread in cakes, whereof a penny serves a week for each; potatoes from August till May, muscles, cockles and oysters, near the sea; eggs and butter made very rancid, by keeping in bogs. As for flesh, they seldom eat it, notwithstanding the great plenty thereof, unless it be of the smaller animals, because it is inconvenient for one of those families to kill a beef, which they have no convenience to save. So as 'tis easier for them to have a hen or rabbit than a piece of beef of equal substance.

Their fuel is turf in most places; and of late, even where wood is most plentiful, and to be had for nothing, the cutting and carriage of the turf being more easy than that of wood. But to return from whence I digressed; I may say, that the trade of Ireland, among 19 in 22 parts of the whole people, is little or nothing, excepting for the tbacco above-mentioned, estimated worth about 50,000*l.* forasmuch as they do not need any foreign commodities, nor scarce any thing made out of their own village. Nor is above one-fifth part of their expense other than what their own family produceth, which condition and state of living cannot beget trade.

And now I shall digress again to consider, whether it were better for the Commonwealth to restrain the expense of 150,000 optimates [i.e. nobles] below 10*l. per ann.* each; or to beget a luxury in the 950,000 plebians, so as to make them spend, and consequently earn double to what they at present do.

To which I answer in brief, that the one shall increase the sordidness and squalor of living already too visible in 950,000 plebians, with little benefit to the Commonwealth; the other shall increase the splendor, art, and industry of the 950,000 to the great enrichment of the Commonwealth.

Again, why should we forbid the use of any foreign commodity, which our own hands and country cannot produce, when we can employ our spare hands and lands upon such exportable commodities as will purchase the same, and more.

Third. The keeping or lessening of money, is not of that consequence that many guess it to be of. For in most places, especially Ireland, nay, England itself, the money of the whole nation is but about a 10th part of the expense of one year; viz. Ireland is thought to have about 400,000*l.* in cash, and to spend about 4 millions *per ann.* Wherefore it is very ill husbandry to double the cash of the nation, by destroying half its wealth; or to increase the cash otherwise than by increasing the wealth *simul et semel.*

That is, when the nation hath one-tenth more cash, I require it should have one-tenth more wealth, if it be possible. For there may be as well too much money in a country, as too little. I mean, as to the best advantage of its trade; only the remedy is very easy, it may be soon turned into the magnificence of gold and silver vessels.

Lastly, many think that Ireland is much impoverished, or at least the money thereof much exhausted, by reason of absentees, who are such as having lands in Ireland, do live out of the kingdom, and do therefore think it just that such, according to former Statutes, should lose their said estates.

Which opinion I oppose, as both unjust, inconvenient, and frivolous. For first, if a man carry money or other effects out of England to purchase lands in Ireland, why should not the rents, issues and profits of the same land return into England, with the same reason that the money of England was diminished to buy it?

I suppose one quarter of the land of Ireland did belong to the inhabitants of England, and that the same lay all in one place together; why may not the said quarter of the whole land be cut off from the other three sent into England, were it possible so to do? And if so, why may not the rents of the same be actually sent, without prejudice to the other three parts of the interessors thereof?

If all men were bound to spend the proceed of their lands upon the land itself; then as all the proceed of Ireland ought to be spent in Ireland; so all the proceed of one county of Ireland ought to be spent in the same; as of one barony, in the same barony; and so parish and manor; and at length it would follow, that every eater ought to avoid what he hath eaten upon the same turf where the same grew. Moreover, this equal spreading of wealth would destroy all splendor and ornament; for if it were not fit that one place should be more splendid than another, so also that no one man should be greater or richer than another; for if so, then the wealth, suppose of Ireland, being perhaps 11 millions, being divided among 1,100,000 people, then no one man having above 10*l.* he could probably build no house worth above 3*l.* which would be to leave the face of beggary upon the whole nation: and withal such parity would beget anarchy and confusion.

Of the Religion, Diet, Cloths, Language, Manners and Interest
of the several present Inhabitants of IRELAND.

We said, that of the 1,100,000 inhabitants of Ireland, about 800,000 of them were Irish; and that above 600,000 of them lived very simply in the cabins afore-mentioned. Wherefore I shall in the first place describe the religion, diet, etc. of these, being the major part of the whole; not wholly omitting some of the other species also.

The religion of these poorer Irish is called Roman Catholic, whose head is the Pope of Rome, from whence they a are properly enough called Papists. This religion is well known in the world, both by the books of their divines, and the worship in their churches: wherefore I confine myself to what I think peculiar to these Irish. And first, I observe, that the priests among them are of small learning, but are thought by their flocks to have much, because they can speak Latin more or less, and can often out-talk in Latin those who dispute with them. So as they are thereby thought both more orthodox and able than their antagonists.

Their reading in Latin is the lives of the saints, and fabulous stories of their country. But the superior learning among them, is the philosophy of the schools, and the genealogies of their ancestors. Both which look like what St. Paul hath condemned.

The priests are chosen for the most part out of old Irish gentry, and thereby influence the people, as well by their interest as their office.

Their preaching seems rather bugbearing of their flocks with dreadful stories, than persuading them by reason, or the scriptures. They have an incredible opinion of the Pope and his sanctity, of the happiness of those who can obtain his blessing at the third or fourth hand. Only some few, who have lately been abroad, have gotten so far, as to talk of a difference between the interest of the Court of Rome, and the doctrine of the Church. The common priests have few of them been out of Ireland; and those who have, were bred in convents, or made friars for the most part, and have humble opinions of the English and Protestants, and of the mischiefs of setting up manufactures, and introducing of trade. They also comfort their flocks, partly by prophecies of their restoration to their ancient estates and liberties, which the abler sort of them fetch from what the Prophets of the Old Testament have delivered by way of God's promise to restore the Jews, and the kingdom to Israel. They make little esteem of an oath upon a Protestant Bible, but will more devoutly take up a stone, and swear upon it, calling it a book, than by the said book of books, the Bible. But of all oaths, they think themselves at much liberty to take a land-oath, as they call it: which is an oath to prove a forged deed, a possession, livery of seisin [i.e. legal token of possession], payment of rents, etc., in order to recover for their countrymen the lands which they had forfeited. They have a great opinion of holy-wells, rocks, and caves, which have been the reputed cells and receptacles of men reputed saints. They do not much fear death, if it be upon a tree, unto which, or the gallows, they will go upon their knees towards it, from the place they can first see it. They confess nothing at their executions, though never so guilty. In brief, there is much superstition among them, but formerly much more than is now; forasmuch as by the conversation of Protestants, they become ashamed of their ridiculous practices, which are not *de fide*. As for the richer and better educated sort of them, they are such Catholics as are in other places. The poor, in adhering to their religion, which is rather a custom than a dogma among them seem rather to obey their grandees, old landlords, and the heads of their septs and clans, than God. For when these were under clouds, transported into Spain and transplanted into Connaught, and disabled to serve them as formerly, about the year 1656*, when the adventurers and soldiers appeared to be their landlords and patrons, they were observed to have been forward enough to relax the stiffness of their pertinacity to the Pope, and his impositions. Lastly, among the better sort of them, many think less of the Pope's power in temporals, as they call it, than formerly; and begin to say, that the supremacy, even in spirituals, lies rather in the Church diffusive, and in qualified General Councils, than in the Pope alone, or than in the Pope and his Cardinals, or other *juncto*.

The religion of the Protestants in Ireland, is the same with the Church of England in doctrine, only they differ in discipline thus, viz.

The legal Protestants hold the power of the Church to be in the King, and that Bishops and Archbishops, with their clerks, are the best way of adjusting that power under him. The Presbyterians would have the same thing done, and perhaps more, by classes of Presbyters national and provincial. The Independents would have all Christian congregations independent from each other. The Anabaptists are independent in discipline, and differ from all those afore-mentioned in the baptism of infants, and in the inward and spiritual signification of that ordinance. The Quakers salute not by uncovering the head, speak to one another in the second person, and singular number; as for magistracy and arms, they seem to hold with the Anabaptists of Germany and Holland; they pretend to a possibility of perfection, like the Papists; as for other tenets, 'tis hard to fix them, or to understand what things they mean by their words.

The diet of the poorer Irish, is what was before discoursed in another chapter.

The clothing is a narrow sort of frieze, of about twenty inches broad, whereof two foot, called a bandle, is worth from 8½d. to 18d. Of this, seventeen bandles makes a man's suit, and twelve make a cloak. According to which measures and proportions, and the number of people who wear this stuff, it seems, that near thrice as much wool is spent in Ireland as exported; whereas others have thought quite contrary, that is, that the exported wool is triple in quantity to what is spent at home.

As for the manners of the Irish, I deduce them from their original constitions of body, and from the air; next from their ordinary food; next from their condition of estate and liberty, and from the influence of their gover-

---

*Time of the Cromwellian land confiscations.

nors and teachers, and lastly, from their ancient customs, which affect as well their consciences as their nature. For their shape, stature, colour, and complexion, I see nothing in them inferior to any other people, nor any enormous predominancy of any humour.

Their lazing seems to me to proceed rather from want of employment and encouragement to work, than from the natural abundance of phlegm in their bowels and blood. For what need they to work, who can content themselves with potatoes, whereof the labour of one man can feed forty; and with milk, whereof one cow will, in summer time, give meat and drink enough for three men, when they can everywhere gather cockles, oysters, mussels, crabs, etc. with boats, nets, angles, or the art of fishing; and can build an house in three days? And why should they desire to fare better, though with more labour, when they are taught, that this way of living is more like the patriarchs of old, and the saints of later times, by whose prayers and merits they are to be relieved, and whose examples they are therefore to follow? And why should they breed more cattle, since 'tis penal to import them into England? Why should they raise more commodities, since there are not merchants sufficiently stocked to take them of them, nor provided with other more pleasing foreign commodities, to give in exchange for them? And how should merchants have stock, since trade is prohibited and fettered by the statutes of England? And why should men endeavour to get estates, where the legislative power is not agreed upon; and where tricks and words destroy natural right and property?

They are accused also of much treachery, falseness, and thievery; none of all which, I conceive, is natural to them; for as to treachery, they are made believe, that they all shall flourish again, after some time; wherefore they will not really submit to those whom they hope to have their servants; nor will they declare so much, but say the contrary, for their present ease, which is all the treachery I have observed; for they have in their hearts, not only a grudging to see their old properties enjoyed by foreigners, but a persuasion they shall be shortly restored. As for thievery, it is affixed to all thin-peopled countries, such as Ireland is, where there cannot be many eyes to prevent such crimes; and where what is stolen, is easily hidden and eaten, and where 'tis easy to burn the house, or violate the persons of those who prosecute these crimes, and where thin-peopled countries are governed by the laws that were made and first fitted to thick-peopled countries; and where matter of small moment and value must be tried with all the formalities which belong to the highest causes. In this case there must be thieving, where is withal neither encouragement, nor method, nor means for labouring, nor provision for impotents.

As for the interest of these poorer Irish, it is manifestly to be transmuted into English, so to reform and qualify their housing, as that English women may be content to be their wives; to decline their language, which continues a sensible distinction, being not now necessary, which makes those who do not understand it, suspect, that what is spoken in it is to their prejudice. It is their interest to deal with the English, for leases, for time, and upon clear conditions, which being performed they are absolute freemen, rather than to stand always liable to the humour and caprice of their landlords, and to have every thing taken from them, which he pleases to fancy. It is their interest, that he is well pleased with their obedience to them, when they see and know upon whose care and conduct their well-being depends, who have power over their lands and estates. Then, to believe a man at Rome has power in all these last-mentioned particulars in this world, and can make them eternally happy or miserable hereafter, 'tis their interest to join with them, and follow their example, who have brought arts, civility, and freedom into their country.

On the contrary, what did they ever get by accompanying their lords into rebellion against the English? What should they have gotten if the late rebellion* had absolutely succeeded, but a more absolute servitude? And when it failed, these poor people have lost all their estates, and their leaders increased theirs, and enjoyed the very land which their leaders caused them to lose. The poorest now in Ireland ride on horseback, when heretofore the best ran on foot like animals. They wear better clothes than ever; the gentry have better breeding, and the generality of the plebeians more money and freedom.

---

*The series of risings begun with the Ulster rebellion of 1641 and crushed by the Cromwellian campaigns of 1649-1650.

John Stevens

A JOURNAL OF MY TRAVELS IN IRELAND SINCE THE REVOLUTION,
Containing a Brief Account of the War in Ireland

After the events related in this journal, John Stevens (d. 1726) affected the title Captain, but he was no soldier before or after the Williamite war in Ireland. Little is known of his earlier life, though the journal indicates that he had been in Ireland before. His father had been in service to the Queen Dowager, Catherine of Braganza. Evidence suggests that Stevens travelled in Spain and Portugal in his youth. He was a collector of excise at Welshpool in Wales in 1688, when Parliament invited William of Orange to assume the throne. Catholic and Jocobite in sympathy, Stevens followed James II to France, where the Jacobite forces assembled and organized French support for a campaign to reclaim the monarchy through Ireland.

These selections from the journal follow Stevens from his landing at Bantry on May 2, 1689, and then, after the defeat of the Jacobites at the Boyne on July 1, 1690, toward Limerick. Limerick survived an initial seige, but after the disasterous Battle of Aughrim it fell to a second seige on October 3, 1691. James's supporters, Stevens among them, were given the choice of the oath of allegiance or exile to the continent. Most, including Stevens, chose the continent. Since the bulk of the defenders of Limerick were Irish, the effect of the mass exile was to deprive Ireland of its old loyalist gentry and such protection as it afforded the native Gaelic culture and population of the country.

John Stevens spent the rest of his life as a prolific though undistinguished translator of Spanish and Portugese histories. The journal selections reprinted here display some power of expression but, like the translations, are characteristically diligent and evenhanded. Although his Stuart bias is apparent, and must be considered in weighing his praise of the Irish soldiery, Stevens is capable of describing in a very straightforward manner aspects of Irish life treated by other English writers with condescension, revulsion, or even hilarity. In his very credible view of poverty as the cause of rebellion, for example, he differs from more self-satisfied English commentators who explained Irish poverty as a simple and direct effect of rebellion. Of course, Stevens' is yet another perspective on Ireland and in no way definitive in itself. But it suggests the possibility of images of the Irish alternative to those that predominate in this collection. That, in turn, serves as a reminder of the arbitrariness and fallibility probable in any colonist account of the colonized. These selections are adapted from the original publication of *A Journal of My Travels Since the Revolution*, edited by Robert H. Murray (Oxford: Clarendon Press, 1912). The journal entries begin on January 16, 1689 and end on July 1, 1691. As the shifting tenses and anticipations of future events indicate, the journal is not the day-to-day diary its form suggests but was written in large part in retrospect. Hence no attempt has been made to unsnarl the confusing chronology of the entry dates.

T hursday the 2nd: we landed at Bantry, which is a miserable poor
place, not worthy the name of a town, having not above seven or
eight little houses, the rest very mean cottages. The least part of
us could not be contained in this place, so most were sent two or three miles
round to no better cottages to quarter. Two nights that we continued here
I walked two miles out of town to lie upon a little dirty straw in a cot or
cabin, no better than a hog-sty among near twenty others. The houses and
cabins in town were so filled that people lay all over the floors. Some gentlemen I knew who took up their lodging in an old rotten boat that lay near
the shore, and there wanted not some who quartered in a sawpit. Meat the
country brought in enough, but some had not money to buy, and those who
had for want of change had much difficulty to get what they wanted, the
people being so extreme poor that they could not give change out of half a
crown or a crown, and guineas were carried about the whole day and
returned whole. Drink there was none, but just at our landing a very little
wort hot from the fire, which nevertheless was soon drunk; and good water
was so scarce that I have gone half a mile to drink at a spring. About half
a mile from this is the old town of Bantry, much like the new. Upon a hill
over the town and creek is a fort built by Cromwell, now gone to decay but
never of any considerable strength.

Friday the 3rd: we continued in this miserable place. Both days were
spent in landing the arms and ammunition that came with us. The Earl of
Clancarty's Regiment came to town, and during our stay had no better
quarters than the open fields without tents.

Saturday the 4th: Much of the morning was spent in looking for horses;
at last with much difficulty Mr. Lazenby, afterwards a captain in Colonel
Butler of Kilcash's Regiment, bought a little nag, on which we laid his,
Captain afterwards Major Price's, and my clothes in two portmanteaus,
and having loaded our horse marched afoot driving him before us twelve
miles to Dunmanway, a place consisting of only one gentleman's house
and some scattering cabins. The road is all mountains very high, steep and
rough, with few or scarce any houses near the way. Having sent before to
take quarters we prevailed for money to get a good barn, where we made
fire and had clean straw to lie on, conveniences that very many met not
withal who were forced to stay all night in the open fields.

Sunday the 5th: marched six miles to Enniskeen, the first three like the
day before, the other much plainer. This is a tolerable town, and appeared
much the better to us after coming from the miserable places before
mentioned. Here we only refreshed ourselves, and went on six miles farther
to Bandon, a considerable walled town, where we found good entertainment, though at this time it was ill-inhabited many of the richest being fled,
after the king had most graciously pardoned their unnatural rebellion in
presuming to take up arms and shut out His Majesty's forces upon framed
fears and pretences.

Monday the 6th: marched twelve miles to Cork; in all this way there is not so much as a village unless such as consist of ten or twelve poor cots or cabins, inhabited by the miserable country people, who live only upon their potatoes and sour milk. The road is all rough mountain rocky way. Having marched these three days afoot I had great difficulty to reach Cork, both by reason of my weariness, as also the soreness of my feet, which kept me in excessive pain and anguish. I gave God thanks that I reached the town, where providence ordained we were stopped two days, by order to wit.

*   *   *

Saturday the 5th: on our march we passed by Clonamicklon, a house of the Lord Ikerrin about a mile from Kilcooly, and rested five miles farther at Killenaule, a small poor village on the mountain, whence we travelled to Cashel which is six miles. It is an archbishopric and the metropolitan see of Munster, and one of the ancientest in the kingdom. The cathedral seems not so beautiful as ancient and stands like a castle on the top of a rocky hill out of town, I thought it not worth time to go up to see it, being satisfied with the outward appearance. All manner of refreshment was hard to be had here but necessity overcame all difficulties. Hence we travelled five miles to a gentleman's house upon the road, where was plenty of all provisions. Some few of our stray officers, being got in before, endeavoured to make good the house against us, the confusion of the time which ought the more to have endeared us to each other, being fellow sufferers in the same cause, making some men rather inhuman and barbarous to those they should relieve and support. Insomuch that one who was within the house would not admit his own brother who came with me to the gate, and where such near ties of blood could not prevail, it is not to be thought our being fellow officers in the same regiment could have any influence. Fair means being of no effect, necessity obliged us to use violence, and with much difficulty we forced our way into the house, where was such plenty as might have contented the entire regiment, much more about a dozen that we were in all, and yet those first few possessors thought all too little for themselves.

Sunday the 6th: we travelled four miles to Cullen, a small town, where we heard mass, the church being then in the possession of the Catholics. Hence is seven miles to Cahirconlish, a small village, where was assembled a great number of the country people armed with roperies to receive the Duke of Tirconnell, thence a mile to Carrick, and from this four miles to Limerick. In the suburbs we met some of our fellow officers who acquainted us there was no accommodation in the town for man or horse, whereupon we turned back and took quarters at a good farm-house a mile from the town, where we found good entertainment and, what was very pleasing, civil reception, in this place as many others, which was a dainty, the best drink was milk and water. The reason no room could be had in town was that most of the best was taken up by the principal officers, and they that came first had taken possession of whatever small places the great ones had rejected. We continued here Monday and Tuesday suffering hourly and furious assaults on our quarters from all who passed that way, which with much difficulty we made good. Some, but few, of our regiment came up during this time; but vast numbers of all sorts of people flocked to town. Hitherto all things remained in confusion, no resolutions being taken and consequently all left to their liberty without any command.

Wednesday the 9th: orders were given to all officers to endeavour to gather the remains of their regiments, and to ours in particular to march four miles to the westward of Limerick to a village called Carrigogunnell and the adjacent places, there to quarter till the rest of our dispersion came up and we received fresh orders. The most remarkable thing in this march was that the number of officers exceeded that of the private men, and yet not one-half of the former were present. These quarters proved very refreshing after our long fatigue, the people being generally very kind, as some thought partly for love, but in my opinion most through fear. For most certain it is few are fond of such guests as soldiers upon free quarter, especially such as ours were ravenous and unruly, but it is the wisest course to make a virtue of necessity, and offer that freely which otherwise would be extorted forcibly.

We had here plenty of meat and barley bread baked in cakes over or before the fire and abundance of milk and butter, but no sort of drink. Yet this is counted the best of quarters, the people generally being the greatest lovers of milk I ever saw, which they eat and drink above twenty several sorts of ways, and what is strangest for the most part love it best when sourest. They keep it in sour vessels and from time to time till it grows thick, and sometimes to that perfection it will perfume a whole house, but generally speaking they order it so that it is impossible to boil it without curdling four hours after it comes from the cow. Oaten and barley bread is the common fare, and that in cakes, and ground by hand. None but the best sort or the inhabitants of great towns eat wheat, or bread baked in an oven, or ground in a mill. The meaner people content themselves with little bread but instead thereof eat potatoes, which with sour milk isd the chief part of their diet, their drink for the most part water, sometimes coloured with milk; beer or ale they seldom taste unless they sell something considerable in a market town.

They all smoke, women as well as men, and a pipe an inch long serves the whole family several years and though never so black or foul is never suffered to be burnt. Seven or eight will gather to the smoking of a pipe and each taking two or three whiffs gives it to his neighbour, commonly holding his mouth full of smoke till the pipe comes about to him again. They are also much given to taking of snuff.

Very little clothing serves them, and as for shoes and stockings much less. They wear brogues being quite plain without so much as one lift of a heel, and are all sewed with thongs, and the leather not curried, so that in wearing it grows hard as a board, and therefore many always keep them wet, but the wiser that can afford it grease them often and that makes them supple.

In the better sort of cabins there is commonly one flock bed, seldom more, feathers being too costly; this serves the man and his wife, the rest all lie on straw, some with one sheet and blanket, others only their clothes and blanket to cover them. The cabins have seldom any floor but the earth, or rarely so much as a loft, some have windows, others none. They say it is of late years that chimneys are used, yet the house is never free from smoke. That they have no locks to their doors is not because there are not thieves but because there is nothing to steal. Poverty with neatness seems somewhat the more tolerable, but here nastiness is in perfection, if perfection can be in vice, and the great cause of it, laziness, is most predominant. It is a great happiness that the country produces no venomous creature, but it were much happier in my opinion did it produce no vermin. Whether nastiness or the air be the cause of it I know not, but all the kingdom, especially the north, is infected with the perpetual plague of the itch.

In fine, unless it be the Scotch no people have more encouragement to be soldiers than these, for they live not at home so well at best as they do at worst in the army both for diet and clothes, and yet none will sooner murmur and complain of hardship than they. It is not through prejudice I give this account, but of love to truth, for few strangers love them better or pity them more than I do. And therefore to do them justice, I cannot but say it is not to be admired they should be poor having been so long under the heavy yoke of the Oliverian [i.e. Cromwellian] English party, whose study it was always to oppress and if possible to extirpate them. Poverty is a source from whence all other worldly miseries proceed. It makes them ignorant not having wherewithal to apply themselves to studies. It enervates the spirits and makes them dull and slothful and so from race to race they grow more and more degenerate, wanting the improvements of a free and ingenuous education, and being still brought up in a sort of slavery and bondage. This may be easily evinced by such of their gentry who having been abroad become very accomplished men either in learning warlike affairs or the more soft and winning arts of the court. Though the Scotch abroad be not inferior to them, yet at home they are as poor, as ignorant, more brutish and more nasty without any excuse for it, having never been oppressed or kept under as the others by a foreign yoke. This I have found by long and dear-bought experience and thought it not unworthy of observation in these few days of respite from labour, having nothing else to divert my melancholy thoughts during this small breathing after so great a series of misfortunes. Our scattered forces daily gather to Limerick being thence directed each regiment to their respective quarters.

* * *

Thursday the 17th: quarters were assigned us, in some houses one, in some two companies. Limerick, being the principal city at this time and long after that, held out for the king, and consequently there being often occasion, and that on account of many memorable occurrences, to speak of it, having been long quartered in it during that season, I will endeavour to give a true and exact description of it, but as brief the small compass of this journal requires.

Limerick is seated in a plain on the banks of the River Shannon, a branch whereof runs through and divides it into two, the one called the English, the other the Irish town, and encompasseth the former together with a considerable spot of ground without the walls called the King's Island, and so falls again into the main body of the river. The English town, by some as being the principal distinguished by the name of the city; is seated within the island made by the Shannon. It is encompassed by a stone wall in most places four, in some but three, foot thick. The houses are most of stone strong built and generally high, the whole consists but of one large street, the rest being all narrow lanes. Within the walls are two churches and two chapels. Our Lady's Church, which is the cathedral, is large and has a high tower, and was in the hands of the Catholics all the time of our residence there, and the body of it towards the latter end made a magazine of meal. St. Munchin's, over against the bishop's house, small and inconsiderable, before our time decayed, first made by us a place for gunsmiths to work in, after a magazine of warlike stores. The Dominicans had built a new chapel in the place called St. Dominic's Abbey in the upper part of the city, the Augustines had another on the river near Ball's Bridge. On the east side without the walls down to the water was a large suburb, and St. Francis's Abbey, at that time possessed by the Franciscans, the most part ruined, but the body of the church which was very large then in use, the other ruined parts being cut off. On the west side is the quay, though narrow in compass yet considerable for that upon high tide vessels of two hundred tons come up to it. Without the island gate stood a house of entertainment with a bowling-green and pleasant gardens. At our coming there were only the ruins of a small fort in the island, the rest being partly a common walk for the citizens and let out for grazing, this land being of the perquisites belonging to the constable of the King's Castle.

Over the Shannon is a very large stone bridge called Thomond Bridge, at the end whereof was another considerable suburb and a hill that overlooks all the city and renders it not tenable if that be possesed by an enemy. Within the city adjacent to the bridge is the King's Castle, the walls thereof like to those of the city, but strengthened with square towers or bulwarks whereon were several good pieces of cannon. This castle, the bridge, and walls of the city were the work of King John. Over that branch of the Shannon which compasses the island is Ball's Bridge, of stone but small, the river being narrowest there; this joins the two towns and leads into the principal street of the Irish, the rest as in the other being all but narrow lanes. From the bridge this street runs to St. John's gate, the principal entrance of the town, joining to which is the citadel; to the cityward it is square of small compass and has two small platforms, without it makes a half-moon; the whole work of stone but weak, and was then furnished with only a few small pieces of artillery. On the other hand, not far from the gate is St. John's Church, the parish, wherein nothing worthy of note. Between this and Mungret Gate was the Capuchin's chapel, so new it never was completely finished. The whole length of the east side under the wall was all tanyards, besides many more in the island, the tanning trade being here very considerable. In the angle made by the great street and Mungret Lane stands Thom Core Castle, reported to be built by the Danes, but in reality is nothing but a high stone house, in nothing that I could perceive differing from many others of the town.

The walls of this town are everywhere four foot thick strengthened with several towers; there are four gates Mungret, East and West Water, and St. John's. Without this was a very large suburb the main street whereof reached to Cromwell's fort, which is near a quarter of a mile southward, and the road to Kilkenny. It runs also a considerable way to the eastward and on the other side westward, till it joined that of Mungret Gate and came almost down to the body of the Shannon, so that it compassed almost the whole town. In digging this latter part for the fortifications were found vast numbers of skulls and bones of men, but I could not meet any could give an account how they came there. Though the buildings of the suburbs were not for the most part equal to those within the walls, yet there were many very fine houses and I believe the suburbs on all sides were larger and contained more inhabitants than both the towns within the walls.

Yet all these at our first coming, except that small part about St. Francis's Abbey in the island, were laid level with the ground for the better defence of the place and all the gardens and orchards utterly destroyed. Nor did the ruin stop at the suburbs, for upon the approach of the enemy our dragoons burnt all round, far and near, and at several times the country before very well peopled and improved was almost turned to a desert, the fury of war destroying in one year the improvements of many years' peace, but hereof I shall speak more in the proper place. I shall only add that when first I saw this city, about four years before, it was inferior to none in Ireland but Dublin and not to a very many in England, and I have lived to see it reduced to a heap of rubbish, the greatest and best part utterly demolished and scarce a house left that sustained not some damage. Such are the defects of war and such the fruits of rebellion.

* * *

Wednesday the 30th: between twelve and one in the morning the general beat, and again ordered that no man upon pain of death should stir from his post in marching. We marched through a very thick wood and extraordinary rough stony way long before the least light appeared, and the road being so uncouth was exceeding troublesome in the dark. We had many falls and that sometimes in the water, some stony brooks crossing the wood and nobody seeing where they set their feet. When day appeared we were out of the wood and in a better way. Soon after day we halted to gather our scattered men and march again with some lighted matches. Now it appeared very many of our men had left us and among them some who had the reputation of being very brave, many of which upon occasions of danger I have found to be the backwardest of all, and that they gained a name only by being mutinous troublesome fellows, always in private broils, yet durst not look upon the common enemy. Having marched seven miles this morning we made a considerable halt to refresh the men at Quin, a small village, where are some considerable remains of an ancient church and abbey, then possessed by the Franciscan friars.

Whilst we halted some men of each regiment were sent with officers to look out for provisions in the neighbourhood to bring to the men, who were commanded to pay for what they had. There was no other neighbourhood to seek anything, but those they call the creaghts, which are much like the Tartar hordes, being a number of people some more some less, men, women and children under a chief or head of the name or family, who range about the country with their flocks or herds and all the goods they have in the world, without any settled habitation, building huts wherever they find pasture for their cattle and removing as they find occasion. This is a custom much used in Ireland, especially in time of war as now, when thousands of all sorts fled from the dominion of the usurper and had no other manner of living but this. But the custom I believe is immemorial and was doubtless in use among them before the conquest by the English. They have small cars and garrons, or little horses, to carry their necessaries and live most upon the milk of their cows. With what they can spare they buy bread and other necessaries, or in these times of confusion make no scruple of taking where they find it. Particularly in gathering cattle they are industrious, for many who came from their habitations in Ulster with only one or two cows by the time they came to the neighbourhood of Limerick were increased some to fifty, some a hundred, and some more head of black cattle. They examine not whose ground they encamp in, and when they march drive all the cattle that comes in their way, and in some places I have heard them complained of as more grievous and burdensome to the country than the army, which seemed to me improbable and almost impossible, but that the country people affirmed the robberies and insolences of the soldiers were much inferior to the extravagant barbarities of those people. In short if they came first they left nothing for the army, and where they came after they carried away whatever the army had left. And though the irreconcilable hatred between Ulster and Munster be cause enough for those people eternally to reproach and slander each other, and that they are never wanting in that part, yet certain it is the creaghts were worse to the country than the professed enemy of their costly friends, the king's army, and even in this the two provinces strove to be upon equal terms, the one always railing and the other always giving fresh occasion to rail. But it must be observed there were creaghts of the other provinces as well as Ulster though not so numerous, yet, whatever was done the Ulster had the name of it.

*   *   *

Thursday the 16th: we returned to Limerick. Here I continued in quarters with the regiment all the winter, during which time there happened very little or nothing of note, for our forces being very inconsiderable and much harasssed, there was no possibility of gaining any advantage upon the enemy, who at the same time made no other of our weakness but to live the more at ease. The weather, it must be confessed, for the most part, was not fit for any action, yet considering how much they were superior to us they might without much difficulty have taken opportunities to straighten us in our quarters, which in a small time must have reduced us to extremity, and would consequently have saved the expense of another campaign, and the lives of many men they lost in it. But they seemed to be stupefied or wholly devoted to their ease, leaving us in quiet possession of the whole province of Connaught, besides the entire county of Kerry and the greatest part of the county of Limerick. These counties maintained the greatest part of our small army, especially with flesh and potatoes, for all sorts of grain was very scarce.

In Limerick, which was the head-quarters, we lived most of the winter upon salt beef allowed out of the stores, and had once ammunition of bread made of all sorts of corn put together allowed in a small quantity, but for the most part instead of bread we received half a pint of wheat for officers, and the soldiers the same quantity of barley or oats in grain, to make our own bread. Of salt beef the allowance was half a pound a day. As for pay a small part of the winter we received subsistence money in brass, which was equivalent almost to nothing, for a captain's subsistence which was a crown a day would yield but one quart of ale and that very bad, whereas for four Irish halfpence there was much better drink to be had. Wine and brandy bore prices proportionable and so everything else in that coin, for with silver necessaries might be had at reasonable rates, but there were few who had any of that metal.

To instance something more of the value of brass money we gave a crown for a loaf of bread very little bigger than a London penny loaf when corn is cheap. I gave five pounds in brass for a pair of shoes, nor could I have purchased them at that rate, but that the shoemaker was allowed a wretched garret to lie in the house where my company quartered; for it is to be observed that most of the garrison was quartered by companies or greater numbers in empty houses, only the officers quartering in those that were inhabited. After this having got cloth, lining, and buttons out of the king's store to make me a suit of clothes, and employing a soldier who was a tailor and managed all things the most frugal way to make it, the expense of making or the tailor's bill came to eighteen pounds, and yet was there not a needleful of silk in the suit, all the seams being sewed with thread, and the buttonholes wrought with worsted.

But to proceed, before Christmas all the brass was consumed, so that nothing remained to coin money, and there being no duties or taxes to be raised because the small territory we had was in no capacity of paying any, the army from that time never received any pay whatsoever, and to say the truth they were better satisfied without it than with such as they had gone before, for the brass was accounted to them as if it had been gold or silver, and at the same time was worth nothing, whereas now as they received nothing so they had nothing to account for. It is really wonderful, and will perhaps to after ages seem incredible, that an army should be kept together above a year without any pay, or if any small part of it they received was, as has been said, equivalent to none. And what is yet more to be admired, the men never mutinied nor were they guilty of any disorders more than what do often happen in those armies that are best paid. Nor was this all they might have complained of. In Limerick as has been said all the garrison lay in empty houses, where they had neither beds nor so much as straw to lie on, or anything to cover them during the whole winter, and even their clothes were worn to rags, insomuch that many could scarce hide their nakedness in the daytime, and abundance of them were barefoot or at least so near it that their wretched shoes and stockings could scarce be made to hang on their feet and legs. I have been astonished to think how they lived and much more that they should voluntarily choose to live so, when if they would have forsaken the service they might have been received by the enemy into good pay and want for nothing. But to add to their sufferings the allowance of meat and corn was so small that men rather starved than lived upon it.

These extremities, endured as they were with courage and resolution, are sufficient with any reasonable persons to clear the reputation of the Irish from the malicious imputations of their enemies; and yet this is not all that can be said for them. We have already seen them defend an almost defenceless town against a victorious disciplined army, and we shall see them the following summer under all these hardships fight a battle [i.e. Aughrim] with the utmost bravery, though overcome by numbers rather than valour. Let not any mistake and think I either speak out of affection or deliver what I know not; for the first I am no Irishman to be anyway biased, and for the other part I received not what I write by hearsay but was an eyewitness.

As for the city of Limerick, which I said was almost defenceless, it had no other but an old stone wall made against bows and arrows, I mean the first siege, and a poor covered way we made in a month's time. The enemy delayed coming to attack us, for when we came to the place it was all encompassed for a great way with suburbs and gardens, and had no other work but the bare wall I have mentioned. All the works there were, we made in that short space of time, by which any man may judge what they were, and the better to satisfy such as cannot form a true notion of them, they must understand that the French regiments we had with us at the Boyne, and who assisted in raising these very works, when they heard that the enemy drew near, utterly refused to stay in the town and stand a siege, alleging, and with good reason, that the place was not tenable, and this because they had seen fortified towns and by their strength were sensible of the weakness of this, whereas the Irish who had never seen a place well fortified thought this an impregnable fortress, and I have heard almost as much said by Irish officers, some of whom in private I undeceived as having been abroad and knowing more of that particular than they. As for the battle in which I say the Irish were overcome by numbers, this I can positively affirm, having myself taken the numbers of each regiment when drawn out, that we did not make 17,000 in all horse, foot and dragoons, and that in all places we had three to two against us. This I am sure of: in the foot and in the horse I believe the odds was much greater. But I must not here anticipate upon what happened so long after. The battle of Aughrim which is that I have made the last observation upon will be mentioned in its own place and with more particulars. Let us now return to our hard winter in Limerick, where the poor men, besides all the other difficulties they had to struggle with of hunger, nakedness, etc., in the severest of all the season for rain and storms were set to work upon repairing the breach and raising a new bastion without it.

18TH CENTURY IRELAND

THE

𝔇ublin 𝔖cuffle:

BEING A

CHALLENGE

SENT BY

𝔍ohn 𝔇unton, Citizen of *London*,

TO

𝔓atrick 𝔠ampbel, Bookſeller in *Dublin*.
Together with the ſmall Skirmiſhes of
Bills and Advertiſements.

To which is Added,

The *Billet Doux*, ſent him bv a 𝔠itizens 𝔴ife
in *Dublin*, Tempting him to Lewdneſs.

WITH

His Anſwers to . Her.

ALSO

Some Account of his 𝔠onverſation in 𝔍reland,
Intermixt with particular Characters of the
moſt Eminent Perſons he Convers'd with in
that Kingdom; but more eſpecially in the
City of *Dublin*.

*In ſeveral Letters to the ſpectators of this ſcuffle;
With a Poem on the whole Encounter.*

I wear my Pen as others do their Sword.——Oldham.

London, (Printed for the Author) and are to be Sold by
A. Baldwin, near the Oxford-Arms in *Warwick-Lane,* and by
the Bookſellers in *Dublin.* 1699.

Title page of the first edition of John Dunton's *Dublin Scuffle* (1699),
including an early version of the 'Conversation in Ireland'.

John Dunton

DUNTON'S CONVERSATION
IN IRELAND

John Dunton (1659-1733) was an early English journalist and genuine Whig literary character. His father educated him for the clergy, but Dunton was such an insolent child that the father, with apparent relief, apprenticed him at age 14 to a bookseller. By the early 1680s, Dunton was a successful bookseller himself, due to ingenuity in combination with shameless exploitation of hack writers. Among his most notable ventures was the *Athenian Gazette*, a weekly that mixed contributions from writers such as Defoe, Swift, and William Temple with notes and queries on matters such as the date of the origin of angels. Dunton was perpetually embroiled in financial disagreements, and the famous 'rambles' he speaks of here were mostly fund-raising expeditions or hasty flights from creditors. He travelled to Boston in 1686 to claim perceived debts and unload a stock of books; there his introduction to American Indians whetted an appetite to see other 'savages', such as the Irish. He arrived in Dublin in 1698, selling books and fleeing a disgruntled mother-in-law. The books were sold at auction by one Patrick Campbell, whom Dunton never allowed peace again. The first result of the Irish ramble was *The Dublin Scuffle* (1699), and the second, this 'Conversation', was included in his autobiography *Life and Errors* (1705); both mix raucous descriptions of Ireland with reflex attacks on Campbell. In this extract Dunton refers to Campbell by first name, and it was his habit to call everybody by pet names, including his companion here, 'Climeme', and his second wife Sarah, here 'Valeria'. By about this time, as the *Dictionary of National Biography* notes, 'his flightiness became actual derangement; and his later writings are full of unintelligible references to hopeless entanglements'. Among his later productions was *Dunton's Whipping Post, or a Satire Upon Everybody* (1708).

Dunton's visit to Ireland fell insignificantly before 1700, but it is part of the 18th century experience of Ireland after the Battle of the Boyne in 1690. As happens at several junctures of Irish history, an event of some finality alters English perceptions of Ireland far more than it immediately alters Ireland itself. The defeat of the Stuart sympathizers in Ireland seems to have tamed the face of Ireland for the English visitor. Much of the matter of Dunton's description is common to reports back to Elizabethan times, such as the descriptions of the cabins and keening. Indeed, the descriptions themselves indicate that very little had changed in the lives of the peasants over more than a century. But the cabins and keening that had been described as indications of savagery are now increasingly treated as kinds of naivete. Dunton's account marks a stage in this shift. He is capable of calling the Irish 'vermin', but for the most part they are 'disarmed rebels', domesticated sufficiently to merit for the first time the tag name Teague, an early version of Paddy.

This is an edited selection from 'Dunton's Conversation in Ireland' as printed in the second volume of a later printing of *The Life and Errors of John Dunton, Citizen of London* (London: J. Nichols, 1818).

I n such discourses as these, we passed away the melancholy day, till we came to Ballimany, our intended quarters. It is a small village of poor cabins, and an old castle, of which there is abundance in Ireland, built, it is said, by the Danes, long before the coming of the English into it; they are square strong buildings of stone, with a small door, and stone stairs, and windows like spike-holes, purposely for strength; for, as the Danes enlarged their frontiers, they built these castles on them as curbs to the neighbouring Irish. I have often had occasion, in some of my letters, to mention these cabins, or huts, but now take the description of them.

They build them by putting two forked sticks of such length as they intend the height of the building, and at such distance as they design its length; if they design it large, they place three or four such forks into the ground, and on there they lay other long sticks, which are the ridge timber; then they raise the wall, which they make of clay and straw tempered with water, and this they call *mud*. When the wall is raised to a sufficient height, which perhaps is four feet, then they lay other small sticks, with one end on the ridge piece, and the other on the wall; these they wattle with small hazels, and then cover them with straw, or coarse grass, without any chimneys; so that, when the fire is lighted, the smoke will come through the thatch, so that you would think the cabin were on fire. Another sort of their cabins is made by laying one end of the stick upon the bank of a ditch, and the other upon a little bit of a mud wall; and then, when it is wattled, they cover it with heath-straw, or scraws of earth; and into this miserable place will half a dozen poor creatures creep for shelter and lodging. But their beds are upon such a firm foundation, that nothing but an earthquake can move them; instead of feathers or flocks, they use rushes or straw, which serves them without changing. Sheets they never provide; and, to tell the naked truth, unless they can purchase a poor cadow [i.e. cloth], which is not often, they lie together like Adam and Eve before the Fall, not a rag to cover them but themselves; which may be one reason why they so multiply, each little hut being full of children. They seldom have any partitions, or several rooms; but sleep in common with their swine and poultry; and for second or third story, you may look long enough ere you find any.

But, as the buildings of Versailles are so very magnificent as not capable of such a description that may give a just idea of them; so these, in the other extreme, are so very wretched things, that perhaps the pen of the noblest Architect would be very defective in describing them. Behind one of their cabins lies the garden, a piece of ground sometimes of half an acre, or an acre; and in this is the turf-stack, their corn, perhaps two or three hundred sheaves of oats, and as much peas: the rest of the ground is full of their dearly beloved potatoes, and a few cabbages, which the solitary calf of the family, that is here pent from its dam, never suffers to come to perfection. Madam, I should more exactly have described their dwellings, or cabins, if I durst have adventured oftener into them, or could have stayed in them, when I was there.

But to proceed in my *Rambles*. Next morning early, without regarding any ceremony, we made our visit to a Popish Father, who was just up, and wiping his eyes. The weather was very fair, and we stayed at the door (which had a little green field before it) until the room within was swept to receive us. The dew lay in pretty spangles on the grass, made by refraction of the sunbeams. I had a mind to try the Father's Philosophy, and inquired 'what the dew was?' He told me, 'It was a vapour that fell upon the ground in the night season, and that the Sun drew it up again in the day.' But Climene told him 'it was an old and vulgar notion, and exploded by the newest Philosophers, who were of opinion it might be either the moisture which the horses of the Sun shake from off their manes, when they were put into his chariot rising out of the Sea; or that more probably it was the sweat of the grass and herbs, condensed by the cold of the evening air.' Her notions made us all laugh; and the Priest swore, by St Patrick's hand, 'she was as witty as she was pretty;' and put some other compliments on her, the best of which were much beneath what she truly deserves. The house was now ready, and the maid came to call us in, where we broke our fast, and prevailed with Father A——— to accompany us to Kildare, where we were going to be merry. His palfrey was presently saddled, and we mounted.

We soon came to the Curragh, so much noised here. It is a very large plain, covered in most places with heath: it is said to be five and twenty miles round. This is the Newmarket of Ireland, where the horse-races are run; and also hunting-matches made; there being here great store of hares, and moor-game for hawking; all which are carefully preserved. They have a tradition (I fancy it was taken from the Story of Dido's purchasing so much ground as she could surround with an ox-hide, on which she built Carthage) that St. Bridget, the great Saint of Kildare, begged as much land from one of the Irish Kings, for a common pasture, as she could environ with her frieze mantle. The Prince laughed at her, and bid her take it; she cut her mantle into so many small shreds, as, when tacked together by their ends, surrounded all this Curragh, or Downs.

Kildare is an ordinary country town, not near so good as Naas: yet it gives a name to the County, and is an Episcopal See, though but of small revenues; and is now therefore united to the Deanery of Christ Church, which is the King's Royal Chapel in Dublin, as the Bishopric of Rochester is to the Deanery of Westminster in England. It has in it the Cathedral Church, with two or three Inns, and those very sorry ones. It has two fairs yearly, and a weekly market, and sends two Burgesses to the Parliament; yet, after all, it is but a poor place, not lying in any road, and not having any trade belonging to it. There are some shops, with hops, iron, salt, and tobacco, and the Merchant not worth forty pounds. This County gives the title of Earl to one of the Family of the *Fitzgeralds*, formerly called *Geraldines*, who came over into Ireland among the first adventurers in Henry II's reign, and is now the first Earl here, as *Oxford* is with you. Here we dined on a dish of large trouts, and, with some bottles of wine, made ourselves merry. When we took horse, our landlord told us, 'we must accept of a *deoch a' dorais* from him;' which is a drink at the door. He had a bottle of brandy under his arm, and a little wooden cup, with which he presented each of us a dram. From hence we went about two miles backward towards the King's county, to view the Earl of Kildare's chair. It is an old castle, built on the side of a hill, which overlooks all the neighbouring country. I was told it was built by some of the Earls of Kildare, as a watch tower, for which purpose it was very well placed. We had hence a lovely prospect towards the North, of a noble vale, part of which was covered with corn, and part with cattle, with some woods; among which were seen some houses of good bulk and shew raising their heads; beyond these were hills, on which stood several great houses; a fine river ran through the valley; on another side, the greatest part of the Curragh lay open to our view, which indeed is a noble plain.

After we had satisfied our eyes with staring about, we steered our course towards the Bog of Allen; which, though it be the greatest in Ireland, yet never was so famous as the last rebellion, where the *Rapparees* (who are a loose undisciplined people) had their rendezvous, when they designed any mischief on the country, to the number of five or six hundred, and where they easily hid themselves when pursued; for, as I am informed, this bog is near fifty miles long, with many woods in it, and some islands of very good and profitable land; as the Island of Allen, which they say is worth 800*l.* a year.

His Majesty, for encouragement to breed large and serviceable horses in this Kingdom, has been pleased to give 100*l.* a year out of his Treasury here, to buy a Plate, which they run for at the Curragh in September. The horses that run are to carry twelve stone each; and therefore there are several fine horses kept hereabouts for the race, in stables built on purpose. There is another race yearly ran here, in March or April, for a Plate of a hundred guineas, which are advanced by the subscription of several gentlemen; and the course is four measured miles.

On Thursday, Sept. 13, was the day of the race this year for the King's Plate. There was a vast concourse of people to see it, from all parts of the Kingdom. My Lord *Galway* (one of the Lords Justices) was present at the race, and other persons of great quality. I met on the Curragh (where the race was run) with my worthy friend Mr. *Searl*, and several others that I knew in Dublin. After the race was over, our company rode to Ballimany. At this village is a little thatched house, like one of our English country houses, built by the Earl of *Meath*. After we had seen all the rooms in this nobleman's thatched house, we left Ballimany, and dined that day at the

Naas, and reached Dublin about nine in the evening.

But, Madam, if the predictions of Astrologers be true, such men as I am are very *Mercurial* folks (I mean the Planet, not the Mineral). I had not been long in Dublin before the itch of *rambling* broke out again upon me, though I once thought the fatigue of my Curragh Ramble would have abated the sharpness of it: but what is bred in the bone will never out of the flesh; and I, among other Sons of Adam, am in a literal sense born to great travels; and some people are surely so much delighted with the variety of change, that, like other Epicureans, they will purchase the fancied pleasure through thousands of difficulties that attend the acquisition.

Not impertinent to this is what I remember to have read in the celebrated Mr. Boyle* of one who was born blind, because of the adhesion of her eye-lids; and her parents living far in the country, from any physicians or surgeons, thought her malady incurable, until the time she was about eighteen years old; when, being called to London about some business likely to require a long attendance, he brought his blind daughter with the rest of his family to town, where the union of her eyelids being separated by a surgeon's lancet, she immediately perceived a thousand pleasing objects; she beheld every minute new things with admiration; and, not satisfied with seeing, as soon as she could conveniently go abroad, she was every day on the ramble, as if she intended to make up for the losses she suffered by her former darkness; and when she became acquainted with the objects of the town, she begged leave to roam about the country, not without expressions of some inclinations to satisfy her eyes with a view of the world could afford her. Of this girl's humour my landlord found me; for now (after I had settled the affairs of my auction) I travelled, East, West, North, and South; and, Madam, should I tell you what Irish cities, towns, and villages I next saw, I should lead you such a *Wild-Goose-Chase*, I should tire you quite, but not myself, for I am never weary with travelling. But (as much as I love rambling) I have just now received a letter from Valeria (crowded with desires to see me) which will shorten my Ramble some thousand miles. I will see but Europe, Asia, Africa, America, or so – that is all – and be in London by Plato's year; not but I am a huge lover of travels, and would gladly view the Globe Celestial too (as I told the ingenious D———ne) before I return; I mean, climb so high as 'to hang my Hat upon one Horn of the Moon, and touch the North Pole with my Middle Finger, But, seeing you admire I ramble thus, let me go down from the Moon a little, to tell your Ladyship, that, had you but seen Italy, and those other countries I am bound to, you would rather envy than pity my rambling fate.

Alas! Madam, to change my bed troubled not me; for I could sleep

*Probably Robert Boyle (1627-1691), of Cork, one of the founders of The Royal Society, the scientific academy established in 1645 and chartered under that name in 1662.

contentedly in America, Ireland, Wales, etc. or in any place; for, if I had the hardest lodging, I could dream of my Valeria with as much satisfaction as if I had been sleeping on a bed of down; and, when I awake, I please myself with thinking, that in a little time I shall see her again. And wherever I ramble, I am still content; for there is a wheel within a wheel, and nothing comes to pass by chance.

As to my very Auctions; if things went prosperously there, I looked upon it as an effect of Divine Favour, and returned God the praise; if otherwise, it put me on examining myself, and humbling of my soul before my Maker; and I look on all cross accidents as trials of my patience. And indeed still, upon self-reflections, I rather wondered that things went so well, than found myself concerned they went no better. When *Patrick* took my Auction over my head, it was for him that I was troubled most, that he should deal so barbarously with one that never gave him any cause for it. I was well satisfied in my own innocence, and thought I was concerned to make the world so, by letting them know the truth of things; and then to leave the issue to that wise Providence that best knows how to order all things for his glory and my good.

You may suppose, perhaps, Madam, there are no beggars in Dublin, since I have all this while been so silent, and said nothing of alms-giving: but assure yourself, Madam, to the contrary; for, to the best of my knowledge, I never saw them so thick anywhere else in the whole course of my life; and how to carry myself in respect to these wretches has been a matter which often disturbed me. To give unto all, is impossible; for a man then must be richer than Crœsus; and not to give at all, is unchristian: but the main difficulty lies in the right distribution, and to relieve those who are most necessitous. But who can know this? For I have heard Bishop *Hall* say (he that was Bishop of Oxford) that once walking through Moorfields, a beggar followed him with great importunities, and 'desired him, for Christ's sake, to give him something, for he was ready to starve.' The Bishop (not thinking him a fit object for charity) told him, 'if he refused to give him any thing, he believed he would curse him.' 'No,' said the Beggar, 'indeed, Sir, I will not.' 'Well, then,' said the Bishop, 'I will try thee for once' upon which the Beggar fell a cursing and swearing at him like a very devil.' Madam, when I meet with such vile beggars as these, I serve them as the Bishop did: but I am, if I do not flatter myself, naturally compassionate, easily affected with the miseries of other men, in any kind, but much more when I see old age go a-begging; and it is such that have been the principal objects of my charity; and next to them the blind. I never conceive the beggar-man the more necessitous, by being the more importunate and querulous; and of this sort, no man, I believe, has been attended with a much greater train: indeed, I have heard your old Eleemosynaries, who have been trained up to the trade from their younger years (as I am satisfied many have been, both in England and Ireland), can, by long experience and constant observation, readily distinguish, even in a crowd of men, a compassionate face; and will single him out, as I may say, to be the object of their importunities. But, after all, Madam, in matters of the distributions of charity, the right hand is not to know what the left does.

And now, Madam, having given you some account of my 'Conversation in Ireland,' both in city and country, and also given you some *hints* of my several Rambles in it, and what I observed in them; perhaps you may think by this time I have seen enough of Ireland to be able to give your Ladyship some general character of it. I confess, Madam, I am very bad at descriptions: but a general character of the *dear Joys* being what I formerly promised the ingenious D———ne, I shall now send it to you, her other self; and hope your goodness will be as willing to pardon all my mistakes in it, as hers would have been, had she lived to have read what I here send you. Then give me leave to tell you in rhyme:

Off in the Seas, and downfall of the Skies,
With water compass'd round, a Nation lies;
Which, on the utmost Western Ocean hurl'd,
Fixes the *ne plus ultra* of the world.
Water the bowels of this land does clog,
Which the weak Sun converts into a bog.
The Sun, whose great and generous influence
Does life and warmth to ev'ry place dispense,
O'ercome by th' innate venom of this air,
Can't draw it out, but leaves the poison there:
So true is what the Natives vainly boast,
No poisonous thing lives on the Irish Coast;
Because their air is with worse poison fill'd:
So has a Toad been by a Spider kill'd.

Perhaps, Madam, you may think I am too poetical, and may expect a more particular account of the country and people where my *conversation* at present lies; so I shall now proceed to a prose character of the *dear Joys*. And here I shall give you a glimpse of the Country; or, as it were, a general view of my Irish Rambles: and, as an Irishman is a 'living jest,' it will be merry and pleasant; but a little mirth must be forgiven to a traveller, who has little else to keep him alive.

Then to proceed to the Prose Character of poor *Teague*. And here I must first acquaint you that the gentleman* who tripped lately to Ireland calls it 'the Watering-pot of the Planets'; and the French have characterized it

---

*Here, and below, the author Dunton refers to is Laurence Echard (or Eachard) whose *An Exact Description of Ireland* was printed in London in 1691.

as 'seldom dry, but often running over, as if the Heavens were a wounded eye, perpetually weeping over it.' It is said there is but one good thing in Ireland, and that is the Wind, as it is generally Westerly, and sets fair to carry one out of it; which makes good the old saying, 'It is an ill wind blows no good.'

Some of their chief Cities are tolerably good; but most of them more populous than rich, Dublin excepted: for though they are thronged like hives, yet, being for the most part drones, they rather diminish than increase their stock; and were it not for the English, and strangers amongst them, I am persuaded in process of time they would be all starved; so that of all the places I have yet seen, give me Ireland to wonder at. For my part, I think it is a sort of *White Friars** at large, and Dublin the *Mint* to it. In every street you pass, you will either meet with some highway tailor, or some arrant unsatisfied pug, that drinks nothing but wicked sack. But at Dublin they have a Recorder, who at present is Mr. *Handcock*; who, besides the reputation that he has for his knowledge of the laws, has also acquired that of a courageous and just Magistrate, impartially putting them in execution against lewd and wicked people, without regard to any degree of quality or riches; instances of which are frequently seen in his punishing swearers with two shillings for each oath, according to a new Act of Parliament; and setting insolvent persons in the stocks. And many of the strolling courteous ladies of the town have, by his orders, been forced to expose their lily-white skins at a cart's tail; by which he is become at once the fear and hatred of the lewd, and love and satisfaction of sober persons. Both churchmen and dissenters are joined in this noble work of exposing vice, and all little enough. Such things as chastity, wit, and good-nature, are only heard of here. Such virtues as temperance, modesty, and strict justice, which your Ladyship possesses in so high a degree, have the same credit with the beaus of Ireland, which the 'Travels of Mandeville' find with us.

I do not hereby design any thing of the true gentry or nobility, amongst whom there are persons of as great valour, as fair estates, as good literature and breeding, and as eminent virtues, as in any of the most polite countries. But really, Madam, if you go into the country as far as Galway, they are as bad, if not ten times worse, than I relate them. There is scarcely a town without a pillory in it; Ballimany has one or two; Carlow has two or three, I think, the strongest I saw in Ireland; Kilkenny, I think, as many; it was here I lost my ring, my gloves, and my very comb; and when I charged them with it, they cry, 'the Devil burn them if they are thieves;' and swear, 'by Chreest and Shaint Patrick,' that 'they never saw it.' I lay at Kilkenny but four nights; but here is such a den of pick-pockets, that I think the thieves in Drogheda are saints to them.

---

*A Carmelite convent in London whose sanctuary was reputedly the refuge of debtors and deviants.

I saw in my Ramble to Kilkenny that enclosures are very rare amongst them; much of their land is reserved for grazing and pasturage; and there, indeed, 'the grass being very sweet, and holding a constant verdure, it is,' as a late author observes, 'in many places so indented with purling brooks and streams, that their meadows look like a new green-carpet, bordered, or fringed, with the purest silver.' Yet hay is a rarity among them, and would cost them more pains than they can well afford towards the making of it; therefore they seldom or never trouble their heads or hands about it. And then for 'their arable ground,' as the same author observes, 'it lies most commonly as much neglected and unmanured as the sandy deserts of Arabia.'

Their women generally are very little beholden to Nature for their beauty, and less to Art; one may safely swear they use no painting, or such like auxiliary aids, being so averse to that kind of curiosity, though they have as much need thereof as any I ever yet beheld, that one would think they never had their faces washed in their whole lives. Amorous they are as doves, but not altogether so chaste as turtles. There needs no great ceremony or courtship, for they generally yield at first summons. The men, as birds of the same nest and feather, differ only in the sex, not in their good humour and conditions. Bonnaclabba and mulahaan, *alias* sour milk and choak-cheese, with a dish of potatoes boiled, is their general entertainment; to which add an oat-cake, and it completes their bill of fare, unless they intend to shew their excessive prodigality, and tempt your appetite with an egg extraordinary.

Thus, Madam, have I given you a brief but general character of Ireland, which I have intermixed with what I found by the *dear Joys:* and what I say of these, I send to you as the character of the better sort of *Teagues*; for as for the wild Irish, what are they but a generation of vermin? If you peep into forty cabins, they are as spacious as our English hogsties, but not so clean; you will scarcely find a woman with a petticoat can touch her knee; and of ten children not one has a shoe to his foot. And these Irish parents are so proud, that, rather than dishonour (as they call it) their sons with a trade, they suffer them to beg for their daily bread; and for themselves, they are so lazy, that those of them that are not thieves live by the drudgery of their poor wives.

But, however careless they be of the living, they are mightily concerned for the dead; having a custom of *howling* when they carry any one to burial; and screaming over their graves, not like other Christians, but like people without hope: and sooner than this shall be omitted, they do hire a whole herd of these crocodiles to accompany the corpse; who, with their counterfeit tears and sighs, and confused clamours and noise, do seem heartily to bemoan the departed friend; though all this is with no more concern and reality, than an actor on the theatre for the feigned death of his dearest in a tragedy. Instead of a funeral oration, they bawl out these or the like querulous lamentations, 'O hone! O hone! dear Joy, why didst thou die, and leave us? Hadst thou not pigs and a potato-garden? Hadst thou not some sheep and a cow, oat-cake, and good usquebaugh to comfort thy heart, and put mirth upon thy Friends? Then, wherefore wouldst thou leave this good world, and thy poor Wife and Children? O hone! O hone!' – with much more such stuff; to all which *dear Joy* lending but a deaf ear, sleeps on till Doomsday; while home they go, to drink, and drown the present sorrow; till the melancholy fit comes upon them afresh; and then they resort to the grave, and bedew it again with tears; repeating and howling their *O hones* with as much deep sense and sorrow as before.

They have many other extravagant customs daily practised at their weddings and christenings: but I reserve these for my 'Summer Ramble.' So I will conclude their character with only saying, they are a nest of disarmed rebels; that have a will, though not the power to cut our throats.

I should next speak of their priests (fit shepherds for such wolves); but you will meet them often in my *Malahide Ramble*, with my conferences with them: so I will drop them here; but will send you a further account of my 'Summer Ramble' by the next post: for, Madam, my mind is always with you and my dear friends in England; though at present I am in the country of wrath and vengeance. But my ink is too clean for a further description. Yet, Madam, if you would see the picture of poor Teague more at large, I would refer you to a Book called 'The Description of Ireland;' that ingenious Author being the person I so often quote.

Thus, Madam, by what I have said, you see what an excellent country Ireland is for a young traveller to be first seasoned in; for let him but view it as much as I did, and I dare undertake he shall love all the rest of the world much better ever after, except Scotland and France, of which more when I get thither.

John Bush

HIBERNIA CURIOSA
A Letter from a Gentleman in Dublin to his Friend at Dover in Kent, Giving a General View of the Manners, Customs, Dispositions, etc. of the Inhabitants of Ireland, Collected in a Tour Through the Kingdom in the Year 1764

Historians as different as the English Victorian J. A. Froude and the modern Irishman James Carty have quoted *Hibernia Curiosa* with approval, but no information appears to survive about its author, John Bush. His tour began in London, and the text suggests a possible connection to Tunbridge Wells. In the book he declares his domain to be natural history, though he takes as expansive a view of that study as any late 18th century Englishman. Bush is extremely knowledgeable about the Irish

A view of Kinsale from the Old Fort.

agricultural economy, which might suggest a substantial amount of time spent in Ireland. However, he was an enthusiast of written descriptions of Ireland; that is clear from a prefatory tirade on tour writers and booksellers by way of introduction of his own claim to have 'copied immediately from nature, without the least implicit reliance on any accounts whatever'. A relatively limited actual experience of Ireland would also explain occasionally surprising comments such as that below on the 'universal sameness' of dialect from north to south. Bush promised a sequel if *Hibernia Curiosa* were successful; no such work appears to have been printed.

It is easy to understand later appreciation of Bush's moderation. He is genuinely sensible of the misery of real poverty, and he presents a coherent argument for general idleness being an effect rather than a cause of endemic poverty. He is also an early commentator on the detrimental effects of absentee landlordism, one of the first English visitors to attribute the misery of the Irish to an insensitive and remote economic system and not to their own faults. Yet his observations on what is 'disagreeable' to the English traveller, such as his devotion here to the clean stabling of his horse, serve as reminders of the limitations of any attempt to describe, as Bush in his preface claims to have done, 'with candour and ingenuity, untinctured with prejudice or partiality'.

The selection is from the first edition (London: Flexnry, 1769).

An 18th century print: idyllic image of industrious Irish farmers, supportive families, and, in the distance, the cultural and civic benefits of industry.

U pon my word, Sir, the inhabitants, in general, of this kingdom are very far from being what they have too often and unjustly been represented [as] by those of our country who never saw them, a nation of wild Irish. Since I have been in Ireland, I have traversed from north to south and from west to east the three provinces of Ulster, Leinster, and Munster, and generally found them civil and obliging, even amongst the very lowest class of the natives. Miserable and oppressed, as by far too many of them are, an Englishman will find as much civility, in general, as amongst the same class in his own country; and, for a small pecuniary consideration, [they] will exert themselves to please you as much as any people, perhaps, in the king's dominions. Poverty and oppression will naturally make mankind sour, rude and unsociable, and eradicate, or, at least, suppress all the more amiable principles and passions of humanity. But it should seem unfair and ungenerous to judge of, or decide against, the natural disposition of a man reduced by indigence and oppression almost to desperation. For a peasant of Ireland to be civil and obliging is a work of supererogation.

> Need and oppression stare within their eyes,
> Contempt and beggary hang upon their backs;
> The world is not their friend, nor the world's law.*

What respect for law or government, what dread of justice or punishment, can be expected from an Irish peasant in a state of wretchedness and extreme penury in which, if the first man that should meet him were to knock him at head and give him an everlasting relief from his distressed, penurious life, he might have reason to think it a friendly and meritorious action. And that so many of them bear their distressed, abject state with patience is, to me, a sufficient proof of the natural civility of their disposition.

The province of Connaught, the most western province of Ireland, and in form and situation, not much unlike Wales in England, is the least inviting to a traveller of any part of the kingdom. Our curiosity carried us only through the eastern counties of Roscommon, Sligo, Galway, and Clare, that border on the Shannon, which are the best and most civilized parts, and as far on as to Galway, the capital of the province.

The province of Connaught is the thinnest of inhabitants of any part of Ireland. Their agriculture is chiefly grazing. There are immense numbers of sheep and bullocks bred in this province; particularly in the counties of Clare and Galway. We were at one of the largest stock fairs, at Ballinasloe, a small town in the eastern part of the province, that perhaps is to be seen in the king's dominions, which continues for a week. The toll of the stock

Romeo and Juliet, V. i. 70-72, slightly adapted.

brought to this fair, which is kept twice in the year, in the Spring and at Michaelmas, is worth, to the possessor, on an average, 600 pounds per annum. I think it is a penny a head for bullocks, and sixpence per score for sheep, for all that are brought. The most distant parts of the kingdom are supplied in general from this fair.

The Shannon is the greatest river in the kingdom, and considerably larger than any river in England, running from north to south upwards of 300 English miles; and, in its course, spreads out into many large and beautiful lakes of different extent, from five to ten and fifteen miles, ornamented, some of them, with fertile and beautiful islands. There are several considerable towns situated upon this river, the principal of which are Limerick and Athlone.

The river abounds, also, with salmon and pike, etc., of very large size. But the navigation is stopped at about 60 or 70 miles up the river by a cataract, or fall of the water over a ridge of rocks that extends across the river about 20 miles above Limerick. If in any part of the kingdom there are any wild Irish to be found, it is in the western parts of this province, for they have the least sense of law and government of any people in Ireland, I believe, except that of their haughty and tyrannic landlords, who, in a literal sense, indeed, are absolute sovereigns over their respective towns and clans, which the western part of this province may not improperly be said to be divided into. Their imperious and oppressive measures, indeed, have almost depopulated this province of Ireland. The will and pleasure of these chiefs is absolute law to the poor inhabitants that are connected with them, and under whom the miserable wretches live in the vilest and most abject state of dependance.

This account, however unfavourable, is not exaggerated, I assure you, for it is taken from some of the more sensible people of the very province. Too much, indeed, of this is seen throughout the kingdom to be pleasing to an English traveller. I never met with such scenes of misery and oppression as this country, in too many parts of it, really exhibits. What with the severe exactions of rent, even before the corn is housed, a practice that too much prevails here among the petty and despicable landlords, third, fourth, and fifth from the first proprietor (of which inferior and worst kind of landlords this kingdom abounds infinitely too much for the reputation of the real proprietors, or the prosperity of agriculture); of the parish priest, in the next place, for tithes, who not content with the tithe of grain, even the very tenth of half a dozen or a half a score perches of potatoes, upon which a whole family, perhaps, subsists for the year, is exacted by the rapacious, insatiable priest. I am sorry to tell you the truth, that too many of them are English parsons. For the love of God and charity, send no more of this sort over, for here they become a scandal to their country and to humanity. Add to these, the exactions of, if possible, the still more absolute Catholic priest, who, though he preaches charity by the hour on Sunday, comes armed with the terrors of damnation and demands his full quota of unremitted offerings. For, unhappily for them, the lowest class of inhabitants in the south and west parts of the kingdom are generally Catholics, and by that time they are all satisfied, the poor, reduced wretches have hardly the skin of a potato left them to subsist on. I make no doubt, this has been the principal source of the many insurrections of the White-boys, as they are called, in the south, from my own observations and inquiries in the midst of them, and likewise drives them, in swarms, to the high roads, which, throughout the southern and western parts, are lined with beggars; who live in huts, or cabins as they are called, of such shocking materials and construction, that through hundreds of them you may see the smoke ascending from every inch of the roof, for scarce one in twenty of them have any chimney, and through every inch of which defenseless coverings, the rain, of course, will make its way to drip upon the half naked, shivering, and almost half starved inhabitants within.

This is no exaggeration of the whole truth, upon my honour, and it is the most disagreeable scene that presents itself to an English traveller in this kingdom. Happy would it be for the lowest class of people (whom oppression and want of employment too often and unjustly subjects to the imputation of being idle) if the method of parochial provision in England were introduced into this country, especially the southern parts of it, where the poor really are infamously neglected. And the case of the lower class of farmers, indeed, which is the greatest number, is little better than a state of slavery, while the priest and subordinate landlords, in ease and affluence, live in haughty contempt of their poverty and oppression, of which the first proprietors are but too seldom, indeed, for the interest of this kingdom, spectators. The natural consequences of this scene of things among the inhabitants is visible even upon the lands in this country in general; which, though by nature, a very considerable part of them, rich and fertile, yet they almost universally wear the face of poverty, for want of good cultivation, which the miserable occupiers really are not able to give it, and very few of them know how they were: and this, indeed, must be the case while the lands are canted (set to the hightest bidder, not openly, but by private proposals, which throws every advantage into the hands of the landlord) in small parcels of 20 or 30 pounds a year, at third, fourth, and fifth hand from the first proprietor. From the most attentive and minute inquiries at many places, I am confident, that the produce of this kingdom, either of corn or cattle, is not above two-thirds, at most, of what, by good cultivation, it might yield. Yet the gentlemen, I believe, make as much or more of their estates than any in the three kingdoms, while the lands, for equal goodness, produce the least. The consequences of this, with respect to the different classes, are obvious. The landlords, first and subordinate, get all that is made of the land, and the tenants, for their labour, get poverty and potatoes.

With respect to grazing, which is, at present, the most profitable kind of agriculture and which annually extends in this kingdom (and is an inexhaustible supply of Irish chairmen in London) that insatiable avarice of most of the stock farmers, as they are called here, after black cattle (bullocks) will, in time, spoil much of the best pasturage in Ireland. The advantages of grazing, I should imagine, would be much greater if sheep-grazing, which is almost confined to the province of Connaught, and two or three counties beside, were more extensively introduced and understood.

Ireland would, indeed, be a rich country if made the most of, if its trade were not reduced by unnatural restrictions and an Egyptian kind of politics from without, and its agriculture were not depressed by hard masters from within itself.

Indeed, how the increasing wealth of this kingdom, from whatever source, should be injurious to England, with which it is so closely connected, or that the putting it into the power of the former to derive such immense additional sums to the public wealth, in which both kingdoms must participate, should be injurious to the general welfare of either, I own is entirely beyond my comprehension.

To prohibit the importation of such commodities [until] our own country shall be already sufficiently provided with [them] must, even to an Irishman, appear just and reasonable, but that they should be excluded from, or restricted in their trade [from] almost all the rest of the world, is a species of policy, the wisdom of which, with deference to our administrators of the Hibernian department, I own, is to me not easily intelligible. However, this is a subject I by no means profess to be a competent judge of, and have only thrown together a few observations on the subject, as they were suggested to me from a general view of the state of things in the country.

And thus much for trade, agriculture, and poverty, which, in this kingdom, appear to have too great a connection, either for its own interest or that of any country it is connected with.

As to the customs and dialect of the inhabitants in general of this kingdom, there is such a universal sameness almost from north to south that Ireland affords the least entertainment in this view of it, perhaps, of any country of like extent in the king's dominions. I have met with greater variety in some two or three counties in England, in these respects, than in all the three eastern provinces of Ireland.

English is the universal language of the country among people of any fortune, and very few of the lowest class are met with that cannot speak it. In regard to language, indeed, they exceed the highest sort of people, who, in general, are too genteelly bred to understand anything of the language of their native country, which seems to be the nearest to the Welsh of any language upon earth; whereas you'll meet with thousands of the lowest rank who speak both English and Irish with equal ease; and, what you will hardly credit, perhaps, they really speak better English than the same class in England. The reason is obvious. Here, the lowest class have, many of them, learned it from schools, in which there may be supposed a general sameness throughout the kingdom.

But this superiority is, in my opinion, far from being discoverable among the people of higher rank anywhere. Though the inhabitants of Dublin, indeed, have the ridiculous vanity of pretending to speak better English than those of London. From the most attentive and frequent observation, however, on the language of the coffee-houses, and places of public business, in Dublin, compared to that of similar places in London, I can see not the least reason for this vain presumption: as little does it appear from a comparison of the language of the pulpit or of the courts of judicature in both cities. The language of the theatres I exclude from the comparison, for that is all prescription in both. And if their English be even as good, their pronunciation, I am sure, is much worse, even amongst the genteelest of them. I should not have taken such particular notice of this circumstance, but from hence, that an Englishman can hardly pass a day in Dublin, if he much frequents the coffee-houses, without finding this the topic of conversation somewhere, in one or other of them, the superiority of the Dublin English to that of London.

Nor is this the only pre-eminence which the citizens of Dublin, in particular, arrogate to themselves to those of London. If you will believe them, their gentility as much exceeds that of London as their language. For invariably, almost, whenever the subject is introduced, if the gentility of Dublin is spoken of, with any view to a comparison with that of London, it is with an air and manner that plainly bespeaks a presumed superiority on the side of Dublin. Indeed, I have often thought there was something characteristic in this Hibernian importance, as I would choose to call it, or, in the language of orator [John] Henley, this Dublin assurance, that, if anything among them can be thought so, is really original. But how the Devil the inhabitants of this metropolis, whose dress, fashions, language, and diversions are all imported from London, should come at a superiority in either, unless from a natural genius or capacity to improve upon their originals, is beyond my comprehension. That Hibernian importance, which I have taken notice of, I make no doubt includes in it a presumption of such a capacity. But here, likewise, as well as in the matter of fact, that they really have made such improvements, they must forgive me if I take the liberty of dissenting; nor will I pay such a compliment to their vanity at the expense of my own country, as to suppose that their talents or genius for improvement upon any originals whatever are in any degree superior to those of the English.

You will readily conceive that the observations from which I have made the preceding remarks were taken of, and entirely refer to, the middling class of gentry, and the people in trade. For it must be between the classes of these ranks that, in the present question, any comparison can be made. The nobility, and people of quality, in, or rather of this kingdom, are to all intents and purposes, almost, very Londoners. This is too well known in Ireland.

That part of the kingdom whose inhabitants, in their manners and dialect, are the most like those of the English, is the province of Ulster; which including within itself almost the whole, or by far the greater part, of the linen manufactory, the best branch of trade in the kingdom, they have consequently the greatest intercourse with England: an Englishman in some parts of it, indeed, will imagine himself in his own country, from the familiarity of their language and manners.

The roads of this kingdom are generally tolerably good for riding, but by no means equal to the English for a carriage. Turnpikes are established on all the principal roads in the kingdom; and at the inns, though they are very far from making the appearance of those in England, yet the English traveller will universally, almost, meet with civil usage, good provisions in general, and, for himself, clean decent lodging. But an English horse, could he speak as well as Balaam's ass, would curse the country, for most of these articles. Their oats, indeed, are, for the most part, tolerably good; but their hay and litter are the worst I ever met with; for excepting two or three counties in the east of Leinster, and one or two in Ulster, almost every handful of straw the earth produces goes on upon their houses and cabins. Their litter is generally the bottoms of their haystacks and the spoiled hay from the rack, which the greater part of it often is before it comes there, from their injudicious method of harvesting it. The provision of the rack is seldom much better than what goes under their feet, and thither one half of it, at last, generally goes.

I absolutely did not get above one bed of clean dry straw for my horse in the three eastern provinces; and that was at a farmer's who kept an inn at Lurgan, near Lough Neagh in the county of Armagh, one of the prettiest little market towns in the north, and the most like some of our spacious thoroughfare towns on the high roads near the capital of any that I met with in all the country. His men happening to be threshing barley and throwing the straw out plentifully just by the stable door, I was determined that once in the kingdom my horse should have a clean and warm bed. I don't exaggerate, I assure you, nor depart in the least from truth, when I tell you, that excepting at my landlord's, at, if I mistake not, the Crown and Wheatsheaf, at Lurgan, I did not once get anything like a good bed of straw for my horse in the kingdom. It may seem a little remarkable this, but it is no less true, nor do I intend by it a reflection upon the rest. In general, they have not the requisite provisions for a horse upon the road. They are very far from having a sufficiency of straw, and their hay is almost universally badly harvested. But they might have plenty of both very good;

and 'tis an infamy to the proprietors of this fertile country that they have not, who suffer some of the best land in the king's dominions to be torn to pieces, and cultivated in the vilest manner by a set of abject, miserable occupiers that are absolutely no better than slaves to the despicably lazy subordinate landlords.

We are generally apt to think everything favourable of a place where we have been agreeably entertained. Not only those of our horses, but our own accomodations likewise, at the Wheatsheaf were so remarkably decent, comfortable, and friendly, the disposition to oblige us in our agricultural host and hostesses was so conspicuous, that I cannot help wishing to perpetuate the memory of a place where we spent two or three days with as much pleasure as in any town in the kingdom. They seemed indeed to exert themselves to support the reputation of their town, which, from the similarity of its general figure, of the language, manners, and dispositions of its inhabitants to those of the English, had for many years acquired the name of Little England. And an Englishman at Lurgan, indeed, will think himself in his own country.

Irish cottage industry, as portrayed in the late 18th century. Home spinning linen was mythologized at the same time it was rendered obsolete by mill industry.

Richard Twiss

A TOUR IN IRELAND
IN 1775

Richard Twiss (1747-1821) had the dubious distinction of being, of all the English writers of accounts of Ireland, the most notorious to the Irish themselves. Wealthy and underoccupied, he had begun his career as a travel writer with *Travels Through Portugal and Spain in 1772 and 1773*, which was praised by Samuel Johnson in Boswell's *Life*. On the crest of that success he travelled to Ireland in 1775 and a year later privately printed in London *A Tour in Ireland*. The book was soon in great demand in Dublin editions because of its unpopularity.

The causes of offence are clear from these modernized selections from the first London edition. Scornful of nearly everything in Ireland but the landscape, this self-proclaimed 'judicious traveller' was frankly contemptuous of 'the Irish species' he found 'a distinct race from the rest of mankind'. The Irish, at the same time, gleefully enjoyed the fact that such a superior visitor was gullible enough to swallow tales about, among other things, women catching leaping salmon in their aprons. Even in the context of this anthology Twiss is salient for the severe limits of his proud liberality, an ideal that in the 18th century replaced the earlier English one of civility. A small but telling indication of the hypocrisy of Twiss' liberality concerns his high dudgeon at unscrupulous Irish printers and booksellers; in fact, this very work was barbarously pirated, but by the Englishman William Mavor in his *The British Tourists* (1800). The note of self-congratulation that ends these selections and the work itself points to a far broader tangle of distinctly illiberal assumptions.

After the encounter in Ireland, Twiss concentrated on a book about *Chess* (1789), *A Trip to Paris* (1792), and a disastrous investment in speculation on making paper from straw. His reputation survived in Dublin because of the manufacture of chamberpots with his portrait painted inside. The motto around his picture read: 'Let ev'ry man p-ss/On lying Dick Twiss'. In 1776 a Dublin poet named William Preston (1753-1807) published satires of Twiss. The first was called 'Heroic Epistle to Mr. Twiss by Donna Teresa Pinna y Ruiz', a lament of Twiss's stay in Ireland away from the Spanish lady. Preston's second poem was 'An Heroic

Answer from Richard Twiss', which lamented the ceramic commemoration:

> Without, a foliage crowns the polish'd frames,
> And burnish'd gold on flowers of purple flames;
> Within, the potter plants thy Richard's face,
> And bids him stare, in horrible grimace.
> Thro' lakes of amber as the face appears,
> The face repentant seems bedew'd with tears.

Even in America, by about 1780, a privately printed blank verse, *Dick Twiss: A Poem*, used the Twiss urinal as a muse.

These selections from *A Tour in Ireland in 1775* are from the first edition (London, 1776).

T he entrance into the harbour of Dublin is one of the most beautiful in Europe; though inferior to the bay of Naples, were it merely from the terrific grandeur of Mount Vesuvius, which there forms a most striking object.

I landed in Ireland with an opinion that the inhabitants were addicted to drinking, given to hospitality, and apt to blunder or make bulls; in which I found myself mistaken. Hospitality and drinking went formerly hand in hand, but since [then] the excesses of the table have been so judiciously abolished, [and] hospitality is not so violently practiced as heretofore, when it might have been imputed to them as a fault.

> Each person now may drink and fill
> As much, or little as he will,
> Exempted from the bedlam rules
> Of roaring prodigals and fools:
> Whether, in merry mood or whim,
> He takes a bumper to the brim,
> Or, better pleas'd to let it pass,
> Grows cheerful with a scanty glass.

Some years ago (perhaps half a century), when the English language was but little understood by the common Irish, it was not to be wondered at that they frequently used improper words, and blundered, because, as the Irish was their native tongue, and the English an acquired one, they thought in one language and expressed themselves in another, the disadvantage of which is obvious. But as at present almost all the peasants understand the English language, they converse with as much propriety as any persons of their class in England, or anywhere else.

Gaming and duelling are also attributed to the Irish, but probably with little foundation. As to the science of gaming, possibly it may prevail in Dublin, as it does in every great city in Europe. And with regard to the art of duelling, a prudent traveller may as easily avoid any such disagreeable encounters there as elsewhere. National reflections are always both illiberal and unjust; and Churchill was undoubtedly in the right when he said,

> Long from a country ever hardly us'd,
> At random censur'd, and by most abus'd,
> Have Britons drawn their sport, with no kind view,
> And judg'd the many, by the rascal few.

> — Rosciad.*

---

*Charles Churchill (1731-1764); *The Rosciad*, a satire (1761).

*   *   *

In the year 1749, it was computed that in the city and liberties of Dublin there were two thousand alehouses, three hundred taverns, and twelve hundred brandy shops. In 1766 the number of houses in Dublin was thirteen thousand, one hundred and ninety-four; so that it is probable that the number of inhabitants surpasses one hundred thousand.

There are many single-horse, two-wheeled chaises, which constantly ply in the streets in Dublin; they are called noddies. These, as well as the hackney-coaches, are so insufferably bad, and even dangerous, as to afford the matter of surprize that they are permitted to be used.

Goods are conveyed about the city on small two-wheeled cars drawn by a single horse; the wheels are thin round blocks, each about twenty inches in diameter. The wheels of those cars which are used in the country are placed at a greater distance from each other than those of the city cars. They are frequently used as vehicles for the common people on their parties of pleasure. A bed, or a mat, is at such times placed on the car, and half a dozen people sit on it, with their legs hanging a few inches from the ground; they are generally dragged at foot-pace. There are many mules made use of in and about Dublin.

The outskirts of Dublin consist chiefly of huts, which are termed cabins. They are made of dried mud, and mostly without either chimney or window; and in these miserable dwellings far the greater part of the inhabitants of Ireland linger out a wretched existence. There is generally a small piece of ground annexed to each cabin, which produces a few potatoes; and on these potatoes, and milk, the common Irish subsist all the year round, without tasting bread or meat, except perhaps at Christmas once or twice. What little the men can obtain by their labour, or the women by their spinning, is usually consumed in whisky, which is a spirituous liquor resembling gin. Shoes and stockings are seldom worn by these beings, who seem to form a distinct race from the rest of mankind. Their poverty is much greater than that of the Spanish, Portuguese, or even Scotch peasants, notwithstanding which they appear to exist contentedly.

The indigence of the middle class of people is visible even in Dublin, where there are many shops which serve at once for two different trades, such as silversmiths and booksellers, sadlers and milliners, etc. The stock in trade of the petty shop-keepers consists of half a dozen of eggs, a platter of salt, a few pipes, a roll of tobacco, a yard of tape, a ball of twine, a paper of pins, etc.

Neither is the keenness of necessity less conspicuous with regard to literature, for every printer in the island is at liberty to print, and every bookseller to vend, as many, and as vile editions of any book, as they please. Thus by using brown paper, saving the expence of a corrector of the press, and being at none for copy, they make shift to gain a few shillings by selling their editions at half, or at a quarter, of the price of the originals. Two magazines are published monthly in Dublin, in each of which any new pamphlet, which is sold for a shilling or eighteen pence in London, is given entire. There are likewise eight Dublin newspapers, which are curiosities by reason of their style and spelling. The orthography of the inscriptions on the signs, and of the names at the corners of the streets, is equally faulty, but might more easily be corrected.

During my stay in Ireland, I frequently had an opportunity of experiencing that 'kind of intellectual retrogradation, by means of which the more I heard the less I knew'*, as the second answer to a question usually annihilated the information supposed to be acquired by a first. Were I to say that the Irish in general have 'obtained a mediocrity of knowledge, between learning and ignorance, not adequate to the purposes of common life', it might be thought too severe. But when it is considered that they are lately emerged out of a state of dissensions and party broils, which left but little leisure for improvement of the mind, the above quotation may not appear totally inapplicable nor invidious.

The climate of Ireland is more moist than that of any other part of Europe. It generally rains four or five days in the week, for a few hours at a time; thus rainbows are seen almost daily. To this moisture and to the temperature of the air, being never in the extremes of heat or cold, is owing the beautiful verdure of the grass, which is seldom parched or frozen. But that moisture and the numberless lakes, rivulets, and springs are the causes of those bogs which so greatly abound in Ireland. These are far from being useless, as they are inexhaustible sources of fuel for the inhabitants, which is obtained at little or no expence. It is called turf, and is of the nature of the English peat and of that turf which is cut in Holland. The Irish turf consists chiefly of fibres of grass, moss, and weeds, with a small quantity of earth, and is easily consumed to ashes. The Dutch turf is wholly of mud, which when dry is heavy, burns a considerable time, and leaves a fine charcoal. In these bogs, some of which are twenty-eight feet in depth, trunks of trees are frequently found, at various depths, which have probably lain there many centuries: the marks of the hatchet are still to be seen on some of them. Many other substances have been found in the bogs, such as iron utensils, sword blades of a kind of brass, and horns of the moosedeer. Sixty or seventy pair of these have been discovered, the largest of which measured near fourteen feet from the tip of one horn to that of the other. A pair is deposited in the British Museum, another in the museum of the Royal Society, and another in Warwick Castle, etc.

There are no snakes, nor any venomous animals or insects in Ireland; neither are there any toads, moles, or molecrickets. Frogs are very

---

*See Dr. Johnson's *Hebrides*. [Twiss's note].

plentiful, and were first imported in 1699.†

To assign any reason for this peculiar exemption from noxious animals would be difficult, as conjecture alone would be the basis of such reason, and could never be satisfactory. It cannot be owing to the moisture of the soil, because the most enormous serpents are generated in the swamps of North America. Snakes have been imported into Ireland, and have always perished in a short time.

As to the customs peculiar to the Irish gentry, I know of only three:

The first is that of having constantly boiled eggs for breakfast with their tea (the Scotch eat marmalade and sweetmeats to their bread and butter).

The second is the universal use of potatoes, which form a standing dish at every meal. These are eaten by way of bread, even the ladies indelicately placing them on the tablecloth, on the side of their plate, after peeling them. The filthy custom of using water glasses after meals is as common as in England. It may possibly be endeavoured to be excused by pleading the natural unsociableness of the British, who if obliged to withdraw to wash would seldom rejoin their company. But then it may be urged that no well-bred persons touch their victuals with their fingers, and consequently such ablutions ought to be unnecessary.

The third custom is that of forging franks, which is pretty universal. The ladies in particular use this privilege. They endeavour to excuse them-selves; some by saying that the members of parliament have given them leave to use their names; others, who, it is presumed are staunch patriots, by pleading that the revenues of the post office are misapplied, and that they think it meritorious to lessen those revenues; others, that the offence is trivial and harmless and that there is no law against it, in which they are mistaken, as there is an Act of Parliament which renders it a felony of septennial transportation. I could not convince them that these fine reasons were inconclusive and unsatisfactory; but was myself convinced of the truth of what I assert, by seeing more than one lady of rank counterfeit the signatures of many persons, with so perfect an imitation that I must do them the justice to say that they could scarcely be distinguished from the originals. However, it is not every lady that has either the talent or the inclination to make use of this ingenious art: and as a futher alleviation, I have been informed that all the inhabitants of a town have sometimes had leave to frank letters in their Member's name.

There are several lotteries in Ireland, many of the tickets of which are

---

†'In O'Halloran's *History of Ireland* is the following passage, "We never had frogs in Ireland till the reign of King William. It is true some mighty sensible members of the Royal Society, in the time of Charles II, attempted to add these to the many other valuable presents sent us from England, but ineffectually; as they were of Belgic origin, it would seem they could only thrive under a Dutch prince; and these with many other exotics were introduced at the happy Revolution." This conclusion is as absurd as it is illiberal: the author is a Roman Catholic.' [Twiss's note].

sent to England to be sold, in open defiance of several Acts of Parliament.

As to the natural history of the Irish species, they are only remarkable for the thickness of their legs, especially those of the plebeian females.

Saint Patrick is the patron and tutelar saint of Ireland. He was born about the middle of the fourth century. In his *Life* I find it recorded that he daily rehearsed the whole Psalter with a great number of prayers, and that he mortified himself by 'saying every night fifty psalms in water'. He is said to have been canonized for having illustrated the Trinity by the comparison of a shamrock, or trefoil. And in honour of this apostle, Paddy is the popular christian name of the Irish.

*   *   *

I then proceeded to Dunleer. The country produces potatoes, wheat, flax, and oats. The enclosures are mostly of loose stones piled on each other. Over the door or chimney (the same opening serving for both) of many of the cabins I observed a board with the words 'good dry lodgings'; however, as I was sure that hogs could not read, I avoided mistaking them for sties.

The brass coins of the Isle of Man are current all along this coast. The beggars here are not exorbitant in their demands, most of them offering a bad half-penny, which they call a 'rap', and soliciting for a good one in exchange.

I observed about a dozen bare-legged boys sitting by the side of the road scrawling on scraps of paper placed on their knees. These lads, it seems, found the smoke in their school or cabin insufferable. It might perhaps be better that the lowest class of people throughout Europe were neither taught to read nor write, excepting those few who discover evident marks of genius; those acquisitions only creating new wants, and exciting new desires, which they will seldom be able to gratify, and consequently rendering them less happy than otherwise they might be.

*   *   *

To enjoy the diversions of angling or shooting, perhaps there is not a spot in Europe which exceeds this lake [Lough Erne]. Several seats contribute to ornament the shores; among them Castle Hume is the most conspicuous. On one of the islands is the most complete round tower in Ireland.

While straying along its solitary shores I felt a kind of pleasing melancholy. I then compared the beauties of this, with those of other lakes which I had seen: such as the Loch Lomond in Scotland; the Lake of Geneva, which receives much grandeur from the immense snow-clad mountains that bound it on the Savoy side, and much beauty from the vines on the opposite shore; the lakes near Naples, which are all classic scenes. And though I afterwards saw the celebrated Lake of Killarney, Lough Erne did not suffer by the comparison.

The cheapness of the necessaries of life in these parts is remarkable. Salmon is fixed, as before mentioned, at six shillings per hundred weight. The other kinds of fish may be had for the trouble of catching them. A couple of rabbits are sold for three-pence, a turkey or goose for a shilling, ducks and fowls two-pence or three-pence a piece, veal is at three pence or three-pence halfpenny, and beef about two-pence a pound. Potatoes, when I was there, were at a single shilling per barrel of forty-eight stone, though it must be confessed that they never have been so plentiful, nor so cheap, as during that season. For on an average the price is eight or ten shillings per barrel. After the frost of 1740 they were sold at thirty-two, and even in 1761, after a failure of the crop, at twenty-nine shillings. Whisky is sold at a shilling a quart. The most expensive articles are tea, sugar, grocery wares (which are sold as in England), and wines, port and claret bearing the same price, which is two shillings per bottle.

Neither is house rent less moderate. So that provided a family can forego the sweets of society, and be content to vegetate in dull tranquility, there is scarcely a spot more suitable for economical retirement. But as it is difficult to divest ourselves of that love, which we naturally have for the place of our birth, or where our childhood has been passed, and to abandon all former connexions, I am not apprehensive that the foregoing remarks will cause a new colony to be planted here. They are chiefly intended to point out to the native inhabitants their own happiness, of which they do not seem to be sufficiently sensible, as most of those whose fortunes enable them to choose their residence unaccountably prefer residing in England, or anywhere else, to living upon their own estates, where they would be respected as petty princes; whereas by squandering away their fortunes among strangers, they not only impoverish their own country, but live unbeloved, and die unlamented.

O fortunatos nimium, sua si bona norint!
— Virgil

*   *   *

I afterwards passed through the filthy town of Knoctopher, and arrived at Waterford. The town is built on the south side of the river Suir, which is broad and rapid, and without any bridge. It is about eight miles from the sea, and is the most convenient port to traffic with Bristol, by navigating with a due westerly wind without any variation. The quay is half a mile in length, and of a considerable breadth, and the largest trading vessels load and unload before it. Smith, in his *History of Waterford*, says, 'this quay is not inferior to, but rather exceeds the most celebrated in Europe'. He probably knew nothing of that of Yarmouth, nor of the magnificent quay of Rotterdam, both of which are much superior to that of Waterford. Here are two churches, besides the cathedral.

The counties of Kilkenny, Waterford, Wexford, and Carlow are overrun with ruffians called Whiteboys. These are peasants, who do not choose to pay tithes or taxes, and who in the nighttime assemble sometimes to the number of many hundreds, on horseback and on foot, well armed, and with shirts over their clothes, from whence their denomination is derived, when they stroll about the country, firing houses and barns, burying people alive in the ground, cutting their noses and ears off, and committing other barbarities on their persons. The objects of their revenge and cruelty are chiefly tithe and tax gatherers, and landlords who attempt to raise their rents. They never rob; neither do they molest travellers. Rewards of forty and fifty pounds are continually advertised in the papers for apprehending any one of them, and from time to time a few of these deluded wretches (as the advertisements term them) are hanged, and escorted to the gallows by a regiment of soldiers. Excommunications are likewise read against them by their priests from the pulpit, but as they are so numerous it is not likely that they will soon be extirpated.

A few years ago a like set of insurgents, who wore oak leaves in their hats, and called themselves Oakboys, rose in the north of Ireland. These gentry refused paying the tithe of their potatoes, telling their priests that they ought to be satisfied with their tithe of what grew above the gound. The disturbances which they caused are now at an end; as I was informed that they carried their point by being so numerous, and that at present their potatoes are tithe-free.

On leaving Waterford I ferried over the Nore at New Ross and arrived at Wexford. This town chiefly consists of a main street, and in size, situation, and dirtiness, is much like Falmouth.

I was informed that to the south of Wexford a tract of land, called the Barony of Forth, was inhabited by a colony which was planted in Henry II's time, and still retained peculiar customs and manners, but I had no opportunity of visiting them. Neither did I go into that quarter of Ireland called Connaught, which comprehends the counties of Mayo, Sligo, Leitrim, Roscommon, and Galway, as I was assured that they were inhabited (especially along the coast) by a kind of savages, and that there were neither roads for carriages nor inns. Undoubtedly the chief towns of those counties are more civilized.

* * *

After having attentively considered the advantages which may be acquired by travelling, we ought, on the other hand, to reflect, that the more knowledge a man possesses, the less satisfaction he will find in his intercourse with the generality of mankind, the majority being composed of ignorant or vicious people; and that his taste will be so refined by having contemplated the various beauties of nature and art, that most of those which occur to him during the course of a settled life will appear trivial or insipid, and that he will have little relish for the greatest part of those things which are generally termed pleasures.

To conclude: if we suppose the judicious traveller to be an Englishman; when, after having visited Europe, he reflects on the different climates, productions, and governments peculiar to the various nations; that some are parched by droughts which continue half the year; that others appear as if situated under a dropping sponge; others buried in snow; subject to earthquakes; exposed to the ravages of volcanos, or to irresistible inundations; and others overrun by wild beasts and venomous animals; he will then be sensible that in England he may spend a greater number of days in the open air than in any other country. And when he considers the arbitrary and tyrannic governments, the unnatural power of the inquisition, and the slavery and poverty of the lowest class of people, the pride and ignorance of the highest, and the superstition and bigotry of both, which prevail in different countries, and compares them with the advantages which so eminently distinguish his own country, where the climate is temperate, the earth fruitful, the government mild, the inhabitants (of both sexes) intelligent, and the women remarkably beautiful, he will then rest contented with the happiness he enjoys, by having it in his power to spend the remainder of his days in England.

Arthur Young

A TOUR IN IRELAND
With General Observations on the
Present State of That Kingdom

Arthur Young (1741-1820) was the most prolific and influential British agriculturalist of his day, when the scientific imagination of necessity extended its bounds from heavy industry to the large-scale agricultural pursuits required to feed a centralized population. His agricultural theories were indebted to contemporary ideas of political economy, and his *Political Arithmetic* (1774) shared its title with a work from the previous century by another author anthologized here, William Petty. Young's most important work was the agricultural survey *Travels in France* (1792), whose quality was enhanced by its timeliness: in great demand in London for its portrait of France on the eve of revolution, it was also translated into French in Paris in 1793 by the Convention as an indictment of the old monarchy. Among other activities too numerous to list, Young also edited 47 volumes of the then definitive *Annals of Agriculture* (1784-1819), of which he wrote a fourth himself, and maintained correspondences with political leaders of the stature of George Washington and Lafayette.

    A Tour in Ireland (1780) was an early work, from a period when the great agriculturalist was casting around for means of income to compensate for his own dismal personal ventures in farming. The tour was suggested by the Earl of Shelburne, later Prime Minister, and others with Irish interests who saw in an agricultural prescription a certain means to economic and political prosperity for Ireland. Young arrived in Ireland in 1776, completed a tour, and lost the journal of it in the theft of a trunk by a new servant. He returned in 1777 and lasted two years as Lord Kingsborough's agent in Cork, leaving that venture, like his own farms, saddled with debt.

    Despite observations such as that hurling is 'the cricket of savages', Young's description of Ireland was respected by the most knowledgeable ascendancy residents of Ireland, including Maria Edgeworth, whose novels were the first to present an image of the peasantry in fiction. To some extent his popularity certainly derived from his useful propensity to make several, often quite contradictory, observations on the same facts. His notice here, for example, of the wretched poverty of the peasantry, and subsequent inference that their poverty was more apparent than real, is at best diplomatic. *A Tour in Ireland* is representative of a period of enlightened and sometimes quite stubborn optimism, when the ideal of greater gross agricultural product held a promise since disproven. This is an ideal that, in Young's hands, instantly transforms Whiteboys, agrarian insurrectionaries, into 'happy little cottar[s]' whose 'industry has no bounds'. Against such fanciful notions, however, one must weigh Young's other rather progressive reflections on the need for employment and the evils of landlordism.

The passages reprinted here are edited selections from the first Dublin edition, printed in the same year, 1780, as the first London edition. The opening selection is from the 1776 part of the journal proper, written by Young from his 'minutes'. The later selections are from Part II of the published work, 'Observations on the Preceding Intelligence', with Young's headings. Ellipses in the text represent omission of statistical data.

T o Sir William Osborne's, three miles the other side of Clonmell. From a character so remarkable for intelligence and precision, I could not fail of meeting information of the most valuable kind. This gentleman has made a mountain improvement which demands particular attention, being upon a principle very different from common ones.

Twelve years ago he met with a hearty looking fellow of forty, followed by a wife and six children in rags, who begged. Sir William questioned him upon the scandal of a man in full health and vigour, supporting himself in such a manner: the man said he could get no work. [To this Sir William replied] come along with me, I will shew you a spot of land upon which I will build a cabin for you, and if you like it you shall fix there. The fellow followed Sir William, who was as good as his word: he built him a cabin, gave him five acres of a healthy mountain, lent him four pounds to stock [it] with, and gave him, when he had prepared his ground, as much lime as he would come for. The fellow flourished; he went on gradually; repaid the four pounds, and presently became a happy little cottar: he has at present twelve acres under cultivation, and a stock in trade worth at least 80 pounds. His name is John Conory.

The success which attended this man in two or three years, brought others, who applied for land, and Sir William gave them as they applied. The mountain was under lease to a tenant, who valued it so little, that upon being reproached with not cultivating, or doing something with it, he assured Sir William that it was utterly impractical to do anything with it and offered it to him without any deduction of rent. Upon this mountain he fixed them; he gave them terms as they came determinable with the lease of the farm, so that everyone that came in succession had shorter and shorter tenures; yet are they so desirous of settling that they come at present though only two years remain for a term.

In this manner Sir William has fixed twenty-two families, who are all upon the improving land, the meanest growing rich, and finding themselves so well off, that no consideration will induce them to work for others, not even in harvest. Their industry has no bounds, nor is the day long enough for the revolution of their incessant labour. Some of them bring turf to Clonmell, and Sir William has seen Conory returning loaded with soap ashes.

He found it difficult to persuade them to make a road to their village, but when they had once done it he found none in getting crossroads to it, they found such benefit in the first. Sir William has continued to give them whatever lime they come for, and they have desired 1000 barrels among them for the year 1776, which the landlord has accordingly contracted for with his lime-burner, at 11 pence a barrel. Their houses have all been built at his expense, and done by contract at 6 pounds each, after which they raise what little offices they want for themselves.

Sir William, being prejudiced against the custom of burning land, insisted that they should not do it, which impeded them for some time. But upon being convinced that they could not go on well without it, he relaxed, and since that they have improved rapidly. He has informed them that upon the expiration of the lease they will be charged something for the land, and has desired that they will mark out each man what he wishes to have; they have accordingly run divisions, and some of them have taken pieces of 30 or 40 acres: a strong proof that they find their husbandry beneficial and profitable. He has great reason to believe that nine-tenths of them were Whiteboys, but are now of principles and practice exceedingly different from the miscreants that bear that name . . . .

Their cattle are feeding on the mountain in the day, but of nights they house them in little miserable stables. All their children are employed regularly in their husbandry, picking stones, weeding, etc., which shows their industry strongly, for in general they are idle about the country. The women spin.

Too much cannot be said in praise of this undertaking. It shows that a reflecting, penetrating landlord can scarcely move without the power of creating opportunities to do himself and his country service. It shows that the villainy of the greatest miscreants is all situation and circumstance: employ, don't hang them. Let it not be in the slavery of the cottar system, in which industry never meets its reward, but by giving them property, teach the value of it; by giving them the fruit of their labour, teach them to be laborious. All this Sir William Osborne has done, and done it with effect, and there probably is not an honester set of families in the county than those which he has formed from the refuse of the Whiteboys.

*   *   *

CLOTHING

The common Irish are in general clothed so very indifferently that it impresses every stranger with a strong idea of universal poverty. Shoes and stockings are scarcely ever found on the feet of the children of either sex, and great numbers of men and women are without them. A change, however, in this respect, as in most others, is coming in, for there are many more of them with those articles of clothing now than ten years ago.

An Irishman and his wife are much more solicitous to feed than to clothe their children: whereas in England it is surprizing to see the expence they put themselves to to deck out children whose principal subsistence is tea. Very many of them in Ireland are so ragged that their nakedness is scarcely covered, yet are they in health and active. As to the want of shoes and stockings, I consider it as no evil, but a much more cleanly custom than the beastiality of stockings and feet that are washed no oftener than those of our own poor. Women are oftener without shoes than men; and by washing their clothes nowhere but in rivers and streams, the cold, especially as they roast their legs in their cabins till they are fire spotted, must swell them to a wonderful size and horrid black and blue colour always met with both in young and old. They stand in rivers and beat the linen against the great stones found there with a beetle [i.e a wooden mallet].

I remarked generally that they were not ill dressed of.Sundays and holidays, and that black or dark blue was almost the universal hue.

HABITATIONS

The cottages of the Irish, which are all called cabins, are the most miserable looking hovels that can well be conceived. They generally consist of only one room. Mud kneaded with straw is the common material of the walls. These are rarely above seven feet high, and not always above five or six. They are about two feet thick, and have only a door, which lets in light instead of a window, and should let the smoke out instead of a chimney but they had rather keep it in. These two conveniences they hold so cheap that I have seen them both stopped up in stone cottages built by improving landlords. The smoke warms them, but certainly is as injurious to their eyes as it is to the complexions of the women, which in general in the cabins of Ireland has a near resemblance to that of a smoked ham. The number of the blind poor I think greater than in England, which is probably owing to this cause.

The roofs of the cabins are rafters, raised from the tops of the mud walls, and the covering varies. Some are thatched with straw, potato stalks, or with heath, others only covered with sods of turf cut from a grass field, and I have seen several that were partly composed of all three. The bad repair these roofs are kept in, a hole in the thatch being often mended with turf, and weeds sprouting from every part, gives them the appearance of a weedy dunghill, especially when the cabin is not built with regular walls, but supported on one, or perhaps on both sides, by the banks of a broad dry ditch. The roof then seems a hillock, upon which perhaps the pig grazes. Some of these cabins are much less and more miserable habitations than I had ever seen in England. I was told they were the worst in Connaught, but I found it an error. I saw many in Leinster to the full as bad, and in Wicklow some worse than any in Connaught. When they are well roofed, and built not of stones ill put together, but of mud, they are much warmer, independently of smoke, than the clay or lath and mortar cottages of England, the walls of which are so thin that a rat hole lets in the wind to the annoyance of the whole family.

The furniture of the cabins is as bad as the architecture; in very many consisting only of a pot for boiling their potatoes, a bit of a table, and one or two broken stools. Beds are not found universally, the family lying on straw equally partook of by cows, calves, and pigs, though the luxury of sties is coming in Ireland, which exludes the poor pigs from the warmth of the bodies of their master and mistress. I remarked little hovels of earth thrown up near the cabins, and in some places they build their turf stacks hollow, in order to afford shelter to the hogs.

This is a general description, but the exceptions are very numerous. I have been in a multitude of cabins that had much useful furniture, and some even superfluous: chairs, tables, boxes, chest of drawers, earthen-ware, and in short most of the articles found in a middling English cottage. But upon inquiry, I very generally found that these acquisitions were all made within the last ten years, a sure sign of rising national prosperity.

I think the bad cabins and furniture the greatest instances of Irish poverty, and this must flow from the mode of payment for labour, which makes cattle so valuable to the peasant that every farthing they can spare is saved for their purchase. From hence also results another observation, which is, that the apparent poverty of it is greater than the real. For the house of a man that is master of four or five cows will have scarce anything but deficiencies. Nay, I was in the cabins of dairymen and farmers, not small ones, whose cabins were not at all better, or better furnished, than those of the poorest labourer. Before, therefore, we can attribute it to absolute poverty, we must take into the account the customs and inclina-tions of the people. In England a man's cottage will be filled with super-fluities before he possesses a cow. I think the comparison much in favour of the Irishman. A hog is a much more valuable piece of goods than a set of tea things; and though his snout in a crock of potatoes is an idea not so poetical as:

> Broken tea cups, wifely kept for shew,
> Rang'd o'er the chimney, glisten'd in a row.

Yet will the cottar and his family, at Christmas, find the solidity of it an ample recompence for the ornament of the other.

*   *   *

OPPRESSION

Before I conclude this article on the common labouring poor in Ireland, I must observe that their happiness depends not merely upon the payment of their labour, their clothes, or their food. The subordination of the lower classes, degenerating into oppression, is not to be overlooked. The poor in all countries, and under all governments, are both paid and fed, yet is there an infinite difference between them in different ones. This inquiry will by no means turn out so favourable as the preceding articles. It must be very apparent to every traveller through that country that the labouring poor are treated with harshness and are in all respects so little considered that their want of importance seems a perfect contrast to their situation in England, of which country, comparatively speaking, they reign the sovereigns. The age has improved so much in humanity, that even the poor Irish have experienced its influence, and are every day treated better and better. But still the remnant of the old manners, the abominable distinction of religion, united with the oppressive conduct of the little country gentlemen, or rather vermin of the kingdom, who never were out of it, altogether bear still very heavy on the poor people, and subject them to situations more mortifying than we ever behold in England.

The landlord of an Irish estate, inhabited by Roman Catholics, is a sort of despot who yields obedience, in whatever concerns the poor, to no law but that of his own will. To discover what the liberty of a people is, we must live among them, and not look for it in the statutes of the realm. The language of the written law may be that of liberty, but the situation of the poor may speak no language but that of slavery; there is too much of this contradiction in Ireland. A long series of oppressions, aided by many very ill judged laws, have brought landlords into a habit of exerting a very lofty superiority, and their vassals into that of an almost unlimited submission: speaking a language that is despised, professing a religion that is abhorred, and being disarmed, the poor find themselves in many cases slaves even in the bosom of written liberty. Landlords that have resided much abroad are usually humane in their ideas, but the habit of tyranny naturally contracts the mind, so that even in this polished age there are instances of a severe carriage toward the poor which is quite unknown in England.

A landlord in Ireland can scarcely invent an order which a servant, labourer, or cottar dares to refuse to execute. Nothing satisfies him but an unlimited submission. Disrespect or anything tending towards sauciness he may punish with his cane or his horsewhip with the most perfect security. A poor man would have his bones broken if he offered to lift his hand in his own defence. Knocking down is spoken of in the country in a manner that makes an Englishman stare. Landlords of consequence have assured me that many of their cottars would think themselves honoured by having their wives and daughters sent for to the bed of their master: a mark of slavery that proves the oppression under which such people must live. Nay, I have heard anecdotes of the lives of people being made free with without any apprehension of the justice of a jury. But let it not be imagined that this is common. Formerly it happened every day, but law gains ground. It must strike the most careless traveller to see whole strings of cars whipped into a ditch by a gentleman's footman to make way for his carriage; if they are overturned or broken in pieces, no matter, it is taken in patience. Were they to complain they would be horsewhipped. The execution of the laws lies very much in the hands of justices of the peace, many of whom are drawn from the most illiberal class in the kingdom. If a poor man lodges a complaint against a gentleman, or any animal that chooses to call itself a gentleman, and the justice issues out a summons for his appearance, it is a fixed affront, and he will invariably be called out. Where manners are in conspiracy against law, to whom are the oppressed people to have recourse? It is a fact that a poor man having a contest with a gentleman must — but I am talking nonsense, they know their situation too well to think of it. They can have no defence but by means of protection from one gentleman against another, who probably protects his vassal as he would the sheep he intends to eat.

The colours of this picture are not charged [i.e. exaggerated]. To assert that all these cases are common would be an exaggeration. But to say that an unfeeling landlord will do all this with impunity is to keep strictly to truth. And what is liberty but a farce and a jest if its blessings are received as the favour of kindness and humanity, instead of being the inheritance of right?

*   *   *

MANNERS AND CUSTOMS

It is but an illiberal business for a traveller, who designs to publish remarks upon a country, to sit down coolly in his closet and write a satire on the inhabitants. Severity of that sort must be enlivened with an uncommon share of wit and ridicule, to please. Where very gross absurdities are found, it is fair and manly to note them; but to enter into character and disposition is generally uncandid, since there are no people but might be better than they are found, and none but have virtues which deserve attention at least as much as their failings. For these reasons this section would not have found a place in my observation had not some persons of much more flippancy than wisdom given very gross misrepresentation of the Irish nation. It is with pleasure, therefore, that I take up the pen on the present occasion, as a much longer residence there enables me to exhibit a very different picture. In doing this, I shall be free to remark wherein I think the conduct of certain classes may have given rise to general and consequently injurious condemnation . . . .

The only divisions which a traveller who passed through the kingdom without making any residence could make, would be into people of considerable fortune and mob. The intermediate division of the scale, so numerous and respectable in England, would hardly attract the least notice in Ireland. A residence in the kingdom convinces one, however, that there is another class in general of small fortune — country gentleman and renter of land. The manners, habits, and customs of people of considerable fortune are much the same everywhere; at least there is very little difference between England and Ireland. It is among the common people one must look for those traits by which we discriminate a national character.

The circumstances which struck me most in the common Irish were vivacity and a great and eloquent volubility of speech. One would think they could take snuff and talk without tiring till doomsday. They are infinitely more cheerful and lively than anything we commonly see in England, having nothing of that incivility of sullen silence with which so many Englishmen seem to wrap themselves up, as if retiring within their own importance. Lazy to an excess at work, but so spiritedly active at play that at hurling, which is the cricket of savages, they shew the greatest feats of agility. Their love of society is as remarkable as their curiosity is insatiable, and their hospitality to all comers, be their own poverty ever so pinching, has too much merit to be forgotten. Pleased to enjoyment with a joke, or witty repartee, they will repeat it with such expression that the laugh will be universal. Warm friends and revengeful enemies, they are inviolable in their secrecy and inevitable in their resentment; with such a notion of honour that neither threat nor reward would induce them to betray the secret or person of a man, though an oppressor, [but] whole property they would plunder without ceremony. Hard drinkers and quarrelsome, great liars, but civil, submissive, and obedient. Dancing is so universal among them that there are everywhere itinerant dancing masters, to whom the cottars pay sixpence a quarter for teaching their families. Besides the Irish jig, which they can dance with a most luxuriant expression, minuets and country dances are taught, and I even heard some talk of cotillions coming in.

Some degree of education is also general. Hedge schools, as they are called (they might as well be termed ditch ones, for I have seen many a ditch full of scholars) are everywhere to be met with, where reading and writing are taught. Schools are also common for men. I have seen a dozen great fellows at school and was told they were educating with an intention of being priests. Many strokes in their character are evidently to be ascribed to the extreme oppression under which they live. If they are as great thieves and liars as they are reported, it is certainly owing to this cause.

If from the lowest class we rise to the highest, all there is gaiety, pleasure, luxury, and extravagance. The town life at Dublin is formed on the model of that of London. Every night in the winter there is a ball or a party where the polite circle meet, not to enjoy but to sweat each other: a great crowd crammed into twenty feet square gives a zest to the *agrements* of small talk and whist. There are four or five houses large enough to receive a company commodiously, but the rest are so small as to make parties detestable. There is, however, an agreeable society in Dublin, in which a man of large fortune will not find his time heavy. The style of living may be guessed from the fortunes of the resident nobility and great commoners: there are about thirty that possess incomes from seven to twenty thousand pounds a year. The court has nothing remarkable or splendid in it, but varies very much according to the private fortune or liberality of disposition in the Lord Lieutenant . . . .

But I must now come to another class of people, to whose conduct it is almost entirely owing that the character of the nation has not that lustre abroad, which I dare assert, it will soon very generally merit. This is the class of little country gentlemen; tenants, who drink their claret by means of profit rents; jobbers in farms; bucks [i.e dandies], your fellows with round hats, edged with gold, who hunt in the day, get drunk in the evening, and fight the next morning. I shall not dwell on a subject so perfectly disagreeable, but remark that these are the men among whom drinking, wrangling, quarreling, fighting, ravishing, etc., etc, etc., are found as in their native soil; [and] once to a degree that made them the pest of society. They are growing better, but even now one or two of them got by accident (where they have no business) into better company are sufficient very much to derange the pleasures that result from a liberal conversation. A new spirit, new fashions, new modes of politeness exhibited by the higher ranks are imitated by the lower, which will, it is to be hoped, put an end to this race of beings, and either drive their sons and cousins into the army or navy or sink them into plain farmers like those we have in England, where it is common to see men with much greater property without pretending to be gentlemen. I repeat it from the intelligence I received, that even this class are very different from what they were twenty years ago and improve so fast that the time will soon come when the national character will not be degraded by any set.

That character is upon the whole respectable: it would be unfair to attribute to the nation at large the vices and follies of only one class of individuals. Those persons from whom it is candid to take a general estimate do credit to their country. That they are a people learned, lively, and ingenious, the admirable authors they have produced will be an eternal monument. Witness their Swift, Sterne, Congreve, Boyle, Berkeley, Steele, Farquhar, Southern, and Goldsmith. Their talent for eloquence is felt and acknowledged in the parliaments of both the kingdoms. Our own service both by sea and land, as well as that (unfortunately for us) of the principal monarchies of Europe speak their steady and determined courage. Every unprejudiced traveller who visits them will be as much pleased with their cheerfulness as obliged by their hospitality and will find them a brave, polite, and liberal people.

George Cooper

LETTERS ON THE IRISH NATION
Written During a Visit to That Kingdom in the Autumn of the Year 1799

George Cooper was a young student of law when he toured Ireland in 1799 with his friend James Clark. He was called to the bar at Lincoln's Inn in 1801, when his *Letters on the Irish Nation* was going into a second edition. Otherwise, his name survives in contemporary records only for authorship of two legal treatises on chancery court law that were published in 1809 and 1815.

Cooper visited Ireland on the brink of the Act of Union, ratified in 1800. The union of the parliaments of Ireland and Great Britain, so fundamental to British politics of the 19th century, was a process that took on an air of inevitability at the close of the 18th century. As Cooper wrote in the preface to the first edition of his *Letters*, 'I thought it a laudable curiosity to inquire a little into a nation with which Great Britain was about to become most closely united'. In the preface to the second edition he fairly gloated over the fact that the union itself, and 'consequences which have already ensued from it', fully confirmed his own opinions on the proper management of Ireland.

Cooper's reference to Ireland as a 'nation' is a telling indication of the profound distance still separating the Irish and the English two hundred years after the Elizabethan visitor's first descriptions. His concentration is on a new gentry, but otherwise his revulsion at Catholicism as the source of rebellion and the Celtic race as notable for barbarity is congruent with Elizabethan accounts. Cooper's opinions are distinctly of their time, however, for their enlightened emphases on the Irish as simply behind the English on some Platonic scale of progress and on the paternal role English improvers must perforce adopt to protect the Irish from their own nature. His literary form — letters — would become increasingly popular in the 19th century.

This excerpt picks Cooper up in an extended discussion of historical chivalry. He speaks throughout as a rather dilettantish philosopher, and the text is relentlessly allusive to the writings of such as Paley, Gibbon, and Voltaire. For all his efforts at a global perspective, Cooper becomes most apparently ideological when he descends from the upper strata of moral philosophy to practical observations on what nature might be presumed to prove 'good habits'.

The first edition of Cooper's *Letters* was privately printed in 1800; the second, from which this selection is taken, was printed in London in 1801.

Ireland in rebellion: *The Massacre of Scullabogue*, engraving by George Cruikshank (1792-1878). The subject is an event in the rebellion of 1798 and so of the 18th century. The illustration was prepared for *Maxwell's History of the Rebellion of 1798*, published in 1845, and so is Victorian in perspective.

T he ancient world were strangers to this romantic kind of attach-
ment to women; but it must also be remembered that they were
strangers to the abuses of those laws of honour which chivalry has
left behind. Against these laws moralists cannot too much declaim, or
legislators too carefully guard. In proportion to the influence which they
obtain, it has been invariably found that all other laws and regulations are
weakened and undermined. In France, where this principle was carried to
its highest pitch, it is well known that the most wanton attacks on private
happiness were considered as no reproach to the character of a gentleman.
Seduction and adultery were carried on in the spirit of the old knight-
errantry, and in the most open and unreserved manner. Indeed the fair sex
always appreciated their [own] consequence by the number of suitors in
their train. Gallantry, which is perhaps but another name for chivalry,
seemed to have altered even the unalterable nature of virtue itself,
amongst the people of France under the old government. It created new
merits and glossed over old vices. How far the revolution in politics which
has been effected will alter them in these respects, experience alone can
demonstrate.

Setting aside for our future correspondence the subjects of the religious
and political differences of the Irish, I cannot better account for the slack
system of morality which is so observable in Ireland by any other principle
than the one above mentioned. There is a profaneness, a neglect of public
worship and private devotion, a cruel oppression of the tenantry, and a
general want of charity towards the poor, more striking amongst the Irish
gentry than anywhere I ever saw or heard of. Religion has done little or
nothing towards the civilization of the Irish. To it, as a softener and
improver of their manners, they may well renounce all obligation. But
though I have pictured this general state of immorality, yet there is one
particular to which in justice to their character I must acknowledge that
the charge does not apply. I allude to conjugal infidelity; instances of
which are much less frequent than in England. The women have the
character of being virtuous; I am sure I should be sorry by any insinuation
to rob them of that brightest jewel in the female character. That they are
many of them beautiful I have seen and often felt, and that they are chaste
I most fully believe: but the evil of chivalry (for I am on the subject, and
must proceed with it) which has not extended to the corruption of the
women, has made full amends for the deficiency by the ravages it has
made, in this particular, in the characters of the men. Although their
debaucheries may not be so evident in their own country, yet in England
and in foreign nations they have always been highly distinguished for
them.

The reason of this state of immorality, particularly with reference to its
effects on the lower orders of society in Ireland, such as I have described
them, has been well given by an excellent philosopher. 'The laws of

honour,' says William Paley, 'only prescribe duties towards equals, without attending either to those which are due to the Supreme Being, or to our inferiors.'

I conclude the observations which suggest themselves to my mind on the character of the higher class of people in Ireland, with remarking that there is not only a general neglect of religion amongst them, but even a frequent derision of it in others. This derision mounts into persecution, where the religion professed by others happens to differ from that which is established by law. The rich have all the intolerancy of bigots, without any of their piety. I think that you will agree with me that these are sufficiently striking traits of character to distinguish the wealthy from the lower classes of the people in Ireland.

It is in general remarked, and with great truth, that the manners of a nation alter considerably from one age to another; either by revolutions in government, by the mixture of strangers amongst them, or even by that inconstancy to which all human affairs are subjected by nature. But perhaps this observation will be found to be exclusively inapplicable to three-fourths of the Irish nation. As the earliest records of the commencement of the connexion between the two countries inform us that they then were — so will they be found at present — an illiterate and uncivilized people. I pass over their legendary tales of ancient refinement, having nothing to do with a period three thousand years before Christ, which rests upon little more than oral tradition. I have observed that the relative situation of one state with another must, without doubt, have great influence on the manners, and even sentiments, of both nations. Civilization has gradually travelled from the South to the North; opposing itself, as it were, to the ordinary progress of conquest. Asia taught Europe, giving lessons to Greece, her firstborn child; and that lovely female, the darling pride of nature, communicated her knowledge to Italy. The conquerors of the world spread civilization through Gaul, till at last it reached the most northern points of Britain. Thule, at last, has indeed had her historian and rhetoricians. The relative situation of one state with another has thus always demonstrated its influence on the manner, and even sentiments, of its neighbour. France has certainly operated considerably, in these respects, upon England. It is said, and with truth, to have forwarded our refinement, directed our taste, and, in every sense, to have been a cradle and nursery to the nation — *gentis incunabula nostrae.*

This principle will well account for that portion of civilization which I have observed is actually found amongst the rich and powerful in Ireland. Our colonists have carried it over from the mother country, and the education of the child has followed up that of the parent. But this refinement of manners has never crept into the great mass of the people. Other nations have advanced in all the arts of polished life by insensible degrees; but the bulk of the Irish nation is still almost at a stand. The native of that country, the descendants, as it seems probably, of its aborigines, still remain the same rude barbarians that our earliest accounts describe them. I shall have little difficulty in describing this character, as it may be depictured in the same few words with that of all nations who have been seen in a state of ignorance and barbarity.

If we study the manners of the ancient Germans, in Tacitus; or of the Tartar tribes, as described by the French missionaries and travellers; or of the modern American Indians, as they have been often seen by our colonists in the North and circumnavigators in the South; it is impossible that we should not be struck with the resemblance which they bear to each other. The cause may be traced to the plain and simple operations of nature. 'As the appetites of a quadruped,' says [Edward] Gibbon, 'may be more easily ascertained than the speculations of a philosopher; so the savage tribes of mankind, as they approach nearer to the condition of animals, preserve a stronger resemblance to themselves and to each other. The uniform stability of their manners is a natural consequence of the imperfection of their faculties. Reduced to a similar situation, their wants, their desires, their enjoyments, are all the same.' Some speculative writers in considering this subject have gone so far as to say that perhaps it would sometime be a happy circumstance if a certain depravity in human nature did not prevent a perfect similitude between the barbarian and the process of instinct in the brute creation.

It must undoubtedly be conceded that there are certain advantages which instinct must be allowed to possess, even over the most boasted refinements of civil society. It was the opinion of Plutarch, that the simplicity to be met with in the actions of our fellow creatures shews nature pure and untainted; neither disguised with art, nor clouded with passion; neither dashed with philosophy, nor corrupted with a multiplicity of contradictory opinions. The celebrated philosopher of Geneva [i.e. ,Voltaire] would no doubt have coincided with this sentiment. Indeed he seems to have proceeded upon it in several of the extraordinary opinions respecting the state of nature, which he has published to the world. If simplicity in morals or in politics is indeed the criterion of excellence, we shall find that if we carry the analogy from the brute to the vegetable creation, it is there still farther discernible. It is obvious that the vegetable world is in a manner tied down by the root to preserve a uniformity of nature, without sense or even instinct to mislead it. But these analogies are absurd in their application and dangerous in their consequences. It is the object of morality to lift human nature still higher than it is, rather than to debase it still lower. But morality is insufficient for this purpose without the aid of religion. Unassisted reason is the most fallacious of all guides. Although it is styled the great director of the human species, it is always hunting after new roads to happiness and is never content with the old ones; a sufficient proof (if proof were wanting) of its complete inadequacy and insufficiency.

But to return from this digression, into which the hypothesis of Plutarch insensibly led me, it will not require that great writer's zeal for parallelism to discover almost the same traits of character in the poor peasantry of Ireland, which distinguish every uncivilized people. The influence of nature has not been subdued, but in many respects perpetuated, by the operation of moral causes. And yet this is extraordinary, when we come to consider the subject. Africa, Tartary, and Siberia have always been countries in a state of barbarism; and the reason which has been assigned for it by Adam Smith is that 'they are inland countries, neither enclosing large seas and gulfs in their bosoms, like the Baltic and Mediterranean, nor rivers capable of carrying commerce and commmunication through them by the means of navigation'. But Ireland is bountifully supplied by Providence with almost every advantage of this sort. Her harbours are almost innumerable, and her navigable rivers superior, both in number and magnitude, to those of Great Britain. How her semi-barbarism (as it has been called) should then still exist, may appear inconceivable. But I shall explain this seeming paradox in my two next letters. At present I content myself with observing, that, though the condition and manners of the Irish do not present us with that appearance of an associated band of warriors which the political society of German tribes formerly gave them, and which is still seen in North America; nor with that pleasing idea of a numerous and increasing family, which the Tartar tribes have always suggested to the minds of the philosopher; although they [are] more approximate to the degraded state of a horde of Hottentots: yet I am persuaded, that in the three important articles of habitation, diet, and disposition, there will be found a great resemblance. If the effects of government and religion could be suspended, the parallel would be perfect. They would, under different circumstances, present us with the picture of the shepherd and the warrior.

The Irish peasant lives in a low, narrow hut, called a cabin; which is built of the slightest materials, cemented with clay, and thatched with straw. It is generally without glass to its windows, or a door to shut out the wind and rain. It seldom enjoys the convenience of a chimney, so that the smoke is seen ascending through every quarter of the roof. In this cold and comfortless habitation, the two sexes promiscuously herd together. These narrow precincts must not only afford shelter to a wife and family, but they must also enclose within them his livestock, if indeed the peasant rises in worldly fortune to the possession of a cow or a pig. These enjoyments of property are thus, like all other human advantages, tempered with a proportionate share of inconveniences. They deprive him of so much room in his cabin. The whole family are obliged to live under the same roof. Children and pigs may indeed, and always do, eat, drink, and sleep together. But a stall must be provided for a cow, by portioning off part of the cabin. The peasant, though he may possess half a rood of land, cannot parcel it off for the purpose, because it would rob him so far of the source of his subsistence. This naturally leads me to consider that subject.

The diet of the Irish peasantry is chiefly vegetable; his subsistence depending on a small spot of ground, which he generally sows with potatoes. Bread, which consitutes the ordinary and wholesome food of a civilized people, he is almost a stranger to. It can only be obtained by agriculture, which is here at its lowest ebb; the lands being, as I have before observed, almost wholly thrown into pasture for cattle. But perhaps it might therefore be reasonably expected, that the peasant would often enjoy the nourishment of animal food. But the fact is otherwise: he is almost a stranger to it. His poverty will not allow him to live upon that which is one of the great trading commodities of the country. If he possessed cattle, he must sell them to make up his heavy rents: when he is without them, where can he obtain the means of purchasing them? The consequence of this is that the peasant starves in the midst of plenty. Whilst the beast of the field is fattened, the man is often seen famishing. And yet, notwithstanding this scarcity of animal food, and entire dependence on roots for subsistence, it must be confessed that the peasantry are naturally a healthy and robust race of men. Their limbs are well formed, and they possess great strength of body. The medical world may with reason consider these two circumstances as convincing proofs that a vegetable diet is at least as fully congenial to nature as any other.

If we proceed from these external circumstances to examine the furniture of the peasant's mind, his disposition, and the qualities of his heart; we shall find him miserably destitute of fear, reason, and often of humanity. His poverty and oppression necessarily make him a prey to the mean and ferocious vices. He is the slave of ignorance and superstition, which will generally be found inseparably connected together. The Roman Catholic priest is the petty tyrant of each village. But his authority does not create that religious, orderly, decent, and dignified conduct which Christianity produces in England. There is nowhere to be seen that orderly observance of the Sabbath, which, to a traveller in Great Britain, bespeaks the mild influence of religion. On the contrary, the lower classes of the people are a prey to that gross, irrational sort of superstition which has little tendency to enlighten the mind, to curb the passions, or to regulate the conduct. The empire of the priest is founded on the fears and observances of his followers. It is a throne whose 'stubble pillars' are concealed by the gloomy darkness of ignorance and credulity. The ceremonies of worship are mere mechanical operations, consisting of exterior practices, in which the mind has no concern, and which have therefore been often compared to the pagan idolatry of antiquity. It is founded on the passions, and its effects are most visible in creating and keeping alive a bitter spirit of intolerance. I know that the heart of man cannot in any country, generally speaking, bear a religious void; but here it seems supplied by a system of blind and implicit reliance on the directions of a godly father. He regulates their wants in this life, and directs their fears or hopes of the next. He sells them the absolution of their sins, or resigns them to the pit of damnation. They can entertain little dread of incurring stains which may be easily wiped away. It is faith, rather than works, which, to judge from their characters and conduct, seems to be considered as achieving the glorious reward of salvation. On the assurance of a mortal man, and that often a venal one, they build their hopes of divine favour. On the worship of a few wooden images (false idols, before which they bow), the imaginary patronage of some tutelary saint, stated fastings, prayers, together with a few other absurd rites and ceremonies, they rest their hopes of a blessed immortality.

If this system of religion could make the people more sober, devout, and orderly, it would deserve the highest commendation. If it could remove that intemperate behaviour so universal, and harmonize the manners of three millions of people, the gratitude of the enlightened part of mankind would unite them in its commendation. The philosopher must approve of every religion which makes a better man. Perhaps neither the Talmud, nor the Koran, deserve reprobation, when considered in a worldly point of view, as a code of laws, and apart from truths of a more sublime and celestial nature. But the effect of the Catholic superstition on the Irish is to plunge their minds in the darkness and gothic ignorance of the 13th century. Had Great Britain still continued the prey of papal tyranny, it is probable that it would have been at present buried in that same gloomy ignorance. We should not have been able to boast of our Bacon, our Locke, or our Newton. The philososphy of the latter we undoubtedly should never have had produced, since it is well known that Galileo, who went upon the same principles with the system of Copernicus, was obliged to renounce them as a dangerous and damnable heresy because they seemed inconsistent with the motion of the sun as mentioned in the Old Testament. But it is not merely as a barrier to knowledge that I disapprove of this religion in Ireland. What is perhaps of equal importance is that it makes them the dupes of artful demagogues, who assume the cloak of the ecclesiastical profession. It is the character of every rude nation to be led by its priests. By this religion are often inflamed those fierce passions which sometimes break out with the most fanatical fury in all the horrors of civil war.

There is but one feature more which I have to add to this degraded character, and which we shall invariably find to characterize the manners of a people in a state of ignorance and poverty. I mean that extraordinary indolence, so much against the Irish nation. A leading cause of this vice is a characteristic to which I have before at some length adverted. This is that extraordinary national pride and that vanity of high descent which so prevails amongst the people. Perhaps there is nothing which is so much calculated to palsy the arm of virtuous industry as the pride of birth, notwithstanding it is often, as I have before allowed, a preventive of crime. But this political effect, this destructive idleness which seems almost inseparable from it, may undoubtedly be counteracted by moral causes. To agriculture and trade and civilization we can alone look for a removal of the defect. Industry is nothing but a habit, and these are capable of leading to the formation of it. They are the principles which expand and exercise the faculties of the mind, and 'off that lethargy which creeps over the senses of barbarous nations'. Whether we trace the character of the German, as delineated by the pencil of Tacitus, or actually behold the Irish boor; we shall find them both the same slothful beings. When the uneasiness which such a state of existence must naturally create leads them to action, it must often be to acts of murder and rapine [i.e. plunder]. Their dispositions accomodate themselves in an extraordinary manner to the opposite extremes of indolence and turbulent aggression. The moment they cease to be despicable, they become objects of dread and danger. An eloquent writer who well knew and commiserated [with] the condition of these unfortunate men, in describing their excesses, accounts at the same time for the cause of them in these words: 'The nation,' says [Edmund Burke], 'is at present divided into two almost distinct bodies, with little common interest, sympathy, or connexion. One of these possesses all the franchises, all the property, all the education: the other is composed of drawers of water and cutters of turf for them. Are we to be astonished, that when they are reduced to a mob, if they happen to act at all, they will act exactly like a mob, without temper, measure, or foresight?'

I have now finished that hasty sketch of the features which seem to me, since I have been in Ireland, to stamp the character of the lower classes of the people and separate them from the rich part of the nation. I may draw this conclusion from the examination of them both: the polished minority of the nation is one hundred years behind England in refinement, and the rude majority of it is at least five. With many noble qualities of the heart, there is still much remaining for the slow operation of laws and civilization to effect. The virtues of courage and generosity are dimmed and obscured by a cloud of vices. With the rich, a relaxed system of morality is aided by the artificial varnish of fashionable manners and those advantages which I have allowed that the laws of honour may and do carry with them, notwithstanding their mixture of evil. With the poor it is replaced by the grossest superstition. How much the rich have benefited by the exchange, I leave you to determine. As for the poor, I think they must be acknowledged dreadful losers by it. Perhaps there is some truth in the opinion of Lord Verulam [i.e. Francis Bacon], that 'atheism is better than superstition; for a man is then left to sense, to philosophy, to natural piety, to laws and to reputation; all which may be guides to an outward moral virtue. But superstition dismounts all these, and erects an absolute monarchy in the mind of men'.

Civil discords have also injured the cause of religion, and increased the natural ferocity of the Irish character. Their tendency is to banish the milder qualities of the heart, and to familiarize the mind to reflections at which it would naturally revolt with horror. A proportionate degradation of the morals and manners takes place, till at length the individual contemplates or engages in scenes of massacre and devastation without feeling any emotions or fear or remorse.

For my own part, I cannot conclude this long letter (which is short, considering how extensive the nature of the subject of it is), without again repeating, that I do not know of any country where the character of the people is more fitted by nature, than is that of the Irish, for the highest attainments in moral or intellectual excellence. The bountiful hand of the Almighty has given the materials; it must be the care of a legislator to form and fashion them. That there is a great portion of talent given them may be judged of from the numerous and bright line of examples which they have given to the world. There is a long list of poets, philosophers, and historians whose very names compose a galaxy of shining stars in the firmament of literature. With what pleasure could I dwell on the learning of Archbishop Ussher, the wit, eccentricity, and knowledge, of Swift; the penetration, judgement, and benevolent patriotism of Bishop Berkeley; the artless simplicity and *naivete* of Sterne; the versatile talents of the good-natured Goldsmith; the splendid eloquence and excellent morals of Burke; not to mention a crowd of elegant poets, classic writers, and sprightly dramatists, some of which are now living, but many more gone to swell the list of departed Irish worthies.

It is true that within these few years the Irish have highly distinguished themselves in literature, but it has generally been under the fostering hand of British governments. At home they have seldom made any figure. Even the Royal Irish Academy has never yet brought to light anything extraordinary for genius, taste, or learning. A leading cause of the very few works of merit which appear in Ireland remains to be mentioned. This is the want of an act of the legislature to protect the copyright of authors. It is unnecessary to add that genius will always best flourish, and learning be most cultivated, where the rewards of it are least liable to uncertainty either in their nature or their continuance.

That this should never have been sufficiently attended to in Ireland appears to me extraordinary, when I consider the talents and knowledge which are often found there. There may be more good sense in England, but there is wanting the life and energy of the Irish character. 'Strong passions awaken the faculties, and suffer not a particle of the man to be lost'. That they possess those warm passions and sentiments which may be directed to the highest moral energies, I have already made appear. Virtue has been shewn to be nothing but passions disciplined by reason and good habits. Aristotle has even called it 'reflecting appetite', and 'impassioned intellect'. From this association then proceeds all that is amiable, and all that is honourable, in society. From this cooperation the head acquires wisdom, and the heart temperance, fortitude, and justice. Whether you consider the happiness of individuals or of nations, it will be found in both to arise from the same sources. If you improve the man in knowledge and virtue, you thereby improve the state in them. By this a state arrives at that which is the standard of polish and urbanity; of that elegance without luxury, and that refinement without effeminacy which Pericles thought the peculiar glory of his age and country. There is a chain in society, which plainly accounts for it. 'Men form the rudiments of families; families constitute the elements of states; and in every system the parts will be found by their respective excellencies to promote the perfection and harmony of the whole.'

I am, &c. &c.

George Cruikshank's engraving *The Murder of George Cooper and his Grandaughter*, for Maxwell's *History of the Rebellion in 1798*. As in the previous Cruikshank illustration, the event was in the 18th century and the rendering is Victorian, especially in prognathous facial caricature of the Irish.

IRELAND
FROM UNION TO FAMINE

The Scalp, a natural formation near Enniskerry: 'the first grand and extraordinary object' John Carr met on his journey south from Dublin. Carr composed sketches from which engravings were made for *The Stranger in Ireland.*

John Carr

THE STRANGER IN IRELAND
Or, A Tour in the Southern and Western
Parts of that Country
In The Year 1805

'Green Erin's knight and Europe's wandering star' was Byron's description, in a suppressed passage of *Childe Harold*, of John Carr (1772-1832). A lawyer by education, Carr became a travel writer for reasons of health and a successful one for reasons beyond any contemporary's comprehension. His first works were *The Stranger in France* (1803), *A Northern Summer* (1805), and then, in 1806, *The Stranger in Ireland*. In its review of his Irish tour book *The Annual Register* conceded that it was 'a very pleasant and humourous compilation', surely a revealing commentary on contemporary expectations for the new vogue in Irish travel books. A less amicable response was an effective satire, complete with caricatures, by Edward Dubois called *My Pocket Book, or Hints for a Ryght Merrie and Conceited Tour in Quarto to be Called 'The Stanger in Ireland' in 1805*. Carr brought suit, to no effect. Some, at least, thought *The Stranger in Ireland* less than ridiculous: Carr was knighted in 1806 by the Duke of Bedford, then Lord Lieutenant of Ireland. Carr's tour in Ireland followed the Act of Union, and the conceits and condescensions characteristic of his book are representative of a newly domesticated image of the Irish. His title is a rich one, evocative of the sense of being 'a stranger' felt by many earlier visitors to Ireland and a phrase that occurs in their accounts of it with more than coincidental frequency. But after 1800 the union and improved transport for visitors combined to give Ireland an aura of new accessibility. Among the consequent effects is Carr's confidence in his discovery of the genuine character of the 'Irish rustic' as hospitable, docile, amusingly ingenious, and endearingly curious. A further effect is his even more remarkable confidence that now once and for all 'ridiculous misrepresentations' can be cleared away; a modern reader's own confidence in that may be shaken by the fact that the observation comes in advance of a completely contemptuous dismissal of any Irish claim to legitimate and respectable ancestry. These selections extricate as much as possible Carr's own observations from the mass of quotation he marshals in support of them. The text is the first edition, printed in London in 1806 and photo-reproduced by the Irish University Press in 1970.

A stranger, in his progress from the Pigeonhouse to the capital, cannot fail of being shocked by a sudden contrast to the beautiful scenes he has just quitted, exhibited in a little town called Ringsend, one of the most horrible sinks of filth I ever beheld. Every house swarmed with ragged, squalid tenantry, and dung and garbage lay in heaps in the passages, and upon the steps leading to the cellars: that such a nuisance should be permitted to remain in the neighbourhood of such a city is astonishing. Upon the road we saw several carriages peculiar to the country; that which struck me most was the jaunting car, an open carriage, mounted upon two small wheels, drawn by one horse, in which the company sit back to back, and hence the Irish, in badinage, call it an Irish *vis-a-vis*; whilst, on the other hand, considering the position of the parties and of the coachman, who is elevated in front, I have heard it more appropriately, though less delicately, nominated the *cul-a-cul*. This carriage is very convenient and easy, and will carry six persons besides the coachman. It much resembles the Russian carriage called the droshka. The entrance to the capital was through one of the barriers which were erected in the rebellion over one of the canals, which form an admirable protection to the city; and, after passing through several noble streets, we stopped at the mail-coach office, and I proceeded to the Royal Hotel in Kildare Street.

As I passed along, I could not help reflecting upon the ridiculous misrepresentations which have so strong a tendency to divide men from each other, and to perpetuate the antipathy which frequently too fatally separates one country from another. It was not above forty years since that an English nobleman, who was compelled, on account of the settlement of some large estates, to pass some time in Ireland, ordered his *avant-courier* to hire for him one of the best houses in Dublin, and to take especial care that it was not *thatched*. In Spenser's time, the wild Irish were believed to have wings sprouting from their shoulders, and it was lawful to shoot them like any other wild winged animal; and even to the present moment, the genuine character of the Irish is but little known to their brethren on this side of the water.

As Sir Isaac Newton has set his face against the authority of tradition beyond one hundred years of age, I shall not detain the reader to enquire whether Jason and the Argonauts sailed from the Bosphorus to Ireland, or whether the neighbouring nations received their alphabets through the medium of that country, or whether the Irish are descended from Magog the son of Japhet, the son of Noah, whether Brian Boru overwhelmed and expelled the Tuatha De Danann with all the artillery of their magic and witcheries. I would disturb no people in their fancy for national antiquity and pre-eminence. In God's name let the Peruvians derive themselves from the sun; let the Chinese boast of the existence of their empire eight thousand years before the creation of the world according to our calculation; let the Laplander, uncontravened, maintain that his dusky groves, shut up for nine months in polar winter, are the most rural in the world, and that the only honest men and good strawberries, created or grown, are to be found in his country. If the Irish prefer a Carthaginian origin, and the honour of having peopled Scotland, instead of being derived from her, or from Great Britain, or any other country; let her enjoy all the happiness attached to the origin she prefers. However powerful or weak her pretensions to Milesian pedigree may be, for being no antiquarian, I care but little for the matter; this I know, that if she were not able to push her genealogy beyond a century, she would at least be, as the chief of her orators, [Henry] Grattan, has finely said, 'Like some men, possessed of certain powers, who distinguish the place of their nativity, instead of being distinguished by it. They do not receive, they give birth to the place of their residence, and vivify the region which is about them.'

My attempt is to sketch the modern Irish, and principally to describe what I saw.

* * *

The following little anecdote will prove that magnanimity is also an inmate of an Irish cabin. During the march of a regiment, the Honourable Captain P———, who had the command of the artillery baggage, observing that one of the peasants, whose car and horse had been pressed for the regiment, did not drive as fast as he ought, went up to him and struck him. The poor fellow shrugged up his shoulders, and observed there was no occasion for a blow, and immediately quickened the pace of his animal. Some time afterwards, the artillery officer having been out shooting all the morning, entered a cabin for the purpose of resting himself, where he found the very peasant whom he had struck, at dinner with his wife and family. The man, who was very large and powerfully made, and whose abode was solitary, might have taken fatal revenge upon the officer, instead of which, immediately recognizing him, he chose the best potato out of his bowl, and presenting it to his guest, said, 'There, your honour, oblige me by tasting a potato, and I hope it is a good one, but you should not have struck me, a blow is hard to bear.'

In the neighbourhood we saw the arbutus or strawberry tree in great perfection, and many fine myrtles growing in the open air. Wherever we moved in the course of our Wicklow tour, we were equally surprised to find such excellent roads, and no turnpikes. The cabins which lay in our route were also neat, generally whitewashed, and an air of comfort and plenty breathed throughout; before each door were the finest pigs and poultry. The peasant and his wife were tolerably well dressed; and their children, of which every cabin has a bountiful quota, looked fat, fresh, and ruddy. Here, as in every part of Ireland which I visited, a dog was almost always one of the inmates of every cabin. The association seemed to be formed by sympathy, and fidelity appeared to be the common principle which bound the master and his favourite.

An Irish cabin, in general, is like a little antediluvian ark; for husband, wife, and children, cow and calf, pigs, poultry, dog, and frequently cat, repose under the same roof in perfect amity. A whimsical calculation sometime since ascertained that in eighty-seven cabins there were one hundred and twenty full grown pigs, and forty-seven dogs. The rent of cabin and potato plot in the county of Wicklow and neighbourhood, is from one to two guineas; the family live upon potatoes and butter-milk six days in the week, and instead of 'an added pudding', the Sabbath is generally celebrated by bacon and greens. In those parts I found the price of potatoes to be eight shillings and fourpence the barrel (twenty stone to the barrel) and three quarts of butter-milk for a penny. The price of labour was sixpence-halfpenny per day.

Insufficiency of provision, which operates so powerfully against marriage in England, is not known or cared about in Ireland; there the want of an establishment never affects the brain of the enamoured rustic. Love lingers only until he can find out a dry bank, pick a few sticks, collect some furze and fern, knead a little mud with straw, and raise a hut about six feet high, with a door to let in the light and let out the smoke; these accomplished, the happy pair, united by their priest, enter their sylvan dwelling, and a rapid race of chubby boys and girls soon proves by what scanty means life can be sustained and imparted.

Upon an average, a man, his wife, and four children, will eat thirty-seven pounds of potatoes a day. A whimsical anecdote is related of an Irish potato. An Englishman, seeing a number of fine florid children in a cabin, said to the father: 'How do your countrymen contrive to have so many fine children?' '*By Jasus it is the potato, Sir,*' said he.

Three pounds of good mealy potatoes are more than equivalent to one pound of bread. It is worthy of remark to those who live well, without reflecting upon the condition of others to whom Providence has been less bountiful, that one individual who subsists upon meat and bread, consumes what would maintain five persons who live on bread alone, and twelve who subsist on potatoes; and if such individual keeps a horse, he maintains an animal for his pleasure, for whose subsistence more land is necessary than for that of his master. In China the men are said to have nearly eaten out the horses, and hence it is usual for travellers to be carried along the high roads to the greatest distances by men.

The mode of planting potatoes is as follows. The potato is cut into several pieces, each of which has an eye. These are spread on ridges of about four or five feet wide, which are covered with mould, dug from furrows on each side, of about half the breadth of the ridge. When they dig out the potatoes in autumn, they sow the ridge, immediately before digging, with bere [i.e. barley], and shelter the crop in a pit, piled up so as to form a sloping roof. Potatoes are said to be very propitious to fecundity; and I have been told that some investigators of political economy, enamoured with the fructifying qualities of the precious vegetable, have clothed it with political consequence; and in Ireland have regarded it like Cadmus's teeth, as the prime source of population. So that hereafter, the given number of potatoes necessary to the due proportion of vital fluid being found, it will only be necessary to have due returns of the potato crops, in order to ascertain the average number of little girls and boys, which have for the last year increased the circle of society. It has been considered that the cultivation of rice was the most favourable to population, not only on account of its nutrition, but because it employed a great number of men, and scarcely any part of the work could be done by horses; but it has been since admitted, that more persons can subsist upon potatoes. I am ready to acknowledge the nutritious quality of the potato, and that it may be sufficient for the purposes of mere existence with an Irish rustic, who having little to do, does little. But an enlightened and experienced medical friend of mine assured me, that it could not supply the frame with its necessary support under the pressure of violent exercise. A workman in an ironfoundry would not be able to endure the fatigue of his duty for three hours together, if he had no other food than potatoes.

As the peasants and cabins, in the neighbourhood of Dublin, are more respectable and neat than those in many other parts of Ireland, I shall reserve any further remarks upon either, till they are suggested by the objects I meet with in the course of my tour. Poor as the cabin is, do not, reader! think that hospitality and politeness are not to be found in it. The power of shewing these qualities, to be sure, is very slender; but if a stranger enters at dinner-time, the master of the family selects the finest potato from his bowl, and presents it, as as flattering proof of welcome courtesy.

After a day of high gratification, we returned to Newrybridge, where we sat down to a couple of delicious fowls, for which, as for poultry of every description, and for its veal, this county is very famous: we had also trout, and excellent wine, particularly port. In England it is a very rare piece of good fortune to get good port-wine at any inn, and the vilest stuff sold under that name, is to be found at the places of the greatest public resort. On the contrary, in Ireland excellent wine is to be had in the poorest public houses. A friend of mine travelling in that country, came late at night to a little inn, which was so wretched that it had not a single bed for him or his servant, yet, to his surprise, the ragged host produced him a bottle of very fine claret.

After a refreshing repose in clean beds, we rose to renew our rambles. At our breakfast we had excellent honey and eggs; the latter the Irish have certainly the merit of having introduced to the English tables. Not many years since, even their neighbours the Welsh were so unaccustomed to the

Mrs. Grattan's Cottage, from *The Stranger in Ireland*. Carr described it as an 'elegant and romantic little summer retreat'. It brought to his mind Milton's line, 'Verduous wall of Paradise upraised'.

Owen Gray's Farmhouse, from Jonathan Binns's *The Miseries and Beauties of Ireland* (1837). Like John Carr, Binns composed his own sketches to accompany a written account of Ireland. The term 'farmhouse' here is more patronising than intentionally ironic.

sight, that upon an Irishman ordering some eggs for breakfast, the waiter asked him whether he would have a rasher of bacon with them. So much do the Irish consider their own eggs to be superior for sweetness and flavour, that some Irishmen will not allow that an English hen can lay a fresh egg.

Under a cloudless sky, we proceeded to Cronroe, about two miles from Newry, the seat of Isaac Ambrose Eccles, Esq., a gentleman of fortune, of considerable classical acquirements, and of the most amiable private character. This gentleman has edited three of Shakespeare's dramas, upon a *liberal* and extensive plan. The great natural curiosity of Cronroe is a vast rock, which rises perpendicularly from some beautiful woods behind the house, to the top of which we ascended, and enjoyed an exquisite prospect of an extensive, undulating, and highly cultivated country, and the sea. One part of the view was enlivened by the busy movements of a crowded fair.

After a display of hospitality, which in Ireland is no novelty, although always charming, we parted with our enlightened host, and proceeded to our chaise, which waited for us in the fair. Here all was bustle; shoes, stockings, hats, pigs, sheep, and horses, were exposed for sale to the best advantage.

It is always a source of pleasure to listen to the conversation of the lower Irish; at these places, wit, drollery, or strength of expression is sure to be the reward of it. 'I am very bad, Pat,' said one poor fellow, rubbing his head, to another. 'Ah! then may God keep you so, for fear of being worse,' was the reply. If Pat falls, his drollery is the first to rise up and laugh: the following instance of it was communicated to me by a very dear friend of mine, who personally knew it to be a fact. An Irishman, an assistant-labourer to a master bricklayer, who was building a house for a gentleman in England, fell through the well-hole from the top of the unfinished dwelling, and alighted very fortunately in a large quantity of mortar that lay at the bottom, which saved his life. The moment he had recovered himself, the only observation he made was, 'By Jasus, I had like to have hurt myself.'

*   *   *

I have in the course of this tour mentioned some circumstances to illustrate the character of the low Irish; and a little closer view of it may not be unpleasant. In this class of society, a stranger will see a perfect picture of nature. Pat stands before him, thanks to those who ought long since to have cherished and instructed him, as it were 'in mudder's (mother's) nakedness'. His wit and warmth of heart are his own, his errors and their consequences, will not be registered against *him*. I speak of him in a quiescent state, and not when suffering and ignorance led him into scenes of tumult, which inflamed his mind and blood to deeds that are foreign to his nature. We know that the best when corrupted become the worst, and that the vulgar mind when overheated will rush headlong into the most brutal excesses, more especially if in pursuing a summary remedy for a real or supposed wrong, it has the example of occasional cruelty and oppression presented by those against whom it advances. The lower Irish are remarkable for their ingenuity and docility, and a quick conception; in these properties they are equalled only by the Russians. It is curious to see with what scanty materials they will work; they build their own cabins, and make bridles, stirrups, cruppers, and ropes for every rustic purpose, of hay. And British adjutants allow that an Irish recruit is sooner made a soldier of than an English one.

That the Irish are not naturally lazy, is evident from the quantity of laborious work which they will perform when they have much to do, which is not frequently the case in their own country, and are adequately paid for it, so as to enable them to get proper food to support severe toil. Upon this principle, in England, an Irish labourer is always preferred. It has been asserted by Dr. Campbell,* who wrote in 1777, that the Irish recruits were in general short, owing to the poverty of their food. If this assertion were correct, and few tourists appear to have been more accurate, they are much altered since that gentleman wrote. For most of the Irish militia regiments which I saw exhibited very fine-looking men, frequently exceeding the ordinary stature; and at the same time, I must confess, I do not see how meagre diet is likely to curtail the height of a man. Perhaps the Doctor might have seen some mountaineer recruits, and mountaineers are generally less in all regions, according to the old adage – 'The higher the hill, the shorter the grass'.

If I was gratified by contemplating the militia of Ireland, I could not fail of deriving the greatest satisfaction from seeing those distinguished heroes, the Volunteers of Ireland. This army of patriots, composed of Catholics as well as Protestants, amounts to about eighty thousand men; when their country was in danger, they left their families, their homes, and their occupations, and placed themselves in martial array against the invader and the disturber of her repose. They fought, bled, and conquered; and their names will be enrolled in the grateful page of history, as the saviours of their native land.What they have done, their brethren in arms on this side of the water are prepared and anxious to perform; and whenever the opportunity occurs, will cover themselves with equal glory.

The handsomest peasants in Ireland are the natives of Kilkenny and the neighbourhood, and the most wretched and squalid near Cork and Waterford, and in Munster and Connaught. In the county of Roscommon the

*Thomas Campbell, *A Philosophical Survey of the South of Ireland*, first edition Dublin, 1778.

male and female peasantry and horses are handsome; the former are fair and tall, and possess great flexibility of muscle. The men are the best leapers in Ireland. The finest hunters and most expert huntsmen are to be found in the fine sporting county of Fermanagh. In the county of Meath the peasants are very heavily limbed. In the county of Kerry, and along the western shore, the peasants very much resemble the Spaniards in expression of countenance and colour of hair.

The lower orders will occasionally lie, and so will the lower orders of any other country, unless they are instructed better; and so should we all, had we not been corrected in our childhood for doing it. It has been asserted, that the low Irish are addicted to pilfering; I met with no instance of it personally. An intelligent friend of mine, one of the largest linen-manufacturers in the north of Ireland, in whose house there is seldom less than twelve or fifteen hundred pounds *in cash*, surrounded with two or three hundred poor peasants, retires at night to his bed without bolting a door, or fastening a window. During Lady Cathcart's imprisonment in her own house in Ireland, for twenty years, by the orders of her husband, an affair which made a great noise some years since, her Ladyship wished to remove some remarkably fine and valuable diamonds, which she had concealed from her husband, out of the house. But having no friend or servant whom she could trust, she spoke to a miserable beggar-woman who used to come to the house, from the window of the room in which she was confined. The woman promised to take care of the jewels, and Lady Cathcart accordingly threw the parcel containing them to her out of the window. The poor mendicant conveyed them to the person to whom they were addressed; and when Lady Cathcart recovered her liberty some years afterwards, her diamonds were safely restored to her. I was well informed, that a disposition of inebriation amongst the peasantry had rather subsided, and had principally confined itself to Dublin.

The instruction of the common people is in the lowest state of degradation. In the summer a wretched uncharactered itinerant derives a scanty and precarious existence by wandering from parish to parish, and opening a school in some ditch covered with heath and furze, to which the inhabitants send their children to be instructed by the miserable breadless being, who is nearly as ignorant as themselves. And in the winter these pedagogue pedlars go from door to door offering their services, and pick up just sufficient to prevent themselves from perishing by famine. What proportion of morals and learning can flow from such a source into the mind of the ragged young pupil, can easily be imagined, but cannot be reflected upon without serious concern. A gentleman of undoubted veracity stated, not long since, before the Dublin Association for distributing Bibles and Testaments amongst the poor, that whole parishes were without a Bible.

With an uncommon intellect, more *exercised than cultivated*, the peasantry have been kept in a state of degradation, which is too well known, and which will be touched upon in a future part of this sketch.

Their native urbanity to each other is very pleasing; I have frequently seen two boors take off their hats and salute each other with great civility. The expressions of these fellows upon meeting one another, are full of cordiality. One of them in Dublin met a camrogue, in plain English, a boy after his own heart, who, in the sincerity of his soul, exclaimed, 'Paddy! myself's glad to see you, for in troth I wish you well.' 'By my shoul, I knows it well,' said the other, 'but you have but the half of it', that is, the pleasure is divided. If you ask a common fellow in the streets of Dublin which is the way to a place, he will take off his hat, and if he does not know it, he will take care not to tell you so (for nothing is more painful to an Irishman than to be thought ignorant). He will either direct you by an appeal to his imagination, which is ever ready, or he will say, 'I shall find it out for your honour immediately'; and away he flies into some shop for information, which he is happy to be the bearer of, without any hope of reward.

Their hospitality when their circumstances are not too wretched to display it, is remarkably great. The neighbour or the stranger finds every man's door open, and to walk in without ceremony at meal-time, and to partake of his bowl of potatoes, is always sure to give pleasure to every one of the house, and the pig is turned out to make room for the gentleman. If the visitor can relate a lively tale, or play upon any instrument, all the family is in smiles, and the young will begin a merry dance, whilst the old will smoke after one another out of the same pipe, and entertain each other with stories. A gentleman of an erratic turn was pointed out to me, who with his flute in his hand, a clean pair of stockings and a shirt in his pocket, wandered through the country every summer. Wherever he stopped the face of a stranger made him welcome, and the sight of his instrument doubly so. The best seat, if they had any, the best potatoes and new milk, were allotted for his dinner; and clean straw, and sometimes a pair of sheets, formed his bed; which, although frequently not a bed of roses, was always rendered welcome by fatigue, and the peculiar bias of his mind.

Disembarking for a tour of Ireland, from William Wilson's *The Post-Chaise Companion, or Traveller's Directory Through Ireland*. First printed in 1784, the book was a great success with late 18th century English travellers in Ireland, and it continued in new editions through 1813. It was the first English tour book of Ireland published in Dublin as well as in London.

J. C. Curwen

OBSERVATIONS ON THE STATE OF IRELAND,
Principally Directed to its Agriculture and Rural Population; in a Series of Letters Written on a Tour Through that Country

John Christian Curwen (1756-1828) became the Member of Parliament from Carlisle, Cumberland, in 1796. His own family name was Christian, but he adopted his heiress wife's name. By education he was an agriculturalist, and as a politician he concerned himself with that area and its logical extension into social welfare. Several pamphlets, probably transcripts of speeches, appeared under his name on subjects such as the corn laws, the feeding of stock, and a 'Plan for Bettering the Condition of the Labouring Classes'. All preceded *Observations on the State of Ireland* (1818).

The occasion of Curwen's tour in Ireland was his retirement from parliament. Though his continuing interest in agricultural reform is apparent in all these letters, his purpose, as described in the opening one, was 'to divert my thoughts from home, and the happy current of their accustomed channel'. In the period following the Act of Union, Ireland represented a convenient diversion for a reform-minded vacationer. As Curwen wrote in that opening letter, 'What an inexpressible pleasure should I partake — how lasting would be the gratification, should any suggestion of mine be the fortunate means of conferring on the Irish peasant the luxury of one comfort, or in any way to improve the abject state of this generous, brave, and feeling people.'

Thus charity neatly dovetails with self-gratification. Like so many tourists of the period, Curwen is inspired by the landscape and troubled by the people. Obviously an aficionado of the aesthetic sublime, he is transported by the landscape into pleasurable reflection. Just as obviously a concerned liberal, he is provoked by the people into more somber, but perhaps just as pleasurable, reflections on the national character and the improvement it wants. In the early 19th century, as here in Curwen and above in John Carr, the term 'lower Irish' replaced the older denomination 'mere Irish'. That is an entirely appropriate neologism for an age and a type of visitor to Ireland devoted to the improving spirit and shocked by Irish deficiency in it. Curwen's *Observations* are characteristic of the period between Union and famine, a period when 'industry', as applied to the Irish, carried far more moral than material freight.

The text, slightly edited, is letters XXI and XXII of the first two-volume edition (London, 1818).

Illustration from *My Pocket Book* (1807), Edward Dubois's satire of John Carr's *The Stranger in Ireland*. It shows Carr on route to ship, overcome with emotion on leaving Ireland, and his valet, overburdened with the successful author's writing implements.

LETTER XXI.

Donegal, August 30, 1813.

T he town of Raphoe appears to have little to engage the attention: had the accommodations there been better, still we had not any object to induce a protracted stay. The spinning of linen yarn is carried on to some extent, and much flax is grown in the neighbourhood. On walking round the town, rather late in the evening, the general decorum and decency which prevailed were pleasing; we did not see or hear any thing in the public houses that indicated the least inebriety or want of good order. There is a considerable endowment for a school, which has some reputation.

On climbing the hill, at the end of the town, this morning, we had a most extensive view of the vale towards Derry; whence a more direct road passes hither through a very beautiful country. The husbandry on this side of Raphoe is tolerably well conducted.

Mr. Montgomery's seat, at Convoy, has the appearance of a fine place, surrounded with extensive woods. Cultivation is carried on to a considerable height on the sides of the hills; the use of lime is very general, and the rent of the land from forty to sixty shillings per acre. On quitting the village of Convoy, we got into a wild country, with a view of one still more alpine before us.

There are two distinct causes whence the mind derives infinite satisfaction in exploring a new country. The one is that of beholding all its resources made available, and the surface under a good system of cultivation; the other, is in estimating the improvements of which it may appear to be capable. Thousands of the neglected acres we have already seen might be advantageously appropriated to the growth of wood. In a circuit of one hundred and forty Irish miles, we have not met with a single experiment of modern planting sufficiently important to entitle the individual to a record of his name as a planter.

I cannot describe to you the pleasure I felt on the first glance of Mr. Stewart's plantations at Tyrehallam. This gentleman has clothed the sides of an extensive range of hills, including many hundred acres, with plantations of young trees, which had a general appearance of being in a thriving state. I much regretted I had no means of introduction to Mr. Stewart, with whose valuable improvements I should have been delighted in an opportunity of becoming better acquainted. As we passed a farm-house building by this gentleman, I could not resist requesting the workmen to convey to their employer the sentiments of admiration his plantations had inspired in the breast of a brother planter. This is by far the most spirited improvement we had yet seen in Ireland, and the first of magnitude to induce inquiry after its author.

By the side of a bog we observed a few miserable merino sheep. On dry and elevated pasture they might make a tolerably good shift; but on wet low ground thriving is not to be expected.

Two miles further on is a small town, the creation of Mr. Stewart, recently sold to Lord Montgomery. The crops are much later here than even in the county of Antrim. Mr. Arthur Young states, that there were no wheel cars in this part of the country when he visited it. At present a sledge is not to be seen; the Scotch carts being very common. In less than twenty years the Irish car will exist only in recollection.

Ballybofey being the only resting place, we were obliged to avail ourselves of it, though only seven miles from Raphoe. Although the town is small, yet from the number of new houses erecting, it has the appearance of being in an improving state. Mr. Brazil has a fine place, called Drumboe, opposite the town, about which there is much noble timber. The Foyle here, over which we passed, is a very handsome river.

After a steep ascent, for more than two miles, on leaving Ballybofey, we found ourselves on a wild, extensive range of flat bog, with a numerous insulated population scattered over its surface. In spite of a bright sun and clear sky, the scene was cold and melancholy. The cabins here at all times must be difficult of access, as there are no roads into the bog; and in the winter it should seem that its inhabitants must be entirely cut off from all communication with the lower country. This circumstance, which to us seemed to be a great misfortune, was by the natives considered as the peculiar advantage of their situation, and which, by the illicit practice of distilling, is turned to a good account. The bog furnishes abundance of fuel, and the difficulty of access enables them to brave the laws with impunity. The manufacture of poteen, or whiskey, made in small stills, is here carried on to a considerable extent, and the produce is held in high estimation. The trade, though lucrative, is, like most other contraband pursuits, in the end not often profitable.

While the lottery has enriched a few, it has impoverished and been the ruin of thousands. The appearance of the cabins by the side of the road, and the state of the potato grounds, bespoke the absence of industry; while the looks of the children, nearly in a state of nakedness, left nothing to conjecture as to the extent of wretchedness in which the parents existed. I made some inquiries of a little boy, which he answered in Gaelic; this furnished me with a pretence for following him home. His mother was employed in the cabin, by attending to four other children. In this miserable hut there was no division of apartments; the cattle occupied one end, the family the other; near the fire was a bed, which apparently served for the repose of all the human beings. I addressed some inquiries to the women, which she either could not, or would not comprehend. Her husband's attention was seemingly directed to the cows and pigs at the other end: contrary to the usual disposition of the Irish, he was by no means solicitous of any intercourse. The most extreme poverty and wretchedness were manifestly apparent, with the absence of what we had everywhere else constantly found, kindness and hospitality. As a further proof of their deplorable condition, we evidently afforded them relief when we quitted the cabin: even the potatoes, as if distempered by poverty, did not seem to thrive. Whether this was owing to the elevation of the ground, or to the want of management, I know not; possibly it might be imputable to both.

There was but one other cabin beyond this, before we entered on an immense tract, which seemed to be desolate and wholly uninhabited. As we advanced towards this dwelling, we observed a female running, with her hair dishevelled, in great haste along the high road, towards us. When she reached the cabin she stopped, and we were sufficiently near to note what passed. She seemed much agitated, and her information evidently produced great alarm in the man and his wife, who came to the door. The messenger had quickly told her tale, and was proceeding on her way by the time we came up; on which, a conversation of a few seconds ensued between the pair, and the woman came forward with a request for our assistance. The still hunters were at hand, and they should be ruined. They had a sack of malt belonging to a neighbour, which could not be removed without our assistance to lift it on her husband's back, which she was incapable of doing – as well she might, for the sack most probably contained six bushels. Strong incitement bestows a power of eloquence to feeling, that speaks irresistibly to the heart. The alarm and dismay of this hapless couple banished every other consideration, and though we might hazard a visit to Sligo gaol, we could not refuse our help. The sack was placed on the poor fellow's shoulders, – he bore its enormous weight with alacrity down an adjoining burn – was soon out of sight, and the good woman relieved from the threatened danger.

The confidence with which our assistance was asked is characteristic of that honorable principle which is eminently distinguishable among the lower Irish; an informer is rarely to be met with, from the detestation in which the character is held. So much confidence reposed in such utter strangers had something in it very grateful to our feelings; yet when the occurrence was afterwards subjected to reflection, it did not appear in a point of view quite so agreeable.

It was about the middle of the twelfth century, that the distillation of ardent spirits was introduced. These for a long time were only used medic-inally, under the name of '*Aqua vita or eau de vie*'. 'What is made in England,' says [Fynes] Moryson, 'is nothing so good as that which is brought out of Ireland; and the usquebagh is preferred to our *aqua vita*, because the mingl-ing of raisons, fennel seeds, and other things, mitigating the heat, and making the taste pleasant, makes it less inflame, and yet refresh the weak stomach with moderate heat and good relish.'

Illicit distillation augments the misery of the lower classes in Ireland, by destroying the habits of industry; while the baneful effects of indulging in spiritous liquors at a cheaper rate than otherwise they could be procured, injures their moral character. The defalcation sustained by the revenue is, comparatively, the least important concern; misery and crime, the consequences of inebriety in the people, are a sad reproach to our policy, and must so continue while tacitly promoted by the state. Can the apology of the half-starved apothecary, our 'poverty, but not our will, consents,' be received as a national excuse from the government, for the degradation of the subject? Surely this would be as ill-founded as the usual pretence for intoxication, – 'to drive away care'. Admitting its noxious influence to be capable of drowning for a moment the sorrows of the afflicted, the suspension of misery is purchased by subsequent increased torture to the sufferers, as well as to their families and friends. The flash of lightning in a night of darkness affords a momentary illumination, to render the obscurity more frightful. If any human being can be deemed excusable in seeking consolation from inebriety, it is the slave, who has no hope of release, or even of any mitigation of his sufferings – the consequence of sordid avarice and inhumanity on the part of others, unconnected with crime, or deserved punishment, on his own. As neither courage nor contrivance can relieve so unfortunate a being, to forget his privations for a time is a blessing – yet this alleviation may be obtained at too great a price, when purchased at the expense of mental and bodily force, which lessens the power of contending afterwards against the evil it was intended to remove.

On our arrival at the uninhabited region, to which I before adverted, one solitary hovel only was seen at a distance, standing in the midst of this extensive field of desolation, nearly opposite to Lough Alowin, a mile and a half in length, and half a mile in breadth. Here we entered the grand and awful pass of Barnmoor, a quarter of a mile wide, and three miles long, formed by mountains which rise to a considerable height on each side of a deep glen, the rugged tops and rocky sides of which contributed to the sombre appearance, by being partially blackened with heath. The gloom and chillness of the air, occasioned by the exclusion of the sun's rays – the death-like silence which here appeared to reign, impressed the mind with an indescribable solemnity and awe. For though there was little to comprehend from the destruction which nature held impending over our heads, and as little to dread from predatory man, yet there was something so truly inhospitable, melancholy, and desolate in the scene, that the passing moments were attended by feelings of a painful description, until we became relieved by the sight of some habitations at the bottom of the hill, yet two miles to the end of this dismal pass.

Appalling and forlorn as was the situation, it had allured a human being, though with scarcely human semblance, here to establish himself.

The cabin in which he and his wife exist is scarcely large enough to afford them shelter. He said, and I verily believe him, there were few who durst inhabit such a spot during the winter months, as the violence of the wind when rushing through the pass, had sometimes proved fatal to travellers, of which there had been instances in the two last winters of his residence. What possible choice could induce a human creature to fix his solitary abode in so frightful a place? The dread of most mortals – the envy of none – and where the glorious rays of the sun never penetrate? His answer in one word was explanatory and conclusive – necessity! – forced out of his former abode, friendless and forlorn, he had sought the occupation of a spot where he might continue undisturbed, a spot which no one should reclaim – and in making his election here, he had, assuredly, been successful. Repulsive as was the countenance of this unfortunate man, it were impossible not to compassionate his miserable situation: ill usage might have conspired to give a savage ferocity to his features, which his seclusion, and the terrific scenery about him, were not calculated to render more mild or hospitable.

Great as are the pleasures resulting from a contemplation of the sublime, and imposing as are the dismal objects in the scenery of this extraordinary pass, we were extremely happy to change our prospect, and once again enter into the habitable world. A number of cabins have been recently erected at the termination of the pass, where the land has been let at four shillings an acre, on leases for lives, and thirty years beyond their duration. As a proof of the profitable application of ashes, the luxuriant appearance of the potatoes and oats surprised me. The cultivation on the southern side of the mountain is carried to a great height; on the more elevated parts of which, a number of goats, belonging to the cabins below, were seen browsing.

As we descended into the plain, we had a magnificent view of the Ross mountains. Lough Eske is at the head of the valley which communicates with Donegal. This lake is of inconsiderable extent – the mountain at its head is rendered more sublime by being thickly covered with wood at its base. The scenery, on the whole, possesses much character, and is really beautiful. Mr. Young has a very pretty place at the foot of the mountain bordering on the lake. Char are taken here, and the water is reported to be of great depth. We understood that the red deer are found as inhabitants of the mountains. From this engaging spot we had the same distance to travel as through the pass of Barnmoor; but the undulations of our road, and cheerful richness of the scene, formed a most complete contrast to that melancholy drive.

It is from trifling incidents, that conclusions may not less frequently than justly be drawn of the general character of a people. As we approached the town of Donegal, we had a specimen of the deportment of individuals, somewhat elevated above the level of the commonality, to their supposed inferiors. A person of the former description was supplicated by a poor man who attended him for several hundred yards, urging his petition with his hat in his hand, and so he continued, though a number of people were passing, as long as they remained in our sight. The feelings with which I witnessed such conduct to a fellow creature were with great difficulty suppressed – I could scarce refrain from expressing my indignation and anger.

Donegal is a small town; the market-place is spacious: at one extremity of it is the ancient castle, the residence of the O'Donnells, now the property of Lord Arran. By the favor of Mr. Young we obtained a sight of its interior. The chimney-piece in one of the public rooms is very perfect, and from the appearance of the arms upon it, which are still entire, it should seem to be of modern date; on ascending to the battlement, we had a fine view of Donegal Bay.

Near the town is a mineral spring, which with the convenience of sea-bathing, draws much company to the place. There are great indications of wealth among the inhabitants. The salubrity and mildness of the climate have counterbalanced the numerous privations the people here have had to encounter from the earliest times. There is a tradition preserved in one of their ancient chronicles respecting longevity. The Irish report, and will swear it, that towards the west, they have an island where the inhabitants live so long, that when they are weary and burthened with life, their children in charity bring them to die on the shore of Ireland, as if the island would not permit them to die upon it. In modern times the Countess of Desmond, who lived to the age of about one hundred and forty years, is said to have been able to go on foot, four or five miles to the market town, and was accustomed weekly so to do in her last years. Not many years before she died, she had all her teeth renewed.

The port is accessible to vessels of two hundred tons burden; and in the bay, there is a considerable herring fishery. Within half a mile of the town are the ruins of a Franciscan monastery, founded in 1474, by Odokoe O'Donnell and Penelope his wife; it is a favorite burial place of the Catholics. The site of the building is very beautiful. The quarries in this neighbourhood yield the best millstones of any procured in Ireland, and a considerable number of them are annually exported. We understood there were a great number of protestants in this neighbourhood, whence to Ballyshannon being ten miles – I must bid you farewell.

J.C.C.

LETTER XXII.

Ballyshannon, August 31, 1813.

The road for the first four miles afforded neither a view of the country nor any thing worthy of remark, excepting some fine quarries of white free stone, which we were informed were the roof to coal that had recently been discovered. Generally speaking, the stratification of Ireland, in those places where the limestone does not prevail, is too much broken to afford a reasonable hope of finding any extensive field of this valuable mineral.

We had a long and tiresome ascent to Scotch Thomond, without any indication of our labors being requited on gaining the summit; when, however, a most surprising view burst suddenly on us, resembling in effect that of a panorama. The sublime, the beautiful, and picturesque, all contributed, with a descending sun and clear atmosphere, to exhibit a distinct prospect of no common or usual description. The first object that attracted our attention, and indeed the most singular one, was the foreground; this consisted of a double row of hills below us: in the upper range, I could distinguish eleven of beautiful rotundity, covered with ripening grain and potatoes; and in some instances, where they were enclosed with a few trees, they had more the appearance of Fairy Land than a portion of Ireland. The length occupied by these hills might be about two miles, the breadth something less. There appeared to be little interval or separation between the two rows: the hills of the outward row gradually sloped down to the sea. The irregular strips of grain and potatoes, the crops of which were exuberant, had a singular effect; giving some of the hills the appearance of a harlequin's dress. I cannot express the sensation produced on my mind by this group of mountains in miniature, which would form a most unique and beautiful landscape. To our right, about two miles below the station we had taken, was seen the spacious bay of Donegal; probably not less than six miles from shore to shore, and fifteen from its termination to the ocean, where the magnificent mountains of Ross end in a promontory, and form the entrance on one side, while the Sligo hills form on the other the opposite and more distant boundary of the bay: among the latter, Benbulben is particularly conspicuous.

The declining rays of the sun, irradiating the surface of the sea, presented to our view an extensive sheet of burnished gold; and in reflecting its warm and glowing tints over the nearer objects, completed the magic of a scene which would have kindled enthusiasm and rapture in the coldest and most insensible individual. The first sensation with which I became affected was astonishment – this was succeeded by the inspiration of unbounded admiration! The effects of both can never be effaced from my recollection. Reluctantly did I bid this delightful prospect farewell; and nothing but the rapid approach of night could have compelled us to quit a scene of such novelty and fascination. As far as we could judge, the remainder of the road was through a poor and ill-cultivated country.

The valley of Ballyshannon is very fertile, as appeared by the excellence of the crops of grain. The town stands on the declivity of a hill sloping to the river Erne. The church is on a rising ground above the town, and is a fine object. A great number of new houses are building, and every thing indicates Ballyshannon to be an improving place. An island of rock above the bridge, which is handsome, divides the current of the river, where are placed coops for taking the salmon, some of which are cured on the spot; this is understood to be a fishery of considerable importance. Lands near the town let from five to eight pounds an acre.

It was our wish to have taken post-horses to Enniskillen, and to have seen Lough Erne. We were, however, for some time unable to procure a conveyance of any kind. At length, a post-boy, who was in attendance on a party, with some difficulty was prevailed on to let us have one of his horses, on a positive engagement that it should be back by nine o'clock. We started at five; but the badness of our hired animal prevented our reaching the distance we proposed going; and we proceeded no farther than Belleek. Church Hill was yet two miles from us; this it was impossible to accomplish without forfeiting my word: we were consequently obliged to relinquish our promised view of this favorite lake. The falls of the Erne at Belleek are very picturesque, and, under any other circumstances, would have well repaid the trouble of the visit.

The general description given of Lough Erne induces a supposition that it possesses more of the characteristics of beauty than any of the other lakes in Ireland. We had now great reason to regret that our original arrangements for this tour had not been better made; having started too late in the season for such a journey as we had undertaken. At Belleek are the remains of an unfinished canal. The completion of this work would have been attended with many advantages to the country.

We were yesterday somewhat surprised with the new character assumed by the mendicants, who travel here *en famille*. The heads of each party are furnished with sacks, cans, and sometimes tea-kettles. Few refuse to supply them either with potatoes or butter-milk. So extended are the rights of hospitality in this country, that any stranger entering a house at meal times may, without ceremony, sit down and partake with the family. Distress never fails to moisten the eye, and wants no advocate to reach the heart of an Irishman.

There is a vivacity in the common people that both interests and amuses – great fertility in expedients, and consummate good humour in tolerating grievances. John Bull would be out of patience, and often out of humour, before he found a remedy for evils which are here constantly met by an expedient! Whilst I write, a proof of the fact is at my elbow. A chest of drawers in which the paraphernalia of the females, as well as the table linen, clean and dirty, are kept, has no lock; the want of this security is supplied by the absence of handles, so that whenever the drawers are resorted to, recourse is had to some new expedient. Three times have I been disturbed – the first essay for a rummage was by the assistance of a fork – this failing, the damsel went in search of a key, which on her return proved to be the sugar breaker! Equally judicious were the other attempts, none of which were made, but in full confidence of a successful expedient! Simple as is this instance, it presents a strong trait of the Irish character. The want of method and order, and the careless indifference in not profiting by the experience of the past, produce and establish inconveniences that get confirmed, and descend to succeeding generations: 'Sufficient for the day is the evil thereof', is here construed literally into taking 'no thought for the morrow'. The same want of reflection and forethought seems to pervade all persons, and every department. How different are the arrangements of an inn in England, where the presence and superintendence of the master and mistress keep their servants attentive to their duty, and every thing in due order. Here there appears to be no check on servants – no solicitude or care in the master – all is left to hazard; and while landlords must suffer prodigiously by such negligence, their guests are greatly inconvenienced – but complaining avails little. We have twenty miles to Sligo, without any inn conveniently placed at which to stop. Adieu.

J.C.C.

A pre-famine image of available and reliable economic resources: the Custom House and the Corn Exchange of Dublin in an 1820 engraving.

Henry D. Inglis

A JOURNEY THROUGHOUT IRELAND
During the Spring, Summer, and
Autumn of 1834

Henry David Inglis (1795-1835) was born in Edinburgh, the only son of a
Scottish lawyer. Although trained for a business profession, he discovered
his true talent at the age of thirty, when he published the travelogue *Tales
of the Ardennes* under the pen name Derwent Conway. In the remaining ten
years of his life, he established himself as one of the most popular travel
writers of his day. Under his own name he published records of his travels
in Norway, Switzerland, Spain, and the Tyrol, as well as a novel called *The
New Gil Blas*.

Inglis's *Journey Throughout Ireland* was published in the year of his death
in London. The book was a great success: as the *Dictionary of National
Biography* notes, it was 'quoted as an authority by speakers in Parliament
in 1835 and reached a fifth edition in 1838'. The *Journey Throughout Ireland*
is an exhaustive, two-volume report of his itinerary. The first portion
excerpted below comes from the 'Introduction', which describes the
contrast between wealth and poverty in Dublin in details surprisingly
graphic for a time accustomed to reports of Dublin wealth and Irish
country squalor. The second portion, Chapter XII of the complete work,
is a description of a County Clare 'assizes', or general court. Inglis' distaste
for the residual legal codes of Ireland is a muted version of the outright
disgust expressed two and a half centuries earlier by the Elizabethan
visitors and a reminder of the longevity of Irish customs presumed by some
to disappear on introduction of self-evidently superior English ones.

Inglis is a fairly benevolent interpreter of the scenes he witnessed.
Ultimately, however, like his contemporaries he can find no possible
explanation for the mores of Irish life than defects of character (i.e. morality). Like Thackerary after him, Inglis sketches the evidence of these
defects, even brutal faction fighting, in fairly farcical fashion. Hence the
machinations of 'liars and cheats' are presented in the comical mode of
O'Sullivan assaulting 'O'something else'. It is in such a phase of English
interpretation of the Irish that the laughable belief in fairies becomes, quite
suddenly, a staple of a new stereotype.

The text of both excerpts is that of the first edition (London: Whittaker
& Co., 1835).

William Makepeace Thackeray's illustration of an Irish assizes, which is also a subject of Henry D. Inglis. Thackeray watched assizes in Waterford. 'The court-house is as beggarly and ruinous as the rest of the neighborhood', he wrote in *The Irish Sketch Book*, 'smart-looking policemen kept order about it'.

Early on a fine spring morning, I crossed the bay of Dublin, and entered Kingstown [i.e. Dun Laoghaire] harbour a little after sunrise. The bay of Dublin has been so often described, that it needs neither description nor eulogy from me. I will only observe, that if it be deficient in some of those attractions which characterise the rival bays of more southern climes, it will yield to none, in the extent and depth of its arch, or in the form and character of its mountain boundaries.

When I stepped on shore at Kingstown, I looked around me with the same curiosity and interest which I have been accustomed to feel on setting foot on other foreign lands; for my ignorance of Ireland might well justify me in looking upon Ireland as a foreign land, and upon her people as foreigners. This I consider an advantage: for unless a country be so regarded, I question if the traveller will be likely to record those minute and common things, which often throw so much light upon the genius and condition of a people; and by the omission of which, the graphic character of a work is so much impaired. It was somewhat too early in the morning to find much food for observation. I saw beggars as importunate and as needy as elsewhere – porters as loquacious, but more orderly – waiters as eloquent in urging the claims of their hotels – and a new race, the drivers of the jaunting-cars, vociferous in their recommendations of the superior advantages of their vehicles, in convenience and cheapness, over all rival and more ambitious conveyances.

First impressions of Dublin are decidedly favourable. Entering from Kingstown, there is little to be seen that is unworthy the approach to a capital; and without passing through any of those wretched suburbs which stretch in many other directions, one is whirled at once into a magnificent centre, where there is an assemblage of all that usually gives evidence of wealth and taste, and of the existence of a great and flourishing city.

A stranger arriving in Dublin in Spring, as I did, will be struck, even less by the architectural beauty of the city, than by other kinds of splendour: I allude to the indulgences of luxury, and the apparent proofs of wealth that are everywhere thrust upon the eye – the numerous private vehicles that fill the streets, and even blockade many of them; the magnificent shops for the sale of articles of luxury and taste, at the doors of which, in Grafton Street, I have counted upwards of twenty handsome equipages; and in certain quarters of the city, the number of splendid houses, and 'legion' of liveried servants. But a little closer observation and more minute inquiry, will in some measure correct these impressions; and will bring to mind the well-known and well-founded proverb, that 'it is not all gold that glitters'.

And if caution be necessary in drawing conclusions respecting the wealth of Dublin from what meets the eye, tenfold caution is required in drawing any conclusion respecting the condition of Ireland, from even the *real* prosperity of Dublin. I saw comparatively few shops closed, comparatively few houses untenanted. No one complained of want of business: and it is a fact, that all the coachmakers were in such full employment, that no contract could be obtained for building coaches on the Dublin and Kingstown railroad. But for my own part, I would rather see a lack of employment among the coachmakers, if this were a proof that Irish landlords remained on their estates, and ran jaunting-cars in place of carriages through their counties; and I would rather see less competition for fine houses, and smaller fines paid for leases of shops, if this were a proof that there was less influx of country gentry into Dublin.

But this appearance of even Dublin prosperity, is somewhat deceptive. I have already hinted that 'it is not all gold that glitters'; by which, I mean, that the Dublin tradesman sets up his car and his country-house, with a capital, that a London tradesman would look upon but as a beginning for industry to work upon: and I believe it may be asserted with truth, that there is less profitable trade in Dublin now, than was found some years ago. Dublin formerly possessed an extensive, safe, and very lucrative commission trade from both the West Indies and England; but the facilities of steam-navigation are now so great, that the country dealers throughout Ireland, who formerly made their purchases in Dublin, now pass over to England and there lay in their stocks. This may possibly be good for the public – I do not know whether it be or not, – I merely state a fact not favourable to the prosperity of Dublin.

In walking through the streets of Dublin, strange and striking contrasts are presented between grandeur and poverty. In Merrion Square, St. Stephen's Green, and elsewhere, the ragged wretches that are sitting on the steps, contrast strongly with the splendour of the houses and the magnificent equipages that wait without: pass from Merrion Square or Grafton Street, about three o'clock, into what is called the Liberty, and you might easily fancy yourself in another and distant part of Europe. I was extremely struck, the first time I visited the outskirts of the city in the direction of the Phoenix Park, with the strong resemblances to the population of Spanish towns, which the pauper population of Dublin presented. I saw the same rags, and apparent indolence – the result of a want of employment, and a low state of moral feeling: boys with bare heads and feet, lying on the pavement, whose potato had only to be converted into a melon or a bit of wheaten bread, to make them fit subjects for Murillo; and houses and cottages in a half-ruined state, with paneless windows or no windows at all. I was also struck with the small number of provision-shops. In London every fifth or sixth shop is a bacon and cheese-shop. In Dublin, luxuries of a different kind offer their temptations. What would be the use of opening a bacon shop, where the lower orders, who are elsewhere the chief purchasers of bacon, cannot afford to eat bacon, and live upon potatoes?

As I have mentioned the lower orders in Dublin, I may add, that the house in which I lived in Kildare Street, being exactly opposite to the Royal Dublin Society, which was then exhibiting a cattle-show, I was very favourably situated for observing among the crowd collected, some of those little traits which throw light upon character and condition. I remarked in particular, the great eagerness of every one to get a little employment, and earn a penny or two. I observed another less equivocal proof of low condition. After the cattle had been fed, the half-eaten turnips became the prerequisite of the crowd of ragged boys and girls without. Many and fierce were the scrambles for these precious relics; and a half-gnawed turnip, once secured, was guarded with the most vigilant jealousy, and was lent for a mouthful to another longing tatterdemalion, as much apparently as an act of extraordinary favour, as if the root had been a pine-apple. Yet these mouthfuls were freely given; and I have seen, that where two boys contended who should take charge of a gentleman's horse, the boy who obtained the preference and got the penny or twopence, divided it with his rival. These were pleasing traits; and were indicative of that generosity of character which displays itself in so many kindly shapes; but which is perhaps also in some degree the parent of that improvidence, to which the evils of absenteeism are partly to be ascribed.

*   *   *

A small Irish county town, during assizes, presents a spectacle that is never seen in England; for even supposing the calendar to be as long, in an English as in an Irish county, which it never is, the difference in the character of the cases to be tried, materially affects the aspect of the town and its population. In England, a case of murder or manslaughter, brings to the country town only the near relations of the party to be tried, and perhaps, of the party prosecuting; but in Ireland, things are on a different scale. The English murder is a private act, perpetrated by some ruffian for the sake of gain: the Irish homicide has been committed for no reason at all; and not by one cold-blooded ruffian, but by a crowd of demi-barbarians, who meet for the purpose of fighting; and who have no other reason for fighting, than because one half of the number are called O'Sullivan and the other O' something else: so that when a manslaughter is to be prosecuted at an Irish assize, the case does not bring up merely the accused and his one or two witnesses, but it brings half the 'boys' in the county who bear the same name as the accused; and as many more, of the same name as the man who was killed, every one of the former, ready to kiss the book, and swear that the boy accused of the homicide, never handled a shillelagh, or lifted a stone, or was seen in a 'scrimmage' in his days; and every one of the latter as ready to swear, that the boy that was killed, was the most peaceable boy that ever bore his name, and that he was killed for no reason at all. Besides these homicide cases, which are peculiar to an Irish assize, prosecutions of any kind bring together a greater number of persons than in England – for be it a robbery, or a rape, or any other crime, of which a man is accused, all his relations come forward to swear an alibi. It may be easily conceived, therefore, what a motley crowd fills the streets of an Irish county town at the time of an assize.

Nor is it only the number of persons, but their eagerness also, that strikes a stranger. Besides the groups that throng every part of the open streets, and who are always in earnest talk, dense crowds are collected at the door of every attorney's office, and no one of this brotherhood can walk a yard, without having his sleeve pulled by half-a-dozen 'boys' or women, all interested for or against somebody; and entreating his honour to get them justice: which may mean, either to get a man hanged, or to save a man from hanging.

The most numerous class of cases at most Irish assizes, is that which is facetiously denominated *fair* murders; that is, homicides committed at fairs; and I do not know any means, by which so much insight is to be obtained into the character of the Irish peasantry, and into the condition of the country, and state of things among the lower classes of society, as by listening to these prosecutions for *fair* murders. There were many of these prosecutions at the Ennis assizes; and, although I had already heard much of the factions, into which the peasantry are divided, I had no conception of the extent of this evil, nor of the bitterness with which this spirit of faction is attended. However these factions may have originated, there is now no distinction among their adherents, excepting that which arises from the possession of a different name. The O'Sullivans are as distinct a people from the O'Neills, as the Dutch from the Belgians. The factions have chiefs, who possess authority. Regular agreements are made to have a battle; the time agreed upon is generally when a fair takes place; and, at these fights, there is regular marshalling, and 'wheeling'; and, as for its being a crime to break a 'boy's' head, such an idea never enters the brain of any one.

The spirit of faction is brought into court by almost every witness in these prosecutions. I saw a witness, a woman, brought in support of the prosecution for a homicide committed on some cousin, who, on being desired to identify the prisoners, and the court-keeper's long rod being put into her hand, that she might point them out, struck each of them a smart blow on the head. As for finding out the truth, by the mere evidence of the witnesses, it is generally impossible. Almost all worth knowing, is elicited on the cross-examination: and it is always, by the appearance and manner of the witness, more than by his words, that the truth is to be gathered. All the witnesses, examined for the prosecution, were, by their own account, mere lookers on at the battle; nor stick, nor stone had they. *Their* party had no mind to fight that day; but, in making this assertion, they always take care to let it be known, that, if they had had a mind to fight, they could have handled their shillelaghs to some purpose. On the other hand, all the witnesses for the prisoner aver just the same of themselves; so that it is more by what witnesses won't tell, than by what they do tell, that truth is discovered. Half the witnesses called, on both sides, have broken heads; and it is not unfrequently by a comparison of the injuries received on both sides, and by the evidence of the doctor, that one is helped to the truth.

It will be easily seen, from what I have said, that I found ample confirmation of what I had often heard, – the small regard for veracity among the Irish peasantry, and their general disregard of an oath. To save a relation from punishment, or to punish any one who has injured a relation, an Irish peasant will swear anything. This would be called, by some, hatred of the law; but, although, in swearing falsely, the Irish peasant wishes to defeat the ends of justice, he does not do so, merely because he hates justice and the law, but because he thinks he is bound to save his relation, or any one of his faction. If the name of the man who was killed be O'Grady, then every witness, who comes up to be sworn for the prosecution, is also an O'Grady; or, if they be women, they were O'Gradys before they were married; and, if the name of the prisoner be O'Neill, then all the witnesses, for the defence, are O'Neills; or, if there be any exceptions in name, still there is a relationship of some kind.

The factions, which occasion the atrocities of which we, in England, know very little, (for the cases reported from the Irish assizes, in the English papers, are, generally, cases in some degree political, and are seldom, or ever, the homicides arising out of fights at fairs), have never been energetically met by the law and the magistracy. Some years ago, when trading magistrates were common, their non-interference was purchased by services performed. If a magistrate, living in the vicinity of a place where two great factions wished to try their strength, had a meadow ready for mowing – or a field of wheat ripe for the sickle – or wished to lay in his winter's turf – twenty or thirty men, of both factions, would volunteer their labour, and refuse, not only pecuniary recompense, but refreshment even: the fight was suffered to go on; and the breakers of heads were leniently dealt with. These days, I believe, are passed, or fast passing; but there is still far too little energy shewn in putting down faction. It is true, that in many remote places – and it is often in the remotest spots that these encounters take place – there are no military, and few policemen; but a resident magistrate, if he be a man fit for his office, may always be previously informed upon these matters. He knows that a faction exists in his neighbourhood; he knows that the fair is drawing near; he knows, that at every fair, a fight takes place; and where any agreement has been made to fight out the quarrel at the fair, he may, without any difficulty, obtain the most accurate information; and every one knows how easily a mob, especially an Irish mob, is reduced to obedience by a very trifling display of firmness and force. I look upon it as most essential to the prosperity of Ireland, that these factions should be put down. They are nearly as inimical to the investment of capital, and nearly as much encouragers of absenteeism, as many of those other kinds of agitation, which are more familiar to us: and I will again take the liberty of repeating my belief, that the substitution of a stipendiary, for an unpaid magistracy, is essential to the peace of Ireland. It is quite unreasonable to expect that an unpaid magistracy, situated as that magistracy is in Ireland, should do their duty. But, to return to the Ennis assizes.

The most numerous classes of cases (with one exception), and the most important class, as throwing the greatest light on the character and state of the people, were those homicides of which I have spoken. The exception in point of number of cases, is rape: of these cases, I think nearly forty were entered for trial; but only a very few of that number were heard; and all of them terminated in acquittal. In nine cases out of ten, the crime is sworn to, merely for the purpose of getting a husband; and the plan generally succeeds. The parties are married before the cause is called for trial; and I have myself seen an earnest negotiation carried on under the piazzas of the court-house, a little while before the case was called. There was the 'boy' indicted for a capital crime, but out on bail, as he generally is; and the girl, about to swear away a man's life; and the attorneys, and a large circle of relations, all trying to bring about a marriage, before Pat should be called to appear, and answer to the indictment that he, 'not having the fear of God before his eyes, and being instigated by the devil', did so and so. In the case to which I was a listener, Pat and the fair one could not agree: the trial went on; and Pat was acquitted.

The number, and nature of these cases, certainly indicate no very high state of morals; for in every one of them, circumstances have occurred, which afford to the prosecutrix *some* ground of charge; and the amicable termination of these cases, shews how small the ground of the *capital* charge is. In these cases too, the want of veracity is strongly displayed; and it certainly impresses a stranger with no very favourable idea of female character, to find a girl falsely swearing a capital charge against a man whom she is willing at that moment to marry.

I saw tried, one of those singular cases of abduction, which very frequently occur in Ireland; and which also throw considerable light on the state of society among the lower ranks. Sham cases of abduction are frequent. The 'boy' and the girl are agreed; but the girl's relations being dissentient, owing to her being an heiress, and entitled to a better match, it is made up between the young people, that the girl shall be carried away by apparent force. The youth makes known the case to his friends, and collects a number of associates: they come during the night to the house of the girl, force open the door, seize upon the maid, who, though 'nothing loth', screams and makes all the opposition in her power, place her on horseback, and, after escorting her a sufficient distance, deliver her over to the 'boy', on whose account the abduction was got up. The charge of abduction which I saw tried at Ennis, was a real abduction however, and a very shameless one, attended with circumstances of great cruelty; and originating, as indeed they always do, in love of money. These abductions are most detrimental to the peace of the country; because a feud is instantly generated, between the relatives of the girl, and those of the aggressor; and many subsequent fights invariably result from these outrages.

One of the cases tried at the Ennis assizes, was in many respects similar to that celebrated case, which was the foundation of that excellent novel, 'The Collegians'.* A man was tried for the murder of a girl whom he had seduced; he killed her, and buried her in a peat-rick; and the similarity is the stronger, inasmuch as he was at the time, in treaty to marry another, not so high-born a damsel indeed, as Anne Chute; but high enough and rich enough, to induce him to sacrifice *his* Elie O'Connor. In this case, one of the witnesses, on being desired to identify the prisoner, and being asked the question, 'Is that the man?' turned round and recognizing the prisoner, said, 'That's him', and added, 'How are you Paddy?' nodding familiarly and good-humouredly to the accused. The man was convicted, and hanged.

Another case tried, arose out of one of those disputes, which so frequently originate in the possession of, and competition for, land. It was a case wherein a widow paid an enormous rent for a bit of potato land; and the rent not being paid, and the mischievous power of distraining [i.e., repossession] being resorted to, the possessor endeavoured to save some portion of the potatoes. This gave rise to a fight; and the fight occasioned manslaughter. In this case, there was much false swearing, and much difficulty in arriving at the truth; and the case strongly impressed upon me the conviction, that the power of distraining, in the hands of the lower orders, is a most mischievous power.

I noticed, that great importance is attached to kissing the book; and sometimes, this ceremony is required, for greater security, to be performed two or three times. Without kissing the book, a witness looks upon his oath as very imperfectly taken; and it is necessary that in the act of kissing, the witness be narrowly watched, lest he kiss his own thumb – with which he holds the book – in place of the book itself.

I noticed also, in the examination of one of the witnesses, a proof of the prevailing belief in the 'good people', or fairies. A witness, being asked upon his oath, whether a certain individual could have made his way out of a room, the door and windows of which had been fastened, said, with the utmost gravity, it was impossible he could have got out, unless by enchantment; meaning by this, without the assistance of the good people.

To attend an Irish assize, is certainly not the means by which a stranger is likely to obtain favourable impressions of Irish character. Few of its favourable traits are exhibited there; while all the darker shades are made

---

*Popular novel, published 1829, by Gerald Griffin (1803-1840).

but too manifest. Want of veracity, on the most solemn occasion on which veracity is ever called for, is but too plainly established. We find the reverse of that straight-forwardness, which is so delightful to see exhibited in the examination of a witness. If positive falsehood will serve the end, it is unhesitatingly resorted to; and as for telling the *whole* truth, I saw no one instance of it.

But the most striking defect of character which is brought to light, is a perfect contempt of human suffering, and an utter disregard even of the value of human life. Weapons, of the most deadly description are brought into court as evidence – sticks and whips loaded with lead and stones that might crush the head of a horse. A ruffian may occasionally be found in England, who would slay a man to become possessed of his purse; but I greatly question, whether out of Ireland, fifty men could be found in any one parish, in any country in Europe, ready to beat one another's brains out with sticks and stones, and all but glorifying in the deed. And, as I have already observed, the same ferocity which has been exhibited at the fight, is brought into court: false oaths are the substitutes for weapons; and by these, witnesses seek to avenge the death of a relative who has been more unfortunate, but probably not more criminal, than the accused.

I was much struck at Ennis, as I had been at Traleee, with the acuteness and talent of the Irish attorneys. Their cross-examinations of witnesses were admirable: certainly not surpassed by the very best cross-examinations I ever heard from the mouth of an English barrister.

A day or two before the conclusion of the Clare assizes, I left Ennis for Limerick; returning by a road different from that by which I had gone to Ennis, and through an equally interesting and fertile country.

By a Cosmopolite

THE SPORTSMAN IN IRELAND

In the 19th century the term 'cosmopolite', for a citizen of the world free of national prejudice, was customarily opposed to the term 'patriot'. This sportsman-cosmopolite believes that because he is above the partisan politics underlying 'the Irish problem' the country and its people will reveal themselves to him 'as they are, and not as political partisans would paint them'. Of course, such an attitude is itself inseparable from its place in the history of English relations with Ireland. This is an accessibility presumed because of parliamentary union, which renders shores 'artificial', and not yet definitively demolished by famine. The sheer unexamined arrogance of this remarkable document's endeavor to 'unite the pleasure of wild sports with the philosophy of statistical observation' explodes its own pretension to true cosmopolitanism. It would have interested Spenser, for example, to know that the only preparation needed for a thorough anatomy of Ireland was a good wool suit.

The sportsman here is notably parochial in his sentimentalizing of the Irish, an operation that throughout this two-volume work typically takes the form of dwelling on children and of treating Irish adults as juveniles. Such an operation, of course, usefully implies a paternal role for the English, who astonishingly enough are admonished here for their 'indiscriminate generosity'. In the immediate context here that role has been exercised by the Poor Relief Act of 1838, which extended the English poor law system of workhouses to Ireland, and by Catholic Emancipation of 1829, which was effectively extended to political representation by the Municipal Reform Act of 1840. These are the underpinnings of the sportsman's magisterial final suggestion that the Irish can be 'nurtured and cherished by kindness and education'.

These selections are taken from the first and fifth chapters of the first edition of *The Sportsman in Ireland*, published in London in 1840.

Thackeray's 1843 sketch of market day in Dunmanway for *The Irish Sketch Book*: 'swarms of peasants in their blue cloaks'.

W|ho that has heard of the resources and beauties of the Emerald Isle – who that has listened to the torrents of abuse levelled against those who are at once termed her patriots and her destroyers, her liberators and enslavers – who that has heard of the trackless mountains, the rushing torrents, the splendid rivers unsullied by a line, or of the wild birds that are undisturbed on her desolate coasts; the honest generosity of character, the hospitable feelings, yet, albeit, the murderous villany, the bloodthirsty relentlessness of her children – who that has only *heard* of all these, but will determine at once to be convinced of the truth or falsehood of the accounts put forth – will at once seize his rod and his gun, and, delivering himself up for fortune, make his journey unite the pleasure of wild sports with the philosophy of statistical observation?

I, at all events, will for one; and, ere I revisit the artificial shore of my birth, the Irish as they are, and not as political partisans would paint them, shall be known to me.

My preparations were simple; and let me entreat all those who follow me to make their own so.

In the first place, let no London fly or rod maker impose on them by the delicate manufacture of their wares, but by all means let the gun-maker have his chance; take a good double-barrel, powder, and casts for bullets, and leave the rest to fortune and my direction; also a good woollen suit, one change for dress, a mackintosh, a well-strapped wallet – for there is much in its being well strapped.

These are all that can be required by or desirable to those who would really make the tour of a sportsman through Ireland. Every desirable comfort will follow in its proper place; and it should not be forgotten that the greatest inconvenience of travelling is the travelling with too many conveniences. But, as I hate people who would have to make their arrangements all tending inevitably to embarrass their progress and restrict their independence, we will suppose the usual horn-blowing has taken place, the usual number of now despised coachmen have been *feed*, and that we find ourselves half asleep and half awake at Bristol.

We judge of the distance of places by the time consumed in reaching them; in fact, time *is* distance, and Bristol is a heavy journey. Bristol itself is a sort of a *slow coach*. It has, by its paltry efforts at inordinate gain in the harbour dues, wrapped itself up in a dignified independence, while all other ports have surpassed its accommodations, and withdrawn its trade. Even the Great Western does not help it: we must still be bugled down, and cramped in four insides. But we are there.

And this is the Irish packet? You need not answer – I perceive it is. Those shoeless wretches, shivering under the March blasts, and crouching midst the packages for a momentary protection – the surly officers who have just presented them with their *free* passage to their native land; the hopeless gaze of that suffering mother, who deprives herself of her ragged shawl that she may shelter her still more suffering infant; all these proclaim the destination of the vessel. Midst the hoarse orders of the bluff comman-der she moves in stately grandeur down the river, and carries with her the farewells, the hopes, the happiness of many!

It is needless to describe the Clifton Rocks. I perceive the pencils of the lady passengers are at work, while the obsequious gentlemen surrounding them gaze on the performances, and admire the wonders of nature, but more those of art.

The massive rocks of the extended scene give rise to general hilarity, and the ever-varying range on each side calls forth the admiration of the Creator's works.

But the sea-breeze now breaks on us The hitherto stately vessel yields to the coming tide. Now shawls and cloaks are in requisition, and the sketches are left for future finishing and future encomiums. Less is heard of the beauty of surrounding objects, and more of personal comfort.

The cabin is sought by some, where fires, books, and all the comforts which the gaudy packet can afford, are at hand. The sea rises – the scudding squalls dash over the angry spray – there is more silence and more self among the previously gay and joyous crowd on the front deck; each looks to himself; while the storm increases, and the rains descend.

Let us survey the deck. Not one of the many, now wrapped in all the comforts which art can supply, has condescended to do so. Each passenger has selected his bed, and made his inquiries for dinner; but where is to be *your* bed – where *your* dinner, ye homeless, hapless wanderers – cursed in your birth-place – whose crime is that you are the offspring of a doomed land! A land, beauteous to the eye, fertile in its resources, yet whose shipless harbours yawn in hospitality without a guest – upon whose shores the wild sea howls, and the angry billows alone unite to break the silence of a gloomy solitude!

See that father and mother, with their helpless race of children; behold them shivering in the bleak March blast, and now and then submitting to the spray which dashes over their half-covered limbs! That child, squalid and bare, crouching beneath the mother's scanty rags; behold her! She is human – those blue eyes seem to speak intelligence; she looks wistfully, beseechingly, yet modestly. It is for food she asks. Inquire their little history: it is the history of all. That father is strong, active, and not deficient in intelligence. You see he does not want feeling for those dependent on him; he has covered the children with his grey frieze coat, and bears the falling rain with a manly defiance. Unable to discharge the heavy imposts of his landlord and the tithe, he has been expatriated; he has sought what he imagined was the golden land; he has sought the English coast. Prejudice and the poor-laws have been his unconquerable foes. Employ-ment was nowhere to be found; and, after a year's travelling from place to place, during which the hedge and the sheep hovel have been his only covering, and the covering of his wife and little ones, he has at length been found guilty of being destitute, and condemned to – his native country. The surly officer, whom you saw speaking to him at Bristol, was employed to ship him and his family safely off by the packet. Their sea-store was supplied, their passage was paid. The bundle, which the enduring woman has hanging from her arm, contains potatoes; they have been already cooked, and you will see the father frequently distributing a portion among his trembling children – God help them! But their native land is now in sight. A joyous exclamation is heard among some – it is among the cabin passengers. Each runs to gain a glimpse of land – of Ireland – the place of our destination.

All are pleased, except only the miserable family whose patient endurance of the long sea passage, whose hunger the lowest of human food has barely appeased; – and from them, and those who surround them, no sound of delight is heard. The countenance of the oppressed father, as he shiveringly looks down upon his children, is marked by a stern misery; his native land is indifferent to his view; it almost excites horror. For him, alas, and his, no home is there prepared. He has no spot whereon to lie! No store, from which the wants of his little ones shall be supplied! To him, his native shores present only the barren rocks of desolation and despair. This is strange, and its cause is worth inquiry; for a cause there must be, why the child of a free country, able and willing to labour – asking only the meanest reward for his toil and zealous exertions – stained by no crime – should look to that free country, and demand but bread, yet be refused. There is a cause – a deep and damning one – 'if philosophy could find it out.'*

The morning broke; and who that has voyaged by steam or coach does not shrink at the remembrance of the peeping morn of March? The face of the ocean presents a cold cheerlessness, which even the sluggish sunrise does not dispel; its rays seem rather to render still more visible the ravages of watchfulness or inebriety. Every face is without a smile; the features are paralysed; even the mind is benumbed and depressed, and misery looks still more miserable.

The lower deck of the steamer was the parade of those who had known no other couch during the night. The wretched family I had before observed were still crouching under the packages; the father standing, in silent suffering, over them!

* * *

Affection, filial affection, is the strongest trait in the Irish character. In the course of all my travels never did I see that sacred affection violated. In the number of their children do the Irish peasantry rejoice – in the hope of an

---

Hamlet, II, ii, 392.

early family do they marry young. They calculate on their children as their wealth, and look upon their offspring as the resources from whence, in age and in sickness, they must derive their subsistence and their happiness. As yet there are no poor-laws – Nature steps in and supplies the place of legislation by the warm gratitude of the child to the parent. In every cottage may be seen the decrepit and the infirm of the family peacefully passing the remainder of their days, their wants supplied by their children; and I believe nothing would appear to an Irish mountaineer more unnatural than the neglect of filial duties. In England, the father, tired of the burden of his children, seeks to be freed from the alliance; and the child, not unfrequently seeking amidst the world a better home, neglects that of his infancy, and forgets the claims of those to whom his being and early nurture are owing. Too frequently may be seen the parents supplied by the parish with those necessaries which would have been unnoticed in the luxurious household of the child.

Nor does this state of things seem to create surprise, or to excite reflection on an ingratitude so generally shared. In Ireland it is otherwise; the *ban* would be put on that child who should neglect to nurture and provide for the authors of his being; and, though other virtues be neglected, no quarter would be shown to him who should forget the duties of the child to the parent.

By four in the morning Owen was on the alert, and, with pipe in mouth, rod in hand, was ready for the sport. We fagged up the stream about a mile above the bridge, where we found a broad expanse of water, not dignified by the name of a lake, but designated the *Inch*. Here I changed my roe for flies, and, after the second cast, found myself tolerably well engaged with a white trout. Not, however, quickly reeling up, I was suddenly astonished by a heavy weight, for which I was little prepared. I was not long in ignorance: a pike had taken a fancy to my trout. Of course I troubled him little. My fly-gut stood till I had convinced myself of the determined voracity of the creature, which would rather suffer himself to be restrained by the line than abandon his prey.

Owen had secured a tolerable salmon, and, as usual, the rains descended almost in heavy sheets of water rather than in separated particles. We agreed, therefore, to abandon our post at Ballyvourneen, and push on for Killarney.

To this end our arrangements were soon made. Leaving Owen to bring on the pony, I mounted the Cork and Killarney coach.

We soon reached the river Flesk, at the point where Clydagh pours in its waters, which form by their junction a broad and rapid stream, falling into the bosom of Killarney. On ascending one of the hills, the whole view at once burst on the sight. Lakes of immense extent, here and there dotted with islands, covered the expanse, and called forth the liveliest feelings of admiration. The wild beauties of Switzerland seemed here blended with a more sober variety of objects; while the anticipations of the sportsman are excited by the beauteous variety of water and mountain.

We now passed one of the prettiest modern objects in the neighbourhood of Killarney – a castle on an abrupt ridge of the Flesk, which, at the distance of the road, presents a very imposing appearance. It is named, from the builder and master, who has exhibited considerable taste in the choice of the site, Coltsman Castle.

Although the Flesk, which runs by the Castle, is at certain seasons celebrated for the variety of its fish, it is by no means a river to which I would direct the angler's attention. In the summer, when the waters get low, no fish are to be found beyond the smallest species of trout; but, in the autumn, when the mountain floods begin to descend, the whole tribe from the lakes of Killarney push up to sandy and gravelly beds to lay their spawn. This is the time when the spear is in requisition, as the large trout and salmon may be found in the shallowest parts, digging holes with a determination and strength that would hardly be ascribed to them. They are easily taken, but are out of season; and, though I have frequently fished this stream through the autumn, I never took one fish which was not sickly and poor. It would appear that the extensive waters of the lakes are necessary to the renovation of trout, as the sea is to the salmon after spawning.

As we approached the miserable cluster of houses which constitute the town of Killarney, there was a manifest alteration in the appearance of the peasantry; and the baleful effects of an indiscriminate generosity (if it may be so dignified) in the visitors to this spot, became everywhere conspicuous. There were two gentlemen on the coast, armed with every implement for the destruction of game and fish, but evidently as yet unseasoned to the climate. It was not difficult to collect that they were perfect gentlemen, their conduct throughout the journey from Cork having evinced irrefragable proofs of their claims. As the coach passed the ragged and shoeless creatures, one amused himself by throwing halfpence, and at length challenged a miserable-looking youth, who had pursued the coach, by the offer of half-a-crown if he would keep up with us a mile. The road was newly covered with broken flint, and the lad's anxiety to select the shortest way wholly overcame the caution which should have directed his steps. He had almost achieved the undertaking, when the loss of blood from his wounded feet, and want of power to continue the exertion, overcame all his efforts, and he sunk on the road amid the violent laughter of the liberal patron who had excited his attempt.

There is altogether a new character observable among the poor, and they are the chief inhabitants of Killarney; there is idleness exemplified in its most intense degree; and the effects of it, among all classes of expectants, are almost sufficient to deter the visitor from any long stay at these beautiful lakes.

Although, throughout Ireland – that is, in all places where the diffuse and indiscriminate extravagance of Englishmen has not yet polluted it – I had reason greatly to respect the general character of the Irish peasantry, I must except that numerous herd which has suffered from the baleful effects of a residence in Killarney. In general, the good feeling which exists among the Irish poor, the affection they appear to entertain for each other, and the general hospitality they, in their humble way, show to their destitute neighbours, is worthy of imitation. The contrast between the Irish and English peasantry is, indeed, very striking. In England the clown will answer the inquiries of the traveller with a bluntness which he mistakes, perhaps, for independence. He answers the inquiry, indeed, but without suffering himself to be for one moment diverted from his employment. In fact, the Englishman is from his cradle taught to care for no one; he walks the high road with a surly doggedness which bespeaks his utter independence of all whom he may meet; he feels that he has at least a right there, and will take the wall of any. Not so the Irish peasant. With many of the best qualities of the human heart, he will be found without independence. Address him by the road-side – he immediately throws down the implements of labour to attend your commands. He does not point out the way, but accompanies you on it. He is your servant, and if you please, your slave. Use to him expressions of anger or disappointment – he never answers; abuse his conduct and condemn his labour – he says nothing, or extenuates his fault by the humblest submission. In all intercourse with superiors you find him servile to a fault, an adept at flattery, and not unmindful of the wrong which he endures with perfect serenity. He says, indeed, nothing; but he treasures all your unjust upbraidings in his heart, and, when the opportunity arrives, a wild feeling of revenge, which might, by proper culture, be trained to high honour and acts of heroism, hurries him into the commission of crime, and the wrong-doer is waylaid in his journey by a ball from a hidden hand.

Although the Irish are most religiously instructed, their morality is lost sight of. It must unhappily be admitted that, though there is scarcely one who would not deem his salvation at stake, should he neglect a mass or forget a filial duty, yet few would hesitate to succour a murderer, or to conceal the perpetrator of most atrocious crimes. A hundred will be present at the slaughter of an unarmed man; yet is not one found to denounce the agent.

Inconsistent, indeed, is the general character, but not difficult of solution is the incongruity. Not only should the administration of the laws be impartial, but they should appear so! I cannot concur with those who think that Protestant ascendancy must necessarily induce partial and unjust administration of the law; yet, I cannot conceal from myself the fact, that the difference in character between the Irish and the English peasantry has wholly arisen from that opinion. At an early period of our history, when the lower orders were emancipated from the thraldom of the feudal lords, the protection of the poor against the tyranny of the rich became the object of a boastful admiration. Soon were the middle classes capable of making stand against their more wealthy and ennobled masters or employers, and independence became the feature of the people. The aid of that people in all contests was sought with avidity, and their protection became an object embracing many advantages. Some were so destitute as to be deprived of the protection of the law, which was, as time and knowledge advanced, more and more equally dealt out, and impartially framed. At length, the poor began to have confidence in the law, which they found protected them, and felt that no man was great enough to oppress or wrong them with impunity. A natural jealousy of the wealthy was disseminated; and the severest civil wars, which evinced the power of the mass of the people, taught them also to feel that they had a redress, let the spoiler be ever so strong. If you were to threaten a breaker of stones on the road in England, he would smile with contempt on you; he would, in all probability, return your opprobrious epithet with interest, and defy you to put in practice your threats; conscious, as he is, that his redress would be in the law. Is that so in Ireland? The threatened would fear the execution of your threats, and would not reply to your abuse. He is convinced that wealth and Protestantism are the only safeguards in his misgoverned country.

Wealth and Protestantism alone engross the fears of the Irish peasantry. If their assailant be a Protestant, the Irish peasant must bear in secret his contumely; if he be wealthy, he has probably the means of punishment delegated to him; while no redress presents itself to his prejudiced mind, in any application to a magistrate, who (at least for a long period) has been appointed such, solely for his possession of wealth, and his profession of an alien religion. The peasant thinks, however unjustly, that he has no appeal; that his story would not be believed in opposition to that of his religious enemy! He hopes nothing from justice, administered by such obviously partial hands as a Protestant magistrate. He, therefore, bears your injustice with patience, but not without feeling; he estimates to the full the wrong that is done to him, and the hopelessness of legal redress; but the time may, and, perhaps, will arrive when he may satisfy his wild and savage justice, by directing a bullet to your heart, when you little suspect the lurking ambush.

Legislators, is this wonderful? Behold the effect a religious ascendancy has caused in the natural character of a people imbued with all the elements of the finest race in the English dominions; who possess qualities which, if nurtured and cherished by kindness and education, would adorn human nature, and raise the character of man.

Dunmanway, in West Cork, as portrayed in *The Illustrated London News* in 1847. John Stevens found little to report of Dunmanway in 1689 (page 131). Thackeray also sketched Dunmanway (page 234). In this image buildings and human figures present a spectrum of elements.

William Makepeace Thackeray

THE IRISH SKETCH BOOK

William Makepeace Thackeray (1811-1863) came to Ireland as a fairly obscure journalist, before he wrote his major novels. Born in Calcutta, he had attended English schools through a brief stay at Trinity College, Cambridge. He travelled in France and Germany before beginning a career in journalism in 1833. Thackeray's inheritance was lost to bad investments by the time he married in 1836. To support his family he turned to satirical sketches and travel writing. *The Paris Sketch Book* was assembled from periodical contributions in 1840, and its success brought a contract for an Irish tour book. The trip to Ireland was delayed, however, by the mental breakdown of his wife. Once she was settled apart from the family, Thackeray proceeded to Ireland in the summer of 1842. Later, he used Ireland for the setting of his first novel, *The Luck of Barry Lyndon* (1844). His major novels begin with *Vanity Fair* in 1848.

Thackeray arrived in Ireland under great personal stress and at a time when the country had well begun its spiral into famine. In whatever proportion, these circumstances conjoined with his professional exigences to produce a resolutely 'merry cockney' in *The Irish Sketch Book*. As is typical of the period, the book often sentimentalizes the Irish, particularly in scenes of religious devotion, for Catholicism is no longer thought threatening. Yet there are apparent tensions in the work attributable to his own sensibility and to the crux of the times. The most shocking passages here concern beggers. Thackeray's condescension and even cruelty toward them indicate the worsening economic plight of the country and also his own growing awareness of a disturbing inability to comprehend their existence. He attempts to maintain a cheerful disposition throughout, but even this brief selection includes references to the rebellion of 1798, to the tithe wars, and to other civil unrest. Most suggestive of all is the kind of tension already seen in the same period in John Carr. The contemporary assumption was that Ireland was spiritually as accessible to the English tourist as it physically was on the rapidly improving coach routes. Thackeray for the most part assumes this. Yet in *The Irish Sketch Book* there is a consistent self-consciousness of being English, of being a stranger in a country that may be fundamentally opaque to the English visitor. As he says elsewhere in this work, Ireland is 'a country far more strange to most travellers than France or Germany can be'.

The Irish Sketch Book, with Thackeray's own illustrations, was published in London in 1843. This text of its third chapter is taken from The University Edition of *The Complete Works* (Boston, 1881).

William Makepeace Thackeray's sketch of the Claddagh in Galway, from *The Irish Sketch Book* (1843). It is conspicuously more scenic and less populous than Francis B. Head's account of 1852.

T he next morning being fixed for the commencement of our journey towards Waterford, a carriage made its appearance in due time before the hall-door: an amateur stage-coach, with four fine horses, that were to carry us to Cork. The crew of the 'drag', for the present, consisted of two young ladies, and two who will not be old, please heaven! for these thirty years; three gentlemen whose collected weights might amount to fifty-four stone; and one of smaller proportions, being as yet only twelve years old: to these were added a couple of grooms and a lady's-maid. Subsequently we took in a dozen or so more passengers, who did not seem in the slightest degree to inconvenience the coach or the horses; and thus was formed a tolerably numerous and merry party. The governor took the reins, with his geranium in his button-hole, and the place on the box was quarrelled for without ceasing, and taken by turns.

Our day's journey lay through a country more picturesque, though by no means so prosperous and well cultivated as the district through which we had passed on our drive from Dublin. This trip carried us through the County of Carlow and the town of that name: a wretched place enough, with a fine court-house, and a couple of fine churches: the Protestant church a noble structure, and the Catholic cathedral said to be built after some continental model. The Catholics point to the structure with considerable pride: it was the first, I believe, of the many handsome cathedrals for their worship which have been built of late years in this country by the noble contributions of the poor man's penny, and by the untiring energies and sacrifices of the clergy. Bishop Doyle, the founder of the church, has the place of honor within it; nor, perhaps, did any Christian pastor ever merit the affection of his flock more than that great and high-minded man. He was the best champion the Catholic Church and cause ever had in Ireland: in learning, and admirable kindness and virtue, the best example to the clergy of his religion: and if the country is now filled with schools, where the humblest peasant in it can have the benefit of a liberal and wholesome education, it owes this great boon mainly to his noble exertions, and to the spirit which they awakened.

As for the architecture of the cathedral, I do not fancy a professional man would find much to praise in it; it seems to me overloaded with ornaments, nor were its innumerable spires and pinnacles the more pleasing to the eye because some of them were out of the perpendicular. The interior is quite plain, not to say bare and unfinished. Many of the chapels in the country that I have since seen are in a similar condition; for when the walls are once raised, the enthusiasm of the subscribers to the building seems somewhat characteristically to grow cool, and you enter at a porch that would suit a palace, with an interior scarcely more decorated than a barn. A wide large floor, some confession-boxes against the blank walls here and there, with some humble pictures at the 'stations', and the statue, under a mean canopy of red woollen stuff, were the chief furniture of the cathedral.

The severe homely features of the good bishop were not very favorable subjects for Mr. [John] Hogan's chisel; but a figure of prostrate, weeping Ireland, kneeling by the prelate's side, and for whom he is imploring protection, has much beauty. In the chapels of Dublin and Cork some of this artist's work may be seen, and his countrymen are exceedingly proud of him.

Connected with the Catholic cathedral is a large tumble-down-looking divinity college: there are upwards of a hundred students here, and the college is licensed to give degrees in arts as well as divinity; at least so the officer of the church said, as he showed us the place through the bars of the sacristy windows, in which apartment may be seen sundry crosses, a pastoral letter of Dr. Doyle, and a number of ecclesiastical vestments formed of laces, poplins, and velvets handsomely laced with gold. There is a convent by the side of the cathedral, and, of course, a parcel of beggars all about, and indeed all over the town, profuse in their prayers and the invocations of the Lord, and whining flatteries of the persons whom they address. One wretched old tottering hag began whining the Lord's Prayer as a proof of her sincerity, and blundered in the very midst of it, and left us thoroughly disgusted after the very first sentence.

It was market-day in the town, which is tolerably full of poor-looking shops, the streets being thronged with donkey-carts, and people eager to barter their small wares. Here and there were picture-stalls, with huge hideous-colored engravings of the saints: and indeed the objects of barter upon the banks of the clear bright river Barrow seemed scarcely to be of more value than the articles which change hands, as one reads of, in a town of African huts and traders on the banks of the Quorra. Perhaps the very bustle and cheerfulness of the people served only, to a Londoner's eye, to make it look the more miserable. It seems as if they had no *right* to be eager about such a parcel of wretched rags and trifles as were exposed to sale.

There are some old towers of a castle here, looking finely from the river; and near the town is a grand modern residence belonging to Colonel Bruen, with an oak-park on one side of the road, and a deer-park on the other. These retainers of the Colonel's lay in their rushy green enclosures, in great numbers, and seemingly in flourishing condition.

The road from Carlow to Leighlinbridge is exceedingly beautiful: noble pure hills rising on either side, and the broad silver Barrow flowing through rich meadows of that astonishing verdure which is only to be seen in this country. Here and there was a country-house, or a tall mill by a stream-side: but the latter buildings were for the most part empty, the gaunt windows gaping without glass, and their great wheels idle. Leighlinbridge, lying up and down a hill by the river contains a considerable number of pompous-looking warehouses, that looked for the most part to be doing no more business than the mills on the Carlow road, but stood by the roadside staring at the coach as it were, and basking in the sun, swaggering, idle, insolvent, and out-at-elbows. There are one or two very pretty, modest, comfortable-looking country places about Leighlinbridge, and on the road thence to a miserable village called the Royal Oak, a beggarly sort of bustling place.

Here stands a dilapidated hotel and posting-house: and indeed on every road, as yet, I have been astonished at the great movement and stir; – the old coaches being invariably crammed, cars jingling about equally full, and no want of gentlemen's carriages to exercise the horses of the 'Royal Oak' and similar establishments. In the time of the rebellion,* the landlord of this 'Royal Oak', a great character in those parts, was a fierce United Irishman. One day it happened that Sir John Anderson came to the inn, and was eager for horses on. The landlord, who knew Sir John to be a Tory, vowed and swore he had no horses; that the judges had the last going to Kilkenny; that the yeomanry had carried off the best of them; that he could not give a horse for love or money. 'Poor Lord Edward!' said Sir John, sinking down in a chair, and clasping his hands, 'my poor dear misguided friend, and must you die for the loss of a few hours and the want of a pair of horses?'

'Lord *What?*' says the landlord.

'Lord Edward Fitzgerald,' replied Sir John. 'The Government has seized his papers, and got scent of his hiding-place. If I can't get to him before two hours, Sirr will have him.'

'My dear Sir John', cried the landlord, 'it's not two horses but it's eight I'll give you, and may the judges go hang for me! Here, Larry! Tim! First and second pair for Sir John Anderson; and long life to you, Sir John, and the Lord reward you for your good deed this day!'

Sir John, my informant told me, had invented this predicament of Lord Edward's in order to get the horses; and by way of corroborating the whole story, pointed out an old chaise which stood at the inn-door with its window broken, a great crevice in the panel, some little wretches crawling underneath the wheels, and two huge blackguards lolling against the pole. 'And that,' says he, 'is no doubt the very post-chaise Sir John Anderson had.' It certainly looked ancient enough.

Of course, as we stopped for a moment in the place, troops of slatternly, ruffianly-looking fellows assembled round the carriage, dirty heads peeped out of all the dirty windows, beggars came forward with a joke and a prayer, and troops of children raised their shouts and halloos. I confess, with regard to the beggars, that I have never yet had the slightest sentiment of compassion for the very eldest or dirtiest of them, or been inclined to give them a penny: they come crawling round you with lying prayers and loathsome compliments, that make the stomach turn; they do not even

---

*In 1798, Edward Fitzgerald, MP, served as liaison to the French invading force; after the failure of the rising he was captured in flight and mortally wounded.

disguise that they are lies; for, refuse them and the wretches turn off with a laugh and a joke, a miserable grinning cynicism that creates distrust and indifference, and must be, one would think, the very best way to close the purse, not to open it, for objects so unworthy.

How do all these people live? one can't help wondering – these multifarious vagabonds, without work or workhouse, or means of subsistence? The Irish Poor Law Report says that there are twelve hundred thousand people in Ireland – a sixth of the population – who have no means of livelihood but charity, and whom the State, or individual members of it, must maintain. How *can* the State support such an enormous burden; or the twelve hundred thousand be supported? What a strange history it would be, could one but get it true – that of the manner in which a score of these beggars have maintained themselves for a fortnight past!

Soon after quitting the 'Royal Oak', our road branches off to the hospitable house where our party, consisting of a dozen persons, was to be housed and fed for the night. Fancy the look which an English gentleman of moderate means would assume, at being called on to receive such a company! A pretty road of a couple of miles, thickly grown with ash and oak trees, under which the hats of coach-passengers suffered some danger, leads to the house of D ———. A young son of the house, on a white pony, was on the look-out, and great cheering and shouting took place among the young people as we came in sight.

Trotting away by the carriage-side he brought us through a gate with a pretty avenue of trees leading to the pleasure-grounds of the house – a handsome building commanding noble views of river, mountains, and plantations. Our entertainer only rents the place; so I may say, without any imputation against him, that the house was by no means so handsome within as without – not that the want of finish in the interior made our party the less merry, or the host's entertainment less hearty and cordial.

The gentleman who built and owns the house, like many other proprietors in Ireland, found his mansion too expensive for his means, and has relinquished it. I asked what his income might be, and no wonder that he was compelled to resign his house; which a man with four times the income in England would scarcely venture to inhabit. There were numerous sitting-rooms below; a large suite of rooms above, in which our large party, with their servants, disappeared without any seeming inconvenience, and which already accommodated a family of at least a dozen persons, and a numerous train of domestics. There was a great court-yard surrounded by capital offices, with stabling and coach-houses sufficient for a half-dozen of country gentlemen. An English squire of ten thousand a year might live in such a place – the original owner, I am told, had not many more hundreds.

Our host has wisely turned the chief part of the pleasure-ground round the house into a farm; nor did the land look a bit the worse, as I thought, for having rich crops of potatoes growing in place of grass, and fine plots of waving wheat and barley. The care, skill, and neatness everywhere exhibited, and the immense luxuriance of the crops, could not fail to strike even a cockney: and one of our party, a very well-known, practical farmer, told me that there was at least five hundred pounds' worth of produce upon the little estate of some sixty acres, of which only five-and-twenty were under the plough.

As at H——town, on the previous day, several men and women appeared sauntering in the grounds, and as the master came up, asked for work, or sixpence, or told a story of want. There are lodge-gates at both ends of the demesne; but it appears the good-natured practice of the country admits a beggar as well as any other visitor. To a couple our landlord gave money, to another a little job of work; another he sent roughly out of the premises: and I could judge thus what a continual tax upon the Irish gentleman these travelling paupers must be, of whom his ground is never free.

There, loitering about the stables and out-houses, were several people who seemed to have acquired a sort of right to be there: women and children who had a claim upon the butter-milk; men who did an odd job now and then; loose hangers-on of the family: and in the lodging-houses and inns I have entered, the same sort of ragged vassals are to be found; in a house however poor, you are sure to see some poorer dependant who is a stranger, taking a meal of potatoes in the kitchen; a Tim or Mike loitering hard by, ready to run on a message, or carry a bag. This is written, for instance, at a lodging over a shop at Cork. There sits in the shop a poor old fellow quite past work, but who totters up and down stairs to the lodgers, and does what little he can for his easily-won bread. There is another fellow outside who is sure to make his bow to anybody issuing from the lodging, and ask if his honor wants an errand done? Neither class of such dependants exists with us. What housekeeper in London is there will feed an old man of seventy that's good for nothing, or encourage such a disreputable hanger-on as yonder shuffling, smiling cad?

Nor did Mr. M——'s 'irregulars' disappear with the day; for when, after a great deal of merriment, and kind, happy dancing and romping of young people, the fineness of the night suggested the propriety of smoking a certain cigar (it is never more acceptable than at that season), the young squire voted that we should adjourn to the stables for the purpose, where accordingly the cigars were discussed. There were still the inevitable half-dozen hangers-on: one came grinning with a lantern, all nature being in universal blackness except his grinning face; another ran obsequiously to the stables to show a favorite mare – I think it was a mare – though it may have been a mule, and your humble servant not much the wiser. The cloths were taken off; the fellows with the candles crowded about: and the young squire bade me admire the beauty of her fore-leg, which I did with the greatest possible gravity. 'Did you ever see such a fore-leg as that in your life?' says the young squire, and further discoursed upon the horse's points, the amateur grooms joining in chorus.

There was another young squire of our party, a pleasant gentlemanlike young fellow, who danced as prettily as any Frenchman, and who had ridden over from a neighboring house: as I went to bed, the two lads were arguing whether young Squire B—— should go home or stay at D—— that night. There was a bed for him – there was a bed for everybody it seemed, and a kind welcome too. How different was all this to the ways of a severe English house!

Next morning the whole of our merry party assembled round a long, jovial breakfast-table, stored with all sorts of good things; and the biggest and jovialest man of all, who had just come in fresh from a walk in the fields, and vowed that he was as hungry as a hunter, and was cutting some slices out of an inviting ham on the side-table, suddenly let fall his knife and fork with dismay. 'Sure, John, don't you know it's Friday?' cried a lady from the table; and back John came with a most lugubrious queer look on his jolly face, and fell to work upon bread-and-butter, as resigned as possible, amidst no small laughter, as may be well imagined. On this I was bound, as a Protestant, to eat a large slice of pork, and discharged that duty nobly, and with much self-sacrifice.

The famous 'drag' which had brought us so far, seemed to be as hospitable and elastic as the house which we now left, for the coach accommodated, inside and out, a considerable party from the house; and we took our road leisurely, in a cloudless scorching day, towards Waterford. The first place we passed through was the little town of Gowran, near which is a grand, well-ordered park, belonging to Lord Clifden, and where his mother resides, with whose beautiful face, in Lawrence's pictures, every reader must be familiar. The kind English lady has done the greatest good in the neighborhood, it is said, and the little town bears marks of her beneficence, in its neatness, prettiness, and order. Close by the church there are the ruins of a fine old abbey here, and a still finer one a few miles on, at Thomastown, most picturesquely situated amidst trees and meadow, on the river Nore. The place within, however, is dirty and ruinous – the same wretched suburbs, the same squalid congregation of beggarly loungers, that are to be seen elsewhere. The monastic ruin is very fine, and the road hence to Thomastown rich with varied cultivation and beautiful verdure, pretty gentlemen's mansions shining among the trees on either side of the way. There was one place along this rich tract that looked very strange and ghastly – a huge old pair of gate pillars, flanked by a ruinous lodge, and a wide road winding for a mile up a hill. There had been a park once, but all the trees were gone; thistles were growing in the yellow sickly land, and rank thin grass on the road. Far away you saw in this desolate tract a ruin of a house; many a butt of claret has been emptied there, no doubt, and many a merry party come out with hound and horn. But what strikes the Englishmen with wonder is not so much, perhaps, that an owner of the place should have been ruined and a spendthrift, as that the land should lie there useless ever since. If one is not successful with us another man will be, or another will try, at least. Here lies useless a great capital of hundreds of acres of land; barren, where the commonest effort might make it productive, and looking as if for a quarter of a century past no soul ever looked or cared for it. You might travel five hundred miles through England and not see such a spectacle.

A short distance from Thomastown is another abbey; and presently, after passing through the village of Knocktopher, we came to a posting-place called Ballyhale.

A dirty, old, contented, decrepit idler was lolling in the sun at a shop-door, and hundreds of the population of the dirty, old, decrepit, contented place were employed in the like way. A dozen of boys were playing at pitch-and-toss; other male and female beggars were sitting on a wall looking into a stream; scores of ragamuffins, of course, round the carriage; and beggars galore at the door of the little ale-house or hotel. A gentleman's carriage changed horses as we were waiting here. It was a rich sight to see the cattle, and the way of starting them: 'Halloo! Yoop-hoop!' a dozen ragged ostlers and amateurs running by the side of the miserable old horses, the postilion shrieking, yelling, and belabouring them with his whip. Down goes one horse among the new-laid stones; the postilion has him up with a cut of the whip and a curse, and takes advantage of the start caused by the stumble to get the brute into a gallop, and to go down the hill. 'I know it for a fact', a gentlemen of our party says, 'that no horses *ever* got out of Ballyhale without an accident of some kind.'

'Will your honor like to come and see a big pig?' here asked a man of the above gentleman, well known as a great farmer and breeder. We all went to see the big pig, not very fat as yet, but, upon my word, it is as big as a pony. The country round is, it appears, famous for the breeding of such, especially a district called the Welsh mountains, through which we had to pass on our road to Waterford.

This is a curious country to see, and has curious inhabitants: for twenty miles there is no gentleman's house: gentlemen dare not live there. The place was originally tenanted by a clan of Welshes; hence its name; and they maintain themselves in their occupancy of the farms in Tipperary fashion, by simply putting a ball into the body of any man who would come to take a farm over any one of them. Some of the crops in the fields of the Welsh country seemed very good, and the fields well tilled; but it is common to see, by the side of one field that is well cultivated, another that is absolutely barren; and the whole tract is extremely wretched. Appropriate histories and reminiscences accompany the traveller: at a chapel near Mullinavat is the spot where sixteen policemen were murdered in the tithe-campaign; farther on you come to a lime-kiln, where the guard of a mail-coach was seized, and *roasted alive*. I saw here the first hedge-school I have seen: a crowd of half-savage-looking lads and girls looked up from their studies in the ditch, their college or lecture-room being in a mud cabin hard by.

And likewise, in the midst of this wild tract, a fellow met us who was trudging the road with a fish-basket over his shoulder, and who stopped the coach, hailing two of the gentlemen in it by name, both of whom seemed to be much amused by his humor. He was a handsome rogue, a poacher, or salmon-taker, by profession, and presently poured out such a flood of oaths, and made such a monstrous display of grinning wit and blackguardism, as I have never heard equalled by the best Billingsgate practitioner, and as it would be more than useless to attempt to describe. Blessings, jokes, and curses trolled off the rascal's lips with a volubility which caused his Irish audience to shout with laughter, but which were quite beyond a cockney. It was a humor so purely national as to be understood by none but natives, I should think. I recollect the same feeling of perplexity while sitting, the only Englishman, in a company of jocular Scotchmen. They bandied about puns, jokes, imitations, and applauded with shrieks of laughter what, I confess, appeared to me the most abominable dulness; nor was the salmon-taker's jocularity any better. I think it rather served to frighten than to amuse; and I am not sure but that I looked out for a band of jocular cut-throats of this sort to come up at a given guffaw, and playfully rob us all round. However, he went away, quite peaceably, calling down for the party the benediction of a great number of saints, who must have been somewhat ashamed to be addressed by such a rascal.

Presently we caught sight of the valley through which the Suir flows, and descended the hill towards it, and went over the thundering old wooden bridge to Waterford.

IRELAND
AFTER THE FAMINE

The Ejectment, an eviction scene published in *The Illustrated London News* in 1848. Multiple parties are present: Irish renters, middleman representative of absentee landlord, and British troopers acting as police.

Thomas Carlyle

REMINISCENCES OF MY IRISH JOURNEY IN 1849

Ireland was at the end of famine when it was visited by Thomas Carlyle (1795-1881). He was at the end of his most productive period. His first important works were *Sator Resartus* (1836) and *The French Revolution* (1837). The 1840's brought *Chartism* (1840), *On Heroes, Hero-Worship, and the Heroic in History* (1841), *Past and Present* (1843), *Oliver Cromwell's Letters and Speeches with Elucidations* (1845), and then, after Ireland, *Latter-Day Pamphlets* (1850). That is a remarkable decade's work, especially in conjunction with public lectures. It also represents some of Carlyle's bitterest work, which is difficult to locate in the ordinary scheme of liberal and conservative. Briefly, for readers new to Carlyle, he saw the condition of England in the 1840's as a degraded and dire one, with society's poten-tial abused and further threatened by egalitarian influences such as labor unions and extension of the voting franchise. The solution, he believed, lay in general submission of the community to stern policies and authoritarian leaders. Philanthropy was to be proscribed for its erosion of the recipients' discipline and duty. Carlyle consistently takes such premises to full extremes. 'The time has come when the Irish population must either be improved', he wrote in *Chartism*, 'or else exterminated'.

Carlyle was a Scot by birth and education, but by the time of these *Reminiscences* he wrote from the political perspective of England. Indeed for some time he appears to have believed that Ireland, or the Irish problem, epitomized the English dilemma he addressed. By May 1849 he had decided to tour famine-stricken Ireland. He travelled in the country that summer, from July 3 to August 6. Only on return did he reconstruct his impressions from memory, notes, and letters written to his wife Jane. This was done between October 4 and October 16, 1849.

The *Reminiscences* was not published until 1882, when it was prepared for publication by Carlyle's friend and biographer J. A. Froude, the historian. In his preface, Froude noted that Carlyle 'attributed no importance' to the work, and it is a relatively insignificant part of his personal *œuvre*. But as an indication of English views of Ireland in 1849 it is significant and not at all eccentric for its virulence from a large body of Irish famine tours. In fact, in that same 1882 preface Froude deplored 'the policy of successive minis-tries, which has been precisely opposite to what Mr. Carlyle would have

himself recommended'. Froude further suggested, against the background
of the Home Rule movement, that Carlyle's views 'cannot be injurious,
and may possible be useful'.

This selection is taken from the first American edition (New York,
1882), with its punctuation retained. In this passage Carlyle is leaving
Tuam, cited as 'Chuam' for its local pronunciation. He is travelling in the
company of Charles Gavan Duffy (1816-1903), founder of the Irish
nationalist journal *The Nation*, which was suppressed in 1848.

The Famine in Ireland. Funeral at Skibbereen. From a sketch by Mr. H. Smith, Cork.

S | *aturday, 28th July.* — Hostlers, horses, two rattling windows, finally cocks and geese; these were one's lullabies in 'Chume'; outlook on the ugly McHale Cathedral, and intervening lime-patched roofs, at present moist with windy rain: poor Duffy, in his front 'best bedroom', hadn't slept at all. Hurried breakfast in the gray morning, seven a.m.; Bill — N.B. Bill came to us at *Sligo*, unsettled still, the innkeeper said; and Duffy, with surprise, paid it there too, uncertain whether not a second time! Walker is out, bound for Sligo at an afterhour; appoints us thither for Monday evening. Squabbling of lady passenger about being cheated of change by some porter or boots; confused misarrangement, and noise more or less on all hands, as usual; windy Scotch mist, coming down occasionally in shower; off at length, thank Heaven, towards Castlebar and Westport, *taliter qualiter*. Watery fields, ill-fenced, rushes, rubbish; country bare and *dirty*-looking; weather rather darkening than improving. Simple big Irishman on coach-roof beside me; all in *gray-blanket*, over all; some kind of corn or butter trader, I suppose; as well-dressed kind of natives are very apt to be. 'Father has *taken* the Ballina work-house contract' said one (who got up, farther forward on the road); 'taken it,' Indian-meal at so-and-so. There is something entertaining too in a region of *unadulterated* professed ugliness? Ride by no means uncomfortable in the Scotch mist (wind to *left* and *rear*), with outlook over ill-tilled bare and ragged expanses, road flanked sometimes with beggarly Scotch firs.

Man holding up a fiery peat in a pair of tongs; stop to change horses; fiery peat is for the guard, who leans forward with (dodeen) pipe, *good-natured* Gorgon face, weighed down with laziness, age, and fat: smack, smack! intense sucking, 'bacco being wet, and the saliva came in dewdrops on the big outcurled lips; poor old fellow, he got his pipe to go at last, and returned the tongs and peat by flinging them away. What a pre-established harmony, this of the fiery peat and the Gorgon guard! Bright through the Scotch mist of the future, this fiery peat gleams beacon-like on his soul; there burns for him a little light of hope. Duffy is inside, lady passenger (of the cheating boots), and some poor young gentleman with the bones of his leg broken. Perhaps we didn't change horses at the fiery peat; but only delivered and received parcels there? Next halt there was a change; a great begging, too, by old sibyl woman; a mounting of one or more (grain-dealing?) passengers with fine dresses, with bad broken umbrellas. The morning is getting wetter; stormful, dashes of heavy showers as we approach Castlebar; road running, and *red* streamlets in the ditches on either side. Duffy has proposed that we shall *stop* at Castlebar, and give up Westport; overruled. 'Hollymount', pleasant-looking mansion, with lawns and groves on the left; letter to the owner, but didn't think of delivering it. Lord Lucan's close by Castlebar and on the other side of it too: has *cleared* his ground (cruel monster! cry all people); but is draining, building, harrowing, and leasing; has decided to make this ugly land *avail*, after clearing it. Candor must admit that *here* is a second most weighty consideration in his favor, in reference to those 'evictions'. First-rate new farmstead of his, Scotch tenant (I think), for peasants that will work there is employment here; Lord Lucan *is* moving, at least, if all others lie motionless rotting. Castlebar in heavyish rain; town-green; confusion of confusions, at the edge of that, and looking down the main street; while they tumble the luggage, rearrange themselves, put out the poor broken-legged gentleman at the hospital (rain now battering and pouring), and do at last dash forth towards Westport.

Wind and rain now right ahead; prefer this to stew of inside; Lord Lucan's husbandry seen to each side from under umbrella – with satisfaction, though not unmixed. Gigantic drain; torn through a blue *whinstone* range of knolls, and neatly fenced with stone and mortar; drippings of the abominable bog (which is all round, far and wide, ugly as chaos), run now through it as a brown *brook*. Abominable bog, thou *shalt* cease to be abominable, and become subject to man! Nothing else worth looking at; dirty hungry cottages, in groups or single; bog generally, or low-lying rushy wet ground, with a storm of heavy rain beating it – till certain heights, which overlook Westport. Gorgon guard's face pours water from every angle – careless he, as if it had been an old stone face; talks busily, nonsense, what I heard of it, with some foolish passenger, the only one now. Distressed gigs; one distressed gig; riders and it running *clear* with wet. Tobacco remains to one! Heights at last; Westport big, substantial-*looking* (*Fronti nulla fides!*); 'Croaghpatrick' big mountain-cone amid tumbl-ing cloud masses, glimpses too of the bay, all close at hand now; and swiftly down-hill we arrive, get to our inn (flaring hotel, fit for Burlington Street by *look*), and, in about three quarters of an hour of confused waiting and vicissitude, *get* our luggage, and begin to think of *seeing* the people I had letters for. Waiter despatched accordingly; people gone, people etc. — One little Captain Something, an intelligent commonplace little Englishman (just about to *quit* this horrid place, and here for the second time) does attend us, takes us to Westport Workhouse, the wonder of the universe at present.

Human swinery has here reached its *acme*, happily: 30,000 paupers in this union, population supposed to be about 60,000. Workhouse proper (I suppose) cannot hold above three or four thousand of them; subsidiary workhouses, and out-door relief the others. Abomination of desolation; what *can* you make of it! Out-door quasi-*work:* three or four hundred big hulks of fellows tumbling about with shares, picks, and barrows, 'levelling' the end of their workhouse hill. At first glance you would think them all working; look nearer, in each shovel there is some ounce or two of mould, and it is all make-believe; five or six hundred boys and lads, pretending to break stones. Can it be a *charity* to keep men alive on these terms? In face of all the twaddle of the earth, shoot a man rather than train him (with heavy expense to his neighbors) to be a deceptive human *swine*. Fifty-four wretched mothers sat rocking young offspring in one room: *vogue la galère*. 'Dean Bourke' (Catholic priest, to whom also we had a letter) turns up here: middle-aged, middle-sized figure, rustyish black coat, Hessian boots, white stockings, good-humored, loud-speaking face, frequent Lundyfoot snuff. A mad pauper woman *shrieks* to be towards him; keepers seize her, bear her off shrieking. Dean, poor fellow, has to take it 'asy', I find — how otherwise? Issuing from the workhouse, ragged cohorts are in waiting for him, persecute him with their begging: 'Get along wid ye!' cries he, impatiently, yet without ferocity. 'Doun't ye see I'm speaking wi' the gintlemen! Arrah, thin! I don't care if ye were dead!' Nothing remained but patience and Lundyfoot snuff for a poor man in these circumstances. Wherever he shows face, some scores, soon waxing to be hundreds, of wretches beset him; he confesses he dare not stir out except on horseback, or with some fenced park to take refuge in: poor Dean Bourke! Lord Sligo's park, in this instance. But beggars still, one or two — have climbed the railings, got in by the drains? Heavy square mansion ('1770' architecture): Lord Sligo going to the Killeries, a small lodge he has to the south – no rents at all. I hear since 'he has nothing to live upon but an opera-box'; literally so (says Milnes) — which he bought in happier days, and now lets. — 'Croagh Patrick, won't ye go to it?' Bay — Clew Bay — has a dim and shallow look hereabouts; 'beautiful prospects.' — Yes, Mr. Dean; but, alas, alas! Duffy and I privately decide that we will have some luncheon at our inn, and quit this citadel of mendicancy, intolerable to gods and man, back to Castlebar *this* evening. Brilliant *rose-pink* landlady, reverent of Duffy (proves to be a sister, daughter perhaps, of the 'Chume' one), is very sorry; but — etc. No *bells* in your room; bell often enough broken in these sublime establishments of the West of Ireland. Bouquet to Duffy — mysteriously handed from unknown young lady, with verse or prose note; humph! humph! — and so without accident, in now bright hot afternoon, we take leave of Croaghpatrick (devils and serpents all collected there. Oh, why isn't there some Patrick to do it now again!), and, babbling of 'litera-ture' (not by *my* will), perhaps about 5 p.m. arrive at Castlebar again, and (for D.'s sake) are reverently welcomed.

Tea. Irish country priest, very soft youth, wonderfully like one of our own green parsons fresh from college; the only one I saw of that sort. Out to the Inspector's, Capt. Something, for whom I have a letter: Strelezki there, whom we had seen at Westport too, talk-talking with his bell-voice, and unimportant semi-humbug meaning. 'Strelezki is coming!' all the natives, with inconceivable interest, seemed whispering to one another; a man with something *to give* is coming! This Captain, in his dim lodging a considerably more intelligent young man (30 or so); talk — to breakfast with him tomorrow.

Westport Union has £1100 a week from government (proportion rate-in-aid), Castlebar has £800, some other has £1300, etc., etc.; it is so they live from week to week. Poor-rates, collectible, as good as *none* (£28.14.0. say the books): a peasant will keep his cow for years against all manner of cess-collection. Spy-children; tidings run, as by electric wires, that a cess-collector is out, and all cows are huddled under lock and key — *unattaina-ble* for years. No rents; little or no *stock* left, little cultivation, docks, thistles; landlord sits in his mansion, for reasons, except on *Sunday:* we hear of them 'living on the rabbits of their own park'. Society is at an *end* here, with the land uncultivated, and every second soul a pauper. 'Society' *here* would have to eat itself, and end by cannibalism in a week, if it were not held up by the rest of our empire still standing afoot! Home through the damp streets (not bad streets at all, and a population still partly *clothed* making its Saturday markets); thimbleful of punch over peat fire or ashes, whiff of tobacco, and bed.

Sunday, 29th July.—Breakfast with Capt. *Farrar* (that was the name); sharp, distinct, decisive young soldier; manfully or patient and active in his hopeless position here. On my return, Duffy has been at *mass* and sermon. Priest reproving practices on 'patron days' (pilgrimages, etc., which issue now in *whiskey* mainly), with much good-sense, says Duffy. Car to Ballina. (*Bally* is place, *vallum*); drivers, boots, etc., busy packing. Tuam coach (ours of yesterday) comes in; there rushes from it, *shot* as if by cannon from Yorkshire or Morpeth without stopping, W. E. Forster!* very blue-nosed, but with news from my wife, and with inextinguishable good-humor. He mounts with us almost without reflection, and we start for Ballina; public car all to ourselves; gloomy hulks of mountains on the left; country ill-tilled, some *un*tilled, vacant, and we get upon wide stony moorland, and come in sight of the desolate expanses of 'Lough Conn'.

Police-barrack, excise-barrack, in a loop of the mountain washed by the lake. Picturesque sites, in nooks and on knolls; one ruined cottage in a *nook* (belongs to Lord Lucan), treeless, yet screened from winds, nestled among the rocks, and big lake close by: why couldn't *I* get it for a hermitage! Bridge (I think there must have been), and *two* loughs. Inexpressible solitude, unexampled desolation; bare gray continent of crags, clear sea of fresh-water; some farms and tufts of wood (one mournful ruined-looking place, which was said to be a burying-ground and monastic ruin) visible far off, and *across* the lake always. Clear blue sky, black showery tempests brewing occasionally among the hills. Brother car meets us, brief dialogue, among the crags; little pug-nosed Irish figure in Sunday clothes, had been escorting a comrade, mounts now beside Duffy — proves to be a tailor, I think. Account by him, inexpressibly vague, of certain neighboring localities. 'Archb. McHale', 'John of Chume', was born hereabouts;

---

*William Edward Forster (1818-1886), originally in Ireland in 1846 to direct a Society of Friends' famine relief fund; later chief secretary for Ireland, 1880-1882.

peasant-farmer's son. Given a vivacious greedy soul, with this grim outlook, vacant of all but the eternal crags and skies, and for reading of life's huge riddle an Irish Mass-book only — one had a kind of glimpse of 'John of Chume' — poor devil, after all! Ballina; immense suburb of thatched huts again; solid, broad, unexpectedly handsome main street; corn-factors, bacon-factors, land-agents (attorneys, in their good days, must have done it); halt at the farther end, close by a post-office, and a huge hungry-looking hotel, or perhaps two hotels; into one of which — the wrong one surely if there was a choice — we are ushered, and in the big greasy public room find a lieut. of foot busy smoking.

'Private room' very attainable, but, except for absence of tobacco, not much more exquisite; in fact, this poor hotel was the *dirtiest* in our Irish experience; clearly about *bankrupt*, as one would see. But the poor waiters, the poor people all, were civil; their poverty gave them even a kind of dignity — the gray-bearded head-waiter's final *bow* next day (disinterested bow) is still pathetic for me. Certain Hamiltons, inspectors; the Captain H. an Ulster man; big cheeks and black *bead*-eyes; Calvinist philanthropist; a really good, but also really stupid, man. Write in my back bedroom; annoyed by gusts of *bravura-singing* (Sunday not the less) from the lieut. of foot; sorrow on him, and yet pity on him! To workhouse, to workhouses, with Bead-eye; *subsidiary* workhouses these; boys *drilling* — discharged soldier: one of the drill-sergeants, begs for something of the nature of 'shoes' when it is done. 'There is Cobden, you see?' said poor bead-eyed Hamilton; discharged that man, and now he comes upon *us!*' Kindness *à la* Exeter Hall; this, with strict Calvinism for life-theory, is H.'s style. A *thatched* subsidiary workhouse this; all for the children: really good, had the children been getting bred towards anything but *pauperism!* — pauperism in geometrical progression. Dinner of perhaps five hundred of them — girls, I think. 'Och, sur, it's *four years* I've been here, and this little girl isn't well, yet!' Four years: what a kindness to us, to stay so long! What she now wanted with this girl? 'To get her taken to the salt-water' — a small allowance for that. Brutallest stupidity can hardly be more brutal than these human swineries had now grown to seem to me. Dormitories, etc. — a street nearly all in ruins beside this admirable place; population of it gone to workhouse, to England, to the grave. Other subsidiary workhouse; *continents* of young women; really whole big roomfuls of them (for it was now raining) waiting for dinner. Home with disgust; to have tea with Hamilton in the evening at his house.

After dinner, walk towards his house; moist windy evening, rain has ceased. Correct little house, good and hospitable man; tries to convince me of philanthropy; pauses horror-struck. I decide (in my own mind) that the *less* of this the better. He (I found afterwards) asks Duffy privately 'if I am an atheist or what?' Hospitable promise to go and show us a 'country of evictions' on the morrow; we shall see! and so home to bed. It was going towards his house that a man (Sundayed workman) caught Duffy's hand, and reverently shook it with apologies.

Monday, 30th July.—Worst of Irish beds, worst of Irish nights (noise, etc.), does finally end. At breakfast Hamilton is punctual and appears: 'Not me, thank you kindly', and the rest also didn't go — or only Forster of the rest, and at some other hour. Through the streets with my two inspectors (Hamilton and his cousin the 'Belmullet' inspector, a simple watery man with one arm, Mrs. Dr. Evory Kennedy's brother), towards the workhouse. 'The Scotch Shop', so called; a Glasgow thing, has propagated itself hither from Sligo; dull Scotchman, 'Never so bad a trade as *now*'; building, furnishing of workhouses, always some money going till now; his brother has taken a farm hereabouts (rent seemed *high* with such pauperism); his shag tobacco (nearly unknown in Ireland) is very dear and very bad; adieu to the Scotch Shop, and him! Dulse [i.e. seaweed] in Ballina street market; comes from Belmullet, I hear; gathered there, carted hither, forty-two miles; sold for 2s. here! Wretched huckster, who has no better industry, subsists his garron [i.e. pony] upon the wayside, lodges with some fellow-poor man; goes his eighty-four miles, on these terms, and takes to gathering new *dulse*. Was such industry ever heard of before in this world? Not this poor huckster is to blame for it, first of all; not he first. O heavens! innumerable mortals are to blame for it; which quack of us is *not* to blame for it? — Look into the *areas* of the workhouse with bead-eyed friend; then, for his sake and for my own, I decline to go farther; return to inn, where at least is a sofa, where tobacco and solitude are possible. Car is to go about two o'clock, and I am due at Sligo to-night. Duffy, finding certain 'Dillons' here, decides finally to stay; Forster too stays, flying about in an uncertain way. Col. Something, a great 'exterminator' hereabouts, and a great improver also; that is he, riding into town: stubborn, uncultivated, big red-haired face, and solid military figure, from fifty to sixty; not the worst of Ballina men he. Glimpse of Bourke, with note from somebody (from the Tralee gentleman it was, who had been 'absent at Valentia') — glimpse of Duffy and Dillons; away then, away!

First part of our route, moory, at first symptoms of plantation and improvement, by-and-by none. Col. Something (Gort's?) evictions, long ghastly series of roofless cottages visible enough; big drain, internal, was not visible: poor groom sitting by me on the car was eloquent as to Col.'s 'cruelty'; Col. himself, I understand, asserts that his people went away voluntarily, money and resource being wholly run out. Beggar cottagers need to be supported by public rate; whether the rate is paid them in cottages or in workhouse is really not so material as the second question, What becomes of their land, they having *ceased* to cultivate it? Gort and Lucan answer? Their land becomes *arable*, will be ploughed in all coming years! Not so bad, surely. My groom gets off; *his* master most humane thrice-excellent old Dublin gentleman, driving up now with son-in-law, daughter, etc., in gig; 'no evictions' there, no, no! Son-in-law, fat young gentleman, had a dish-hat, as usual; dish-hats drab-colored, black, brown, and even green, universal wear of young gentlemen here, and indeed in all country parts (Scotland and England too) at present. Flat, flat, waste of moor; patches of wretched oats — then peat bogs, black pools; the roofless cottages not far off at any time. Potatoes — poor cottier digging his little plot of them, three or four little children eagerly 'gathering' for him: pathetic to look upon. From one cottage on the wayside issue two children, *naked*, to beg; boy about thirteen, girl about twelve, 'naked' literally, some sash of rag round middle, oblique-sash over shoulder to support that; stark-naked would have been *as* decent (if you had to jump and run as these creatures did) and much cleanlier. *Dramatic*, I take it, or partly so, *this* form of begging: '*strip* for your parts, there is the car coming!' Gave them nothing.

Stage: 'Dromore' (?), little hamlet; country alters here; sun too is out; beautiful view of the sea, of Sligo Bay with notable mountains beyond, and high (limestone) dry hills on our right too; much indented coast, circuitous road for Sligo, but decidedly a pleasant region, with marks of successful cultivation everywhere, though still too *treeless* (and full of *beggary* below board, as we afterwards found). Small young lady from Dromore going on visit to Sligo, her parasol a little interrupts my view; 'bay of' something ('Ballisadare', it would seem) on this side of Sligo Bay: high fine hill between the two — north side of that, it turns out, is Walker's house. Sligo at last; beautiful descent into it, beautiful town and region altogether. Down, down, to the river-bank, then halt a little to right; Mr. Walker, with servant and nice neat car, is waiting: how charitable to the dusty, heartbroken soul of a pilgrim from his car! No host can do a kinder thing than *deliver* a poor wretch in these circumstances, save him from porters, innwaiters, and the fatal predatory brotherhood! Up, some three miles; then on a pleasant shelf of the big hill or mountain 'Knocknarea', dividing Sligo from the other bay; a trim fertile little estate, beautifully screened and ornamented (or soon about to be so); a neat little country-house, and elegant welcome: thanks, thanks! Elaborate dinner, however, *no* dish of which *dare* I eat; salmon, veal, lamb, and that is *all!* Cold beef supplies every want. Excellent quiet bedroom; to bed utterly done, almost sleeping for an hour before I got away.

The Day After Ejectment, a famine-period engraving. The child on the right points to a round tower, emblem of romantic Ireland.

Harriet Martineau

LETTERS FROM IRELAND

The journalist Harriet Martineau (1802-1876) is said to have contributed to the London *Daily News* 1600 articles, among them the first serialization of these *Letters From Ireland*. Her father was a modest manufacturer, and her homelife was disciplined and intellectual in the contemporary middle-class British fashion. On the death of her father in 1826 she was forced to turn to journalism to help support her family — her deafness rendering impossible the more conventional career in teaching. Initially her literary career focussed on popularizations of contemporary notions of political economy, as in *Illustrations of Political Economy* (1834) and *Illustrations of Taxation* (1834). These were followed by a trip to America, where she contributed to the fledgling abolitionist movement, and her first travel book, *Society in America* (1837).

Martineau was stricken ill on the continent in 1839. With characteristic industry she then produced from her sickbed a half-dozen popular works of fiction in three or four years. She was cured by mesmerism in 1844, and then began to formulate a theological agnosticism that brought her some disrepute. Her principle articulation of her position, published a year before she arrived in Ireland, was *Letters on the Laws of Man's Nature and Development* (1851), an agnostic rationale of moral obligation as a social imperative.

That background helps explain some of the intellectual baggage Martineau brought to Ireland: reliance on statistical tabulation of political economy, an ideology of industry whose ideal is neatness, and a positive view of the principle and potential of the workhouses that so appalled Carlyle. But Martineau was also a women writer of significant willed achievement and profound ambivalence about it. Here that ambivalence extends to the achievement of the women of Ireland: their economic leadership is a 'system of barbarism', but at least it does promote improvement (and neatness). Martineau's insistence on improving conditions in Ireland since the 'sudden, sweeping calamity' of the famine is characteristic of a popular Victorian image of the Irish as victims struggling gallantly, if naively, against a disaster of natural rather than political origins. In her feminization of the Irish she also contributes to an emerging notion, later put into definitive form by Matthew Arnold, of the Irish as a race, Celtic and feminine, fundamentally different from the Anglo-Saxon, masculine ethos. These selections are taken from the first edition of *Letters From Ireland* published in London in 1852.

The Village of Mienies, from *The Illustrated London News*, 1847. Its image of poverty suggests the shift in British popular press treatment of Ireland as the full extent of famine became apparent.

THE WOMEN

August 27, 1852

Considering that women's labour is universally underpaid, in comparison with that of men, there is something very impressive to the traveller in Ireland in the conviction which grows upon him, from stage to stage, that it is the industry of the women which is in great part sustaining the country. Though, in one view, there is moral beauty in the case, the symptom is a bad one. First, the men's wages are reduced to the lowest point; and then, capital turns to a lower-paid class, to the exclusion of men, wherever the women can be employed in their stead. We should be sorry to draw any hasty conclusions on a matter of so much importance; but, recalling what we have seen since we landed, we cannot but declare that we have observed women not only diligently at work on their own branches of industry, but sharing the labours of the men in almost every employment that we happen to have witnessed. As an economical symptom, the employment of the least in the place of the most able-bodied is one of the peculiarities which marks the anomalous condition of Ireland. The famine time was, to be sure, an exception to all rules; but the same tendency was witnessed before, and is witnessed still. At that time, one of the London companies sent directions to their agent to expend money to a certain amount, and on no account to allow anybody on their estates to starve. The agent determined to have a great piece of 'slob' land [i.e. bog land] dug, — employing for this purpose one boy out of every family of a certain number, with a staff of aged men for overseers, to superintend and measure the work. Spades, from a moderate to a very small size, were ordered; and a mighty provision of wheaten cakes was carried down to the place every day at noon. The boys were earnest and eager and conscientious about their engagement. They were paid by the piece, and they worked well. Some little fellows, who were so small that they had to be lifted up to take their wages, earned 5s. a week. They grew fat upon their wheaten food, and their families were able to live on their earnings; and if the company did not gain, they did not lose. But it must have been a piteous sight to see households supported by their children and grannies, instead of by the strong arm of him who stood between. The women were at work at the same time. The women of Ireland so learned to work then that it will be very long indeed before they get a holiday, or find their natural place as housewives.

We do not say recover their place as housewives; for there is abundance of evidence that they have not sunk from that position, but rather risen from a lower one than they now fill. Some years ago, the great authority on

Irish peasant life was Mrs. Leadbeater,*, whose 'Cottage Dialogues' was the most popular of Irish books till [Daniel] O'Connell's power rose to its height. In the suspicion and hatred which he excited towards the landlords, and the aristocracy generally, works like Mrs. Leadbeater's, which proceed on the supposition of a sort of feudal relation between the aristocracy and the peasantry, went out of favour, and have been little heard of since. Elderly people have them on their shelves however, and we know, through them, what was the life of the Irish peasant woman in the early part of the century. We know how, too often, the family lived in a mud hovel, without a chimney, all grovelling on the same straw at night, and perhaps with the pig among them; and at meals tearing their food with their fingers, and so forth. We know how the women were in the field or the bog, while the children were tumbling about in the manure at home. Those who have been to Stradbally, Queen's County [i.e. Laois], where Mrs. Leadbeater lived, are aware of the amelioration in cottage life produced by the efforts of her daughter-in-law, by the introduction of domestic industry in the place of field labour. The younger Mrs. Leadbeater taught fancy knitting to a bedridden woman and her daughters, many years ago, for their support. The example spread. Women came in from the reaping and binding — girls stayed at home from haymaking, and setting and digging potatoes. They kept their clothes dry, their manners womanly, and their cabins somewhat more decent. The quality of the work grew finer and finer, till now we see issuing from the cabins of Stradbally the famed 'Spider Mitts', 'Impalpable Mitts', 'Cobweb Mitts', or whatever else English and American ladies like to call them. Upwards of two hundred women and girls are employed in this knitting; and people who knew Stradbally thirty years ago are so struck with the improvement in the appearance of the place, that they declare that the lowest order of cabins appears to them to be actually swept away.

Stradbally is only one of many such places. In every house of the gentry one now sees sofas, chairs, screens, and fancy tables spread with covers of crochet-work — all done by the hands of peasant women. In the south and west, where the famine was sorest, terrible distress was caused, we are told, by the sudden abolition of the domestic manufactures on which a former generation was largely dependent. The people used to spin and weave linen, flannel, and frieze, which were carried to market, as were the knitted stockings of Connaught. In the famine, the looms and spinning-wheels disappeared, with all other cabin property. It is very well that, when this had once happened, the same manufactures should not be restored, because they are of a kind surely destined to destruction before the manufacturing system. The knitting goes on; and it may long go on, so

---

* Mary Leadbeater (1758-1826), an Irish writer whose *Cottage Dialogues Among the Irish Peasantry* (1811) sold out four editions in two years.

superior as knitted stockings are to woven ones in point of wear. And a variety of fine works are going on, in wild western districts, where the workwomen who produce such beautiful things never saw a shrub more than four feet high. In the south-west, lace of a really fine quality is made in cabins where formerly hard-handed women did the dirtiest work about the potato-patch and piggery. Of the 'hand-sewing', some mention has been made before. We are assured at Belfast — and it only confirmed what we heard in Scotland — that no less than 400,000 women and girls are employed, chiefly by the Glasgow merchants, in 'hand-sewing' in the Irish cabins. Their wages are low, individually; but it is a striking fact that these women and girls earn from £80,000 to £90,000 per week. It is a regular branch of industry, requiring the labour of many men at Glasgow and Belfast, to stamp the patterns on the muslin for the women to work, and, again, to bleach it when it comes in 'green' (that is, dirty — so dirty!) from the hands of the needlewomen. They earn but 6d. a day, poor things! in a general way, though at rare times — such as the exhibition season — their pay amounts to 1s.; but it must be considered that their wear and tear of clothes is less than formerly, and that there must, one would think, be better order preserved at home.

So much for proper 'women's work'. But we observe women working almost everywhere. In the flax-fields there are more women than men pulling and steeping. In the potato-fields it is often the women who are saving the remnant of the crop. In the harvest-fields there are as many women as men reaping and binding. In the bog, it is the women who, at half wages, set up, and turn, and help to stack the peat — not only for household use, but for sale, and in the service of the Irish Peat Company. In Belfast, the warehouses we saw were more than half peopled with women, engaged about the linens and muslins. And at the flax-works, near the city, not only were women employed in the spreading and drying, but in the rolling, roughing, and finishing, which had always till now been done by men. The men had struck for wages; and their work was given to girls, at 8d. per day.

Amidst facts like these, which accumulate as we go, one cannot but speculate on what is to be the end; or whether the men are to turn nurses and cooks, and to abide beside the hearth, while the women are earning the family bread. Perhaps the most consolatory way of viewing the case is that which we are quite willing to adopt — that, practically, the condition of women, and therefore of their households, is rising. If there is something painful in seeing so undue a share of the burdens of life thrown upon the weaker sex; and if we cannot but remember that such a distribution of labour is an adopted symptom of barbarism; still, if the cabins *are* more decent, and the women more womanlike, it seems as if the process of change must be, on the whole, an advance. As to the way out of such a state of things, it seems as if it must be by that path to so many other benefits —

agricultural improvement. The need of masculine labour, and the due reward of it, must both arise out of an improved cultivation of the soil; and it is not easy to see how they can arise in any other way.

While thinking and speaking of cabin life, it occurs to us to notice the remarkable appearance of health among the very lowest of the peasantry whom we have yet encountered. What we may see in the West we cannot anticipate; but we are assured that the same fact will strike us there — that there also we shall see grown people and children grovelling in filth, with a manure-heap on the threshold, a stagnant pool before the door, and rotten thatch dropping on the stale straw on which they sleep, and they nevertheless stout, clear-eyed, and ruddy. From this we except, of course, particular situations and circumstances in which ophthalmia and fever arise, such as crowded dens in towns, and over-peopled workhouses. What this mischief amounts to may be partly judged of by the number of one-eyed people, and persons marked with the small-pox, who may be seen at assemblages like Donnybrook Fair; where we observed more than can easily be seen at once, anywhere out of Egypt. But these people are not usually peasants, living in country cabins. As to the cause of the apparent health, it is said to be nothing else than the antiseptic properties of the peat. We know how charred and powdered peat is valued as a deodorizing agent. Plenty of this crumbled peat lies in and about every cabin, on the mud or flint-paved floor, on the threshold, in the pool, and dropped about on the manure. If this is the real reason of the undeserved healthiness of the ordinary Irish cabin, it is as well that the English should know it, for the same of many thousands of poor fever patients who might be made the better for the 3,000,000 of acres of bog which might be emptied out, greatly to the advantage of Ireland.

* * *

LETTER XX.

THE WORKHOUSES

September 22, 1852.

Before entering an Irish workhouse, the English visitor is aware that the people to be seen within are altogether a different class or race from those whom he has been accustomed to see in workhouses at home. In England, the pauper population, domesticated in those abodes by legal charity, are, for the most part, a degraded order of people. The men and women have either begun life at a disadvantage, or have failed in life through some incapacity, physical or moral; or they are the children of such that we find in workhouses; and we expect therefore to see a deteriorated generation — sickly or stupid, or in some way ill-conditioned. In Irish workhouses it is not this sort of people that are to be found. Indeed, the one thing heard about them in England is that they are ready to die rather than enter the workhouse. They are the victims of a sudden, sweeping calamity, which bore no relation to vice, folly, laziness, or improvidence. In the first season of famine, the inmates were a pretty fair specimen of the inhabitants at large; and they are now the strongest and best-conditioned of those original inmates. They are now the people who lived through the famine which carried off the weak and sickly. The visitor therefore enters the workhouse gates without that painful mingling of disgust and compassion in his mind which is one of the most disagreeable feelings in the world. From afar he sees the great building — solid and handsome, not at all dull or dreary-looking, but lightsome, with plenty of windows, and generally in an airy and cheerful situation. Again and again have we asked one another whether, if we had been hungry peasants, we should have been otherwise than eager to go to those refuges, where food was known to be certainly procurable. We can understand the dislike to the supposed confinement, to the diet, to the cleanliness, to the total change, in any ordinary times, but we should have thought that there had been nothing here that hunger would not have made almost inviting. We have inquired a good deal into this matter; and we have visited several workhouses. With regard to the well-known fact that many thousands died immediately after admission, it is asserted by some persons that a large number had applied days or a week before they could be admitted; but it seems more widely true that admission was at the worst period regarded as a sentence of death; and that, at all times, there is a dread of the food in the first place, and of the confinement and new ways afterwards, so that the request for admission was delayed till too late.

What we have seen now is nothing like what we should have seen in the famine years. The first workhouse we visited was that of Newtown-Limavady, in Londonderry. In the centre of the estates of the great companies is little distress; and in the harvest season we saw only groups of children, healthy and playful, clean and bright; and women and girls spinning, washing, or cooking; and infirm old men and boys,much fewer than the house would hold; and benevolent agents going in very often, to see that they were comfortable. Matters are not so pleasant everywhere, of course; but still they are a vast improvement on what 'S.G.O.'* and others saw a while ago. For instance, we stopped at Ballyvaughan, on Galway Bay. In the course of our afternoon walk, we were struck by the situation of a farm-house on an eminence, with a green field before it, stretching down to the bay. Entering the field, we saw below us a number of women washing clothes, evidently from the workhouse. This house was an auxiliary to the auxiliary house of Ballyvaughan. The prevalence of

---

* Sidney Godolphin Osborne, mentioned by name below; his *Gleanings in the West of Ireland* was published in 1850.

ophthalmia in the house caused this field and dwelling to be hired for an infirmary. Forthwith we went to the larger house, an assemblage of whitewashed buildings, arranged as a workhouse, for the relief of the overcrowded establishment at Ennistymon.

This Ballyvaughan house was prepared to contain 900 inmates. On the day of our visit — at harvest-time — at the most prosperous season of the year, and in a neighbourhood where there is an admirable employer of labour, the number was no less than 667. It was inconceivable to us, when we heard this, what the people could have done when there were no houses nearer than Galway and Ennistymon. People who had come above thirty miles for relief perished for want of it in great numbers — some at home, and some by the roadside. It will not be so again, for there is to be a proper workhouse built at Ballyvaughan, and the question of its precise situation is now under debate. A proprietor in the neighbourhood is draining his lands largely, and with funds borrowed from the Improvement Commissioners, one of whose stipulations is that the labourers' wages shall be paid in cash. If we remember rightly, as many as 200 men are thus employed regularly, and for sufficient pay. How, then, were there 667 in the workhouse in the harvest month? How many were able-bodied men? One official said twenty, but on inquiry it turned out that they were not able-bodied at the moment. Ophthalmia, or other ailment or infirmity, had incapacitated these twenty. Of children there were 300. That was a fact only too easily understood: they were orphaned by the famine. There were many widows and 'deserted women'; the 'desertion' being that their husbands had gone to England for summer work, leaving their families to the union. The expectation was that most of these men would come back, with more or less money. Some would probably go from Liverpool to America, leaving their families where they were till they could send funds to carry them out to the United States. We heard here again of a scandal which we have since encountered more than once. Some of the guardians have turned out young women, all alone, to shift for themselves. In each case the clergyman and the great man of the neighbourhood have rebuked this practice, and put a stop to it: and it is well; for there will be an end of the well-grounded boast of the virtue of the Irish peasant women, if scores of girls are thus set adrift by their so-called guardians. In one case the excuse given was, that there was no particular notice of their being young women, but that they were included among the able-bodied, and ordered off with that class. Twenty were thus got rid of at Ballyvaughan, and thirty at Kilrush, besides many at other places. We heard with much more satisfaction of the efforts made to enable young women to emigrate to Australia. From Kilrush no less than 450 (some of our informants said more) have been sent across the Atlantic, chiefly to Canada.

On the shores of Malbay, in Clare, stands a little sea-bathing place, called Milltown, all glittering with whitewash; and the most glittering part of it is a large house full of thorough lights, which is described in the guide-books of a few years ago as a fine hotel, where sixty beds are made up for visitors. Travellers had better not go there now in expectation of a bed, for this house is at present a workhouse — another auxiliary of Ennistymon — and spoken of with pride for its healthy situation. Yet, on the way to it we saw a painful sight — a cart or truck, loaded very heavily with paupers — chiefly children, with some women — the whole being guarded by three of the constabulary, carrying arms. These were runaways, we were told, who were being brought from gaol to Milltown workhouse. We know nothing of the merits of the case, but the spectacle was not a pleasant one. If the dread of ophthalmia causes any to abscond, we do not wonder at it. The story goes, however, that many put themselves in the way of the disease, actually try to catch it, to avoid work and obtain the superior diet ordered for the patients. The Poor Law Commissioners believe this. We saw the patients at Ennistymon — dozens, scores of them — lying on clean comfortable beds, in rooms coloured green, with green window-curtains, their skins wholesome-looking, and the hair of the young people bright and glossy, but all alike suffering under that painful-looking disease, the consequence of over-crowding, and other predisposing disadvantages.

The aspect of the other parts of the Ennistymon house is anything but depressing. The greatest number receiving relief from its doors at the worst time was 20,000. The house being built to hold 500, of course the chief part of this relief was outdoor, of which there is now none. An incident of the time which happened here explains something of the horror with which the people regarded the workhouse. In order to prevent the sale of the meal given in relief it was wetted by order of the guardians. Much of it became as hard as mortar; and most of it turned sour and caused illness in the already enfeebled people. Popular reports of wholesale poisonings have often arisen from a less cause. Now, however, it is found that the meal and other food agree well with the inmates, whose average of health is high, exclusive of the prevalent ophthalmia. The resident officers spoke cheer-fully of the change since last year. During the fever season last year there were deaths daily to the amount of from twenty to twenty-five in that crowded house, whereas there are now only about three in a week. The breakfast is porridge with milk; and the dinner, soup made of meal, with various vegetables; and an allowance of bread, which suffices also for supper. The people are hoping now to be allowed potatoes twice a week; and great is the pleasure with which they look forward to this treat. There is no regular agricultural instructor of the boys at Ennistymon, but some are promising weavers, under the teaching of a zealous Yorkshireman. The women spin and knit, and the sewing of the household is done by the girls, who are also taught fine work, by which they may make money hereafter.

Long before we entered an Irish workhouse Mr. Osborne's name was uttered to us with blessings, as we find it still wherever we go. There are no two opinions about him, and the blessedness of his visit — as far as we have heard. Gentle and simple, Catholic and Protestant, Tory and Liberal, bid us believe all that he has said — assure us that his information was precisely correct — declare that he is the best of all the good friends of Ireland — and glow while they tell us that what he said was (in the words of a poor Catholic) 'religion, and charity, and truth, all in one'. We had not doubted this before; but this universal testimony strengthened our desire to see the Kilrush house. We there heard, from resident officials, terrible accounts of the famine and fever times, when people were brought in, and died between the outer gate and the door of the house; when they were laid three in a bed (those beds which are comfortable and decent for one, but which still are made to hold two), and the dead and the living were found lying side by side every morning. But enough has been said about that. There have been auxiliary houses opened to a greater extent than are now needed. Three have been lately closed. The house was built to contain 1100, and the sheds 416 more. The number in the house when we were there was 2735, and the deaths during the last twelve months have been 362. There is a farm of twenty-five acres, where the boys are taught to labour. It was Sunday when we were there; and we neither saw the people at work, nor met the master and matron. Colonel Vandeleur and a party of friends were there. After they were gone we went round. We thought the place very clean, and the people, on the whole, healthy-looking; but our impressions of the management, in the hands of subordinate officers (who seemed to us too young), were not very favourable. There was much confusion and inaccuracy in their statements; and the terms they were on with the people, and the manners of the household, did not seem to us so good as we had expected from what we had seen elsewhere. There can be no doubt, however, of the improvement which has been fairly instituted in the Kilrush house, and which is still advancing.

Here and there we meet with some one who wishes to see workhouses made self-supporting. Such persons seldom see any alternative between paupers being absolutely idle and supporting the house by field-labour. There is no need to tell you what we say when our opinion is desired — how we ask whether any industrial enterprise ever answers under corporate management; whether there are not, in the case of pauper labourers, peculiar disadvantages; and whether the whole principle of a legal charity for the helpless is not abandoned when the proposition is made to maintain them by the labour of the able-bodied. Of this we may have occasion to say more, if the subject should again be pressed upon our notice as it has been. Meantime, we have only to say now that we cannot conceive what would have become of the people without the workhouses; and that we cannot conceive what is to become of the workhouses unless some productive industry — farming, fishing, or manufactures — is ere long established in the west of Ireland.

Francis B. Head

A FORTNIGHT IN IRELAND

'Galloping' Francis Head (1793-1875) was a genuine paragon of Victorian determination and derring-do. In the Royal Engineers he survived shipwreck off Tripoli and then the battle of Waterloo. He managed gold and silver mining companies in South America, earning his nickname there for heroic horseback traverses of the pampas. He wrote a book about Bruce of Africa. As lieutenant-governor of Upper Canada he put down an 1837 insurrection with a severity that alienated the home office and necessitated circuitous travel home to avoid assassination. Then he retired to a genteel literary career as a correspondent for the *Quarterly Review*, travel writer, and translator of Apuleius. His entry in the *Dictionary of National Biography* notes that he rode to hounds until the age of seventy-five.

In 1852, as he wrote in the preface to *A Fortnight in Ireland*, 'among a motley crowd of tourists, by the irresistible power of steam, I was injected into the island of Ireland, which I had never before seen. For a week, almost without blinking, I looked it steadily in the face'. The second week of the fortnight was spent collecting statistical data.

Head boasts here that the 'object of my little tour in Ireland was to listen to opinions rather than to impart them'. His journey was predicated by a host of opinions, however, most notable among them the familiar assumption that the real character of the country could be captured in a 'little' tour of a week's duration. So, too, he carries with him an opinion on Irish women's chastity that is as entrenched in the 19th century as the opinion of their indecency was in previous eras. Nor can Head hope to escape the ramifications on his perspective of the fact of recent famine. As his own fairly accurate figures indicate, the problems Head describes did not originate in the late 1840s. Among the things that did happen then was that Ireland, for the English visitor, became a problem to be solved.

This selection is the 'Fifth Day' of the first edition, printed in London in 1852.

Mullins's Hut at Scull: famine victims and visitor, from *The Illustrated London News*, 1847. This illustration shared a page with that of Dunmanway on page 267.

T he seaport town of Galway, the capital of the West, and in point of population the sixth town in Ireland, from its peculiar position has always been a point of great commercial importance. Its bay, one of the finest in the world, is a magnificent funnel, intended by Nature for the reception of vessels from all quarters of the globe. By means of two short canals, already described, an inland water communication of great extent and value is on the point of being effected. Lastly, by the Midland and Great Western Railway, which as nearly as possible bisects Ireland, Galway and Dublin are inseparably joined together by a line of communication, which, besides being the nearest and speediest, is the shortest that could have been devised between the Irish Channel and the great Atlantic Ocean — Nature's thoroughfare between the United Kingdom and the two continents of America.

The connection which formerly existed between Galway and Spain is not only recorded in history — is not only to be traced in the architecture of Lynch's Castle, also in the wide entries, arched gateways, stone-mullioned windows, and outside stairs of several ancient mansions in the town, but the traveller, as he runs, can most legibly read it in the dark eyes, noble features, and high-bred demeanour, that in Galway in particular, and throughout Connemara in general, constantly remind him of the fact; indeed, I repeatedly met men and women whose countenances, to say nothing of their garb, would anywhere have induced me to address them in Spanish rather than in English.

The town is now a medley of streets and buildings of various dates, forming altogether a strange, incongruous, but very happy family of narrow crooked alleys, broad thoroughfares, docks, churches, dispensaries, chapels, banks, gaols, court-houses, nunneries, barracks, monasteries, storehouses, breweries, a union workhouse, distilleries, flour-mills, docks, bridges, a magnificent railway hotel just constructed, several ancient houses just falling, a number of hovels of the most wretched appearance, evidently destined to be replaced very shortly by mansions of wealth and luxury. There are several streets composed almost entirely of immense warehouses, from four to six storeys high, each with a small pent-house-covered crane affixed to its upper stratum. These vast receptacles are now nearly all empty; and, on inquiring the reason, I was briefly informed that Galway, which used to import and bond corn in large quantities, now exports it.

Queen's College [i.e. now University College, Galway], just completed on the outside of the town, is one of the chastest and handsomest public edifices I have ever seen. It is a pity, however, that the lowness of its position prevents it from contributing as much as it ought to the general beauty of the town. In its vicinity is a large poor-house, built eight years ago; and about 100 yards from it, on an elevated plot composed of emerald-green turf and beds of beautiful flowers, stands a school-house, resembling very much a modern villa; and yet, in their immediate neighbourhood are to be seen unroofed huts, miserable cabins, a confusion of tottering, crooked stone walls surrounding small enclosures, many of which are so full of rocks that they really resemble a rising crop of young tombstones, several, like children's second teeth, coming out all crooked.

As I was strolling through the suburbs I came to a potato-market, in which I found, squatted on the ground, a number of women, four or five of whom were suckling ravenous infants. Of the potatoes, which in heaps were before them, it was sad to observe many diseased, some quite rotten. The clothes of buyers, as well as sellers, were also, generally speaking, in the very last stage of consumption. The arms of the jacket of one old man beside me had each been replaced by a portion of coarse grey worsted stocking, in holes; and his corduroy breeches, which had no buttons at the knees, had been mended with pieces of cloth of various hues. Several of the women's red petticoats had likewise been patched with old flannel and rags of so many colours that the garment resembled altogether a printed map of modern Europe, the scarlet bit being, of course, the papal dominions. In a mantilla of old blanket, fantastically shrouded over her head, so as to show nothing of an aged face but an Arab nose, a pair of piercing eyes, and a very small portion of sallow complexion, there sat at my feet a regular Spanish beggar. Before me two fine little barefooted boys, of about five years old, stood for some minutes whapping each other on the head; at last one tried to pull the hair of t'other one, but, as his mother had happened to cut it almost to the quick, the little urchin could grasp nothing, until he bethought himself of catching hold of the yellow side-locks of his comrade, which in dead silence he steadily pulled with all his force. 'And that's the way,' said I to myself, 'that the Protestants of Ireland are said to deal with their Catholic brethren!' In the middle of this group stood erect a stout man, in official charge of an iron triangle, from the apex of which hung scales for weighing potatoes, diseases and all. As I was looking at him, a pretty half-naked child of about two years old tottled up, and in high glee whipped my leg with a stick. 'Och! ye blackguard,' exclaimed an old woman sitting beside me on the ground with her legs sticking out, showing me, when I turned round, ten up-pointed toes and a pair of soles as hard as hide. In all directions was to be heard a deal of very rough female cackling, and occasionally laughter, but no quarrelling. In the midst of the whole stood here and there, with drooping head and motionless thin tail, a donkey, patiently bearing a pannier laden with turf, secured by straw ropes.

After proceeding some way I was gradually assailed by a very strong smell, and, summoning my eyes to the elucidation of this discovery of my nose, I perceived hanging on some rails before me a quantity of salted, conger-eels, split open; in short, I found myself in a fish-market, with mackerel, 'hake' and other beings fresh from the vasty deep, of such

Scene in a chapel at Thurles, *The Illustrated London News*, 1848: humble supplicants, left; social reformer, right.

guttural names that, although they were over and over again pronounced to me, I felt the alphabet had not consonants enough to repeat them. A gentleman who happened to stand near me, pointing to a basket of young herrings about the size of sprats, observed to me, 'It's a great shame they should be allowed to take them so young'. I replied, 'Why, there must be plenty of all ages in the sea!' 'And sure,' exclaimed an old fish-woman at our side, 'the *say* is richer than the land!'

For a few moments I stood gazing at a roofless and almost floorless building, of Spanish architecture, on the curiously worked front of which was inscribed, in old style,

MARTINI BROWN,
1627

A woman passing at the moment gratuitously informed me it was the oldest house in the town.

As I was crossing the great esplanade in front of Kilroy's hotel, I suddenly heard the din of martial music, and soon saw approaching me, preceded by a crowd of ragged, barefooted boys, a regiment of soldiers, whose fine scarlet clothes and white crossed belts formed a striking contrast with the dingy, crooked, narrow street from which they had emerged.

After admiring for some time the dock, which appears to me most admirably constructed, I observed close to it, quite apart from the town of Galway, a little city of cabins, entirely inhabited by fishermen and their families. It is called 'The Claddagh'; and as I had heard much of their strange habits, prejudices, superstitions, and of their being governed almost exclusively by their own laws, with considerable curiosity I slowly dived into it. I must own, however, I was woefully disappointed; for although it certainly was strange to wander by oneself through winding narrow streets of huts, containing a population of nearly 1300 people, yet with this eccentricity there was mixed up so much filth and misery that the amalgam altogether was anything but attractive.

As might naturally be expected, the first thing I ran against in the city of The Claddagh was a tall dirty old woman, with a long fish dangling, as if it had grown there, from her right hand.

On each side of every street the doors of the cabins were wide open. On entering one of them I found, kneeling on the ground in the middle of her chamber, an old woman, with one tooth, preparing, in a wooden bowl, for two little pigs a quantity of potato-parings, which they were eyeing and she chopping very attentively. Around her were walking, and now and then interjectionally hopping, three hens. 'After the disorder,' said the aged creature to me, pointing with her bony dry chin to her two pigs, 'they're very sick!'.

In another cabin I found four women rapidly making nets, and a very old man, in rags, slowly combing his hair.

After passing through several streets of cabins, in which I usually saw, mixed up in different proportions, half-naked children, pigs, fowls, women, and nets, I heard an astonishing cackling of female voices, and on arriving at the hovel from which it proceeded I was suddenly surrounded by ten or a dozen women, of various ages, who — *nem. con.* [i.e. *nemine contradicente*, no one contradicting] — appointed me high-judge and arbitrator in a dispute of apparently extraordinary importance. As, however, they all addressed me at once, in a confusion of tongues that must very closely have resembled that of Babel, I am unable to impart to the reader, simply because I don't know, what in the world it was all about. The only person in the group that said nothing was a poor woman, of about thirty, who, with eyes streaming with tears as she looked at me, and with a countenance of excruciating grief, was bitterly crying. 'Her husbind has been just drowned!' observed to me one old wife. 'That 'oman,' exclaimed to me a stout girl, down whose flushed and violently-heated cheeks tears appeared to be almost hissing as one after another they rapidly fell on the ground — 'that 'oman, yere Arn'r,' said she, pointing to a female on her right, 'horped I might be a cripple!'

'Oh, never mind,' said I to her in a soothing tone; but as I only made her cry more violently, and as her sobs seemed about equally to excite the voices of plaintiffs as well as of defendants, I gave up the cause in despair; and accordingly, turning on my heels, and deferring judgment, I left the court, and in doing so nearly ran against a boy carrying a basket on a naked arm; his right leg was barely covered with blue rags, his left leg with brown cloth; and through both, as also through his jacket, sundry pieces of white skin were peeping at me.

As I wandered I hardly knew where, I entered a tarred-roofed cabin, in which I found hanging round a fire a quantity of drenched blue sailors' clothes, in rags; from the black rafters drooped, in form of a cone, a net which a sturdy woman was mending. While talking to her I heard something breathing apoplectically hard, and looking towards the sound I saw, on a little patch of straw, two very fat piebald pigs; close to them was a heap of mussel-shells, and a smoked wicker cradle containing a sleeping infant begrimed with dirt.

In the pea-green book, to which I have so often had occasion to refer, the English tourist is informed that the people of 'The Claddagh will marry with no one but themselves'. 'I should like to know who'd marry *them!*' said I to myself, rather petulently — principally because at the moment of the intemperate expression I felt something or another crawling on and occasionally biting my legs. In short, of all the dirty places in this world I have ever had occasion to visit, The Claddagh is the worst.

'They really,' I said to myself, improperly irritated by the tingling in my legs, 'should be swept off the surface of the globe, and the easiest and least painful mode of putting them to death,' I added, as with my umbrella I slightly scratched my left ankle, 'would be suddenly to wash them, which, like oil on a wasp, or a drop of prussic acid on the tongue of a dog, would inevitably in an instant render them inanimate.'

On extricating myself from this extraordinary congregation I observed close on the adjoining dock, whose admirable construction had already attracted my attention, a fine hewn stone building, three storeys high, surmounted by a large statue or figure of a fisherman with his hat on, leaning with his left hand on an anchor, and holding in his right hand a flag-staff.

'He'd a fine green flag in thart hand,' said to me with evident pride an old fisherman who had attentively been remarking what I was looking at, 'the day the Lord Liftinunt was here!'

The building in question, on which was inscribed in large letters, 'CLADDAGH NATIONAL PISCATORY SCHOOL, AN. MDCCCXLVI.,' at a cost of 1200l, had been constructed for the children, male and female, of the fishermen of the Claddagh, on a site where a few years ago salmon could be caught.

On entering it I found, barefooted, but with clean faces and in decent attire, about 130 children in narrow rooms, in which the girls were instructed to sew, spin, read, and write; and the boys, in addition, to make nets, etc. On the walls were several pictures, the most striking of which was a very large fish; there were also maps, the model of a ship, etc. The improvement in their appearance was certainly very striking. A very respectable-looking priest, who was in attendance, earnestly solicited me to write my opinion of the school in a book which he presented to me for that purpose; as, however, my object in my little tour in Ireland was to listen to opinions rather than impart them, as courteously as I could, I declined.

Moored to the wharf was a little black steamer with a small raised buff deck immediately abaft the black funnel, which was in midship.

On its stern was the word 'O'CONNELL'. At its prow, with wings extended, was a very large white fat bird with a pouting breast and a hooked bill.

'Is that an *eagle?*' said I dubiously to a small group of the Claddagh fishermen, who, in blue jackets and weather-worn trousers, were standing indolently beside it.

'I don't know,' replied one. 'Yere Arnh'r can judge better than we can!' 'Ut's *like* an agle!' said another. 'I think ut's a doove!' said a third, 'or a goole!'

'Where does this little steamer go to?' I inquired.

'She's been doing nothing, divil a hap'orth, for months. Last wake she took the Lord Liftinunt and his lady up thro' the locks. They stood thegither alone on that deck. The ady-cumps were arl in front. I very soule cheered um. 'Twas a fine sight, yere Arn'r! Ut was, indade!'

From the dock I went to the constabulary barracks, the force of which in Galway consists of one sub-inspector, one head constable, five constables, two acting ditto, 38 sub-ditto.

The sub-inspector was on duty at the Court-house, but from the head constable I learned that the particular duties of the force consisted 'in protecting property, the docks, and the quays, on which arrive a quantity of sea-weed and goods from the country; in attending to emigrant vessels, in keeping returns of emigration, etc.'

During my tour, wherever I went, I had observed that Irish dogs are infected with a wooden log tied round their necks, and which bruises their knees if they attempt to go faster than a trot. 'It's inflicted on um by the aristocricy of England!' said a man of whom I had modestly inquired on the subject. I certainly inwardly laughed at the idea, but, on asking the constable why the dogs of Galway were all tackled in this extraordinary way, he produced to me, to my astonishment, an Act of Parliament, authorising 'all dogs within 50 yards of any public road to be logged'; and moreover under a warrant from the Justice of the Petty Sessions district, any sub-inspector, head, or other constable to 'seize or kill any such dog'. It must, however, be recollected that this log is no doubt wisely intended by Parliament to balance the infliction upon English dogs of the income-tax; and as an English dog runs about unfettered, but *taxed*, and an Irish dog lives untaxed, but *logged*, it would admit of argument, if 'the twa dogs' were to meet, which was the freest animal of the two.

I had now a few questions to put to the constable on a subject of very great importance, on which I was particularly desirous to obtain accurate official information.

From the morning on which I had visited the great model National School in Marlborough Street, Dublin, to the hour of my arrival at Galway, I had remarked in the Irish female countenance an innate or native modesty more clearly legible than it has ever been my fortune to read in journeying through any other country on the globe.

Of the pure and estimable character of Englishwomen, I believe no one is a more enthusiastic admirer than myself; nevertheless I must adhere to the truth of what I have above stated, and I do so without apology, because I am convinced that no man of ordinary observation can have travelled, or can now travel, through Ireland without corroborating the fact.

But I have lived long enough to know that outward appearance cannot always be trusted, and accordingly, wherever I went, I made inquiries, the result of which was not only to confirm, but to over-confirm, my own observation; indeed, from the Resident Commissioner of the Board of National Education in the metropolis, down to the governors of gaols and masters of the remotest workhouses, I received statements of the chastity of the Irishwomen so extraordinary, that I must confess I could not believe them;

in truth I was infinitely more puzzled by what I heard than by the simple evidence of my own eyes.

I resolved, therefore, that before I concluded my trifling tour, the sole object of which had been to inform myself as correctly as possible of the real character of the Irish people, I would, instead of generalities, come to particulars on the subject in question, and I accordingly put to the constable the following questions, the answers to which I wrote as he pronounced them:-

Q. 'How long have you been on duty in Galway?'
A. 'Above nine years.'
Q. 'Have you much crime here?'
A. 'Very little; it principally consists of petty larcenies.'
Q. 'Have there been here many illegitimate children?'
A. 'Scarcely any. During the whole of the eight years I have been on duty here I have not known of an illegitimate child being reared up in any family in the town.'
Q. 'What do you mean by being reared up?'
A. 'I mean, that, being acquainted with every family in Galway, I have never known of a child of that description being born.'
Q. 'Does that fact apply to the fishing village of "The Claddagh"?'
A. 'Particularly so.'
Q. 'Do you mean to say that, to your knowledge, there has never been an illegitimate child in the town of Galway?'
A. 'I have *heard* that a servant-girl has had one, but at the present moment there is no such case in my mind. In the village of "Claddagh" they get their children married very young.'

The above statements appeared to me so extraordinary, that I begged the constable to be so good as to conduct me to his commanding officer (sub-inspector), a well-educated and highly intelligent gentleman, whom we found at the courthouse, seated on the bench with the magistrates. As soon as the business was over I went with him to his lodgings, and, after some conversation on the subject, I asked him the following questions:-

Q. 'How long have you been on duty here?'
A. 'Only six months.'
Q. 'During that time have you known of any instance of an illegitimate child being born in the village of the Claddagh?'
A. 'Not only have I never known of such a case, but I have never heard any person attribute such a case to the fisherwomen of Claddagh. I was on duty in the three islands of Aran, inhabited almost exclusively by fishermen, who also farm potatoes, and I never heard of one of their women — who are remarkable for their beauty — having had an illegitimate child, nor did I ever hear it attributed to them; indeed, I have been informed by Mr.———, a magistrate who has lived in Galway for eight years, and has been on temporary duty in the island of Aran, that he also had never heard there of a case of that nature. These people, however, when required to pay poor-rates, having no native poor of their own in the workhouse, resisted the payment of what they considered a very unjust tax – in fact, they closed their doors, and the rate was only partially collected.'

The officer, seeing that I took great interest in the subject on which I had been conversing with him, sent for some subordinates, who, he observed, had been longer in Galway than himself.

They arrived separately, and the information of the head constable (sergeant), in reply to the same questions I had put to the constable, were as follows:-

A. 'I have been here better than two years, and during that time I have never known of any woman of Claddagh having had an illegitimate child – indeed, I have never even heard of it.'
Q. 'Have you ever known of any such case in Galway?'
A. 'Oh, I think there have been some cases in *town*. Of my own knowledge I cannot say so, but I have *heard* of it.'

The sergeant in charge of the Claddagh station now arrived, and gave his opinion as follows:-

Q. 'How long have you been in charge of the Claddagh village?'
A. 'I have been nine years here, for five of which last March I have been in charge of Claddagh.'
Q. 'During that time has there been an illegitimate child born there?'
A. 'No, I have never heard of it, and if it had happened I should have been sure to have heard of it, as they wouldn't have allowed her to stop in the village.'
Q. 'Have you ever heard of any that occurred *before* your arrival?'
A. 'No, Sir.'
Q. 'During the nine years you have been in Galway, have you known of any cases that have occurred *there*?'
A. 'Well, there were very few: only one that I know, of my own knowledge.'
Q. 'Are the Claddagh people always as slovenly in their persons as I have seen them to-day?'
A. 'Oh, no! on Sundays the fishermen turn our clean and neat, in blue jackets and trousers, and shoes. The women turn out with scarlet cloaks and white caps; the young women with their hair trimmed and bound up very tastily.'

'And yet,' said I to myself, 'what ornament can these poor young people put on equal to that virtuous character which they wear wherever they go, and which, in spite of their poverty, it appears no human power can deprive them of!'

He added, 'But they are very improvident; they make much money in summer. I have known them catch 260 pair of soles in one haul.'

The officer here stated, and the last witness (the sergeant), who had been in charge of Claddagh for the last five years, subsequently of his own accord repeated the assertion, that until lately the crime of theft had been utterly unknown among the fishermen, and was almost so now; 'in fact', added the sergeant, 'no theft has occurred in Claddagh during *my* time.'

From the officers' quarters I hastened to The Claddagh, and, hiring a boat, I desired a couple of boys, who evidently looked upon me as the best fish they had caught for some time, to take me aboard an emigrant ship heavily laden with passengers (they had only yesterday taken leave of all their friends), and lying in the bay, about a mile and a half off.

There was a nice fresh side breeze, and after rolling about for a few minutes, while the youngsters were hauling up the sail, the 15-year-old pilot took the helm, and I and his comrade, aged 17, sat down close by him to windward.

Of course it was the interest and object of these lads to make the most of the haul they had got, and accordingly, said the youngest,

'The *lighthouse* is a very nice place. Would your Arn'r like to see ut?'

'*Art-fry*, there,' said the other, pointing to a desolate-looking spot, more than 12 miles by road from Galway, 'is the nicest place in a' the town. Will your Arn'r go to *ut*?'

'No, I thank you!' I replied, 'I want only to go to that ship; do you know what sort of emigrants are on board of it?'

'They're all from this neighbourhood,' he replied. After pausing for a few seconds, he added, 'They're distroyed out of this land, and must go to Ameriky!'

'How long have you been a fisherman?' said I to the eldest of my crew.

'We're been to *say*,' ejaculated the youngest, 'yere Arn'r, since we were four years awake!' Pointing to the stone ballast in the centre and at the bottom of the boat, he added, 'That's our bed; we're aften out a week wet through in these little boats; for winter we have big boats, of from twelve to fifteen tons; this little one is but four.'

'What do you subsist on while you are out?' I inquired.

'We ate bread, and cook mackerel with turf, and we arlways carry two kegs of warter with us.'

'But,' said I, 'will the fish you catch for sale *keep* for five days?'

'Oh yes, yere Arn'r,' he replied; 'we take the goots and liver out o' um, and then they'll keep a week.'

But by this time we had got close to the black vessel, a 'bark', over whose stern I observed hanging by the heels and gently vibrating twenty-five flaccid-looking cabbages, among which there appeared, written in large white letters,

THE ALBION OF ARBROATH

Over the gunwale were ranged a line of rustic faces, male and female, all quietly looking at us. In a few seconds, however, we were alongside, and I had scarcely stepped among the crowd when, the interest of my arrival having completely ceased, no one took the slightest notice of me; however, on one of the crew passing me, I begged he would tell the captain I would be glad to see him. In about five minutes he came up from below, told me he was very busy serving out provisions, but that I was quite welcome to go over the vessel, and he desired a sailor-boy to accompany me.

New Year's Night in an Irish cabin, from *The Illustrated London News*. Like Francis B. Head's account, the contemporary English view of Ireland modulated in emphasis between economic victimisation and romantic idealisation.

On the deck, besides a number of steerage passengers, were three or four women of superior garb, sitting rather indolently, reading. The boy told me the bark was registered at 302 tons; and he then led me down below between decks, which, as soon as I could see — for at first I fancied I was in almost utter darkness – appeared completely thronged with country people, very poorly but clean and decently dressed; in fact, it was evident they were all in their best clothes.

On each side throughout the whole length of the vessel, without any curtains or compartments to separate them, were, one above the other, two tiers of berths, each 4 feet 8 inches broad by 5 feet 10 inches in length. Each of these beds was nominally for two people.

'What do they pay for them?' I asked the boy.

'Those of full age pay 3l. 10s., under age 3l.', he replied.

'Whart *I* pay', exclaimed a female voice from a berth on my right, 'for myself and two chilthren, one three and the other five, is 8l. 5s. I have here, myself, my two chilthren, and another woman!'

Although I was thus loudly addressed, no one noticed me; in fact, they had not room to do so. In several of the berths I saw powerful-looking men lying indolently; the distance from their faces to the deck above them was 2 feet 7 inches.

After worming my way through a number of women, some of whom were erectly arranging their berths, others stooping to ferret into trunks, and others sitting placidly mending extremely old clothes, I came to the hold, down which a small gleam of sunshine from above was illuminating the red moist face of the captain, who, in a blue superfine jacket, blue foraging cap, and in a clean shirt, but without his stock, was very busily occupied in weighing out, and noting down in a book he held in his hand, meal for his passengers.

After saying but a few words – for I did not like to interrupt him – I proceeded onwards with the boy, who told me that in the several adjoining berths 'cousins, friends, and families go together', until I came to a crowd, which for a few seconds obstructed me. 'Come along out o' thart and let hum pass!' exclaimed the fine manly voice of an emigrant who had observed my predicament. Very shortly another poor fellow, fancying I belonged to the ship, came up to me and asked me something about meal. 'This man,' replied the sailor-boy, 'has nothing to do with *you!*' and my friend accordingly turned aside.

Affixed to one of the berths I observed a placard of printed regulations, which I own appeared to me to have been concocted by someone not very conversant with the various indescribable *désagrémens* of a gale of wind; for instance, it ordained –

'That all the passengers must be out of bed by seven o'clock a.m.; the children to be then washed and dressed: all to be in bed by ten p.m.

'That, when the emigrants victual and cook for themselves, the overseer will see that each family has its regular hour at the cooking place.

'That there be issued to each passenger three quarts of water, not less often than twice a-week. Bread, biscuit, flour, oatmeal, and rice – in all, seven pounds per week. One-half of the supply to consist of bread or biscuit; and if potatoes be used, five pounds to be reckoned equal to one pound of bread-stuff.

'That the washing-days be on Monday and Friday.

'No smoking, gambling, swearing, or improper language to be allowed.

'No sailor to be allowed between decks, except on duty,' etc. etc.

After reading these regulations, and gazing on both sides, and as far as between decks my eyes could reach, at the men, women, and children, who in numerous groups, active, passive, and neuter, were apparently blocking up the thoroughfare, I could not help feeling very keenly how little they were aware of the discomforts of being jumbled together during a sea voyage, and, above all, of the tragic catastrophes that have so often in one relentless gulf buried the cares, sorrows, hopes, and lives of shipload after shipload of poor Irish emigrants – such as were now around me and before me, nursing infants, unpacking and repacking boxes, making beds, and engaged in numberless other little domestic arrangements. On a curtain-less berth beside me, in extreme lassitude, sat a slight, elegant-looking girl, of about seventeen, very poorly dressed; her elbows nearly touched each other – the backs of her hands rested on her lap, on which her eyes also listlessly reposed – her whole attitude appeared collapsed and unstrung. In fact, she was the personification of the word 'Eviction!'

'Erin, my country! though sad and forsaken,
    In dreams I revisit the sea-beaten shore;
But, alas! in a far-distant land I awaken,
    And sigh for the friends who can meet me no more.

Where is my cabin-door, fast by the wild wood?
    Sisters and sire! did ye weep for its fall?
Where is the mother that smiled on my childhood?
    And where is *the bosom friend*, DEARER THAN ALL?'*

The picture before me was on the whole so distressing that I was glad to find myself again in my boat; and as the distance between it and the emigrant bark gradually increased, my mind became engrossed with one simple, single, and natural subject of inquiry – namely, Why are these good people leaving their native homes? 'Why,' said I to myself, as I finally closed the note-book of my little tour – 'why, for so long a period, have the

*'Exile of Erin' by Thomas Campbell (1777-1844), with a quatrain omitted. The poem was inspired not by eviction but by a meeting in Hamburg with one Anthony McCann, exiled for participation in the rebellion of 1798.

inhabitants of Ireland been centrifugally ejected from their country, as if its lovely verdant surface were a land blasted by pestilence, or as if its virtuous and intelligent peasantry were malefactors who had been sentenced to transportation?'

From the year 1620, when the pilgrim fathers went out, up to the present time, not less than 9½ millions of Irish have emigrated from England, Ireland, and the Canadas to the United States of America.

From 1806 to 1851 not less than 4½ millions of the Irish people have emigrated from their country.

From 1841 to 1851 upwards of 1½ million have left Ireland.

In the single year 1851 Irish emigration amounted to no less than 257,372; and even from the Clyde [i.e. in Scotland], of 14,435 emigrants who in 1851 sailed to America, above one-third were Irish!

In London there are more Irish than in Dublin. In Manchester and Salford more Irish than in Cork. In Glasgow as many Irish and descendants of Irish as in Belfast. There are more Irish (born in Ireland) now living in Glasgow than there are living at Belfast Irish who have been born *there*. Of the Anglo-Saxon and Celtic races abroad, nearly one half of the whole are Irish.

Now, in the sacred names of Mercy and of Justice, who, I ask, are the guilty authors of this awful desolation?

By the Special Correspondent of the Times

LETTERS FROM IRELAND, 1886

In 1886 Parliament tabled and defeated Gladstone's first home rule for Ireland bill, two actions that combine to mark an important watershed in the history of English-Irish relations. This anonymous correspondent of the *Times* travelling in Ireland offers insight into popular English opinion on the subject of Ireland at the time when home rule was considered and then refused. In characteristic 19th century fashion, he considers the future of Ireland in the midst of a vacation tour and reports his impressions with intermittent paeans on the splendid scenery. Then, as a hundred years later, the dent civil unrest makes in the tourist industry is of much concern.

Principal among the nationalist political forces in Ireland then was the Land League, founded in 1879 to organize no-rent campaigns against agrarian landlords. Its popular support made possible the boycott, named for a Mayo victim of the tactic. The Moonlighters, as this correspondent implies, adopted more violent means to the same ends. These *Letters From Ireland* also mention assorted local politicians and victims caught up in the general agitation.

These forces are now generally cast in populist terms, a fact that quite naturally owes a great deal to the ultimate degree of success of the Irish nationalist movement. But the English correspondent in Ireland in 1886 casts them instead in terms of the immediate confrontation of colonialism with dissent. First, the forces of dissent appear in this light not as populist at all but as an 'iron rule' of a minority over an otherwise peaceful and hard-working majority. Then, on the occasion of the inevitable generalization on the national character, the forces of agitation are attributed to the 'bad qualities' of the race — improvidence, untruthfulness, 'trickery and deceit'. On that contradictory image of the Irish rests the prescription for the problem: 'to teach them to improve'. Of special interest in the context of 1886 is the general gloom about the prospects for that prescription: 'it is difficult to see how they [the younger generation] are ever to become decent members of society'.

These selections constitute letters III and IV as they were first published in book form, in London in 1887. The copyright page of the first edition carries a blurb from the *Saturday Review* to the effect that 'much valuable information on the Irish question is to be found in the series of *Letters From Ireland*.'

Punch's Irish Frankenstein, 1882. The image is famous for its racial stereotype, though the adaptation from Mary Shelley's novel also suggests creator-guilt. The caption attributes Dr. Frankenstein's words — 'Had I not breathed into it my own spirit?' — to Charles Stewart Parnell.

LETTER III.

Cork, August 25

T he sail down the river from Cork to Queenstown [i.e. Cobh] is worth a visit to Ireland in itself. The well-wooded banks rising up from the shore, the pleasant-looking villas, and the broad waters of the river combine to make it a charming expedition, if only the day be fine. Queenstown itself is beautifully situated on the face of a hill, and before it lies the splendid harbour which bears its name. At Cork the annual races were going-on, which caused some stir in the town, but the attendance was very small as compared with that of former years. The gentry have no money, and the country people seem to have lost their love of sport under a *régime* which proscribes even fox-hunting, of which they used to be so fond. I visited, too, the famous Blarney Castle, with its massive donjon tower, beautifully situated in the well-wooded demesne. The modern residence is as deserted as the old one, the owner, like so many of the great Irish proprietors, having become an absentee within the last few years. In the village of Blarney is a tweed manufactory, carried on by Mr. Mahony, a brother of the celebrated Father Prout.*

In my last letter I gave some account of boycotting as directed against a landlord in the county Tipperary, and in county Cork I have had some opportunity of seeing how it presses upon poorer men. One case, well-known in the West Riding, is that of a blacksmith, whose offence consists in having supplied a car last September to the police, when they were going to a seizure, though he was not aware of their mission at the time. He has suffered from the most virulent persecution, and his wife, who was a short time ago dangerously ill and supposed to be dying, was informed by her friends that the [Land] League would not allow her to be visited while alive, but in the event of her death they would be permitted to attend her wake and funeral; and, although her mother and a large family of brothers and sisters were living within a short distance, so great is the terrorism that they were, with one exception, afraid to come near her.

Another man in the same division of the county, who took a farm from which the former tenant had been evicted, says that whenever he travels outside his farm he is insulted and hooted and called a 'land-grabber'. He cannot go to mass on Sundays for fear of being insulted and assaulted on the way. His outhouses were burnt down last February, and his dwelling-house narrowly escaped destruction, his life and those of his family being nearly lost in the endeavour to save themselves.

A farmer in a very bad part of the county, close to Kerry, writes under date August 1:-

---

*F. S. Mahony ('Father Prout') (1804-1866), poet and satirist.

I beg to inform you that boycotting is still practised towards me, and, I fear, likely to continue as long as I hold the farm at ———, or until the Government proclaim or put down the Land League, whose laws are the only laws acknowledged here. You are, no doubt, aware that I am under police protection, and were these withdrawn I am persuaded that my existence in this world would be limited indeed. I may state that I have not attended Divine service for over twelve months, as my presence there would most certainly lead to bad results. It was only this day (Sunday) that I heard of notices being posted on the Roman Catholic chapel gate threatening a woman in the locality, whose only offence was attending to my daughter-in-law during her recent confinement.

As another instance of the intimidation that is practised, I may give the following letter from a local butcher, also dated August of this year:-

Sir, — I would have sent you a reply long before now, but I was inquiring to know if I could supply you with beef and mutton, and the answer I got from the committee of the Land League was that if I supplied ——— with any beef or mutton I would be hunted out of ———. I hope you won't feel displeased with me for not supplying you, but, as you are aware yourself, the slightest word that is said at present to a man in business will prevent people from dealing with him. I would be only very glad to supply you, and I hope I can supply you before long.

I came across one case of a man who took a farm in 1878, before the Land League was established, the granting of which had been taken the two previous years by a prominent Leaguer, but from which a tenant had formerly been evicted. He was boycotted in 1880, and repeatedly visited by Moonlighters, who endeavoured to intimidate him by firing shots round his house. A police hut was erected on the farm and protection afforded him. He was unable to buy or sell, or to procure the necessaries of life. His family were persecuted and hooted; the master whose school was attended by his children was warned not to receive them, and they had to give up going. After six years of such existence he could stand it no longer. He sold the interest of his farm and sailed for America only a few days ago, and it seems intolerable that honest hard-working men should not be able to live in the country and pursue their avocations in peace.

Two printed handbills, circulated by a local branch of the League in this county have come into my possession. The first is as follows:-

Irish National League.
Bartlemy and Rathcormac.

Shopkeepers, tradesmen, and labourers are requested to have no dealings of any kind with Captain St. Leger Barry, his agent, T. Ryall, and his three sons.

God save Ireland!

The Crisis, frontispiece illustration for *Realities of Irish Life* (1868) by William Stewart Trench (1808-1872). The book was widely respected in Ireland and republished as recently as 1966. The image here combines imminent violence and evident deprivation with need for managerial discipline.

And at the bottom is a written postscript:-

> We expect this caution will be sufficient.

This was followed by another bill calculated to prove more efficacious:-

> ### £5 Reward.
>
> Shopkeepers, Farmers, Tradesmen, Car-owners, and Labourers are strictly requested to have no dealings of any kind with the following persons – viz., that writ-serving little despot O'Riordan, solicitor, of the firm of O'Riordan and Mandeville, of Fermoy and Mitchelstown, and the clique who are assisting him in his dirty work, Captain St. Leger Barry, his agent, T. Ryall, and his two sons, John and Robert Ryall.
>
> The above reward will be paid to any person who shall give such information as shall lead to the detection of the backsliders and others who are assisting the abovenamed in their felonious landlordism.
>
> God save Ireland.

These instances are sufficient to show that the organization of the League is strong in the county Cork, but the action of the Cork Defence Union has been most valuable in supporting boycotted persons and enabling them to live. It purchases their cattle and farm produce, supplies them with men and machinery, as well as food and other necessaries, subsidizes local blacksmiths on condition that they work for any one who wishes to employ them, and counteracts the operations of the League in every possible way. A gentleman who undertook to buy boycotted cattle for the Union in his locality, provided they were brought into the open market, gave me a lively description of his first experience. He came into the fair after a prominent member of the League had gone through pointing out the boycotted cattle, and priced and bought them all. They were driven up to the station surrounded by a cordon of forty police, half of whom were in plain clothes, and followed by a hooting, yelling, and hissing mob, who did their best to separate the cattle and mix them with others, but without success, and he has since been able to buy without active interference. The fact that there are few outrages committed in this county is a testimony to the perfection to which the machinery of the League has been brought. A gentleman who is fully conversant with it said:

> The existing peaceable state of this part of the county may be safely attributed to the fact that the inhabitants are held in the iron grasp of the League, whose orders they dare not venture to disobey, and as long as this reign of terror exists, so long will personal liberty and freedom of action remain suspended.

Another gentleman, who has had some 2,000 tenants under him, as agent, during the last forty years, and has not evicted half a dozen, tells me that from what the people say to him in confidence he believes the suppression of the League would be the most popular act, and that if a genuine poll could be taken 80 per cent. would be in favour of it.

'If it were suppressed,' he said, 'we should get rid of politics and turn our minds to industry. The people are longing to take the vacant farms, and the value they set on the land may be gathered from the sums they are giving for the tenant-right.'

Another gentleman, a Roman Catholic, well acquainted with the country, expressed himself precisely to the same effect. 'I wish in God, sir,' the people say, 'something could be done.' No doubt a considerable number would be glad to be relieved from such an iron rule, and to recover their individual liberty; but it is questionable whether the majority of the farming class would not be the other way, as they feel they have got large reductions of rent through the action of the League, and they hope to get still more.

One gentleman of considerable experience in the South and West, so far from suppressing the League, would allow them to blow off as much steam as they like, but the moment they held any one up as an object for boycotting he would have them prosecuted and liable to summary conviction at the hands of resident magistrates.

It is a remarkable fact that since the decision of the country was given against Home Rule several sales have been effected to tenants under Lord Ashbourne's Act;* and if once the farmers were disabused of the idea that they may get the land for nothing, or next to nothing, many of them would be only too ready to buy, and they would then become the most conservative people on the face of the earth. Some of the larger farmers might prosper well enough as freeholders, but the majority of Irish tenants are too dependent and helpless, and certainly have not as yet shown any of the qualities necessary for success as peasant proprietors; moreover, when once they become owners in fee there would be no check upon subdivision, which has been one of the greatest curses to the country.

It is generally anticipated that there will be a passive resistance to payment of rent in the autumn, and it will be difficult to know how best to meet it. It is easy enough to deal with those who can, but refuse to, pay a fair rent; but there is only too good reason to fear that many of the tenants, whether from their own fault or not, are hopelessly insolvent, and the question is what to do with them. It is to be hoped that the landlords will take care, in the first place, that they are making a reasonable demand, considering the times, as they will then be standing on firm ground. There is no doubt that large reductions have been generally made throughout the country, though the Nationalists speak and write as if there had been none;

---

*The Purchase of Land (Ireland) Act of 1885 to aid tenants become land owners. This letter is dated August, and the first home rule bill was defeated in the Commons on June 7, 1886.

but at the same time some few landlords have shut their eyes to facts, and have in consequence not only suffered severely themselves, but injured the cause of others who have been more considerate, by giving a handle to the National League.* I have seen a letter from an eminent firm of London solicitors to an Irish land agent, from which one would suppose they had not read a newspaper for the last six years, and that there was no difficulty whatever in collecting rents in Ireland. They observe that it is a remarkable fact that English agents have no difficulty in collecting the full rent in Ireland, and request him to be good enough to remit the rents in future without any reduction, though one of their clients has been already practically ruined by pursuing the same short-sighted policy.

It is true that twenty or twenty-five years ago prices were as low as they are now, but the people lived in a very different way. In the good times, when prices were too high, the farmers all increased their way of living, in many cases to an absurd extent. The small farmers took to white bread and tea instead of oatmeal and potatoes, and the large ones began to live like gentlemen. I have seen the wife of a tenant who professes to be unable to pay his rent, driving about in as smart a pony-carriage as any one could wish to see, and I have seen others who say they cannot make up anything for the landlord, living with every appearance of comfort and prosperity. The advice given by the League has, no doubt, been very acceptable. They have been told from a hundred platforms to provide for themselves and their families, and if anything is over they can then think of the landlord. This advice is being repeated now in much the same terms as ever. Dr. Tanner, M.P., speaking at Millstreet, county Cork, on the 15th of August, put it thus:-

Arm yourselves for the fray, keep your pockets tightly buttoned up. You will be obliged to pay your shopkeepers; do so in order to clothe and feed your wives and families. If, of course, when you have done all this, and have and hold sufficient to stock your farms next year, why, if you have then any margin of course give it as rent; but if not, as I should imagine would be the case, why no one can give what he has not got.

And Mr. Gilhooly, M.P., tendered the same advice to his friends at Bantry on the same date:-

Your first duties are to look after your families and to their requirements. If you have money spared after attending to them, pay it to the landlords. If none is spared they are entitled to none, and you are justified in combining to protect your property, should the landlord try to deprive you of it. . . . By combination, unity, and courage, the tenant-farmers will be able to keep themselves and their families in their homes during the coming winter. They have a right to live and thrive on the soil of this country, and if they allow themselves to be driven from their homes for want of unity, courage, and combination, they will not receive, nor do they deserve, the sympathy, respect, or support of their friends in America to better their condition.

---

*A successor of the Land League; founded by Charles Stewart Parnell, its fortunes declined with his in the 1890s.

(Both speeches are reported in the *Cork Examiner* of Tuesday, August 17th.) Many of the tenants have also of late years neglected their farms, their minds have been unsettled by the constant agitation and the prospect of getting their land for nothing; and if an Irishman thinks he can get on without working he will certainly prefer to do so. People complain, too, that the labourers have become demoralized and idle, and that there is no getting a good day's work out of them now.

I have met with some remarkable instances of what may be done by industry as compared with idleness. One was that of a widow living on a wild mountain holding, the rent of which is £2.10s. Her husband died only three years ago, and during the last forty years they have made enough to give three daughters substantial fortunes and to send a son to America. They had no other means of making money but the land, and it was simply the result of patient toil. 'We did make money thin, sir,' said the woman, 'and people can do it by industry'. In another case a man took a farm near Macroom, in 1845, of considerably over 100 acres, on a thirty-one years' lease, and at a rent of £113. He started with four cows, a horse, and £200 which he got with his wife. He prospered, and, in spite of the famine times, took another farm under the same landlord in 1849, at £64, and yet another in the following year at £76. He gave one daughter a fortune of £800, a second £600, and a third £400. He built houses on two of the farms and gave them up, fully stocked, to two of his sons. At his death he left the third farm to another son, and £300 to a fourth, who took a farm also under the same landlord. Those four sons are now hopelessly insolvent; they have given themselves up to idleness and drinking, and one of them, I am told, entertained the Land League with champagne. The landlord has endeavoured to help them by giving enormous reductions, but they seem unable to do anything.

Some landlords would do well to remember that too much indulgence is as bad as none at all, and that there are other ways of helping tenants besides merely giving abatements of rent. The rent is after all nothing as compared with the produce of the land, and the real thing is to teach them to improve, though with Irish farmers it has to be done almost in spite of themselves. It is demoralizing that they should come to look upon abatements of rent as the only remedy for bad times, and that they should not rouse themselves to better methods of farming, and do something to help themselves.

LETTER IV.

Kerry, August 30

At the close of my last letter I alluded to the importance of trying to get Irish tenants to improve their methods of farming, and the difficulty of persuading them to change what they have been always used to. The agent of a very large property in the south-west endeavoured to improve the breed of pigs and cattle on the estate this year by procuring a number of good beasts and offering them as presents among the more prosperous farmers. The first man to whom he sent a boar refused it, the only reason he could give being that his wife would not let him have it; and no one else would take it after it had been once rejected. Another man who had received a present of a fine bull came soon after with a petition that he might be allowed to fatten it for sale. It was pointed out to him that his cattle might be worth £2 or £3 a head more if they were better bred, but he thought 'maybe they'd be too good, and mightn't do on the mountain'. There is hardly any sale now for inferior cattle, the natural consequence when there is a shrinkage being that only the better qualities are in demand, and yet they will not see the necessity of improving their breeds.

In some cases, however, they are being starved into improvements. The low price they have been getting for their butter has driven them to recognize the fact that it is not as good as it might be, and that they must mend their method of making it; and it is a hopeful sign that the Dairy School, which has been lately established at Cork in connection with the Model Farm there, is being largely patronized by the farmers' daughters. They go through a two months' course, paying a fee of £2, which does not cover the cost of their board, and are taught butter-making, not only with the newest and most approved appliances, but also with the ordinary ones which they are likely to use at their own homes. They can, moreover, get instruction in cookery and the economical management of food, accomplishments in which most Irishwomen are sadly deficient. There were other model farms in Ireland besides those now carried on at Cork and Glasnevin under the control of the Education Commissioners, but the farmers did not appreciate them, and but for the Dairy School the institution at Cork might also have been given up. They can take in thirty girls at a time, and the school has not only been quite full all this year, but several applications have had to be refused for want of room.

At Bantry I visited a most prosperous butter factory, which was started about five years ago, and is rapidly developing a very successful business. Irish butter has for a long time had a bad name, chiefly owing to the carelessness and want of method with which it is made. They salt one churning and put it into the firkin and wait for the next, and so on, keeping it meantime perhaps in a place which is neither clean nor well ventilated, the result being that the firkin when complete is composed of butter of different qualities, unevenly salted, and possibly tainted into the bargain. I have heard of one old woman who said she liked to set the milk in her room, because she could skim it from her bed in the morning. The manager of the butter factory buys up the butter from the people just as it is made; the different qualities are then carefully separated, and a batch of one kind is put through four different machines, worked by an engine — two for washing, one for pressing out the water, and one for salting the butter. It is then packed into clean firkins lined with muslin and despatched to London, where the best brand is now well known and commands the highest price. They turn out nearly £2,000 worth of butter a week during the summer and a considerable quantity in the winter, while between the cooperage and dairy work there are nearly 100 hands employed. I saw 180 firkins of the butter which had been bought only the day before ready to be despatched by the next train. Creameries have also been established in various places, in some of which the milk is simply put through the separator, while in others the people bring their cream, which is churned in the ordinary way. One gentleman in county Cork, who carries on dairy farming on the most approved principles, tells me that he gets £1 more per cwt. for his butter than most of the farmers, and seeing that there must be over 200,000 cwt. produced in this county in the year, it affords a slight indication of the increase of wealth rendered possible in the country by the adoption of improvements. In the same way Ireland ought to be able to supply the English market with eggs, but the people seem wanting in the energy and method requisite for developing such an industry. At Bantry I came across a striking instance of a most promising enterprise being nipped in the bud by the action of the League. A few years ago two local gentlemen determined to try and open up the fishing in the bay. They laid out a certain amount of capital and employed a number of men, and at the end of the first month they had £300 worth of fish stored in the town. This was merely the beginning of what might have been developed to almost any extent, and given a large amount of employment among the people; but at the end of a month the promoters of the undertaking were boycotted. They could not sell the fish or procure cartage for sending it away, and it was finally put out on the fields for manure. There are thousands of pounds' worth of fish lying in Bantry Bay waiting to be caught, but with such an example before them no private individuals are likely to repeat so disastrous an experiment, and it is no wonder that those who have had such an experience should think the Irish a hopeless people, and consider it a thankless task to try and help people who will not help themselves.

From Cork to Bandon the railway passes through a fine, well-wooded country, with fertile fields and smiling crops. Just before reaching the station the Duke of Devonshire's Bandon estates are passed, and, just after, the beautiful grounds of Castle Bernard. Not far from Drimoleague may be seen the spot on the road where Mr. Hutchins was shot at five years ago, and his driver killed. Everyone in the district knew the murderer, but there was no one to give evidence against him. Bantry itself is well worth stopping at, though the ordinary tourist rushes on to more popular places. If he climbs the hill beyond the town, he will get a most lovely view of the bay looking inland; and Bantry House, too, well repays a visit, with its wonderful collection of tapestries made by the second lord, including those from the Tuileries bearing the initials of Marie Antoinette. The beauties of Glengariff have often been described, and it is certainly one of the choicest spots on the face of the earth. The blue waters of the bay studded with islands; the rich foliage coming down to the very edge of the sea; and the wild mountains that surround it complete a picture which of its kind is unsurpassed. The drive on to Killarney is also magnificent. The road runs for a considerable distance up a splendid mountain pass, descending to Kenmare, where there is a very handsome chapel and convent, and lace-making is carried to great perfection under the superintendence of the nuns; and the latter part of the drive down through the richest woods to the far-famed lakes is beautiful indeed.

This has been the worst tourist season for many years; indeed, I antici-pated as much from the difficulty I found in procuring a copy of Murray's

This has been the worst tourist season for many years; indeed, I antici-pated as much from the difficulty I found in procuring a copy of Murray's 'Ireland' before leaving London, even Mr. Standford being unable to produce one, not because the stock was exhausted, but because there is no demand for Irish guide books. The hotel keepers say that but for the Americans they might give up, and the people fully realize that the English are afraid to come, though they say, with perfect truth, that they would be as safe as in their native country. The tourist might travel through the south and west without seeing a trace of the evil that exists, unless he set himself to look for it, and it is difficult to believe that the lovely country that surrounds Killarney is the scene of almost nightly raids and outrages.

My first introduction to Kerry was somewhat in the nature of a surprise, as on visiting a well-known land agent I found his hall-door wide open, and that he thought nothing of sitting in his diningroom on the ground floor with the lamp lit and windows open, although he has evicted rather more than two dozen tenants in the last three months. It is, however, a quiet part of the county, and one in which the League has never made much way. He told me the tenants are for the most part paying him, but he has to evict some of the defaulters, or the whole property would be demoralized. My experiences have not all been equally pleasant, as I slept last night in a house guarded by police, and when my host drove me out in his carriage we were followed by an escort on an outside car — a specimen of civiliza-tion in the nineteenth century.

Kerry is certainly in a most extraordinary state. The whole county is in a condition of the most abject terrorism, and the people are domineered over by a handful of village tyrants in each particular place. There are various organizations at work, partly independent of one another, but so interwoven that it is impossible to distinguish between them. There is the National League with its various branches posing as a constitutional organization. There are the Moonlighters acting, it would seem, independently in each locality; and there is the Fenian organization,* which is more or less merged in the others, and supplies materials ready to hand. The League, of course, disclaims all connection with outrages; but though it may not organize or direct them, it is impossible to acquit the local branches of all association with them.

Every Moonlighter is a member of the League, though it by no means follows that every member of the League is a Moonlighter. They are, for the most part, younger sons of small farmers, but directed by men in a better position of life; and as surely as the League denounces a man so surely do they carry the decree into effect, and if a man is had up for outrage or intimidation the local secretary of the League will be seen in court instructing the solicitor for the defence. If an outrage is committed and the murderers are brought to justice, as in the Curtin case, those who secure the vindication of the law are boycotted by order of the League. If a priest denounces outrages at a meeting of the League he probably finds himself deserted by half the members of the League; and those of the farming class who have suffered at the hands of Moonlighters, and with whom I have conversed, attribute all their misfortunes to the action of the League.

The Nationalist leaders repudiate the outrages, but without the outrages their organization would never have attained its present power or position. They say they have used their influence to check boy-cotting, but their agents in each particular place are the active promoters of boycotting. From a report of the proceedings of the Killarney Branch in the *Cork Examiner* of August 17, it appears that at a meeting presided over by Mr. Sheehan, M.P., a fund was started for John Roche, who had been imprisoned for 'alleged intimidation', and that several contributed on the spot; the fact being that Roche had been sent to gaol for a month, having pleaded 'Guilty' before the magistrates.

The worst sign of all is the spirit of the people. I believe there is no doubt that the farmers in Kerry are for the most part heartily sick of the league and the Moonlighting, and the whole agitation, but the younger generation are hopelessly demoralized. They look upon the outrages as an act of war, and the Moonlighters in their eyes are heroes fighting in a noble cause. They have thrown off the restraint of religion and of the priests, and it is difficult to see how they are ever to become decent members of society. I have even heard of cases in which farmers are anxious to have their sons sent out of the country, and to get rid of them altogether. The priest of one parish gave me some remarkable figures to show the falling off of the people in attending to their religious duties. From 1873 to 1879 the number of communions in his parish averaged 39,000 per annum, with a population

*A secret military and nationalist organization also known as the Irish Republican Brotherhood; founded in 1858, it survived to assume a formidable role in the nationalist risings of the 20th century.

of about 10,000. In 1880, the year in which the Land League went ahead, the number fell to 26,000, without any decrease in the population. He also dwelt on the extent to which perjury had increased. In one case, at the Cork Assizes, no less than 19 witnesses attended to prove an *alibi*, and counsel was brought down specially from Dublin, when, to the consternation of his friends, the prisoner pleaded 'Guilty'. In fact, the people are altogether changed, the agitation seems to have brought out all their bad qualities, their untruthfulness, their trickery and deceit, and to have effaced most of the good ones. A Roman Catholic gentleman also told me that infidelity has increased enormously, especially among the men. He said that on the 15th of this month, being Lady-day in harvest, one of the days when they are all expected to go to Mass, he counted about 100 women in his parish chapel, but not a single man except himself.

By a Guardian of the Poor

THE IRISH PEASANT
A SOCIOLOGICAL STUDY

The immediate parliamentary future of home rule effectively ended with the death of Charles Stewart Parnell in 1891. Gladstone's second bill for home rule did pass Commons in 1893, but it was defeated in Lords with stunning finality. Thereafter the nationalist movement shifted toward the activities of the Gaelic League and Sinn Fein that linked political autonomy to cultural revival.

Some time in the years leading to those events this anonymous 'Guardian of the Poor', an Englishman, travelled Ireland in the disguise of an Irish mason. The book is a mysterious affair. The title page notes that it was 'edited from original papers' but says nothing about dates or names. The work has an editor's preface that says of the author that 'he was a real person, anxious only to discover the truth as to a matter in which he felt a deep interest'. Nothing further indicates whether the author was living or dead when the book was published. Many of the people in the book bear absurdly Shavian names, presumably to protect the anonymity of a living author.

When Edmund Campion went to Ireland in 1569 one of his principal concerns was the degeneration of English into English-Irish. This work — however murky its origins — enacts just that sort of degeneration, and the suggestiveness of its premise is not lessened if it records imaginary and not actual experience. This work clearly presents the change as a debasement rather than as a simple transformation. The author just as clearly assumes that he can achieve an authenticity as Irishman that would not be possible for an Irishman to achieve as Englishman. The motivation is frustration at an inability to understand the Irish and also guilt at being thought 'better than other folks'. The goal is a remarkable one in the context of the conclusion of this survey of 300 years of English accounts of Ireland: 'I was bent on mastering the Irish problem, and I determined to discover all that could be seen or known in every direction'.

The Irish Peasant: A Sociological Study was published in London in 1892; this selection is the first chapter, slightly abbreviated.

Thurles on Market Day, from *The Illustrated London News*, 1848. Unlike Thackeray's market scene in Dunmanway (page 234), this suggests prosperity and amity: heaps of produce, pleasant buyers and sellers, helpful police officers. Note the Norman tower in the background, battered symbol of troubled history.

I was born in London, where my father had a house in an old-fashioned and highly respectable square. In due course, I was sent to that ancient university which has turned out so many great divines, statesmen, and men of thought. At the university, I took part in most movements of the day, particularly in those of a philosophical nature, and, having taken a respectable degree, returned to my home. I was not long there until my father died. This was a heavy blow. My mother had long gone before, and I had neither brother nor sister. I was quite alone in the world, and free to do as I liked. My father had been a man of considerable property, all of which had been left to me; part of it was in Ireland, a country in which my mother had been born. I felt puzzled to know where to turn. I could not live on in the gloomy, old house alone. But whither should I go? Suddenly the thought struck me, 'Why not go to Ireland?' it is a beautiful country, now much talked of, and a great field for the friend of progress. I soon acted on my idea, let my house for a term of years, and sailed for Ireland.

After a voyage of several hours in a steamer, I landed at a little seaport on the shores of an Irish loch. Black, savage-looking mountains rose straight from the sea on either hand; their lower slopes were cut up into small patches of tillage, and trees seemed to be unknown. Altogether, the scene was gloomy and depressing. In order to see the shores of the loch, I took a passage in a small steamer which went from the port at which I had landed to a larger town at the head of the bay or loch. I had a full view of either side as we steamed slowly along; one place in particular seemed strange to me who had never before seen such things. This was a mountain-side covered from top to bottom with small houses or huts, dotted over it like a flock of seagulls. The hillside was cut up into small patches of cultivation which ran nearly to the summit. I asked the steam-boat skipper how these people lived: he told me that they were nearly all hawkers, pedlars, and fish-men or fish-women. Some had a donkey and cart, and vended herrings and cockles far and near. Others, who had no donkey, carried baskets and sold, some lemons, some apples, some fish, just as these things were in season. Children began their lessons in hawking by 'taking out a few lemons in a net'. For the hut and 'bit of ground' a trifling rent was paid, and it was useful as a home to return to, or as a shelter in old age. How the land in such bleak, cold regions could be worth working, or be made grow anything, puzzled me.

I was landed at a little village, whence I hired a jaunting car, on which I drove to the small watering-place at which my father used to stay when he visited Ireland. It was a little town or village on the other side of the mountain range I had crossed, and on the open coast. The town was commonplace, being made up of whitewashed houses and cottages, plain and ugly, but slated and neat. Everything was modern. It seemed that at one time there had been nothing but thatched hovels, and a few of these yet stood at one end of the village. I stayed the night at a little inn, having ordered a car to be ready in the morning for a long drive. I intended the first thing to call on a Mr. M'Whirter, whom I had heard my father speak of as a man of great sense and shrewdness. I wanted to advise with him both as to finding a residence, there not being one on my estate, and as to some improvements I intended to make.

On a fine morning in early summer, I started for Mr. M'Whirter's house, which was some twenty-five miles off. At first I drove through a flat country, bare and ugly, ragged, furze fences divided the fields from one another, and long, low, thatched houses were dotted here and there over the country. These houses seemed to be comfortable, and the land looked fertile, and bore good crops of flax, oats, potatoes, and wheat. Having driven for a few miles through this flat district, the country began to rise, and instead of furze ditches were dry stone walls, and the houses were better, many of them being slated. Again the scene changed and I came out on a dismal-looking, upland tract. Here, black-looking hovels stood forth against the sky in hideous nakedness. Drains and pools filled with black and slimy water lay along the road, which was carried at some height above the surrounding country. Road and country had once been on a level, but the peat had all been cut away, save the narrow strip along which the road was carried. Such places as these are very common; no effort seems to be made to improve them; wretched beings squat there and try to make a living by selling the few remaining peats they can cut, and trying to grow a few potatoes in the 'spent moss', or cut-away bog. All this dreary tract, together with miles of craggy hills, covered with poor tenants, belonged to the Earl of Blunderbore, a great absentee landlord. His land was said not to be dear, but between its sterility and the way in which it was subdivided, it seemed to be impossible to make a living on it at any terms. After driving for many miles through this miserable district, we at length came into a fertile-looking country, where there were some large farms and good houses. The driver, pointing to the best of these, said that it was Mr. M'Whirter's, who, it seemed, was farmer, miller and cattle-dealer, all in one.

Accordingly, we drove up a little avenue to the door of Mr. M'Whirter's house. It was a stylish, villa-like abode, well plastered and finished. I pulled a bell handle several times, but no one came to the door. At last, after about half-an-hour, the door, creaking on its rusty hinges, was pushed open about a foot or so, and the frowzy, yellow head of a servant wench was thrust forth. She crossly asked what I wanted. I replied that I wanted to see the master; she then asked me why I could not go to the back door like 'any other body'. I suppose that I must have looked astonished, for she burst out laughing, so did the car-driver. I then found out that gentlemen like Mr. M'Whirter built their houses for show, and not for use. A good house was merely an index or proof that its owner had risen in the world. The old dwelling was left standing joined to the new one at the rear, and in it the master dwelt. The new house was only used on rare, state occasions, when some display was thought to be needful. The front door having been opened with some difficulty, I was shown into a damp room, gaudily furnished. In a few minutes, Mr. M'Whirter came into the room. He was a powerfully built man, with a large, coarse mouth, and small, cunning eyes. His manner was friendly, but not over-polite; he seemed in some way to look down on me. I explained to him my reasons for coming to Ireland, said that I wanted a residence, and wished to carry out improvements and benefit the people. He listened with a pitying smile, and asked me if I wanted his opinion. I replied that I should be glad to have it. 'Well, then,' said he, 'my dacent man, I'll tell you what it is; if you'll be guided by me, ye'll just take yourself off by the next boat that sails, and never show your nose here again. And I'll give you some more advice, too, but first we must have something to drink'. Having ordered in a decanter of whisky, a jug of water, and some glasses, he poured me out about half a tumbler of whisky, and pressed me to drink. Now, I should not have objected to something to eat, but to drink spirits in the daytime, without eating, was contrary to my habits. However, I just raised the glass to my lips and set it down again; this inability to drink spirits seemed to sink me yet lower in M'Whirter's esteem. 'Now,' said M'Whirter, 'I must be quick, I have to be in the mill and have no time to lose. As I was saying, either go back to where you came from, or else, if you do want to live over here, rent a farm on the Blunderbore estate. What would you be doing with a gentleman's residence? Drive your trap, and drink your glass, take off your hat to the agent, and let all your schemes alone.'

'But,' said I, 'I have always been treated as a gentleman, and besides, why should a man with four or five square miles of property settle down as a tenant farmer, and doff his hat to a land agent? Should I not have some standing and influence?'

'Is it you,' said M'Whirter, with huge scorn, 'you're not the style of man for that sort of thing. Now, there's Captain O'Shun-the-Battle, the Blunderbore's agent, there's a man to carry weight anywhere. A lofty, high-minded, military, or, at least, militia-man, wears no end of jewellery, drinks champagne and whisky every day, and the roar of his voice would make you shake in your shoes. What are you with your plain dress and quiet voice beside a man like that? Just nowhere! Why, none of the quality here would have anything to do with you. Or there's M'Swagger, the spinning-mill manager, a yet greater man than O'Shun-the-Battle. That's what you may call a real gentleman, and a high Conservative as well. He's bought a place here that belonged to the Fitzmaurices, a wheen [i.e. lot] of auld, Popish rats, dating from the times of Strongbow. He's levelled the old castle, built a big new house, well plastered, and with plate-glass windows from top to bottom, where the castle stood, and cleared away every scrap of old work about the place. Broke 'em up, indeed, and bottomed the new avenue with them, the right way to serve them.'

'Surely,' said I, 'you don't call a man like that a Conservative?'

'Don't I, indeed,' said M'Whirter. 'Why, do you know what he did last election? He drove five electors up to the poll in a four-horse brake, wi' an orange flag flyin', and a horn blowin', and every one of these men was so drunk when he came back that he had to be lifted out of the brake. Ah,' said my friend, with an air of relish, 'that's a real gentleman, and is out and out the finest man in the county.'

It was quite plain that M'Whirter's views and mine disagreed on everything. It seemed useless to stop longer, so I took my leave, mounted my car, and slowly and sadly drove back to my inn, which I did not reach till late at night.

Next day, I made every possible inquiry about renting a house, but could hear of nothing. I then drove to my estate, which I had not as yet seen. It was in a rough, unimproved part of the country, but the farms were of a good size and the houses slated mostly. My father had been careful to check subdivision, and to have houses well roofed. My first visit was at the house of an old man, who after eyeing me curiously, said, 'You've fine times of it, landlord, drivin' about.' This remark struck me as something new. The people seemed to grudge that anyone should be better off than themselves. I afterwards found that this feeling was quite common. All my tenants seemed to look on me with suspicion and dislike, and I was about as popular a person as a tax-collector. They had nothing to complain of, but a person who wanted rent or money in any form from them could not be otherwise than odious. The steward or bailiff, who was the most civil person I had met with, told me of a man who wished to sell his interest in a cottage, which had been built on the site of an old residence on the property. It then occurred to me that as I could get nothing better, perhaps my best way would be to buy this man's interest and settle down on my own property. I might as well do that as take M'Whirter's advice and be a tenant under the Blunderbore agent, and besides, I might win the confidence of my tenants by living like one of themselves. Having made up my mind to take this course, I went at once to look at the cottage, which I found to be stone-built and slated, having two rooms and a kitchen. We soon struck a bargain with the tenant who had been abroad and wanted to go back. He agreed to clear out at once, and I agreed to take over all furniture and fixtures. These consisted of a table and a few chairs made of beechwood, a bedstead, and bedding, and a few cooking utensils. The owner of these was a bachelor, who had roughed it in back settlements abroad, and his habits were simple. As the few unmarried peasants had old women to keep house for them, I hired a clean, decent-looking old peasant woman, who could bake oatcake and cook a bit of bacon. This was the staple diet of the people, varied by a few potatoes, and on state occasions white bread and tea. Few lived on better fare, almost nobody on worse. I made up my mind to live as the average peasant did, also to walk instead of riding or driving. I could not then be sneered at as being 'better than other folks'. There were thirty or forty acres of land attached to the house; this I determined to keep in my own hands and manage myself.

In a few days I moved into the cottage. At first I found my life a hard one, and wearied of the coarse diet. But it was that of nearly everyone about. In the course of a few days I had been in every farmhouse and cottage on my estate, and found the fare to be nearly alike in all.

Seeing the great need of fences, I hired a country mason to build up the worst place, particularly those by the roadside. This was interesting kind of work. The walls were built of dry stones, and a little mortar was used in coping them. I took daily lessons in this work, to the scorn of all passers-by, who sometimes stood and spoke half-pityingly, half-scoffingly. These walls were well spoken of by the tenantry, as they kept cattle from straying, and saved the cost of 'herding' them. At first the mason did not like my helping him; I was finding out too much; but as I saved him the cost of a man to attend him and gave him his own price for his work, he bore with me. I found the out-door life agreed with me. I grew healthier and had a better appetite for my coarse fare; I slept soundly and felt better in every way than I had done since my boyhood.

Wall-building was work for summer. At other seasons of the year, I spent my time either tending a little flock of sheep which I kept on my farm, or in rambling about my property and the surrounding country. I was bent on mastering the Irish problem, and determined to discover all that could be seen or known in every direction. In the course of two or three years I had gained a fair knowledge of the rural economy of my own neighbourhood and of some thirty miles round about. Coarse attire, rough workingman's hands, and the best attempt I could make at speaking the dialect of the country, all these helped me greatly in my investigations.

Having quite exhausted my own part of the world, I thought of travelling farther afield, in fact of walking across Ireland from its eastern to its Atlantic coast. I had now mastered to some extent the difficulty of Irish dialects, having had good opportunities of learning them. The country round was mixed as to its population, and dialects varied from broad Scotch to the usual Irish sort of talk spoken with a slight northern accent.

One morning about the end of spring or beginning of summer, I set out on my travels, in the character of a mason. I was clad in a coarse suit of country-made tweed, on my feet were hobnailed brogues, and my luggage was contained in a coloured handkerchief slung at the end of a stout walking-stick. My first night was passed in a travellers' lodging in a village about twenty-five miles from home. 'Lodgings for Travellers' in Ireland are in a cottage or cabin in a village street. Outside is posted up a notice, 'lodgings and entertainment'. 'Entertainment' means board. Sometimes the notice runs good 'dry' lodgings — 'dry', here means without board. The accommodation at such places is usually very poor. The beds are generally of straw stuffed into sacks or mattresses, the bedding coarse and dirty, and the food bad. Of course prices are low, the class of persons who travel on foot in Ireland being very poor. They are for the most part beggars, tinkers, navvies, tradesmen out of work, and tramps of different sorts. The aristocracy of these classes who can afford to pay for bed and board stay at lodgings, those who can't afford this luxury put up at the casual ward of the workhouse.

I started from my lodgings very early, and walked all that day. As I got towards the central parts of Ireland, the appearance of the country began to alter. Neat farmhouses and good cultivation became fewer and less. Bogs and cabins became more and more plentiful. From the bogs rose low hills, covered with bright green grass, on which large cattle lazily fed. By the roadsides were grimy-looking cabins, the thatch green with slime and moss, the walls black from age and smoke. The climate had become much damper, and the atmosphere reeked with moisture and peat smoke. Towards nightfall, I stopped at a cabin to ask my way to the nearest village. The woman of the house asked me to come in, and set a chair for me before the fire, beside which the owner of the house was already seated, smoking a short black pipe. There was no lack of fuel, and the fire was heaped with peats — here called sods of turf — and over the fire a big pot of potatoes hung from an iron hook. The master of the house and I soon became friends; my horny hands and coarse dress showed that I was 'one of the people', and there was no reserve or suspicion on my host's part. He showed me two cows, which were tied up in one end of the cabin, separated from the apartment in which we were seated by a mud partition. I now had learnt enough about cattle to know that they were good, useful animals, in by no means bad order. During the daytime they grazed along the roadsides or on patches of herbage among the marshes, at night they got a little coarse hay.

I was now about to leave the cabin and walk on to the next village, but such a thing was not to be heard of — I must stay the night. To this I at once agreed, being curious to know more of the way of living of these people. After a few minutes the pot which hung over the fire was unhooked, the water poured off, and a heap of dry floury potatoes turned out on the table. Each person being supplied with a tin porringer of milk, we began our supper. The meal over, we drew our rush-bottomed chairs to the fire, and smoked and talked. My host smoked the traditional Irish pipe. This is now greatly out of date, so that an account of it may be of interest. This pipe is about two inches in length, and of a dark brown or black hue from age and use. The proper method of filling it is to pack and well press down the tobacco. This is cut from a stick or twist, which has been well soaked with oil to make it heavy and sell well — so at least the country folk say.

There are various ways of lighting the pipe. The old-fashioned way was by a flint and steel, the down of a thistle being sometimes used as tinder. The most common way, perhaps, is by holding a lighted sod of turf to the bowl of the pipe. But of late years lucifer matches have come greatly into fashion. Lighting the pipe is by no means easy, but, once 'started', it does not easily go out. When the pipe is going, the smoker sends forth a puff every one or two minutes, and talks in the intervals between each whiff. The pipe is looked on as a great means of quickening conversation and strengthening friendships.

My host's discourse was practical; he cared little for theorising, and still less for sentiment. He complained of good land being all let to big graziers, and of 'poor men' getting nothing but the bad bits that the others did not want, and 'of prosecutions for grazing on the roadside'. This was something new to me. I had always heard of English lanes being let for the summer grazing by the local authority. But it seemed that in Ireland people could not graze stock by the roadside on any terms, though they were quite willing to pay for the privilege. Cow, donkey, or goat are forbidden to graze by the roadside, and must 'move on', smart policemen having usually a string of such prosecutions at petty sessions.

The sharp little Irish boy or girl who mind the animals keep a good lookout for the 'peeler', and when he is sighted in the distance, the animals are driven along the road. Sometimes the policeman suddenly appears from round a corner, and then the offenders are caught. This law seemed to bear very hardly on poor folk in Ireland, when it is taken into account that there is much more traffic on English lanes and roads than on those in Ireland. In most parts of Ireland there is almost no traffic on the country roads, and the danger arising thereto from animals grazing on the roadside must be very small. These were my host's chief grievances, and he seemed to have good grounds for his discontent. He cared little for politics. A law that would give him a bit of good ground cheap was all he wanted.

Having passed the night on some dried rushes covered with a spare blanket, and breakfasted on the same fare as that on which I had supped, I rose to depart. I wanted to pay something, but the man refused with a look of hurt dignity. He, however, accepted a little tobacco as an offering of friendship. Like many Irish peasants, he was hard and matter-of-fact, yet polite and hospitable. I have described this household because it was a fair type of many others in this part of Ireland. For some days I travelled through a country that seemed to consist of bogs, grazing tracts without habitations, save occasional mud cabins, and poor gravelly ridges of hills, swarming with small peasant holdings. I rambled for some distance to the southward, and then turned north-west. Having travelled in this direction for a few days, I came into a mountainous region. There were nothing but black, boggy-looking mountains, with poor valleys lying between. Having followed the course of a river, I at last reached the head of a bay or loch.

Here was a little town whose main street was filled with emigrants, who had come in from the country, and were going on to a seaport, whence they were to embark for 'foreign parts'. These people were nearly all young men and women, with a sprinkling of married women and children, who were going to husbands and fathers abroad. Their miserable attire seemed ill-suited for a sea voyage. But with most of the peasantry shoddy and cheap finery had supplanted the warm frieze and woollens formerly worn. English people are apt to think that the Irish are always in rags. I cannot say that I have seen many rags in Ireland. But English-made clothes of the vilest shoddy are far too common. These are sold in Irish fairs by dealers in such things. They look cheap for the price asked, and so tempt ignorant young men and lads. Female attire of an equally flimsy and worthless character is sold by the village shopkeepers. I have often thought that many English manufacturers of so-called cheap stuffs must profit well from the folly of young Irish men and women. In out-of-the-way places frieze and coarse cloth of home manufacture are yet worn by the men, and blue cloth cloaks by the older women, and of late years efforts have been made to extend the manufacture of Irish woollens. But they are unable to keep pace with cheap English shoddies, and many people in Ireland think that protective duties ought to be levied on such fabrics.

I stayed the night at this town and in the morning took a road that led along the shores of the loch. Great dark mountains rose on the opposite coast sheer from the water's edge. Everything was on a large scale, unless the huts of the people, here of the smallest size I had seen. They were built of large stones and thatched with heather, tied down by straw ropes, crossed and re-crossed. All day I walked by these gloomy shores, and towards nightfall came to a house to which I had been directed in the town I had left. It was a small, slated farmhouse, where lodgings were let to country-folk, who came to the 'water', as the seaside is called in Ireland. Here I made an arrangement with the owner to work at drystone walls at such times that the weather allowed, or as suited my convenience, the work done to count for so much in my bill for board and lodging. I arranged to stay during the summer, and bargained that on those fine days on which I wished to make expeditions I should not be required to work. I thought it better to keep up the character of working-man, in order that I might be the better able to get to the bottom of things.

Accordingly, next morning I set out for a walk to the mouth of the loch. The little farmhouse was a few miles from this opening, and the road to the open coast wound up a steep mountain-side. When I got to the top of this mountain, the other side descended as a cliff down into the open Atlantic. The view here was a splendid one. The mouth of the loch must have been several miles in width. On either side, especially on the farthermost from me, arose steeply great promontories or heads with cliff-like faces. Against these thundered the huge Atlantic seas, rolling down from the Arctic regions without a check. It was a cloudy day with a strong north-west wind and gleams of sunshine now and then. The sun shone on the great white-crested waves, the spray from which flew far up the steep, black faces of the rugged headlands. Thousands of sea-birds of all sorts were flying around, or sitting ranged in rows on the rocks waiting for the tide to ebb. The whole scene was such as I had never before witnessed; wildness, majesty, and a sort of rugged beauty seemed striving for the mastery.

I spent the summer, working and rambling over the country by turns. Sometimes I spent two or three days from home, particularly on one occasion on which I travelled out to the far western coast, as had been my intention to do at first. Here, as I sat on a big stone by the gloomy ocean, I summed up in my mind all I had seen and heard during my trip from the farmhouse to the western shore. The dismal tales of famine and distress I had heard among the people through whom I had travelled occurred to my mind and weighed down my spirits. Things looked bad enough, but the people seemed to try to make them worse, and to gloat over their own misery. What, indeed, could be done with such districts, hopelessly sterile, drenched by Atlantic rains, and crowded with starving people?

BIBLIOGRAPHY/ACCOUNTS OF IRELAND

A complete bibliography of accounts of Ireland by English visitors would face enormous problems because of the overwhelming quantity and erratic quality of such materials. The list attached here is selective and provisional. Authors known to be of Irish birth, including prominent writers of Irish descriptions such as Mrs. Hall, have been omitted. Purely tabular and statistical accounting of Ireland has been omitted as well. No attempt has been made to deal with the profusion of incidental letters or journals and such on Ireland by figures as prominent as Raleigh and Wordsworth and Scott. Nor does this listing attempt to include essayistic material on Ireland by writers like Shelley or Mill. It emphasizes, instead, accounts of the country written on the occasion of being an English visitor to it. The rough chronological limits of this bibliography are the dates of the first and last selections in this book. Citations are given, wherever possible, for first publication. Writers anthologized in this collection are included, though the text excerpted in this reprint may differ from first publication. Dates in parentheses indicate approximate date of arrival in Ireland or composition when that differs significantly from date of publication and is not indicated in the title.

Anon. *Approved, Good, Joyful News From Ireland Relating How the Castle of Artaine Was Taken From the Rebels.* London, 1641.

Anon. *Brief Description of Ireland.* London, 1692.

Anon. *The Description of Ireland, and the State Thereof As It Is At This Present In Anno 1598.* Ed. Robert Hogan. Dublin, 1878.

Anon. *The Irish Peasant: A Sociological Study, by A Guardian of the Poor.* London, 1892.

Anon. *The Irish Tourist; or, The People and the Provinces of Ireland.* London, 1837.

Anon. *Journal of a Tour in Ireland Performed in August 1804.* London, 1806.

Anon. *Letters From Ireland 1886 By the Special Correspondent of the Times.* London, 1887.

Anon. *Letters From the Irish Highlands.* London, 1835.

Anon. *Notes of a Journey in the North of Ireland.* London, 1828.

Anon. *The Sportsman in Ireland, With His Summer Route Through the Highlands of Scotland, by a Cosmopolite.* London, 1840.

Anon. *Tour Through Ireland By Two British Officers.* Dublin, 1746.

Anon. *Wars of Ireland, By a British Officer.* Dublin, 1873. (1641).

Ashworth, John Hervey. *The Saxon in Ireland; or, The Rambles of an Englishman in Search of a Settlement in the West of Ireland.* London, 1851.

Barrow, John. *A Tour Around Ireland, Through the Sea-coast Counties, in the Autumn of 1835.* London, 1836.

Barry, William Whittaker. *A Walking Tour Round Ireland in 1865, By an Englishman.* London, 1867.

Beacon, Richard. *Solon His Follie, or A Political Discourse Touching the Reformation of Common Weales Conquered, Declined, or Corrupted.* Oxford, 1594.

Becker, Bernard Henry. *Disturbed Ireland: Being Letters Written During the Winter of 1880-81.* London, 1881.

Bennet, William. *Narration of a Recent Journey of Six Weeks in Ireland, In Connexion with the Subject of Supplying Small Seed to Some of the Remoter Districts: With Current Observations on the Depressed Circumstances of the People, and the Means Presented for the Permanent Improvement of Their Social Condition.* London, 1847.

Bicheno, J. E. *Ireland and Its Economy: Being the Result of Observations Made in a Tour Through the Country in the Autumn of 1829.* London, 1830.

Binns, Jonathan. *The Miseries and Beauties of Ireland.* London, 1837.

Boate, Gerald. *Ireland's Natural History.* London, 1652.

Bodley, Josias. *Descriptio Itineris Ad Lecaliam in Utonio Anno 1602.* Trans. C. L. Falkiner. *Illustrations of Irish History and Topography.* Ed. C. L. Falkiner. London, 1904.

Boorde, Andrew. *The First Boke of the Introduction of Knowledge.* London, 1548.

Bowden, Charles T. *A Tour Through Ireland in 1790.* London, 1791.

Brereton, William. *Travels in Holland, the United Provinces, England, Scotland, and Ireland.* Ed. Edward Hawkins. The Chetham Society, 1844. (1635)

Brewer, J. N. *The Beauties of Ireland: Being the Original Delineations, Topographical and Biographical, of Each County.* London, 1825

Brown, Tom. *A Brief Descrition of Ireland; Being a Description of the Country, People, and Manners, As Also Select Observations on Dublin.* London, 1699.

Bush, John. *Hibernia Curiosa: A Letter from a Gentleman in Dublin to His Friend at Dover in Kent, Giving a General View of the Manners, Customs, Dispositions, &c. of the Inhabitants of Ireland, Collected in a Tour Through the Kingdom in the Year 1764.* London, 1769.

Campion, Edmund. *A History of Ireland Written in the Year 1571.* Ed. James Ware. Dublin, 1633.

Carlyle, Thomas. *Reminiscences of My Irish Journey 1849.* London, 1882.

Carr, John. *The Stranger in Ireland: Or a Tour in the Southern and Western Parts of that Country in the Year 1805.* London, 1806.

Chatterton, Henrietta. *Rambles in the South of Ireland During the Year 1838.* London, 1839.

Clarke, E. D. *A Tour Through the South of England, Wales, and Part of Ireland, Made During the Summer of 1791.* London, 1793.

Cooper, George. *Letters on the Irish Nation: Written During a Visit to That Kingdom in the Autumn of the Year 1799.* London, 1800.

Cromwell, T. K. *Excursions Through England and Wales, Scotland and Ireland.* London, 1822.

Curwen, J. C. *Observations on the State of Ireland, Principally Directed to its Agriculture and Rural Population, In a Series of Letters Written on a Tour Through That Country.* London, 1818.

Dalrymple, John. *Memoirs of Great Britain and Ireland.* London, 1773.

Davies, John. 'A Discovery of the True Cause Why Ireland Was Never Brought Under Obedience of the Crown of England'. *Historical Tracts by Sir John Davies, Attorney General and Speaker of the House of Commons in Ireland.* Dublin, 1787. (1613)

De Quincey, Thomas. 'Autobiography From 1785 to 1803'. *The Collected Writings of Thomas De Quincey.* Ed. David Masson. Vol. 1. London, 1896. (1800)

Derricke, John. *Image of Irelande.* London, 1581.

Dewar, Daniel. *Observations on the Character, Customs, and Superstitions of the Irish, and on Some Causes Which Have Retarded the Moral and Political Improvement of Ireland.* London, 1812.

Dickson, M. F. *Scenery on the Shores of the Atlantic.* London, 1845.

Dineley, Thomas. *Observations in a Voyage Through the Kingdom of Ireland.* Dublin, 1870. (1681)

Dufferin, Frederick Temple, Lord. *Narrative of a Journey from Oxford to Skibbereen During the Year of the Irish Famine.* Oxford, 1847.

Dunton, John. *The Dublin Scuffle: A Challenge Sent by John Dunton, Citizen of London, To Patrick Campbell, Bookseller in Dublin.* London, 1699.

————. 'Dunton's Conversation in Ireland'. *The Life and Errors of John Dunton, Citizen of London, With the Lives and Characters of More than a Thousand Contemporary Divines and Other Persons of Literary Eminence.* London, 1705.

————. Unpublished Letters. Ed. Edward MacLysaght. *Irish Life in the Seventeenth Century.* London, 1939. (1699)

Dymmok, John. *A Treatice of Ireland*. Ed. Richard Butler. Dublin, 1842. (1600)

Echard, Laurence. *An Exact Description of Ireland*. London, 1691.

Entick, John. *The Present State of the British Empire*. London, 1774.

Fanshawe, Ann. *Memoirs*. London, 1830. (1650).

Forbes, John. *Memorandums Made in Ireland in the Autumn of 1852*. London, 1853.

Foster, Thomas Campbell. *Letters on the Condition of the Irish People*. London, 1846.

Gainsford, Thomas. *The Glory of England*. London, 1618.

Gandon, James. *The Life of James Gandon From Materials Collected and Arranged by His Son*. London, 1846. (1781)

Gatty, Margaret Scott. *Old Folks From Home, or A Holiday in Ireland in 1861*. London, 1862.

Gernon, Luke. 'Discourse of Ireland Anno 1620'. *Illustrations of Irish History and Topography, Mainly of the Seventeenth Century*. Ed. C. L. Falkiner. London, 1904.

Glassford, J. *Notes of Three Tours in Ireland in 1824 and 1826*. London, 1826.

Good, William. 'Maners of the Irishry, Both of Old and of Later Times'. *Britain, or a Chorographicall Description of the Most Flourishing Kingdomes, England, Scotland, and Ireland. By William Camden*. Trans. Philemon Holland. London, 1610. (1566)

Gookin, Vincent. *The Great Case of Transportation Discussed, or Certain Considerations Wherein Many Great Inconveniences in Transplanting the Natives of Ireland Generally Out of the Three Provinces of Leinster, Ulster, and Munster into the Province of Connaught Are Shown*. London, 1655.

Granville, Mary 'Mrs. Delany'. *The Autobiography and Correspondence of Many Granville, Mrs. Delany, 1700-1788*. Ed. Lady Llanover. London, 1861. (1731)

Grose, Francis. *The Antiquities of Ireland*. London, 1797.

Hall, James. *Tour Through Ireland, Particularly the Interior and Least Known Parts, Containing an Accurate View of the Parties, Politics, and Improvements in Different Provinces*. London, 1813.

Harington, John. 'Report of a Journey into the North of Ireland'. *Nugae Antiquitae: Being a Miscellaneous Collection of Original Papers*. Selected by Henry Harington. Newly arranged by Thomas Park. London, 1804. (1599)

————. 'A View of the State of Ireland in 1605'. *Anecdota Bodleiana*. Ed. William Dunne Mcray. Oxford, 1879.

Head, Francis B. *A Fortnight in Ireland*. London, 1852.

Hoare, Richard Colt. *Journal of a Tour in Ireland A.D. 1806*. London, 1859.

Holmes, George. *Sketches of Some of the Southern Counties of Ireland Collected During a Tour in the Autumn 1797, in a Series of Letters*. London, 1801.

Hooker, John. 'The Chronicles of Ireland'. *Holinshed's Chronicles of England, Scotland, and Ireland*. London, 1587.

Houstoun, Mrs. *Twenty Years in the Wild West, or Life in Connaught*. London, 1879.

Howard, John Eliot. *The Island of Saints, or Ireland in 1855*. London, 1855.

————. *The Protestant in Ireland*. London, 1854.

Inglis, Henry D. *A Journey Throughout Ireland During the Spring, Summer, and Autumn of 1834*. London, 1835.

Lithgow, William. *The Total Discourse of the Rare Adventures and Painful Peregrinations of Long Nineteen Years Travels*. London, 1632. (1619)

Loveday, John. *Diary of a Tour in 1732 Through Parts of England, Wales, Ireland, and Scotland*. Edinburgh, 1890. (1732)

Luckombe, Philip. *A Tour Through Ireland: Wherein the Present State of that Kingdom is Considered*. London, 1783.

Lyttelton, George. *A Month's Tour in North Wales, Dublin and Its Environs*. London, 1781.

Macaulay, James. *Ireland in 1872: A Tour of Observation, With Remarks on Irish Public Questions*. London, 1873.

————. *The Truth About Ireland: Tours of Observation in 1872 and 1875, With Remarks on Irish Public Questions*. London, 1876.

MacKenzie, John. *A Narrative of the Siege of London-Derry, or the Late Memorable Transactions of That City*. London, 1690.

Manners, John. *Notes of an Irish Tour in 1846*. Edinburgh, 1885.

Martineau, Harriet. *Letters From Ireland*. London, 1852.

Moryson, Fynes. *An Itinerary Containing His Ten Years Travel*. London, 1617.

Mulholland. *History of the War of Ireland From 1641-1653, By a British Officer*. Ed. E. Hogan, S.J. Dublin, 1873.

Mulock, Dinah Maria 'Mrs. Craik'. *An Unknown Country*. London, 1887.

Munday, Anthony. *The True Report of the Prosperous Successe which God Gave unto Our English Soldiers Against the Forraine Bands of our Roman Enemies in Ireland in the Yeare 1580*. London, 1581.

Nicholson, Mrs. Asenath. *Lights and Shades of Ireland*. London, 1850.

Noel, Baptist Wriothesley. *Notes of a Short Tour Through the Midland Counties of Ireland in the Summer of 1836, With Observations on the Condition of the Peasantry*. London, 1837.

O'Connell, Catherine M. *Excursions in Ireland During 1844 and 1850, With a Visit to the Late Daniel O'Connell, M.P.* London, 1852.

Osborne, Sidney Godolphin. *Gleanings in the West of Ireland.* London, 1850.

Page, James R. *Ireland: Its Evils Traced to Their Source.* London, 1836.

Parker, George. *A View of Society and Manners in High and Low Life: Being the Adventures in England, Ireland, Scotland, Wales, France, etc., of Mr. G. Parker, In Which Is Comprised a History of the Stage Itinerant.* London, 1781.

Payne, Robert. *A Briefe Description of Ireland Made in This Year 1589.* Nottinghamshire, 1589.

Penn, William. *My Irish Journal 1669-1670.* Ed. Israel Green. London, 1952.

Perrott, James. *Chronicle of Ireland 1584-1608.* Dublin, 1933.

Petty, William. *The Political Anatomy of Ireland 1672.* London, 1691.

————. *Reflections Upon Some Persons and Things in Ireland.* London, 1660.

Plumptre, Anne. *Narrative of a Residence in Ireland.* London, 1817.

Pococke, Richard. *Pococke's Tour in Ireland in 1752.* Ed. G. T. Stokes. Dublin, 1891.

Rich, Barnaby. 'The Anothomy of Ireland'. Ed. Edward M. Hinton. PMLA, 55 (March 1940), 73-101. (1615)

————. *A New Description of Ireland.* London, 1610.

————. 'Remembrances, by Captain Barnaby Rich, Concerning the State of Ireland, 14 Aug. 1612'. Ed. C. L. Falkiner. *Proceedings of the Royal Irish Academy*, 26 (1906-1907), 125-142.

————. *A Short Survey of Ireland, Truley Discovering Who It Is That Hath So Armed the Hearts of the People with Disobedience to Their Prince.* London, 1609.

————. *A True and Kind Excuse Written in Defense of That Book Intitled A New Description of Ireland.* London, 1612.

Rooper, George. *A Month in Mayo, Comprising Sketches (Sporting and Social) of Irish Life.* London, 1876.

Sandby, P. *Tour Through Ireland, In Several Entertaining Letters.* London, 1746.

Scott, Clement William. *Round About the Islands, or Sunny Spots Near Home.* London, 1874.

Senior, Nassau William. *Journals, Conversations, and Essays Relating to Ireland.* London, 1868.

Shand, Alexander Innis. *Letters From the West of Ireland 1884.* Edinburgh, 1885.

Spenser, Edmund. *A View of the Present State of Ireland.* Ed. James Ware. Dublin, 1633. (1580)

Stafford, Thomas. *Pacata Hibernia: Ireland Appeased and Reduced, An Historie of the Late Warres of Ireland.* London, 1633. (1599)

Stanihurst, Richard. 'A Treatise Containing a Plain and Perfect Description of Ireland'. *Holinshed's Chronicles of England, Scotland, and Ireland.* London, 1587.

Stevens, John. *A Journal of My Travels Since the Revolution, Containing a Brief Account of the War in Ireland.* Ed. R. H. Murray. Oxford, 1912. (1689)

Story, George Walter. *An Impartial History.* London, 1691.

————. *A Continuation of an Impartial History.* London, 1691.

Sullivan, D. *A Picturesque Tour Through Ireland.* London, 1824.

Temple, John. *The Irish Rebellion, To Which Is Added The State of the Protestants of Ireland Under the Late King James' Government.* Dublin, 1713. (1641)

Thackeray, William Makepeace. *The Irish Sketch Book.* London, 1843.

Tonna, Charlotte Elizabeth. *Letters From Ireland 1837.* London, 1838.

Trollope, Anthony. *Autobiography.* London, 1883. (1840)

Twiss, Richard. *A Tour in Ireland in 1775.* London, 1776.

Wakefield, Edward. *An Account of Ireland, Statistical and Political.* London, 1812.

Walker, George. *A True History of the Siege of Londonderry in 1689.* London, 1699.

Weld, Charles Richard. *Vacations in Ireland.* London, 1857.

West, Mrs. F. *A Summer Visit to Ireland in 1846.* London, 1847.

Wright, G. N. *Ireland Illustrated.* London, 1832.

————. *Tours in Ireland.* London, 1833.

Young, Arthur. *A Tour in Ireland: With General Observations on the Present State of That Kingdom.* London, 1780.

INDEX